When Ted Kennedy Rallied the Democrats in a GOP Congress

LION
of the SENATE

Nick Littlefield
and David Nexon

SIMON & SCHUSTER

New York   London   Toronto   Sydney   New Delhi

Simon & Schuster
1230 Avenue of the Americas
New York, NY 10020

First Simon & Schuster hardcover edition November 2015

SIMON & SCHUSTER and colophon are
registered trademarks of Simon & Schuster, Inc.

For information about special discounts for bulk purchases,
please contact Simon & Schuster Special Sales at
1-866-506-1949 or business@simonandschuster.com.

The Simon & Schuster Speakers Bureau can bring authors to your live event.
For more information or to book an event contact the Simon & Schuster Speakers
Bureau at 1-866-248-3049 or visit our website at www.simonspeakers.com.

Interior design by Ruth Lee-Mui

Manufactured in the United States of America

10 9 8 7 6 5 4 3 2 1

Library of Congress Cataloging-in-Publication Data

Littlefield, Nick.
   Lion of the Senate : when Ted Kennedy rallied the Democrats in a GOP Congress /
Nick Littlefield. — First Simon & Schuster hardcover edition.
      pages   cm
   Includes bibliographical references and index.
   1. Kennedy, Edward M. (Edward Moore), 1932–2009.   2. United States—Politics
and government—1993–2001.   3. United States. Congress. Senate—Biography.
4. Legislators—United States—Biography.   I. Title.
   E840.8.K35L58   2015
   973.92092—dc23
   [B]   2015008579

ISBN 978-1-4767-9615-4
ISBN 978-1-4767-9617-8 (ebook)

Nick: To my wife, Jenny Littlefield,
and my children, Frank, Tom, and Kate Lowenstein.
I love you.

David: To my wife, Lainey, my son, Dan,
my daughter-in-law, Maia Gemell,
and my granddaughter, Lyra Gemell-Nexon.
All of you enrich my life immeasurably.

Contents

This book had its genesis in several drafts begun by Nick Littlefield in 1998, shortly after he left his position as top domestic policy advisor to Senator Kennedy and Kennedy's staff director for the Senate Committee on Labor and Human Resources. Much of the narrative is based on verbatim notes he took on key meetings he attended and on his personal observations and experiences. The book is told in his voice and from his point of view. When the pronoun "I" is used, it refers to Nick. In 2012, when he was determined to finish the book after Senator Kennedy's death, he asked David Nexon to join the project as his coauthor. David was Senator Kennedy's chief health policy advisor for twenty-two years and was deeply involved in the events described in the book.

Introduction

By Doris Kearns Goodwin

"Everything in Washington is changed by Tuesday's Republican sweep," the *New York Times* noted. "With the Republicans in control of the Senate and the House of Representatives for the first time since 1954, when the Dodgers were still in Brooklyn and a postage stamp cost three cents, and with the Republicans in control of the statehouses in seven of the eight largest states, it is evident that a power shift of major proportions has taken place. But is the transformation permanent?"[1]

At that moment in time, few could have predicted that in two years, a demoralized Democratic Party would not only rally to blunt Newt Gingrich's conservative agenda, but even more surprisingly, would manage to enact important progressive legislation.

Lion of the Senate tells the inside story of how this happened. It is a story of pitch-perfect leadership from Senator Ted Kennedy, of friendships forged across party lines, and of a time, unlike today, when members of both parties worked together on issues that made a difference in the lives of the American people. If it could happen then, it could happen again.

As chief of staff for the Labor and Human Resources Committee, which had been chaired by Senator Kennedy for eight years before the Republican takeover, Nick Littlefield was both a participant in and a keen observer of the dramatic two-year period that followed the Republican victory. And, happily, the verbatim notes Littlefield took during discussions with Kennedy, dinners with fellow senators, and preparations for meetings with President Bill Clinton, create an atmosphere of immediacy and intimacy. By telling the story from beginning to middle to end, Littlefield allows us to experience the legislative struggles as they unfolded, to let us feel as if we, too, are there, walking through the halls of Congress, sitting in on strategy sessions, waiting for key votes, wondering how each battle will turn out.

Right from the start, the book makes clear what the turnover from a majority to a minority party meant not only to Democratic senators and congressmen but also to the members of their committee staffs. The minority party's share in the Labor Committee's budget would automatically be reduced by 50 percent; within days twenty of the forty Democratic staff members would lose their jobs. Offices would change hands along with the power to schedule hearings. Most importantly, the Republicans would now be in a position to set the agenda. And Newt Gingrich had made clear that he intended to follow up on every one of the far-reaching pledges the Republicans had made in their "Contract with America."

Yet, even at this moment when Democrats despaired, Senator Kennedy assumed a leadership role, rallying his colleagues to fight in unison against the most harmful of Gingrich's legislative proposals. At the same time, he reached across the aisle, creating surprising alliances which, against all odds, increased the minimum wage, provided portable health insurance for people who moved from one job to another, and secured health care coverage for millions of low-income children. Without Republican cooperation and cosponsorships, none of these bills could have passed.

With a gift for storytelling, Littlefield details the shifting set of alliances Kennedy forged to pass each of these bills. In the process, he paints a colorful picture of everyday life in the Senate as well as a primer in how the Senate works. Arcane Senate rules—unanimous consent, cloture, perfecting amendments—come to life in the telling of how various senators deployed them to obstruct or facilitate forward movement. Senator Kennedy's mastery of these rules proved an essential weapon in his arsenal.

The ultimate key to Kennedy's success, however, turned on the relationships he had carefully built and nurtured with his colleagues over the years. While he could argue passionately with Republican senators on the floor, he never betrayed impatience or disrespect toward them as individuals. On the contrary, he went out of his way to defer to the feelings of his fellow senators, often walking to their offices for meetings even if his senior position suggested they should come to him. In similar fashion, he would frequently defy protocol by journeying to the House when meeting with individual congressmen.

The stories of how Kennedy built working alliances with his colleagues are comical, instructive, and fascinating. When he wanted government funds to restore and preserve the house of the poet Henry Wadsworth Longfellow in Cambridge, Massachusetts, he set up a meeting with Senator Robert Byrd, who chaired the Appropriations Committee. In the weeks prior to the meeting, he memorized Longfellow's famous poem about Paul Revere's ride on the eve of the battle between the Minutemen and the British at Concord's North Bridge. The poem begins with "Listen, my children, and you shall hear/Of the midnight ride of Paul Revere," and stretches on for ten stanzas and nearly one thousand words. By the end of Kennedy's lengthy recitation, Byrd was only too happy to appropriate the funds!

The relationship Senator Kennedy developed with Senator Orrin Hatch resembled, in Littlefield's words, "an elaborate courtship dance." Though the two men were polar opposites, both ideologically and temperamentally, they were able to work together time and again. Kennedy traveled to Utah for the funeral of Hatch's mother; Hatch came to Boston for Rose Kennedy's funeral. They both considered the Senate their home; they both had staffs willing to work round the clock, and they both loved singing patriotic songs. Indeed, Hatch had written and recorded a number of songs himself over the years, regularly providing Kennedy with cassettes of each new song. To break an impasse over the child insurance bill, Kennedy asked Nick, whose beautiful voice had carried him to Broadway for a few years between college and law school, to start a crucial meeting by belting out one of Hatch's title songs. When the song ended, Hatch turned to Kennedy and smiled: "Nice move, Teddy." An agreement satisfactory to both sides was soon reached.

The portrait of Kennedy painted here is of a man capable of hard, sustained work and extraordinary perseverance. In the give and take necessary to get anything done, he always seemed to know what each individual senator needed or wanted. Once a week, he would hold dinners at his house: sometimes with experts on various issues, but most often with other members of the Senate. At these relaxed dinners, Republicans and Democrats engaged in informal conversation, teasing each other and generally having a good time. The book describes a hilarious episode at one of these dinners when Strom Thurmond, then nearly ninety, revealed that exercise was the secret to his longevity. He then proceeded to entertain the dinner guests by acting out his daily routine in pantomime, squatting down, then, with appropriate grimaces, lifting an imaginary barbell over his head. Beyond learning about Thurmond's daily exercise, Kennedy learned that the senator had a daughter with diabetes and therefore might be amenable to help the Democrats fund stem cell research. The pages of the book are filled with dozens of marvelous stories like this—stories revealing the human side of the Senate, the cooperation and compromise necessary to get anything done.

I did not want the book to end, not only because I so thoroughly enjoyed every chapter, but because I knew, of course, that that story would come to a close in the summer of 2009, when Kennedy would die after battling incurable brain cancer for a little more than a year. "He had been such a big part of my life for so long," Littlefield writes, "that I could not imagine a world without him."

A decade earlier, Nick had begun thinking about a book to chronicle the pivotal years following the Gingrich Revolution. He had spent summer vacations transcribing the copious notes he had taken during his years in the Senate. Kennedy's death renewed his resolve to complete the manuscript. In early 2011, however, he was diagnosed with a very rare progressive neurological disease called multiple system atrophy (MSA), which is a variant of Parkinson's disease but more aggressive. In the fall of 2012, Nick asked his colleague and friend, David Nexon, with whom he had worked on Kennedy's staff, to help him finish the book. David ran the health policy office of the Labor Committee for Kennedy for twenty-two years and was a key participant in the events described in the book. He became a full partner and crucial coauthor in the last few years of writing the book.

During this final stretch, Nick lost mobility. Then nine months ago, his speech and his ability to be understood became seriously impaired. With the help of family, health aides, and communication assistance, Nick managed to complete the final edit of this book, working eleven- and twelve-hour days.

Truly a labor of love, *Lion of the Senate* is also, hands down, the best book I have read about the inner dynamics of the U.S. Senate. In these pages, the daily life of the institution, the complex parliamentary rules, and the personalities of the men and women who work there come to vivid life. Historians, students, and general readers alike will read and revel in this splendid book for generations to come.

The Republican electoral victory on November 8, 1994, shocked the political world. For the first time in forty years, Republicans would control both the House of Representatives and the Senate. The House flipped from a 259–176 Democratic majority to 228–207 for the Republicans, a monstrous swing. The Senate shifted from 55–45 Democrat to 52–48 Republican. To rub salt in the wound, two Democratic senators and a number of House Democrats switched parties after the election, increasing the GOP margins. The governorships reversed themselves completely, from a 30–18 Democratic advantage to a 30–19 Republican advantage. No Republican incumbent congressman, senator, or governor lost anywhere in the country.

East to west, north to south, dozens of Democratic officeholders were unceremoniously tossed out of office, including leaders of the party. On the East Coast, Governor Mario Cuomo of New York was defeated; on the West Coast, Speaker Tom Foley of Washington State fell; in the South, Anne Richards of Texas was defeated by a young first-time candidate for governor, George W. Bush.

The scale of the Republican victory was unprecedented and unforeseen but not inexplicable. Having failed to deliver on their promise to provide health security for all Americans and tarred by congressional banking scandals that had contributed to a perception of corruption, Democrats had spent the fall of 1994 on the defensive in campaigns all across America. President Bill Clinton was unpopular, and many felt that Democrats had controlled Congress for too long. Led by Congressman Newt Gingrich of Georgia and united behind their campaign manifesto, dubbed the "Contract with America," Republicans were on the attack, campaigning vigorously against big government, taxes, welfare, and what they saw as a decline in values that they blamed on Democrats.

The Republicans who won across the country were typically fervent conservatives, promising a revolution to dismantle decades of progressive policies and diminish the role of the federal government in American life. The size of the changes Republicans sought was as vast as their election victory. They wanted to roll back government responsibilities that Americans of all parties had taken for granted since Lyndon Johnson's Great Society, even programs that dated back to the New Deal and to the Progressive Era of Teddy Roosevelt and Woodrow Wilson. Medicare, Medicaid, federal support for education, the minimum wage, the right to organize unions, the Food and Drug Administration, and protection of the environment—all were in the Republicans' sights for weakening, scaling back, or eliminating. Some Republicans went so far in their contempt for government that they bragged about their willingness to shut it down to achieve their goals.

In January 1995 the Republican juggernaut seemed unstoppable. The incoming Republicans in Congress held strong majorities in both the House and the Senate and were backed by a powerful conservative infrastructure of think tanks, media, and business and religious groups that had been built up systematically for over three decades.

During the election campaign, many Democrats responded to Republican attacks by seeking to blur the lines between the two parties, downplaying their identification with low- and middle-income families and their support for an active federal government. Following the election, demoralized, disoriented, and doubting their own convictions, many Democrats still in office argued for accommodation of the Republican legislative agenda. The public has spoken, they thought. People want tax cuts and the size of government scaled back. We can't stop the Republican agenda, and we'll look bad if we try.

Other Democrats disagreed. In the 1994 elections, Senator Edward Kennedy of Massachusetts was challenged by Mitt Romney, the son of the former Michigan governor and presidential candidate George Romney. Mitt was not only the bearer of a famous political name, he was also an aggressive and well-financed opponent. For the first time in his long career, Kennedy faced the very real prospect of defeat. But he chose to fight back, not by trimming his liberalism but by emphasizing it. Three weeks before Election Day at a rally in Boston's historic Faneuil Hall, known as "the cradle of liberty," Kennedy made the defining speech of his campaign: "I reject the laissez-faire notion that all government has to do is get out of the way, and kind, caring, generous, unselfish, wealthy private interests and power will see to it that prosperity trickles down to ordinary people."

It was Kennedy's seventh Senate campaign in Massachusetts. He stuck with what had always been his core message, and in the end Massachusetts voters stuck with him. While Democrats across the country were falling, Kennedy won reelection by seventeen points.

Back in Washington, Kennedy kept up the drumbeat for an activist, progressive Democratic Party. The day after the election he devised a plan to resist the Republican revolution, in effect organizing a counter-revolution. By the end of the 104th Congress in 1996, Republicans in Congress were actually racing to enact Kennedy-led initiatives to regulate health insurance and raise the minimum wage that they had earlier resisted. Kennedy's willingness to fight for the needy and the powerless, for working families and the middle class, turned the tide and kept the country from falling to the extreme right.

Had the Republican agenda succeeded, the country would have changed profoundly. Safety-net programs for the poor, the aged, and the young would have been shredded; protections for minorities and working Americans weakened; the ladder of opportunity for the middle class made rickety and less accessible; health, safety, and environmental rules that protect all Americans debased.

Newt Gingrich and the Republicans reached the brink of enacting their agenda, but against all odds they failed. How they were stopped and how Senator Kennedy went on to make substantial progress on key progressive goals while in the minority is a story worth telling in its own right. But it has special resonance today as a resurgent Republican Party with equally if not more radical views uses similar tactics to try to impose its agenda on the country. And as then, the central challenges America faces today require solutions that cannot wait.

Kennedy was at once the unshakable, dominant liberal of the Senate and one of its most pragmatic members, a highly effective advocate capable of trailblazing bipartisanship. While vigorously opposing the right, he never lost sight of the need to work across the aisle to find common ground and enact solutions to pressing national problems. Kennedy was a convenient foil for Republicans who wanted to rile up the conservative base and generate campaign contributions. They called him a socialist and worse. But when real work needed to be done, they knew he was open to compromise and a man of his word.

I worked and lived in the world of the Senate for nine years as chief of staff for the Labor and Human Resources Committee (now the Health, Education, Labor, and Pensions Committee), which Kennedy chaired for the first five years of my tenure. I worked alongside the senator day after day, taking close notes. In this book I have sought to portray daily life in the Senate, how it works, and how the actions and tone of the institution are shaped by the diverse personalities that make up its membership and staff. Most of all, I have tried to portray Kennedy in action at the peak of his powers in the arena that was the center of his political life and in which he accomplished so much toward his goal of improving the lives of all Americans.

This is the story of how Kennedy worked, what made him so effective, and how he was able to stop a resurgent Republican Party from reshaping the country to fit its conservative ideology.

Chapter 1

ELECTION DAY

GLOUCESTER

When the doors of the Veterans Memorial Elementary School in Gloucester, Massachusetts, opened to admit the first voters at 7:00 in the morning on Election Day 1994, I was standing outside the school holding a
red, white, and blue "Kennedy for Senate" sign, "doing visibility," as they
call it in Massachusetts politics. I had taken two weeks off from my job
working for Kennedy in Washington to volunteer on the campaign. It
was his tradition that for the final weekend and until the polls closed on
Election Day, everyone involved in the campaign would leave the Boston
headquarters and spread out across the state to help in local cities and
towns. I chose to work in Gloucester, an hour north of Boston. Over the
long hours in the early morning New England chill, holding my sign
and saying "Good morning" to voters, I thought about what had brought

me, a fifty-two-year-old lawyer and father of three, to this school and this moment.

I'd grown up in Providence, Rhode Island, and gone to Harvard College. My first job after college was as a Broadway singer in *My Fair Lady* in summer stock and in *Kismet* with Alfred Drake at Lincoln Center in New York. After one year in the professional theater I left to go to law school. I thought law and musical theater were the opposite poles in my life, never imagining that singing would become a great political asset, especially when I worked for Kennedy.

When I was in law school at the University of Pennsylvania, part of a generation urged to go into public service by President John F. Kennedy, I worked on my first political campaign, for Governor John Chafee of Rhode Island, a progressive Republican. I drove Chafee around in a yellow and blue truck with speakers on the roof blasting a campaign ditty I'd written: "Keep the man you can trust in Rhode Island, with Chafee we're moving along. Keep the man you can trust in Rhode Island, and keep Rhode Island strong." Chafee won the election, and I finished law school. In 1968 he asked me to run his reelection campaign, which I did while studying for the New York Bar Exam. His defeat, due to his courageous support for a new state income tax, was my first political disappointment.

In 1970, while working at a New York law firm, I ran the "Lawyers Committee against the Vietnam War," raising money for congressional antiwar candidates across the country. One of these candidates, the brilliant antiwar and civil rights activist Allard Lowenstein, recruited me to run a nationwide voter registration drive called Registration Summer the next year. A constitutional amendment lowering the voting age from twenty-one to eighteen had just passed, and we wanted to register young people, who we hoped would help stop the war with their votes. In 1972 I left my law firm and ran Al's campaign to return to Congress. His loss was another profound disappointment; I was beginning to understand that losses are frequently part of politics and that losing hurts a great deal.

After the campaign the Republican U.S. attorney appointed me an assistant U.S. attorney for the Southern District of New York (Manhattan and the Bronx). There I prosecuted corrupt politicians, drug dealers who were part of the infamous "French connection," tax swindlers, and worked on white-collar and organized crime cases. I conducted over two dozen trials and learned how to make a convincing argument in front of a Manhattan jury, a formidable task for a Bostonian. When my four-year term ended I wanted to go home to New England to reconnect with my family and lifetime friends, so I accepted a job as a lecturer at Harvard Law School. I soon was running Harvard's trial advocacy program, which I did for twelve years; I also taught prosecution and investigations and started a course called "The Government Lawyer" to encourage students to work in government by showing them the excitement and responsibility involved.

In 1978 the Massachusetts legislature established a special commission to investigate corruption in the state's public construction projects. Bill Ward, the president of Amherst College, was appointed head of the commission; on the recommendation of Harvard Professor Archibald Cox and Manhattan District Attorney Robert Morgenthau, whom he knew through Amherst, Ward asked me to become chief counsel and executive director. We wanted to excite public opinion about the costs of corruption, which had become a way of life in Massachusetts. We hoped to convince a reluctant legislature to rewrite the laws and fix the problems we would identify. We decided that presenting evidence of the widespread kickbacks that we uncovered was the best way of doing this. Because there were still afternoon papers as well as afternoon and evening news shows that had to be filled, we determined to try to hold full public hearings every morning, and revelations from these hearings became our signature "bribe a day before lunch." Our eighteen months of public hearings were covered extensively in the media.

One of my favorite bribery cases was that of William Masiello, who ran a pizza parlor in Worcester and decided he could make more money if he opened an architectural firm. Masiello quickly got public work by paying off the Worcester County commissioners and persuading them that there should be a new courthouse in each town in Worcester County, which is why, to this day, that area has four virtually identical courthouses within a radius of fifty miles. Masiello eventually succeeded in winning bribery-greased contracts all over the state.

The Ward Commission served its purpose: the legislature passed criminal laws to strengthen public corruption prosecutions and reform the construction process from bid to completion. It also created a permanent Inspector General's Office to continue our work.

When the Ward Commission ended in 1981, I was married and the father of three, so for financial reasons I had to think about going back to a law firm. I took a job at Foley, Hoag and Eliot and spent almost eight years there. In the fall of 1988 Gregory Craig, an old friend from the Lowenstein campaign, called to tell me he was leaving his job as foreign policy advisor for Senator Kennedy. He told me that it was a tradition in Kennedy's office to find candidates to succeed you when you left, and he was calling to urge me to be his replacement.

The idea of working for Kennedy was very enticing, but I wasn't sure foreign policy was the right fit for me. As I was hesitating about the job, Ranny Cooper, the senator's chief of staff, called to tell me that there was also a vacancy coming up in domestic policy for staff director for the Senate Labor and Human Resources Committee, which Kennedy chaired. The Labor Committee had jurisdiction over health care, medical research, doctor training, people with disabilities, the Food and Drug Administration, and education, including higher education, student loans, and school reform. It also had jurisdiction over jobs and job training, wages, labor, civil rights in the workplace, and even the arts and children's issues, such as Head Start and child care.

I wanted to go back to government, but not as a prosecutor. I had learned from prosecuting two cases in which we mistakenly arrested the wrong person that the truth could be elusive and the consequences of mistakes dire. Although the falsely convicted bank robber and the wrongly identified international drug dealer were ultimately released, I no longer wanted to take the chance of ruining a person's life and spending my time passing judgment on whether what people had done was wrong or criminal. Building people up was more important to me. This was an opportunity to return to a whole different kind of government service, where the goal was no longer being the cop on the beat but using government to try to improve people's lives. It was irresistible.

Ranny arranged for me to be interviewed for the Labor Committee job by Kennedy and his Boston chief of staff, Barbara Souliotis, in Boston. I met the senator in the restaurant of the Harvard Club at 4:00 p.m. on a Friday, just after he'd finished his steam bath treatment for his bad back. This was the first time I had met him. He came upstairs in his well-pressed blue suit and well shined black shoes (he later told me that Kennedys don't wear brown), sat at the table, and turned on the famous Kennedy charm: loud, funny, and warm.

"I want you to come work with me," he said. "This is what we're going to do: health care, raising the minimum wage, fixing the schools, to start."

As it was my habit to take notes in every meeting, I grabbed the only available paper—a cocktail napkin—and jotted down what he said: *Health care, minimum wage, schools.* I felt like accepting on the spot but refrained, instead telling him I would think about it. He said he would see me in Washington.

I flew down for more formal meetings with the staff of the Labor Committee and with Kennedy's personal staff. The staff members were expert in their substantive areas. I was an expert in none, but I would learn, and I knew how to develop and run a campaign. A week later I went to see Kennedy in his office. He took me out onto the balcony, turned to glance up and down Constitution Avenue, over the Capitol, the Supreme Court, the Washington Monument, and, in the distance, the rows of graves in Arlington National Cemetery, where both his brothers were buried (and where he is now buried). Before I could say anything, he asked me when I could start. I said, "How soon do you need me?"

The answer was February 1989. One of the first things Kennedy told me was that nothing could get done in the Senate unless it was bipartisan. The notion of good and bad guys, which I had been focused on for twelve years, was useless; we had to seek out Senate colleagues, Republicans and Democrats, for everything we did. Kennedy had great respect for the other senators and worked hard to build relationships with those across the aisle. This would prove particularly difficult on health care reform, the cause that was so central to Kennedy and that would be an ongoing focus of my career.

Five extraordinary years later, campaigning in Gloucester, I thought over some of our successes: we had passed landmark legislation through the Labor Committee, including the Americans with Disabilities Act, the Civil Rights Act of 1991 (strengthening the laws against discrimination in the workplace on the grounds of race, religion, or gender), the Family and Medical Leave Act, the Ryan White AIDS CARE Act, and the Child Care and Development Block Grant. Nothing was as important to me as Kennedy's reelection.

Gloucester was a good place to spend Election Day, a working-class city of thirty thousand with a proud history that had fallen on hard economic times. The median family income was $32,000, close to the national median of $31,278. I thought that many of the voters I saw that day and had talked to over a weekend of phoning and canvassing neighborhoods had probably benefited from the senator's legislation.

What I'd heard from voters during my time in Gloucester and from the latest polls gave me confidence about the outcome of the election, though the campaign had been the toughest of Kennedy's long career. First elected to the Senate in 1962 at the age of thirty, he'd been reelected five times but hadn't had a serious challenge in at least twelve years, until Republicans fielded the impressive Mitt Romney against him.

KENNEDY DEFEATS ROMNEY

Romney was a fresh and promising new face in Massachusetts politics. He was forty-four, clean-cut, and handsome, with a photogenic family and a lot of money that he was willing to plow into the campaign. He'd come to Massachusetts from Michigan to attend Harvard Law and Business schools in 1971 and stayed to make a fortune in the private equity business.

Several factors were working against Kennedy in this race. The storied Kennedy political organization in Massachusetts was out of practice, the senator himself was older and heavier, and the rape trial of his nephew in Palm Beach three years before had taken a toll on his reputation. Across the country Republicans were united, well-financed, and on the offensive. Kennedy was one of their prime targets; they attacked his politics as obsolete and out of touch. Although Massachusetts is regarded as a reliably Democratic state, the voters had elected a Republican governor, William Weld, in 1990, and were preparing to reelect him in a landslide in 1994, on the same ballot as Kennedy. Polls in the spring had shown that only one third of Massachusetts voters thought Kennedy deserved reelection, and, equally ominous, even one third of Democrats thought it was time for a change.[1]

On the other hand, the senator had one new extraordinary asset: Victoria Reggie Kennedy, whom he had married on July 3, 1992. Vicki was everything he could want in a wife. Beyond being "the love of his life," as he often said, she was politically very astute and as good as most of his advisors at thinking strategically. They loved talking politics, and she was a great sounding board for his ideas. Despite their busy schedules, they ate dinner together practically every night, most meals featuring a vigorous discussion of politics and policy. She quickly became very popular in Massachusetts and helped to bridge the gap between his public persona and who he was personally, as a father and a husband. People got to know him all over again with Vicki at his side.

The Romney challenge had a strong start partly because Kennedy was busy with obligations that kept him from campaigning. For most of 1994, he was required to remain in Washington, carrying out his senatorial duties, especially working on President Clinton's universal health insurance bill, so Vicki pitched in as an eloquent surrogate campaigner. The Senate remained in session through August, when it was normally in recess for elections, and as chairman of the Labor Committee, he took the lead on many issues for Clinton. And before his sister-in-law Jackie Kennedy Onassis died in May of that year, he and Vicki had flown back and forth to New York all spring to visit her. Meanwhile Romney's television advertisements ran throughout the summer without a Kennedy advertising response. A poll taken in September showed Romney leading Kennedy 43 to 42 percent, and internal Kennedy campaign polls showed a six-point spread against the senator. It had never before seemed possible that a Kennedy could lose an election in Massachusetts. Now it did.

Kennedy reorganized his campaign. Ranny Cooper, the seasoned poltical operator and former Kennedy chief of staff who had told me about the Labor Committee job, joined the campaign team. In early October, after Congress adjourned, Kennedy came home and barnstormed the state. His high energy level roused his allies as well as ordinary voters, putting to rest speculation that he was tired or had lost interest in his job. John F. Kennedy Jr., Ethel Kennedy, and many other Kennedy family members, President and Mrs. Clinton, Vice President Al Gore, and Jesse Jackson all came to Massachusetts to campaign for him. Supporters mobilized advertisements, endorsements, voter contact drives, and events. Leaders in Massachusetts health care, education, labor, civil rights, technology, the arts, and even the fishing industry signed on. The breadth of support was remarkable. A few days before the election members of the Massachusetts Carpenters Union joined with the Gay and Lesbian Task Force in an impressive march through Boston, holding Kennedy signs and banners. He began to turn the election around as the campaign reached the homestretch.

Kennedy took out a million-dollar personal loan on his house in Virginia to signal that he would match the Republicans in spending. His first television ad stressed his career-long commitment to improving the living standards of Massachusetts's working families and his achievements in health care, education, jobs, and wages. Then came a big break: the campaign received a call from a labor union in Marion, Indiana, telling us that we should look carefully at how a stationery factory there, acquired by Romney's firm, had been unfair to its workers. The new management cut jobs, increased insurance premiums, and eliminated the union. Kennedy's advertising strategist, Bob Shrum, sent a film crew to Indiana and located and interviewed many of the laid-off workers who were understandably hostile to Romney. Their testimonials about their unhappy fate at his hands, broadcast over and over again, painted Romney as no friend of working people. This tactic was so devastating to Romney that the Obama campaign used it again in 2012.

The challenge for the campaign was to convince voters to reject the Republican wave building across the country and stick with the Democratic values for which Kennedy had always fought. To that end, Kennedy reenergized his campaign with his speech at a packed rally in Boston's Faneuil Hall on October 16. Hearing that speech in person was one of the most memorable moments of the campaign. The text could have been delivered in thirty minutes, but it took an hour because applause interrupted him fifty-seven times. It was a call to battle and an uncompromising assertion of liberal principles.

> I stand for the idea that public service can make a difference in the lives of people. I believe in a government and a senator that fight for your jobs. I believe in a government and a senator that fight to secure the fundamental right of health care for all Americans. I believe in a government and a senator that fight to make our education system once again the best in the world. If you send me back to the Senate, I make you one pledge above all others. I will be a senator on your side. I will stand up for the people and not the powerful.

Kennedy's strategists had hoped to avoid any debates with Romney, as incumbents with healthy leads usually do, but as the polls showed, the race was a toss-up; debates became inevitable. In the first, held on October 25, Romney started out strong, attacking Kennedy as unresponsive to the prevalence of crime. But as the debate progressed, he became rattled. He reiterated a point from his television ads, claiming that the Kennedy family had made millions from federal leases, but the attack backfired when Kennedy responded, "Mr. Romney, the Kennedys are not in public service to make money. We have paid too high a price for our commitment to public service."

As the debate continued, Romney appeared increasingly out of his depth. He seemed to have little grasp of what a senator actually does, of what his own proposals would cost, and even the geography of Massachusetts. Kennedy effectively put his enthusiasm, his record for Massachusetts, his family tradition of public service, his mastery of legislation, and most of all his identification with the needs and interests of working families on full display for the largest television audience for a political debate in Massachusetts history.

When the TV lights went off, the Kennedy campaign staff believed the tide had turned. Viewer polls showed Kennedy the decisive winner, and a week after the debate Kennedy had a twenty-point lead in one poll and a ten-point lead in another. But there had been so much volatility in the polls throughout the campaign that no one took a single poll as the final word. The senator continued barnstorming with great enthusiasm; there was no doubting his zeal for the fight.

When the polls closed at 8:00 on election night I drove straight to the Park Plaza Hotel in the Back Bay section of Boston. Kennedy people arrived from all over the state—the army of volunteers who'd covered each of the 2,500 polling places, as I had in Gloucester. Some had driven from the Berkshires, more than two hours away to the west, others from Cape Cod, two hours to the south. Everyone wants to be with their candidate on Election Night.

I took the elevator to the twelfth floor, where private meeting rooms were reserved for staff and Kennedy had his private suites. Exit polls had Kennedy comfortably ahead, and one of the television stations had projected him the winner. I took the corridor to the Kennedy suite, to see the senator and Mrs. Kennedy and congratulate them before they went downstairs to the ballroom to make their victory speeches. I told the senator things looked good based on my day in Gloucester.

"Good to see you. It looks like we're okay," he said. "Thanks so much for helping. We'll get right back on health care and the minimum wage."

Kennedy hadn't yet heard from Romney. While he waited, he was busy placing calls to Democratic officials and candidates across the country, wishing them well, congratulating those who were already clear winners, commiserating with those who'd lost. For years President Clinton had reminded Kennedy how much it meant to him that Kennedy had been one of the few national figures who'd called him in Little Rock on Election Night in 1980, when Clinton had just lost his first reelection campaign for governor of Arkansas.

Downstairs a stage had been constructed in the ballroom, a band was playing, and balloons and signs were everywhere. On stage were the senator's nieces and nephews, sisters, children and grandchildren. At 10:00 he and Vicki pressed up onto the crowded stage, joyful, waving, the senator punching his fist in the air, Vicki nodding, smiling. Hunched over a bit, like a boxer protecting his chin, he kept waving his arm up by his head, mouthing the words, "Thank you. Thank you." The band was playing louder and faster, and the cheering wouldn't stop. Finally Kennedy waved the crowd to silence.

"I've had a call from Mitt Romney, and he's congratulated us on winning the election," he announced. The crowd erupted again, cheering uncontrollably. Kennedy again put up both hands for silence.

"I want to thank all of you for what you've done. . . . I thank the voters of Massachusetts. . . . I thank my family, my sisters, my nephews and nieces. I want to pay special tribute to the love of my life, Vicki." More cheering. Then he introduced his family. "My daughter Kara, my son Teddy. My son Patrick is not here. He's in Rhode Island tonight, celebrating his election today to the United States Congress. I saw him earlier this evening in Providence." The crowd roared.

The senator brought the crowd to silence once again and enthusiastically belted out his campaign mantra: "We won because people understood what we stood for and what battles we would fight. We will never stop fighting to improve jobs and wages, for better schools, for health care for all." The room erupted with cheers once again. Then the pledge: "We will go back to Washington to carry on the fight to improve the lives of ordinary working Americans. With all the strength I have, I will make that fight." As the cheering continued, the senator made his way down from the stage and into the crowd to thank people in person. The stage emptied behind him, but the euphoria among the packed crowd stayed strong as volunteers pressed forward to congratulate him and Vicki.

When the formal vote count was tallied, Kennedy's victory margin was 58 to 41 percent, close to the average in his five previous elections. The vote total from Gloucester was 6,846 for Kennedy and 4,185 for Romney, a 62 to 38 percent advantage.

By 11:00 the senator was back upstairs, and the ballroom was empty. I found myself wandering across the floor amid the leftover balloons and placards from the celebration feeling a mixture of relief and joy.

REPUBLICANS SWEEP THE NATIONAL ELECTIONS

Before midnight I went upstairs to the staff meeting rooms, where televisions along each wall were tuned in to Election Night coverage. The mood was very different from the euphoria in the ballroom; here people looked shocked. Each close race was coming in against the Democrats, and it looked more and more likely we would lose the majority in the Senate. Democratic incumbents Jim Sasser in Tennessee and Harris Wofford in Pennsylvania had already lost. Open seats previously held by Democrats Donald Riegle in Michigan, Howard Metzenbaum in Ohio, George Mitchell in Maine, David Boren in Oklahoma, and Dennis DeConcini in Arizona had already gone to Republican candidates. Only a few races had not yet been called, and it looked ominous. By midnight the networks were reporting that the Senate had gone to the Republicans, 52–48.

The news on the House elections was even more stunning; if the trends continued into the morning, Newt Gingrich and the Republicans with their Contract with America would be in charge of the new order in the House of Representatives. The conservative revolution was at hand.

It was almost too much to take in at once. I didn't know what it would be like to be in the minority. Republicans had been in control of the Senate from 1981 to 1986, the first six years of the Reagan administration, so some of Kennedy's staff knew the experience firsthand, but back then I'd been a private citizen in Boston.

There would be a Republican majority leader and a Republican chairman of the Senate Labor Committee. So much power lost. I would no longer be staff director to the Committee. Kennedy would no longer control the Committee's agenda. Our plans for more progress in health care, education, and jobs were all in jeopardy. Everything I had known in Congress would be turned upside down.

I went back to my hotel room and slept badly, torn between the joy of the senator's reelection and the disaster of the Republican sweep of Congress, between the sweet and the bitter. The sweet mattered more to me; Kennedy's defeat would have been devastating. But the bitter cast a dispiriting pall over the future.

Early the next morning, the senator and Vicki went to the Park Street subway stop to thank people for their votes. He was thrilled with his victory; he had worked hard and was inspired by his contact with voters. But now he had to go back to Washington, where many of his friends had lost their seats and his party had been handed a devastating defeat. Armed with his unshakable conviction that government is a positive force in American society, he was determined to bring the successful lessons from his campaign to the national party, which was in deep despair over its losses.

Chapter 2

THE CONTRACT
WITH AMERICA

GINGRICH ROLLS OUT THE CONTRACT

If I hadn't been so focused on Kennedy's campaign, I would have had a clearer idea of what was in store for Democrats—and the country—in the new Congress. Newt Gingrich had made it clear on the steps of the west front of the U.S. Capitol six weeks before the election.

September 27, 1994, was a flawless warm autumn day in Washington. A cloudless blue sky above the white marble dome of the Capitol created a picture-perfect background for the made-for-television rally Gingrich had organized to kick off the last six weeks of the election campaign. He had dreamed of this event since 1982, when he watched his idol, Ronald Reagan, bring Republicans from the House and Senate together on this same spot to celebrate the passage of the Reagan tax cut. Gingrich, introducing his Contract with America to the nation, had assembled 350 Republican congressional candidates from across the country to sign it. He was the principal speaker, proclaiming with typical grandiosity, "Today on these steps we offer this Contract as a first step toward renewing American civilization."

The Republicans faced a seemingly insurmountable challenge to take over the majority: they needed to pick up forty seats held by Democrats in the 435-seat House. Gingrich was acting as if his Contract, which would unify all these candidates around a common agenda, together with his many years of work to build the Republican campaign challenge, could actually make it happen.

The signing ceremony itself combined the happy air of a high school reunion class photograph and a pep rally for the big homecoming football game. Dozens of American flags were stationed around the stage. As an army of television cameras filmed their every move, the candidates, mostly young white men, stood on bleachers with Gingrich in the middle, then filed four at a time up to a table festooned with red, white, and blue banners to put their signatures on the Contract.

The Contract with America was a ten-point program of proposed legislation that the Republicans pledged, if they won a majority in Congress, to vote on in the first hundred days of the new session. They said the Contract "would be the end of government that is too big, too intrusive, and too easy with the public's money." For added drama, they threw down a gauntlet: "If we break this contract, throw us out."

When everyone had finished signing the Contract, Dick Armey, a Republican congressman and a member of the party leadership, spoke: "The People's House must be wrested from the grip of special interests and handed back to the people." Gingrich followed, referring to the Contract as an "historic event" that would change the government as much as the New Deal had.

After the rally, the challengers met with Gingrich inside the Capitol for tutorials on campaign strategy. That evening they were guests of honor at a $7,500-per-table fundraiser hosted by the Republican National Congressional Committee. The next morning, before leaving Washington to return to the campaign trail, they met with representatives of corporate political action committees who were evaluating potential recipients of campaign largesse.

The Capitol ceremony was covered widely on all the television news shows that evening and in the next day's newspapers across the country, but Gingrich wasn't content to rely on free media. He used $275,000 from the Republican Campaign Committee to purchase a full-page ad in *TV Guide* with a pull-out card listing the ten items in the Contract with America. Leon Panetta, the president's chief of staff, noted the contradiction between Republicans railing about ridding the House of "special interests" and then retiring to the fundraiser for business lobbyists and political action committees, but the Republicans saw no inconsistency.[1] When they referred to special interests, they meant groups such as women, children, farmers, union members, and seniors. They didn't consider business a special interest.

The Contract with America was the capstone of sixteen years of effort by Gingrich to win a Republican majority. The brainchild of Gingrich, Armey, and their favorite political consultant, thirty-two-year-old Frank Luntz, the Contract was a Republican rallying cry designed to turn the electoral status quo upside down. From his first day in Washington in 1979, Gingrich had worked single-mindedly to overthrow the Democrats. He organized the Conservative Opportunity Society (COS) to harness the energy of young, aggressively conservative Republicans in the House. COS was designed to serve as the focus for opposition not only to the Democrats but also to what Gingrich regarded contemptuously as the moderate "go along to get along" Republican leadership. Republicans had been in the minority since 1948, and Gingrich predicted they would stay there until they distinguished themselves as much as possible from the Democrats and became far more aggressive in advancing conservative ideas and challenging the Democratic majority. He spent hours relentlessly attacking Democrats and organizing his allies to do the same. On the floor of the House after the main business of the day was completed, he used the so-called empty time to bash the "corrupt, liberal, welfare state" represented by the Democratic House leadership. These speeches looked great on the new C-SPAN channel because the camera never panned to the empty hall. When President Clinton was elected in 1992, Gingrich targeted him with equal fervor, calling him "the enemy of normal Americans."[2]

Frank Luntz, Gingrich's partner in developing the Contract, was described by the *Washington Post*'s Michael Weiskopf as "steeped in the power of anger" as a political weapon.[3] Luntz had abandoned President George H. W. Bush in 1992 to work in two campaigns that exploited the anger phenomenon: Patrick Buchanan's challenge to Bush in the Republican presidential primaries, and later that same year Ross Perot's assault on both political parties. But Gingrich was willing to forgive Luntz for his apostasy because his message was what Gingrich now wanted.

In urging Republican leaders to adopt the Contract in early September 1994, Luntz wrote, "To say that the electorate is angry would be like saying that the ocean is wet. Voters in general and our swing voters in particular have simply ceased to believe that anything good can come out of Washington." In his article Weiskopf concluded, "Rather than modulate the anger, Luntz wants Republicans to be a 'megaphone' for it."[4]

Gingrich and Luntz carefully chose their themes to target not only Republicans but swing voters and low- and middle-income Democrats, including blue-collar workers angry about what they thought were free riders on welfare, suburbanites frightened by crime and other urban problems, and the religious right. They chose the concept of a contract because it implied an obligation to follow through on campaign promises, unlike the Democrats, who had been unable to deliver on their promise of expanding health care coverage in America. It was no accident that there were ten items in the Contract just as there are Ten Commandments in the Bible.

Many of the items they put in the Contract were not new but rather a creative repackaging of standard Republican campaign themes: cut taxes, cut spending, fight crime, slash welfare, build up the military, embrace right-wing "family values," and enact term limits. Luntz had made an art form out of identifying particular words to present issues in their most advantageous way. He used focus groups and polling to test different ways of describing the points Gingrich wanted in the Contract.

The trick was to run a highly negative campaign that would exploit voter anger, while appearing to be uplifting and positive. To that end, Luntz and Gingrich chose words that seemed benign but actually masked a startlingly aggressive intent when the fine print was examined. More than just a platform, the Contract was designed for a tactical purpose, to "nationalize the election," in contrast with the Democrats, who were running 435 separate elections without a coherent or common agenda.

The Contract was a remarkably cynical document on a number of levels. Many of the proposals were modest and relatively unobjectionable, though couched in grandiloquent language. But no one relying only on the Contract as a guide to what the Republicans would do if elected would have realized how far-reaching their legislative assault on the social safety net or on basic government responsibilities would be.

The first item in the Contract was the "Fiscal Responsibility Act," the centerpiece of which was the pledge to enact a balanced budget amendment. The not so subtle message of the title was that opposition to the act was a vote for fiscal irresponsibility. Whatever the pros and cons of deficits as a general matter, the Republicans had a second, more fundamental goal in mind. For Gingrich and company, the balanced budget was an engine to drive a dramatic scaling back of government. Tax increases would be banned unless approved by a supermajority of three-fifths of the House and Senate. The first item also provided the president a line-item veto of spending bills, but not bills creating new tax expenditures. This construction was necessary because the Contract also called for large tax cuts—cuts that primarily benefited the wealthy and business. And since the Contract also called for increased defense spending, it was not hard to read between the lines of the Fiscal Responsibility Act to figure out where the burden of the balanced budget would fall.

The Republican route to achieving a balanced budget would have slashed the nation's historical commitment to critical social programs such as Medicare and Medicaid, education, student loans, and nutrition programs. But of course Luntz and Gingrich weren't going to put any of these proposals in the Contract. The titles of some proposals were Orwellian: the first item was called the "Fiscal Responsibility Act" because they weren't about to call it the "Slash Spending on Medicare, Medicaid, Education, and Nutrition Act." It was this masking of the true Republican agenda that made the Contract salable politically, but the failure to enunciate central goals of the conservative revolution also meant that the successful Republican candidates viewed their mandate very differently from the country at large.

Other titles went straight for the angry white voters Luntz and Gingrich saw as a key to electoral victory. For their anticrime item, they chose the "Taking Back Our Streets Act." The focus was heavily on punishment and enforcement. It suggested that our streets were occupied by a dangerous force; for the Contract's target audience, that force was clearly black criminals. And the harsh message was that the only way to deal with criminals was to increase the prison population and the use of the death penalty.

The "Personal Responsibility Act" was a mean-spirited version of welfare reform and built on the anger Luntz found in his polls. Here too there was a racial subtext. Although the majority of welfare recipients were white, the voters Luntz and Gingrich targeted envisioned black single mothers when they thought of "welfare cheats."

Four of the next five items in the Contract promised tax cuts for important constituencies that Gingrich and Luntz wanted to court: the religious right, middle-income families, senior citizens, and especially prime Republican constituencies among investors, corporations, and the wealthy. Despite the lofty language of the Contract, however, the tax benefits for individual families and senior citizens were far smaller than the proposed new tax breaks for businesses and wealthy individuals. The "Family Reinforcement Act" proposed a $5,000 tax credit for families adopting a child. The "American Dream Restoration Act" called for a $500 per child tax credit and reforming the so-called marriage penalty. No Republican agenda would be complete without support for an increased defense budget, and the "National Security Restoration Act" played that role. The "Senior Citizens Fairness Act" was the centerpiece of the Republican proposal for senior citizens; it proposed a modest cut in taxes on Social Security benefits for middle- and upper-income seniors. The Republicans also proposed to raise the amount a senior could earn without losing Social Security benefits.

Gingrich and Luntz saved their largest benefits for their strongest constituencies among businesses and the wealthy, and they disguised them under the title "Job Creation and Wage Enhancement Act." The changes promised by this item would provide significant tax cuts for the wealthy and for businesses and scale back the government's ability to issue regulations to protect workers against unsafe practices, consumers against unsafe products, and the environment against industrial pollution. For investors, the Republicans proposed to cut capital gains taxes by 50 percent. For businesses, they would increase investment depreciation levels and expensing levels for investments and equipment. The next item, which made product liability suits more difficult for plaintiffs, served a different purpose from any of the others in the Contract. It was designed to reward business and insurance companies, a key Republican constituency, and to punish trial lawyers, who were a prominent Democratic constituency.

The final item introduced another dimension to the Republican agenda: an attack on the "discredited and entrenched" Democratic membership in Congress. The "Citizen Legislature Act" called for a vote on limiting members of the House of Representatives to three terms for a total of six years and of the Senate to two terms for a total of twelve years. Unlike the other items in the Contract, there must have been disagreement within the Republican Caucus on how hard to push this item, with senior Republican members not anxious to commit political hari-kari. As a result the Contract did not promise to enact term limits, only to hold a vote on term limits.

Building on this theme of a corrupt Democratic Congress, in addition to the ten legislative initiatives, there were eight congressional reforms that the Republicans proposed. These included conducting an independent audit of Congress for fraud and abuse, cutting committees and staff, opening all congressional meetings to the public, and requiring a three-fifths majority vote to pass a tax increase. The Republicans promised to make these changes on the first day of the new Congress to, in the words of the Contract, "restore accountability to Congress. To end its cycle of scandal and disgrace. To make us all proud again of the way free people govern themselves."

After unveiling the Contract, Gingrich and the Republicans went home to their districts across the country to wage their campaign to take over the House. But they weren't finished with campaign pomp and ceremony. A week later state legislators and candidates gathered on the steps of their state capitols, followed the next week by local candidates at city halls around America, and held similar signing events with their own contracts to limit government and cut taxes at the state and city levels. Gingrich himself campaigned in over 130 districts in the month before the election.

In what would turn out to be a colossal misunderstanding of the voters' mood and of the power of the Republicans' overriding message, Democrats were initially delighted that the Republicans had been so explicit in describing their agenda. But these Democrats misjudged the extent of voter anger and the desire for change in Washington and over-estimated their own ability to pin the Republican candidates with the specifics of what the Contract actually called for.

The Republicans' success was a testament to the failure of Democrats nationally to produce their own agenda, to get off the defensive, to campaign with any kind of coherence or energy. It was, in part, a Republican victory by default.

There was no lack of opportunity for the Democrats. Missing from the Republican Contract was even a nod to compassion. There was no kinder and gentler conservatism, no point of light to take the hard edge off the Contract, as the first President Bush had promised in 1988. The Contract assumed—correctly, as it turned out—that mobilizing voter anger at government, at Democrats who had governed for forty years in the House, and at a Democratic president who had been hovering around a dismal 40 percent favorability rating for the past six months provided everything they needed in the election. The Contract said nothing positive about improving the schools or making college more affordable, about health care, or about easing the pressures on workers and the middle class beyond token tax cuts. It offered nothing to raise their wages or to secure their retirement. You might have thought the absence of any of these initiatives would have left a hole big enough for the Democrats to drive a juggernaut of their own through, since just two years earlier the country had thrown out Bush for being out of touch with the average American, a vulnerability Clinton had emphasized in the election with his "Putting People First" agenda.

Thus the stage was set for January 1995, when the new Congress convened. For the first time in over forty years, Republicans controlled both houses. Emboldened by this historic victory, the new leadership believed it could make dramatic changes in the shape and direction of government even without control of the White House. Republicans thought Clinton would adopt their agenda and cave in the face of their power; in the worst case, they could override his vetoes with the acquiescence, if not outright support, of accommodating Democrats in the House and Senate.

ELECTORAL TSUNAMI

Political shifts of the scale of 1994 are shocking even if foreseen, but the impact of this one was compounded by the fact that neither the Democrats, the press, nor political commentators saw it coming. Most of us had not even imagined such a reversal as a possibility. A forty-seat Democratic majority in the House and a six-seat majority in the Senate seemed irreversible.

Political observers competed to describe the magnitude of the change. "Tuesday was potentially one of the most important days in 20th-century political history," Michael Beschloss, the presidential historian, said the next day. "It could mean that we are headed back into a period of Congressional dominance and Presidential weakness such as we had in the late 19th century."[5] William Kristol, the conservative theorist, voiced a typically expansive Republican assessment when he said, "[Sixty] years of Democratic dominance of American politics, established by Frank D. Roosevelt, have been effectively ended by two years of Bill Clinton."[6] William Safire, the *New York Times* columnist, called the election a *tsunami* and identified the source as "the majority's growing belief that government is growing too big, intrusive, domineering and remote—wasteful of tax dollars at all levels."[7] He didn't mention that the senator who stood most prominently for the effective role of government in enhancing the lives of working families had survived the tsunami.

A House banking scandal, which involved revelations of check-kiting by Democratic members of Congress, undoubtedly played a role in the Republican triumph, but more important was the disappointment and frustration of Democratic voters, who felt the Clinton administration and the Democratic Congress simply hadn't delivered for them. Clinton's performance was perceived as lackluster, and the Democrats in Congress looked divided and impotent. Clinton had backed away from key appointments and had lost the bid for a more tolerant policy on gays in the military. One of his first legislative programs, a $30 billion economic stimulus package to repair and construct roads and bridges in nearly every state, was pulled off the Senate floor when head counts failed to find a majority. Once Republicans saw that the president lacked the nerve to battle one of his first big proposals through to victory or defeat, they were emboldened to bloody him further at every opportunity. And the congressional Democrats' failure to use their majority effectively reflected both on them and on the president. By Election Day, Clinton's approval rating had fallen to a weak 44 percent.

A balanced view of Clinton's first few years, however, would recognize a number of groundbreaking achievements. He signed the Family and Medical Leave Act, which required employers to provide workers with unpaid time off after the birth of a child or to care for a family member who was ill. Bush had vetoed the same bill several months earlier. Some Democrats boasted that the 104th Congress should be known as the Education Congress because it enacted a far-reaching series of education bills. In the summer before the election, Congress passed a Clinton initiative popular with conservatives to put 100,000 more police officers on the streets of communities across the nation, but the measure had to be scaled back considerably after Republicans complained about other crime-prevention programs included in the bill, most notably pro-posals for nighttime basketball leagues to keep at-risk teenagers off the streets. Several gun-control measures banning assault weapons and op-posed by the National Rifle Association were also included in the bill, and votes by Democratic incumbents to support these provisions were used effectively by Republicans and their NRA allies in pro-gun districts. In the biggest legislative struggle of 1993, Clinton passed a tax and deficit reduction bill that laid much of the groundwork for the prosperity that continued for the remainder of his presidency. Yet none of these accom-plishments, not even all of them put together, could offset the political fallout that resulted from the effort to pass a universal health care plan that the president had made the centerpiece of his 1992 campaign and of his first two years in office.

Chapter 3

THE FAILED STRUGGLE FOR HEALTH REFORM

CLINTON'S UNIVERSAL HEALTH PROPOSAL

When President Clinton took office in January 1993, a Democratic proposal for universal health care already existed in the Senate, having been developed by Senators Kennedy, Mitchell, Rockefeller, and others. This legislation was relatively simple, understandable, and ready to go with broad Democratic support. Both employers and employees would contribute to the cost of employees' health care. Employers would either "play or pay": they could either contribute directly to a health care program for all their employees or pay a fee to a general fund that would help cover the costs of insuring workers not covered by company plans. This plan was built on two earlier universal health care proposals sponsored by Kennedy and reported out of the Labor Committee in 1987 and 1989.

For Kennedy, who had made universal health care a top personal and political priority since 1971, the prospects for success had never looked so good. Clinton made enactment of universal health care a central part of his first State of the Union message, as he had made it a central part of his campaign. When he approached Kennedy on the House floor after the State of the Union, Kennedy told him that he "had been waiting thirty years for a president to make that speech."

At that point the momentum for change seemed irresistible. Republican senators such as the minority leader, Bob Dole, and John Chafee of Rhode Island were developing their own proposals for universal health care.

The new White House team was headed by Ira Magaziner, a brilliant management consultant and the president's fellow Rhodes Scholar at Oxford in 1968. First Lady Hillary Rodham Clinton was appointed the overall head of the effort. A large number of task forces was soon in place. Hundreds of health experts were assigned from departmental offices and borrowed from universities to work under Magaziner. Working groups made presentations at marathon "toll gate" sessions chaired by Magaziner; if a presentation passed muster with him, its proposals would pass through the toll gate for further refinement. Clinton invited members of Congress and their staffs to participate in the process of developing the plan. Most chose to stand back and wait for the White House to deliver a proposal that they would then consider—or not—as a starting point for their work. Kennedy, however, saw the offer as a chance to get in on the ground floor and participate in shaping the proposal. At one point, his whole health staff was essentially working two jobs: one for him and one for Magaziner and the task force.

When Congress took up the federal budget resolution in May 1993 for fiscal 1994, Senators Kennedy and Mitchell saw that the best chance of passing universal health care lay in attaching instructions to the legislation that would allow health reform to be included in the subsequent budget reconciliation bill. Under Senate rules, opponents of a reconciliation bill cannot filibuster it, and only fifty-one votes are required to pass it. If health care legislation came to the floor independently and was filibustered, it would take sixty votes to break the filibuster and bring the measure to a vote. However, practically speaking, attaching health care to the budget bill required the consent of Robert Byrd, Democratic senator from West Virginia and chairman of the Appropriations Committee, and he was in principle opposed to such attachments.

Kennedy and Mitchell appealed to Byrd to drop his opposition; the president too appealed to him. But Byrd stood firm. It was a second fatal blow. When the opportunity to attach health care reform to reconciliation evaporated, so did the opportunity to bypass the task force process and produce a bill quickly. Instead, the task forces ground on and on. Kennedy urged the Clintons to move quickly, even if a health care bill could not be attached to the budget, but Clinton's economic team universally advised him against putting forward a big-spending health care bill until his economic program was passed. Kennedy brought polls to the White House showing that even Reagan's approval ratings dropped below 50 percent by the autumn of his first presidential year, but to no avail.

Spring passed into summer. Clinton was putting all of his energy into passage of a tax and deficit reduction bill, which, after eleventh-hour appeals to Senator Bob Kerrey of Nebraska, the Senate Democrats barely managed to pass in July. Even with Kerrey's vote, the bill passed only when Vice President Al Gore broke the 50–50 tie. But Clinton had used up most of his chits with the Senate majority. There was negative fallout in the House as well, where many Democratic members were furious at the administration for forcing them to vote for unpopular provisions in the original legislation, most notably the environmentally sound but politically unpopular BTU tax, that were dropped from the final bill.

The plan specified in the Health Security Act that Magaziner finally brought to Capitol Hill in September 1993 was artfully constructed. Hillary Clinton defended it brilliantly before Kennedy's Labor Committee in the Senate Caucus Room, the same room that had housed the announcements of John and Robert Kennedy's presidential bids, the Watergate hearings, and the second set of hearings on Clarence Thomas's nomination to the Supreme Court.

The plan combined market-based managed care that promised reduction of costs and an employer mandate to finance health care for working Americans. It provided for the pooling of employees from businesses, large and small, into "alliances" that would in turn contract with medical insurers and health care providers. Employers and employees could choose their insurance plans. The benefit package included preventative care and prescription drugs. The plan strengthened Medicare and Medicaid. All Americans would be covered by the year 2000.

HARRY AND LOUISE OPPOSE UNIVERSAL HEALTH

While Magaziner toiled, so did the opposition, led by small business lobbyists and the insurance industry. The length of time it took to produce the administration proposal opened the door for opponents to charge that the White House was secretly drafting a massive bureaucratic takeover of the health care system. As time passed and the president's approval ratings sank, the aura of inevitability around health reform began to evaporate. Interest groups that originally scrambled to find a compromise with the administration now felt emboldened to oppose it. The health insurance industry launched an extensive and effective television campaign depicting a middle-class couple, Harry and Louise, sitting at their kitchen table. Harry and Louise concluded that they would lose the benefits of their existing health insurance and would lose the right to choose their own physicians if the Clinton plan were enacted. They portrayed it as a suffocating bureaucratic monster.

Public opinion, which had remained favorable to universal health coverage well into the fall of 1993, began to turn against Clinton's plan late in the year. The Harry and Louise ads did their damage, but there was also a barrage of carefully planned oppositional radio talk shows, newspaper columns, letters to editors, op-eds, and direct-mail messages. I don't think the country had ever seen the equivalent of the conservative infrastructure of think tanks and foundations coordinated with media that matured just in time for the anti–health bill campaign of 1993–94. Fighting it was swimming against a powerful incoming tide.

As Republicans saw support for the Clinton plan beginning to wane, their tactics shifted, and whatever willingness there had been to compromise began to evaporate. William Kristol, a scion of the neoconservatives and a powerful opinion maker on the right, circulated an influential memo laying out the case that the "predicate" for Republican success in the 1994 elections was preventing Clinton and the Democrats from passing a health plan—any health plan.

By November 1993, when the Clinton plan was finally introduced in legislative language, the country was entering the first phase of the 1994 congressional election campaign. The Republicans' strategy was complete obstruction. Less than two months before Election Day 1994, Republican senators met at their weekly caucus lunch in the Mansfield Room in the Capitol. The 103rd Congress was about to adjourn for good. The Clinton health care plan was dead. Senator Bob Packwood, the ranking Republican on the Senate Finance Committee and floor manager for the Republicans during the health care floor debates, spoke up: "We've killed health care reform. Now we've got to make sure our fingerprints aren't on it."[1]

Democratic Senator Daniel Patrick Moynihan of New York, chairman of the Finance Committee, and usually our strong ally, was very public about his opposition to Clinton's timing for health care. He had been critical of the Clinton plan from the beginning. For him it was a matter of priorities; he wanted Clinton to deal with welfare reform, his particular interest, before health care reform. He made critical statements in the Finance Committee hearings about the financial and budgetary assumptions in the Clinton plan and criticized the Magaziner task force and Hillary Clinton's projections on the financing of the program. Tactically, he decided, and announced publicly, that as chairman of the Finance Committee, whose support was vital to health care, he would not move the Clinton legislation through his committee promptly but would wait until he and Senator Dole, the minority leader, had reached agreement on an approach. The goal of bipartisanship is always a laudable one, but in this case Moynihan effectively gave the Republican Caucus veto authority over any bill. Dole, moreover, had no incentive to reach agreement because the Republicans had become committed to killing all versions of health care legislation.

In the days of the solid South, many southern Democrats were jokingly called "Yellow Dog Democrats" because they were so loyal to the Democratic Party they would vote for a yellow dog if he were on the Democratic ticket. Now, as the Republican Party gained traction in the South, a group of moderate and conservative southern Democrats dubbed themselves the "Blue Dogs" to indicate their independence from the national party—an independence that they hoped would help them with their increasingly conservative constituencies. This group was as likely to vote with conservative Republicans as with liberal Democrats. The Blue Dogs were difficult to hold in support of the health reform program, mainly because of the opposition from small business and because they were vulnerable to charges that the program represented an inappropriate, overregulatory expansion of the role of government.

THE STRUGGLE FAILS

In January 1994 President Clinton stressed universal health insurance in his State of the Union Address. If legislation didn't provide coverage for all, he said, he would veto it. He held up a symbolic "health security card" akin to a Social Security or Medicare card. Progressive Democrats greeted the defiant gesture with applause and cheers. The Republicans sat on their hands. The Blue Dogs shifted uncomfortably.

There was a laudable and sustained effort by the old Democratic coalition—public interest health groups, labor, civil rights activists, women's groups, liberal religious groups—to build support for the Clinton plan. Representatives of over a hundred groups met in Kennedy's Labor Committee hearing room several afternoons a week from early in 1994 through the summer to share information and plan strategies. I became the master of ceremonies for these sessions. In a takeoff on the popular children's Nickelodeon channel programming, they came to be referred to as D.C.'s version of *Nick at Nite.*

Legislation as comprehensive as universal health care invariably comes before more than one committee in both the Senate and the House. In the Senate, Kennedy led the Labor and Human Resources Committee carefully through the Health Security Act, amending as necessary to get majority support, and reported it to the floor of the Senate in early June 1994, after the Committee approved it by 10 votes to 6. Only Senator Jim Jeffords from Vermont among the Republicans voted for approval in the final vote. The Kennedy version provided universal coverage.

The Senate Finance Committee did not take up the Clinton plan until July. A bipartisan group self-labeled "the Mainstream Coalition," led by the Republican Chafee and the Democrat John Breaux of Louisiana, broke away to formulate their own plan, which would have provided expanded but not universal coverage. Their bill set a coverage target of 95 percent of Americans. If that goal were not met, a new commission would report on recommendations to reach the target with procedures for expedited floor consideration of the commission's recommendation. Their alternative passed the Finance Committee, but then it stalled.

Under Finance Committee procedures, unlike most other Senate committees, legislation and amendments are presented and voted on in "conceptual" form—a prose description—rather than actual legislative language. After the markup, Moynihan's staff worked with Senate legislative counsel—nonpartisan legislative draftsmen who work for the whole Senate—to put the conceptual legislation passed into legislative form. Inexplicably, they did not involve Finance Committee members from the Mainstream Coalition in this effort—and Mainstream Coalition members were outraged when they saw the legislative language, believing it did not accurately reflect their bill.

In the House, the Labor and Education Committee reported out a bill similar to the Clinton plan. The Energy and Commerce Committee deadlocked and couldn't agree on any legislation at all. And the Ways and Means Committee reported out a bill that looked less like the Clinton plan and more like a universal Medicare plan. There was much to recommend this approach, building on the acknowledged success of Medicare, but if the Clinton plan worried Harry and Louise (and the insurance industry behind them), the Medicare-like plan would have driven them crazy.

George Mitchell, justly celebrated for his ability to move complex legislation through the Senate, had to decide which bill to bring to the floor: the original Clinton bill, the Kennedy Committee's version of the Clinton bill, or the Mainstream Coalition's bill from the Finance Committee. Since only Jeffords among the Republicans had shown any regard for the Clinton bill or the Kennedy variation on it, and additional Republican cooperation was essential to breaking a filibuster, Mitchell brought up the bill reported out of the Finance Committee for debate and offered an alternative that incorporated many of the Mainstream Coalition's ideas.

But it didn't matter which version of health care insurance Mitchell brought up. The Republicans were extremely well organized in opposition. Each time Mitchell offered a revision to even one page in the bill, the Republicans demanded reprints of the entire thousand-page document, which they then stacked on their desks and ridiculed as "Mitchell 1," "Mitchell 2," "Mitchell 3." They complained the bills were too long and that no one had had a chance to read them. They picked apart each one, searching for vulnerabilities. Each day they highlighted a different criticism. They endlessly paraphrased the dialogue from Harry and Louise. They attacked the president and Mitchell and Kennedy and other proponents of universal health insurance relentlessly. They did not hesitate to distort the provisions of the bill or make outlandish claims about its consequences.

In late August, with no prospect of a vote in sight, Mitchell yielded to a recess over Labor Day weekend and into early September, during which he would try to work out a version of the Mainstream Coalition's proposal that might gain majority support. Staff for Mitchell, Chafee, and Kennedy remained in Washington, trying to assemble a bill that could attract wider support. But the break seemed to do the opposition more good than the proponents. There was no relenting in the Republican ranks, and even Republican participants in the Mainstream Coalition backed away from the program they had previously endorsed.

Meanwhile Democrats facing reelection were worried that the extended debate on health care was preventing them from conducting their campaigns, and they repeatedly urged Kennedy and Mitchell to give up. Kennedy exerted all his influence to bring a health care bill to a vote during the session. Passing a bill would give the Democrats an historic achievement to run on. Even losing the vote would give them political ammunition because they could put the blame on Republicans for defeating universal health coverage. But a significant number of Democrats did not want to vote on the bill, believing that the Republicans had created enough noise around the concept of universal health care that a vote even on a scaled-down bill would hurt them in their election campaigns. On September 26, 1994, just forty-three days before the general election, with no prospect of getting the sixty votes needed to break a Republican filibuster, Mitchell pulled the bill from the floor.

The Senate never voted on universal health care, so there was never a moment when each senator had to stand up and be counted. Until the fall of apartheid in 1996, the United States would remain the only nation in the industrialized world other than South Africa not to guarantee health care as a basic right for all its citizens. The number of uninsured, which during the health care debate was roughly 37 million, was growing by at least one million each year.

The failure of the Clinton health care proposal was central to the outcome of the election. Its passage would have shown the Democratic Congress to be effective and responsive to social needs. Instead, Republican campaigns, right-wing think tanks, and industry lobbyists successfully spun the bill as a threat to the health care that insured Americans already had, a harbinger of a large and intrusive bureaucracy rather than a guarantee of quality care for all. The debate kept vulnerable and threatened Democratic congressmen in Washington when they might have been campaigning, and ended sourly, so dispiriting Democratic voters around the country that enough stayed home to turn the election. Tellingly, for the first time since 1970 more Republicans than Democrats voted.[2]

The day that Mitchell finally pulled the health care bill was the day before Gingrich unveiled his Contract with America on the steps of the Capitol. The high level of enthusiasm and unity at Gingrich's rally should have provided fair warning of the right-wing juggernaut that was rolling toward us. But, like the rest of the Democrats, we were blissfully unaware of what was to come.

Chapter 4

KENNEDY IN
THE MINORITY

HELLO, TEDDY

The day after the election there was one last victory celebration at Kennedy headquarters. All the volunteers who had come to Boston for the campaign showed up early, bleary-eyed and punch-drunk from too little sleep for days, but excited over our decisive victory. We gossiped and hugged and high-fived each other over mounds of bagels and pitchers of orange juice and coffee. The senator and Mrs. Kennedy wandered through the crowd thanking each of us individually. Then a surprise guest appeared. The Broadway star and musical theater legend Carol Channing was performing at the Shubert Theatre in Boston in a revival of *Hello, Dolly!* more than thirty years after her New York triumph in the title role. She arrived at headquarters wearing bright red lipstick and a full-length white fur coat, her snow-white hair in a pageboy cut. She hugged the senator, said how happy she was to be up so early to celebrate his reelection, and began singing, drawing out each word in her trade-mark deep voice.

> *Hello, Teddy, well, hello Teddy,*
> *It's so nice to have you back where you belong.*

She sang several more choruses, then flashed an open-mouthed smile and gave the senator, who was blushing and laughing, another hug. He thanked her and reminded her that he had first seen her in *Hello, Dolly!* at its pre-Broadway tryout in Washington when his brother was president. The staff applauded and cheered enthusiastically, although many of the young staffers probably had no idea who she was. Then she swept out of the headquarters almost as quickly as she had arrived.

After Channing left, the senator thanked the staff again, and we all went back to finishing the food, still in high spirits from the night before. No one mentioned the national drubbing the Democrats had just received or what those of us soon to return to Washington would face when we got there.

BACK TO WASHINGTON

From the party I went directly to the airport for my flight back to Washington. My transition from euphoria to grim reality was about to occur. I was returning to a city that I knew was already changed. For most of the hour-long flight, I stared out the plane window and wondered what was in store when I went back to work in the Senate. Approaching National Airport, I could see all the way down to the nation's stunning Capitol building, dominated by the marble dome at the center and flanked on either side by the Senate and House wings. It was the same U.S. Capitol, the people's building, the heart of our democracy, that I had left two weeks before, but my relationship to what went on there had changed.

In the majority, Kennedy had done much to set the agenda for the party and the country, and through the legislation he had enacted he had made a difference in the lives of millions of Americans. When I joined his staff in February 1989, President George H. W. Bush had been inaugurated a month earlier, and the 101st Congress had just begun. When the Senate Democratic Policy Committee set its legislative agenda for 1989–90, they identified sixty-three priority items for action. Of those enacted into law by the end of 1990, almost half, twenty-eight, came out of our committee: the first minimum wage increase in ten years, reforms to job training and math and science education, and reauthorization of the National Endowment for the Arts and the National Health Service Corps. We passed the Ryan White AIDS CARE bill, created a major new federally supported child care program, and in a step that truly changed our society, passed the Americans with Disabilities Act—a bill of rights for the disabled.

The second Congress under Bush, the 102nd, was somewhat less productive, as Bush moved to the right to try to placate his conservative base. His chief of staff, John Sununu, set the administration's tone when he said, "There's not a single piece of legislation that needs to be passed. . . . In fact, if Congress wants to come together, adjourn, and leave, it's all right with us. We don't need them."[1] But in spite of this, Kennedy still managed some legislative achievements. He and Senator John Danforth of Missouri led the successful effort to pass the Civil Rights Act of 1991, expanding remedies for employment discrimination. The Labor Committee reauthorized the Higher Education Act, which included an important direct loan program to bypass the banks and increase the amount of money that students would get. We reauthorized Head Start as well as a number of other important social programs. We passed the Family and Medical Leave Act, which Bush vetoed but which later became the first law signed by the new president, Bill Clinton. And Kennedy persisted in declaring that jobs, education, and health care all needed government action to address the needs of American families, while Bush focused exclusively on the first Iraq War.

The defeat of universal health care overshadowed just about everything else during Clinton's first two years—the 103rd Congress of 1993 and 1994—but Kennedy was nevertheless extraordinarily successful in advancing important elements of the progressive agenda. When Senate

Majority Leader Mitchell gave his wrap-up speech identifying the principal accomplishments of the 103rd Congress, more than half were Kennedy bills, including Family and Medical Leave, Head Start expansion,
Goals 2000 school reform, the Elementary and Secondary Education
Act, School-to-Work, further reform of student loans, and the establishment of the National Service Program.

Now the environment was very different, and I was going to have
to figure out how to adapt. Democrats would no longer set the agenda.
Instead we would be reacting to the Republican majority's priorities and
searching for ways to exert some influence, a very new experience for me.

I began looking for clues to where the Republicans would try to go
with their new power. An indication came from the first pronouncements of Newt Gingrich, soon to be speaker of the House. When the
election results became known the night before, Gingrich started out
being rather conciliatory. By morning, however, he was focused on reaffirming his party's commitment to enacting the Contract with America.
Then, during the day, he reverted to the posture he had presented during the campaign: the belligerent attack dog targeting Democrats and
liberals. Gingrich adopted all three modes within twelve hours after the
election results became known, and all before anything was heard from
the Democratic president.

Gingrich celebrated Election Night in his congressional district, at a
victory party in a suburban shopping mall in Marietta, Georgia. Maureen
Dowd, the sharp-eyed political satirist of the *New York Times*, was there.
She reported that the mood was one of "vengeful glee." The master of
ceremonies, a local Republican official, "made fun of Mario Cuomo losing his race in New York, and observed that President Clinton was about
to 'feel the pain.' Inside the ballroom little girls waved placards reading
'liberals, your time is up.'" She observed that Gingrich himself was more
statesmanlike, promising to be "Speaker of the House and not Speaker
of the Republican party." He said, "The Republican success in the elections proved Americans wanted the Contract with America enacted," but
he made a point of noting that "at least half of our contract are things
the President supports, that we should be able to work on together." He

urged "the President in the next few days to invite Bob Dole and myself to sit down and let's talk in a candid way and see if there isn't some common ground."[2]

On the television news shows the following morning Gingrich was explicit about his reading of the elections. On *CBS This Morning*, he said, "I think we have an obligation to listen carefully to what was clearly a voice for lower spending, for less government, for lower taxes, for much tougher provisions on criminals." On CNN's morning news show he said, "I think that the American people want very bold dramatic change."[3] In an interview with Maureen Dowd later in the day, he was back on the attack: "Although Mr. Gingrich said it might take a decade, he promised to bury any remnants of what he disdainfully calls the Great Society counterculture, McGovern legacy, and return America to a more black and white view of right and wrong." Gingrich told Dowd "he expected a ten to twelve year battle between conservatives and leftist elites over the direction of the country, before conservatives would be able to recast the government as a force for traditional morals."[4]

Clinton spent Election Night at the White House with the first lady and close friends, according to the *Washington Post*'s Dan Balz.[5] For most of the evening he remained in the family quarters, where he watched the returns on television and placed and fielded phone calls from Democrats around the country, many of whom had already lost. Several times during the evening and night he ventured down to the West Wing, where his staff was tabulating the results and grimly monitoring one bad outcome after another. The next morning Clinton woke to learn that the *New York Times* and *Washington Post* had interpreted the election results as a referendum on him—a referendum that he had lost badly. The *Times* front-page headline was "A Vote against Clinton," and the *Washington Post* lead story was titled "An Historic Election Message of Repudiation to President Clinton and His Party."

There was no public statement from the president until the afternoon. Even then the event was delayed by an hour while Clinton huddled with his aides, deciding what to say. Not surprisingly the president was deeply shocked by the one-sided results. He had campaigned for

Democrats in state after state almost nonstop for several weeks before the election, and everywhere his candidates were losing. He looked haggard and tired at the press conference, which was held in the East Room of the White House. The location gave his remarks the full formality of presidential pomp, to remind the country that he was still president even though his party had been clobbered in the election and it seemed as if the leadership of the country had passed to Gingrich and his Republican allies. The *Post*'s veteran and insightful columnist Mary McGrory described Clinton's mood: "He was pretty much in the Ancient Mariner mode, haunted and babbling. He couldn't stop talking about the shipwreck that had just occurred, but he couldn't think of anything to say either."[6]

Not surprisingly, Clinton pledged, "I will do everything in my power to reach out to the leaders and members of this new Congress." Reaching out was one thing; I was more worried that he seemed to agree with Gingrich on the meaning of the election. He said, "Not enough people . . . believed we were meeting their desires for a fundamental change in the role of Government in their lives. . . . It must be possible for us to give our people a government that is smaller, that is more effective, that reflects both our interests and our values."[7]

By the time I returned to my office in the Senate for the first time since the election, I had read the clues from Gingrich and the president from the day before. The president was interpreting the election the same way as the leader of the radical right, that voters were calling for less spending, fewer taxes, less government. He was saying he wanted to reach out to the Republicans and meet them in the center. In contrast, the Republican leader was talking about bold and radical change, about "burying" the Great Society and "recasting" the government after a ten-year "battle between conservatives and liberal elites." All I could think of was that if one side in any political struggle is hell-bent on achieving total victory and is conceding no ground to the other, and the other is nodding in agreement with its opponent's interpretation of events and priorities and emphasizing how much it will reach out and work with that opposition, the end result will inevitably be dramatic movement in the direction of the more aggressive party.

Passivity usually doesn't work in politics. The party setting the agenda, bringing energy and vitality to the contest, clear in its convictions, beats the party that is confused, sullen, reactive, defensive, incoherent, and accommodating. It doesn't work in policymaking either. In one hundred days in 1933, President Franklin Roosevelt marshaled all his political capital and pushed through Congress the bulk of the New Deal agenda, while a demoralized and disorganized Republican minority watched, consigned to defeat. President Lyndon Johnson used his huge majority after the 1964 election to push through Congress the raft of far-reaching liberal social legislation that became the Great Society. Gingrich was now poised to ram through a radical conservative agenda, and the Democratic president was already conceding ground.

WHAT A DIFFERENCE AN ELECTION MAKES!

Arriving at my office, I was surprised when the door of the Labor Committee administrative office next to mine suddenly opened and Senator Nancy Kassebaum's chief of staff, Susan Hattan, stepped out, nearly running into me. I knew Susan well. After the election Kassebaum would replace Kennedy as chair of the Committee, and she would choose the new staff director. Now change stared me in the face. Susan had been in the Committee office already. She must have been talking to the Committee administrator, making plans for Republican control, scoping out my office, which would soon be hers.

"Susan, congratulations! Would you like to inspect your new office?" I said, being as upbeat as I could be.

A broad grin escaped her normal composure. "No, not now, but I'd like to get together with you soon to talk about the transition."

My instinct was to be as cooperative as possible. "Sure, just tell me when. I'll come over to the Hart Building to your office. I'd like to see where I'll be moving."

Susan was from Nebraska. Having worked for Kansas senators Dole (five years) and Kassebaum (sixteen years at that point), she was an experienced moderate Republican staffer. I am sure she had chafed under Democratic control of the Senate because Kennedy had controlled the Labor Committee agenda and a good deal else. While I was staff director and Kennedy was chairman, I had tried to be accommodating to the Republicans, but being accommodating and cooperative did not mean giving up on our ambitious goals or lessening the intense workload. Now the positions were reversed. Susan was not only liberated; she was poised to lead, to take control herself. At least she wasn't a Gingrich Republican bent on getting even with us or, as Gingrich had put it, "burying" the remnants of our legacy.

I asked Susan what she intended to do about Committee funding for the minority.

"You know Senator Kassebaum is very frugal, and I suspect both the majority and the minority will be facing big budget cuts," she responded. "I'll call you later to set up a time to meet."

My heart sank. I had calculated that our share of the Committee budget would automatically be reduced by at least 50 percent when we went into the minority, but now I feared Kassebaum would cut the whole Committee budget even more. There were over forty staff members working for the ten Democratic senators on the Committee. At least half of them would have to find another job.

Other than Nadine Arrington, the Committee administrator, I was the first in my office that morning. Nadine arrived early most mornings, and I'm sure she especially wanted to be there early today in case Susan Hattan came by. Usually the Committee administrators would change as control shifted from one party to the next, but Nadine had survived at least two turnovers over the past fifteen years. She was an elegant woman whose soft, cultured voice masked an iron determination to see that her job was carried out efficiently and effectively, and I thought it was likely that she would survive this turnover as well.

WHAT WE WILL BE HIT WITH

I called our first staff meeting to assess the impact of Republican control in Washington on the issues each of our staff members worked on and to respond to the matter on every Democratic staff members' mind that day: the future of his or her job.

The impending loss of staff was upsetting, but the threat the Gingrich agenda presented to the continuation of a strong government role in the lives of middle- and low-income Americans was even more so. These families depended on the federal government for health care, college loans and grants, job training, and aid to elementary and secondary schools, among other programs. Millions of others depended on the federal government to monitor safety conditions in the workplace, to enforce the safety of the food, drug, and water supplies, to regulate conditions in the nation's nursing homes, and to assure the security of their pensions. Years later it is hard to remember that Gingrich targeted each of these programs for massive reduction or elimination. Our Committee had jurisdiction over most of these issues, but even in other key areas, such as Medicare and Medicaid, which belonged to the Finance Committee, Kennedy had historically taken a critical leadership role. He—and we—would be at the epicenter of the Republican crusade to reduce the role of government in American life.

The Kennedy staff assembled at lunchtime in the Committee hearing room. The room is very grand, rectangular in shape, with wood-paneled walls, ornate moldings, bronze Art Deco lighting fixtures, tall ceilings, and large, wide windows draped with deep green, heavy, floor-to-ceiling curtains. At the end of the room opposite the public entranceway is an elevated U-shaped stage fronted by a long, U-shaped desk. This stage or dais is where the Committee senators sit in high-back leather swivel chairs for hearings. Along the wall behind the dais are small metal chairs for staff members. In front is a long table for the witnesses; behind that are rows of chairs for spectators, and, on each side, tables for the press. The room is used not only for hearings but also for markups, where bills referred to the Committee are amended and voted on and for press conferences, meetings, and even holiday parties.

The Committee room had been the scene of many memorable events as well as confrontations between Democrats and Republicans over labor, education, and health policy issues. More than any other place this room impressed me with what we had lost. We didn't control the hearing room anymore. We would not be the ones scheduling hearings on issues we chose or moving legislation we wrote or consistently winning votes in Committee on bills and amendments. I looked behind the dais and focused on the row of empty metal chairs along the wall where our staff members sat behind their bosses at hearings. In January many of those seats on the Democratic side would be empty.

The Committee education and health staff arrived together, followed by the labor and employment staff, all from the Hart Senate Building next door. The immigration and judiciary staffs, along with a small contingent focused on children's issues, our general counsel, our oversight staff, and our press staff all came from offices in the Dirksen Building. Legislative Director Carey Parker and Kennedy's foreign policy staff came from the senator's personal office in the Russell Building.

Since I started working for Kennedy I had carried a six-by-nine-and-a-half-inch spiral notebook to every meeting, and I had made a habit of writing down, verbatim when possible, whatever was said in a form of shorthand I had developed while I was a prosecutor writing down witnesses' statements during interviews. My notes from this first meeting of staff after the election debacle reflect the alarm we shared about Gingrich's intentions.

We had all read the newspapers that morning and knew in broad strokes what Gingrich and Dole were intending and that President Clinton was offering to work with them. Every staff member had followed the campaign discussions of their issues and had studied the Contract with America and the policy statements by Gingrich and his allies, which provided details beyond the relatively brief and general provisions of the Contract. Our staff had worked with many of the Republican staff members whose senators were soon to assume leadership roles in shaping the Republican strategy and agenda. In some cases our staff had already met with their counterparts on our Committee and staff of Republicans in leadership roles and had learned more details of what they were planning. So it was likely that the predictions at this meeting were well founded.

"What will we be hit with first?" I asked. We started with education, where the Republican agenda was most menacing. Ellen Guiney, our lead staff person for elementary and secondary education issues, said, "Watch out for an all-out attack on public elementary and secondary school programs. The Republican platform calls to abolish the federal Department of Education. The new majority believes the federal government has no role in public schools." Clayton Spencer, who handled higher education issues for us (in 2014 she became president of Bates College), described the new Republican majority as "hostile to universities that were seen as hotbeds of elitism, liberal intellectualism, and Democrats. Their goals include slashing college student aid and loan programs and grants to researchers at universities and hospitals."

Predictions on health care were just as ominous. David Nexon, Kennedy's longtime chief health policy advisor (and more recently my coauthor), warned, "The guarantee of health care provided by Medicare and Medicaid since 1965, when these programs were enacted, is on the block. Health benefits will be reduced and premiums increased, with an ultimate objective of privatizing or eliminating the programs entirely." Dr. Van Dunn said, "All public health programs are in jeopardy, and funding for training programs for health professionals, for the Centers for Disease Control, and for minority health programs can no longer be taken for granted. The Republican strategy is to cut funding, eliminate and consolidate federal programs on health care into so-called block grants to the states, where the remaining funds will be allotted by state governments under the control of Republican governors and suburban legislators. Cities and the poor will be left out."

On wages, Beth Slavet, a Kennedy labor staff member, told us, "Republicans in the House want to abolish the minimum wage altogether. They are certainly adamantly opposed to our intention to try to raise it." She added, "There will be a steady attack on laws that protect labor unions, and regulations that govern the rights and safety of workers in the workplace." Judy Appelbaum, a women's rights advocate on Kennedy's Judiciary Committee staff, reported, "Nine of the eleven newly elected Republican senators are staunchly opposed to a woman's right to choose and have pledged to outlaw and criminalize abortions." Michael Iskowitz, Kennedy's chief staff member on children's issues, told us, "Programs to help families and young children, such as child care and early childhood education, are viewed as unwarranted intervention by big government in the raising of children. These programs are all threatened." Ron Weich, Kennedy's advisor on criminal justice and mental health issues (now dean of the University of Baltimore School of Law), said, "There will be less funding for drug prevention, less for civil rights enforcement, and less for afterschool crime-prevention programs." Marsha Simon, Kennedy's staff member handling appropriations bills, reported, "A first line of attack by the Republicans will be on the budget. They will seek to make steep cuts in programs in our committee's areas to balance the budget, while following the Reagan model of large tax reductions for upper-income Americans and corporations and large increases in defense spending. . . . I am especially disturbed because as a consequence of the election results, the Clinton administration is already rethinking the budget it was preparing to introduce in January. I have heard noises from the administration about drastic cuts to meet the Republican demands."

There was very little good news. Nexon had talked to the Kassebaum health staff about moving forward on very limited health care reform, but they made it clear that expanding health insurance coverage to the uninsured was off the table. On job training, Kassebaum and her Republican counterpart in the House Education and Training Committee, Congressman Bill Goodling of Pennsylvania, both supported reasonable reform of job training programs, particularly consolidating many different programs spread across offices and agencies into one-stop job search and training centers in each community. This made sense to us. On the budget and appropriations front, the only good news was that Senator

Mark Hatfield of Oregon, the veteran moderate Republican soon to be chairman of the Appropriations Committee, was opposed to Gingrich's budget-slashing strategy.

The discussion went on for several hours. What were the Republicans planning in each area? What programs did we have to extend, or "reauthorize," before they expired? Where could we work with the Republicans? Could we do anything now, in November and December, while Kennedy was still chair of the Committee, to publicize the consequences of what the Republicans were planning? Would anybody listen to a lame-duck chairman if we tried? I requested that each staff member prepare reports for briefings for the senator, which we expected to hold within the next few days on each of the four key areas: health care, education, labor, and children and families. We'd have these memos ready for the next week's briefings.

Then we turned to the grim topic of the Committee's budget for staff. I asked all staff members to come and see me over the next day and a half. We all knew cuts were coming, but I preferred to have these conversations privately so I could work through each individual's situation.

KENNEDY BEGINS TO CHART HIS COURSE

Before attending any other meetings, I was summoned to Kennedy's main office to meet with him. The senator was impatient to get back to work.

No matter how many times I have sat in Kennedy's office with him or with other members of his staff, I still found the experience inspiring. The office itself is imposing, with high ceilings and a handsome marble fireplace along one wall. Behind the senator's desk are French doors opening onto a balcony that runs along the south side of the Russell Building on Constitution Avenue and looks out across the green through Japanese fruit trees and American elms to the Capitol. It was on that balcony that Kennedy had offered me the job in 1989.

The room itself was furnished more like a living room than an office. In the center were sofas and easy chairs arranged in a circle to facilitate discussion among senators and guests and staff. A deep blue, handsomely upholstered couch was on the wall opposite the fireplace, two crimson wing chairs faced each other across an antique coffee table, and three other wooden chairs were arranged around the table. Behind one of the wing chairs in front of the window was Kennedy's desk, the same desk his brother had used in the White House. On one side was an American flag that President Kennedy had saved from his time in World War II. On the other was a flag of the Republic of Ireland. On one wall were pictures of Senator Kennedy with foreign dignitaries: among them, Nelson Mandela, Mikhail Gorbachev, and several presidents of Ireland.

On the other walls of the room were framed Kennedy family mementos: President Kennedy's original dog tag from PT 109, a letter from Senator Kennedy's mother to him when he was a schoolboy, noting that his report card was unsatisfactory because he hadn't gotten all A's, a picture of John F. Kennedy Jr. introducing the senator at the Democratic Convention in 1988 in Atlanta, with the inscription "From the nephew to the uncle, 'you were always there when we needed you.' With love, John." There was a photo of the three Kennedy brothers—president, attorney general, and senator—inscribed to the senator by President Kennedy, and a photo of Senator Kennedy's oldest brother, Joseph Kennedy Jr., who was killed in World War II. There were photos of Kara, Teddy, Patrick, Curran, and Caroline. On another wall were paintings and photographs of Kennedy's sailboat, the *Mya*, on which he could usually be found in daylight hours when his schedule permitted him to return to his summer home in Hyannis Port on Cape Cod. When one met with Kennedy in his office, there was history all around, and somehow that history seemed to elevate the significance of every meeting. (A replica of the senator's office and anteroom has been constructed in the new Edward M. Kennedy Institute for the Senate in Boston and can be visited by the public.)

For our meeting, Kennedy took his accustomed seat in the wing chair in front of his desk. Carey Parker, his longtime legislative director whose office was immediately next door, joined us. We had been talking to other Democrats, and we knew how they were feeling. Those still in office were demoralized and disoriented. Many were at a loss to respond to the election disaster they were now experiencing. Many were already arguing for accommodation to the Republican platform, for acquiescing to their legislative program. Their thinking was that we couldn't stop them no matter what we did, the public had spoken, and we'd only make matters worse if we resisted.

Kennedy didn't agree. He wasted no time in calling for a massive effort to organize resistance to Gingrich. As he always did at important moments, he dissected the problem calmly and strategically: "The biggest problem we'll have in stopping these Republican initiatives will be holding Democrats together. Democrats are shattered by the results of the election. Those who survived are looking over their shoulders at Republican challenges next time. Those who were lucky enough not to have an election this year will be doing the same."

He continued forcefully, "Our only chance of succeeding is to hold the Democrats together. To do that, we must convince them that the election was not a mandate for a drastic scaling back of government. The best strategy for Democrats is to identify the issues that matter to working families—health care, education, jobs, and wages—and hold every Republican action and every Democratic initiative to the standard of how it affects middle- and low-income Americans. Too many concessions, any attempt by Democrats to be more like the Republicans, would have disastrous consequences for these ordinary people. And it will doom the Democrats' political fortunes for the foreseeable future. After this election, there will now be a long and difficult struggle for the soul of the Democratic Party."

Just two days after that devastating election, Kennedy's spirit and resilience made him determined not only to resist the Republican onslaught but to continue moving ahead with our own legislative initiatives. It simply never occurred to him that we should abandon these initiatives in the face of the Republican takeover. He had already identified the political strategy necessary to succeed on our policy priorities and position the Democratic Party for the next election.

Where did this resolve come from? The Republicans seemed to have all the momentum behind their agenda. Many Democrats in Washington were assuming, as Clinton appeared to be, that they would have to lie low. Conventional wisdom suggested that resisting the Republicans would be hopeless. Why, then, was Kennedy instinctively and without hesitation prepared to sail against the wind?

For him, the question of whether the resistance would succeed was secondary; it was just the right thing to do. Using the government as an instrument to improve the lives of the American people—particularly those who needed help the most—was the very reason for his public service and the foundation of his political convictions. It was what he had campaigned on in Massachusetts. It was what he had fought for during three decades in the Senate and one run at the presidency. He could not be true to himself and watch the Republicans repeal the institutions of support and opportunity that had been built by Democrats since the New Deal.

Kennedy knew viscerally what we should do, both in terms of where to stand and the broad strategy and tactics needed to achieve his goals. He was not only a liberal icon; he was one of the canniest politicians in America. With the perspective of thirty-two years in the Senate he knew that there is an ebb and flow in politics. He knew that movements that were ascendant at one time would eventually recede, and other movements would rise to take their place. Eventually the pendulum would swing back toward government activism. The Reagan agenda had been almost as radical as Gingrich's, and while Reagan had done some damage to social programs, he had not been successful in repealing the New Deal and the Great Society—not even close. Giving in made no sense, and resisting made all the sense in the world.

Kennedy also sensed that Republicans—and Democrats—were drastically misreading the public mood. He believed that the election represented dissatisfaction with the Democrats more than a massive voter shift to the right. The American people didn't want Medicare to "wither away." They didn't want government to stop protecting them against unsafe water or polluted air or dangerous pesticides. They wanted the federal government to do *more* to improve education, not *less*. They didn't want senior citizens left to the untender mercies of the nursing home industry, and they wanted health security for their own families and for every other family as well. Fighting against the Gingrich agenda was not only critical for the American people; it was good politics for the Democrats.

Furthermore, people all over the country depended on Kennedy for leadership for their causes: blue-collar workers, minorities, immigrants, the poor, the LGBT community, the elderly, children. These people and their champions in Washington and Massachusetts and across the country had been allies of Kennedy's for years. There was no question that they needed him now, as they were the ones in the sights of the Contract with America. They knew he would not stand aside while the Republicans sought to decimate the programs on which they depended. Other Democrats would help, but Kennedy had to lead the charge.

While Kennedy's powerful convictions were a source of great inspiration to others, he was reluctant to talk about the sources of his own inspiration. It's clear, though, that his identification with those left out or left behind started from the very beginning.

As a freshly elected senator at the age of thirty in 1962, Kennedy's first fight was to challenge the southern Democrats, the barons who controlled the key committees, by leading the opposition to the poll tax, a barrier that stood firmly in the way of African Americans and the poor exercising their right to vote in the South.

From the stories he told about "Grandpa," it was clear that John "Honey Fitz" Fitzgerald, the three-term congressman and mayor of Boston known as a fighter for the working man, was a primary influence in his life. He loved to recall the time he spent with his grandfather when he was twelve and living at a boarding school outside Boston. His grandfather had retired and lived alone in a hotel; Kennedy would take the train in to the city to have lunch with him each Sunday. They would meet at the back door of the hotel. "Grandpa would take me into the dining room through the kitchen. He knew the first names of each waiter and the cooks and the busboys, and he would take me around to each of them and say hello to them by name and introduce me. We almost never went into the dining room until we had spoken to all the people in the kitchen. They were all Grandpa's friends. They were the ones he had always fought for in politics."

SUBSTANCE, POLITICS, AND PUBLIC RELATIONS

After Kennedy made clear he was going to fight, we wasted no time getting to work on the plan. At its core, it was similar to the approach he applied to legislative goals when we were in the majority. He told me to immerse myself in the first step of what would be our defense: gather our ammunition, steep ourselves in the facts, investigate the underlying causes of the drubbing at the polls, master the substance and predict the consequences of the Republican proposals, flesh out our own initiatives, and frame the debate. As usual Kennedy was on the lookout for new ideas, new approaches, new messages, and new ways of stating his position.

Kennedy was a master of the legislative process, so after six years in the majority I had learned something about how legislation moved. There were three components to our strategy that had worked over and over again: substance, politics, and public relations.

The first requirement involved researching the substance thoroughly to get the initiative or strategy just right and to prepare to respond to every question and challenge. Kennedy insisted that there was no substitute for exhaustive research, analysis, discussion, and preparation. He always tried to know more about the subject before him than anyone else, whether the venue was a committee markup, a floor debate, a caucus discussion, or a meeting among senators. He believed that knowledge was power.

The second element was politics, which included an "inside game" and an "outside game." The inside game covered the strategy in the Senate, on the Hill, and in the administration. Here we benefited from Kennedy's ability to gather bipartisan support for whatever he was doing, whether he was in the majority or the minority. He knew the importance of building relationships with Republicans—conservative Republicans at that—and using these relationships to forge important alliances on bills. This inside game also included working with Democrats to make sure they would be supportive, even if they were not as committed to the initiative as we were.

The outside game was equally important. This referred to the grassroots support for the initiative, spread as broadly as possible across the country. We usually started by organizing this support in Washington with the national groups concerned about whatever legislative area we were working on, but quickly expanded the effort through the groups or directly to the grassroots. Here the senator emphasized that legislators needed to hear from their constituents at home to know that the issue was important enough to act on.

The third broad component of our approach was the public relations or marketing effort. Our allies never had as much money as the opposition, so we couldn't run major television advertising campaigns. But recognizing the Washington adage that nothing happened if it didn't happen in the press, we focused on the so-called unpaid media—the free press. Because politicians respond to issues that are in the public eye, we were constantly engaged in organizing public events and drumming up news around each of our initiatives. We worked for endorsements, held rallies, reviewed and publicized polls, sought out—and sometimes developed ourselves—reports and studies that could be released to create news. We held hearings that were designed to generate media interest. Sometimes the effort put into an event seemed immensely disproportionate to the coverage it received, but the cumulative effect was what was important.

The three elements worked together, and each was indispensable to success. Without the substance you couldn't assemble the political coalitions or motivate the public interest allies or fend off the arguments of political opponents. Without the politics you didn't have the support necessary to get anything done. Without a press strategy there was no energy or pressure behind an initiative to cause it to emerge from among the hundreds of other ideas and causes competing for attention.

There was a fourth element to success in the Senate, which Kennedy was better at understanding than anyone else and which he always raised when we developed a strategy. That is the "chemistry" on the floor, in the cloakrooms, and in the caucuses, or, as Kennedy frequently said, the "chemical" situation on the floor, which was one of my favorite Kennedy malapropisms. Which way is the debate going? Who has the momentum? He understood the importance of the chemistry of the Senate and the effect it could have on any and all Senate business, and he used it as his secret weapon.

At this first meeting, Kennedy described a road map for the two months that lay ahead before the new Congress began and Gingrich and the Republicans officially took over. While the basics—substance, the inside and the outside game—had not changed, I had no experience working in the minority, as Kennedy had. But the key question remained: would the strategy work this time, with this majority, and with this president?

On the substance, Kennedy referred to three tasks for action in November and December. His inclination was to give a major speech in early January that would lay out the road map, pulling together in one outline the ideas, themes, and message of the Democratic strategy. But before that moment he would use the results of our research and analysis to guide the conversations he would have with other Democrats, and ultimately with the president, about this agenda.

First, he wanted to understand fully the results of the election, the causes and ramifications of the Democratic defeat. What were voters really saying? Which themes had worked for Democrats, and which hadn't?

Second, he wanted to plow ahead with his own affirmative legislative agenda in health care, education, and increasing the minimum wage. Which initiatives in these areas could work in the new environment of Republican control and without a majority on the Committee or in the Senate?

Third, and most important, we had to be prepared to resist the Contract with America and other Republican initiatives. Kennedy asked me to set up a series of meetings for him over the next month with outside experts, historians, political analysts, and writers. The purpose of these meetings was to assess the causes of the election debacle, to understand the new order in Washington, and to find the best way of leading the minority. This was standard operating procedure for the senator. He was a good delegator. Because his legislative efforts spanned such a broad spectrum, he relied heavily on his staff, and over the years he had been extremely successful at recruiting and keeping talented staffers. But on the big strategic issues, he never relied solely on the inner circle. Instead he reached out broadly to political allies, to the huge network of friends and advisors he and his brothers had worked with over the years, to the best thinkers and writers. Often we would gather a small group over a spirited dinner at his house, to get their ideas, debate with them, sharpen our understanding of what had happened and where we should go from there. In preparing our affirmative agenda, we would bring together discussion groups of outside experts in health care, education, and the economy, but we would also rely on our own staff who were experts in their own right in each of these areas. To understand the Gingrich agenda and the Contract with America, we would also meet with advocates and experts on areas targeted by the Republicans. This would allow us to develop the most effective opposition strategy and response. What would be the impact of budget cuts on health and education? How would we highlight opposition to repealing environmental and workplace safety and wage protection regulations?

Getting the substance of our situation under control was the first task set out by the senator. We would be holding meetings and conducting interviews nonstop for the next two months to prepare for January 1995.

UNITING THE DEMOCRATS

On the politics—inside the Congress—Kennedy had already warned that our biggest challenge would be holding the Democrats together behind a strategy opposing the Contract with America. Without unified Democratic support, the opposition could not succeed. So the first task he proposed was a series of meetings with Democrats in the Senate: in the leadership, on the Labor Committee, and with others who were potential allies on various issues. But of course there was no Democratic leadership yet. Mitchell, the previous majority leader, had not run for reelection. His heir apparent, Jim Sasser of Tennessee, had been defeated in his reelection bid, and Daschle, who, as Mitchell's deputy, would seem to have the inside track on the leadership position, had not actually won the position or picked his leadership team, and it was not clear if he would face any opposition. Democrats would hold their election for leadership positions in early December. Until then, things would be in a state of uncertainty.

Next would be meetings with House Democrats, who were facing an even greater challenge than Senate Democrats. They had lost their majority for the first time in forty years, and they would face the first battle over the Gingrich agenda. The procedural rules of the House strongly favored the majority, but Kennedy wanted meetings set up with the House leaders nonetheless because a unified voice would strengthen his party's opposition.

The most important Democrat in Washington was the president, and he was key to the strategy. He still had the power of the bully pulpit, and his appointees ran the agencies that administered the programs Gingrich would try to dismantle. The Republicans needed his signature on bills unless they could override his vetoes by obtaining a two-thirds vote in both the House and the Senate. But Kennedy wanted to wait on tackling Clinton. "Let's get everything ready," he said, "and then, before he has made any irreversible decision that sets us back on our opposition strategy, let's go see him and make our case. But let's be well prepared."

Kennedy also wanted to start meeting with our allies in the public interest advocacy community—the advocates for children, seniors, women, consumers, workers, education, and health care. These grassroots organizations would be our ground troops for the opposition, so we needed to schedule strategy sessions with them in the next sixty days.

Since it was not just a defensive agenda that Kennedy was contemplating—he still intended to push forward with an affirmative agenda in health care, education, and wage growth, particularly—he also asked me to plan meetings with key Republicans, first those on the Labor Committee and then others with whom he had hopes of striking bipartisan deals to advance new initiatives even while he was in the minority. He wanted to start with the new chair of the Labor Committee, Kassebaum, and follow with Jeffords, next in seniority among Republicans on the Committee. Kassebaum had worked well with Kennedy before, and Jeffords had been an ally on health care and the minimum wage, so there was some hope these conversations could be productive.

The third element of the strategy, the press side, would take longer to plan. The core of Kennedy's message came straight from his own election campaign: Democrats must fight for health care, education, and jobs, and against Republican plans to reduce government efforts in these areas. He would present his blueprint of opposition in his speech in January, but for now he would pull back out of the public eye to prepare for the year ahead and the changes that would come.

STAFF

One of the first tasks was the wrenching job of paring back the Committee staff. Each member of Congress has a budget for personal staff. Chairmen and ranking members also have separate committee budgets because so much of the work of Congress is done in committees. As an activist senator who wanted as large a staff as possible to help drive a wide-ranging progressive agenda and who presided over a committee with far-reaching jurisdiction, Kennedy had managed to engineer a budget for the Labor Committee that was one of the largest in the Senate. As in most committees, this budget was traditionally divided into two-thirds for the majority and one-third for the minority, so we could anticipate a cut of at least 50 percent when the new Congress convened in January. Susan Hattan had already warned me that Kassebaum might want to cut the overall Committee budget further, reducing our share even more—and some Republicans saw cutting back the Kennedy staff as a way to clip the senator's wings. We needed a staff of reasonable size to adequately analyze proposed legislation in our jurisdiction, to manage our legislative agenda, and to oversee executive branch activities—all key responsibilities of Congress under our system of government. Without adequate staff, Congress has to rely almost entirely on outside interest groups or the administration for information and expertise, and its ability to exercise independent judgment is curtailed.

Our Committee's broad authority included jurisdiction over three cabinet departments: the Department of Education, the Department of Labor, and jointly with the Finance Committee, the largest of all executive branch departments, the Department of Health and Human Services. Each of these departments had very large budgets, many programs, and many employees engaged in carrying out their programs.

Even in the majority, we felt our staff resources were slim. While Kennedy was chairman of the Committee, we had two or three—or, at most, four—professional staff people, whom we paid with our Committee budget, in each of the principal areas of jurisdiction: health, education, and labor. Because of our limited ability to hire paid staff, we often supplemented staff on our Committee payroll with interns and other volunteers, individuals on sabbaticals or receiving fellowships from foundations or universities, and so-called detailees, individuals on loan or assignment from the executive branch.

Put in this context, it seems ridiculous that the responsibility for all these functions rests on a paid committee staff of only about sixty individuals working for sixteen senators of both parties. Under Kassebaum's budget reductions, Kennedy's staff would consist of as few as one senior person in each of the three key areas, in addition to my position as minority staff director and possibly several additional senior staff for the areas of oversight and investigations, press, and Committee legal counsel. One person would write the laws, authorize the funding, and oversee the Department of Health and Human Services, with its budget of $640 billion and 127,000 employees; a second person would do the same for programs in the Department of Education, with its budget of $27 billion and 200,000 employees; while a third would have to do the same for the Labor Department, with its budget of $50 billion and 200,000 employees.

Kennedy attracted talented staff because he was the preeminent activist legislator of his time. Those of us who shared his view of an active role for government in society had long known that there was no better person to work for. But just as we came to Washington to further this agenda, there were others who came to stop it. Shortly after I became staff director, I received some candid insight on the Republican view of Kennedy and his staff from David Durenberger, a moderate Republican senator from Minnesota. After a Labor Committee hearing, Durenberger approached me and, to my surprise, invited me back to his office; it was the first time a senator other than Kennedy had asked to talk with me alone.

Sitting in the inner sanctum of his private Senate office, he said, "I'm really interested in why you came to Washington. What was it about working in the Senate that led you to give up your work in a law firm where you were probably making a lot more money? I'm thinking the reason you came must be that you're one of those Kennedy people who really wants to get things done in government. You're coming down here to get bills passed and get things done—that's what Kennedy's all about. You wanted to come to Washington to be like Kennedy: you wanted to pass laws."

When I said yes to all this, he continued, "Well, I want to tell you something, just so you have it in your mind. The Republicans on the Committee and in the Senate come to Washington to make sure that you and Kennedy don't pass any laws. At the end of the day, if they can go home and say to their family or to their constituents that they stopped you from passing a law, that's going to make them totally satisfied. That's their objective. I just wanted you to know."

He seemed like a person with good intentions, and his advice really helped bring home what we were up against. I left appreciative but scratching my head about his motivations. On reflection, I thought that perhaps, since Durenberger was a moderate Republican who did want to get things done, he was trying to send me the message that if Kennedy wanted to work with a Republican partner, he, Durenberger, would be a good choice.

There are trade-offs involved in becoming a Senate staffer, even one for Kennedy, and that's why so many are young. First, the pay is likely to be less than they would earn in the private sector. When I began on

Kennedy's staff, the starting salary on the Committee was about $16,000 a year; my salary was less than one-third of what I had made as an attorney. Second, the hours are extraordinarily long. Working until 3:00 a.m. or later night after night is almost routine before a contentious markup or floor debate. Third, expectations in the Kennedy office for top-flight performance, although rarely stated, are very high, which creates immense pressure to work hard and do well.

Then there are the limitations on congressional staff. We exist to serve the legislative and political causes of the senator for whom we work. The senator has the office and all the power that goes with it; he or she sets the direction and makes the key decisions. The staff does the backup work, the research, and negotiates all day long around all manner of issues with other staff and outside advocates. In a sense, the senator bestows his or her authority on us. It is an unwritten rule that, in return, we will be anonymous. We do everything in the name of the senator for whom we work. Our names rarely appear in the newspaper; the senator's does. We do not go on television; the senator does. For some of us a state of anonymity is almost a relief, as most of the pressure is on the senator. He or she is the one appearing in public; his or her reputation is always on the line. The pressure on us comes from the expectations of the senator and from our desire to further a common purpose. As staff we are part of a closed society, unknown to the outside world. Within our special world we exercise considerable discretion in making hundreds of decisions each day on matters too small, too fast-moving, or too routine for the senator to become involved in.

One area in which a staff director makes decisions in collaboration with a senator is choosing staff. Staff directors recruit, screen, and interview, and then present finalists to the senator for interviews and final decisions. When staff cuts are in order, we are the first to meet with the individuals involved, although once again the senator ultimately chooses who will stay in which position.

Kennedy was not always terribly direct about his feelings toward his staff. Occasionally we received a handwritten notation, such as "Good" or better yet "Very good," on the top of a memo we had sent him. The personal office staff would return such memos to us with the senator's handwritten comment in a nearly illegible scrawl and a gold star on any memo that had a "Good" on it. But that was it. On a day-to-day basis, the senator was all business. At the same time, all of us felt that he appreciated our efforts and appreciated us as people. Occasionally he was effusive with praise and gratitude. He went out of his way to recognize staff at appropriate times. He always sent Christmas gifts with a personal note attached. When a bill passed that we had worked on, he would get the title page framed and present it to us with a handwritten message across the top. When he received a coveted bill-signing pen from the president, that would also be framed and given to the appropriate staff member. Staff members who were hospitalized or ill could count on a call and flowers from the senator. The death of a parent or loved one always resulted in a sympathy call. If he heard something nice about us from another senator or saw a newspaper story that reflected well on something we did, we could count on a call or a note.

Kennedy's expectations for his staff were high. He made his displeasure known if he didn't feel he was getting what he needed or if he felt he wasn't being prepared properly for a meeting or event. But since his demands were fair and reasonable, we appreciated them as challenging and inspiring. We were grateful for his encouragement to press the limits of the possible, to dream up new ideas, and to fight to the end for the dreams we shared. He provided the access, the power, and the political savvy to make achieving our dreams seem possible. Many of us had great personal affection for him, and it was well known that people who ultimately left the office remained part of the Kennedy network for life.

Many former Kennedy staff members have gone on to very distinguished careers. To name just a few, among the chiefs of staff, Paul Kirk became chairman of the Democratic National Committee and was appointed by Massachusetts governor Deval Patrick to serve out the five months remaining in Kennedy's Senate term when he died; Kenneth Feinberg became administrator of the victims' compensation funds for 9/11, the BP oil spill, and the Boston Marathon bombing; David Burke became CBS News chief; and Ranny Cooper became president of public affairs at Weber Shandwick, a large international public relations firm. Among Judiciary Committee staffers, Stephen Breyer became a U.S. Supreme Court justice; Melody Barnes became chief of President Obama's domestic policy staff; Tom Perez was named secretary of labor in Obama's second term; Ron Weich became dean of the University of Baltimore School of Law; and David Boies represented Gore in *Bush v. Gore* and the plaintiffs in the California gay marriage equality case. Among foreign policy advisors, Gregory Craig served as an advisor to both Clinton and Obama and was the lead defense attorney in the Clinton impeachment trial; Jim Steinberg became deputy secretary of state and is currently dean of the Maxwell School at Syracuse University; and Bill Lynn was named deputy secretary of defense. Among Labor Committee staff, Dr. Phil Caper became vice chancellor for medical affairs, chief of the medical staff, and hospital director of the University of Massachusetts Medical School; education advisor Clayton Spencer became the second woman to be president of Bates College; health policy advisor Mark B. Childress became senior counsel for Senate Majority Leader Tom Daschle, deputy chief of staff for President Obama, and U.S. ambassador to Tanzania; Sarah Fox was appointed a board member of the National Labor Relations Board and the State Department's special representative for international labor affairs; Dr. Van Dunn became chief medical officer for the mammoth New York City Health and Hospitals Corporation; and Mary Mundinger became the dean of the Columbia School of Nursing.

The person who stayed with the senator the longest at the highest level was Carey Parker, his legislative director. Carey sat in a tiny office right next to the senator's and was consulted on virtually every important decision. He is a brilliant writer who had a hand in most of Kennedy's speeches, either as the principal author or as an editor. Although Kennedy always cast a broad net when looking for advice, Carey was the person he depended on more than anyone else. Carey had been a law clerk to Potter Stewart in the Supreme Court and went to work for Kennedy in 1969 after his clerkship ended. He had originally planned to stay for a year or two and then go into practice but found working for the senator so rewarding that he never wanted to leave.

Regardless of how distinguished their post-Kennedy careers were, all the staff members I knew treasured the opportunity to work with the senator. We each loved our job, and the prospect of losing it because the Senate changed hands was devastating.

Kennedy himself worked extremely hard. His schedule at the office was always packed—and if it wasn't, he complained. He approved everything before it went on his schedule and was adamant about not wasting time. He always took a lot of work home in a big briefcase we called "the bag," mostly staff memos to review. He would work through them after dinner, often making marginal notes or sending them back with questions.

His mornings started early, often with a speech to the breakfast meeting of an advocacy group, a fundraiser, or some other meeting on the way to the office. Before his marriage to Vicki and their subsequent move into the District he would get up even earlier three days a week to play tennis on the court at his house in northern Virginia. After he discovered that I was a pretty good player, he often invited me to join him for a doubles match. He was a steady player but not terribly mobile because of his bad back, so when I was his partner, I was expected to do a lot of running around to return shots he couldn't reach. His other tennis partners were old friends—people like Tim Hanan, Vince Wolfington, and Lee Fentress. Lee, whom he had known from the time Lee worked for Robert Kennedy in the Justice Department, was a former pro and always the best player on the court.

On tennis mornings you had to arrive at 7:30 sharp, and then you discovered who the other players were—other senators, journalists, or personal friends. Were they good, or was this going to be a social or political game? The senator didn't care if it was rainy or cold, or even if there was ice or snow on the court, and he didn't believe in rallying to warm up; he wanted the competition to begin immediately. He always provided four new balls (I never understood why four balls since balls come in cans of three). He would pick the best player for his own partner—most often, that was Lee. Kennedy always served first and rarely moved over from the serving position. If you were his partner at net and the opposing player hit a drop shot, you had to dash over in front of him to get the ball; if it was one of the rare drop shots he thought he could get and he went for it, you had to swerve to avoid colliding with him; if the ball was lobbed over your head, you had to run back and get it. If I were his partner when Lee couldn't be there, he loved teasing me for not running back to get the ball fast enough. The games were very competitive, and the senator did not like to lose. We played until 8:45 sharp, no matter what the score was, and after showering we'd all gather in his library for breakfast: English muffins with strawberry jam and rashers of bacon, which were replenished often. We would rehash the game, going over each point: who had missed this shot, who had made an exceptionally good one. We laughed the whole time, but when breakfast was over, the senator was all business and eager to get to the office.

The Committee's budget ran from March 1 to March 1 each year, so even though the Republicans were taking over in January there was some possibility we would have flexibility with our budget through the end of February.

A month later, we got the bad news from the Republicans that our budget would be cut not by 50 percent but by 75 percent. Unfortunately that meant we would lose some of our most talented staff members, a profound loss for the committee.

THE DEATH OF LIBERALISM IS ANNOUNCED

In the days and weeks immediately after the election, the press frequently reported on Republicans' ambitions for massive change. Speaker-to-be Gingrich declared that he would read the Contract with America in the House at the start of business every day for the first hundred days and would work around the clock if necessary to pass every single item in it in those same hundred days. Three days after the election, the *New York Times* quoted him as saying, "I am prepared to cooperate with the Clinton administration. I am not prepared to compromise."[8] Three days later he suggested that poor children who weren't doing well with their parents should be removed from their families and sent to orphanages.[9]

Within days of the election, Congressman Bill Archer of Texas, soon to become chairman of the critical House Ways and Means Committee, said that he intended to replace the income tax with a national sales tax. The first week after the election, Gingrich said he would move a prayer in schools amendment promptly through Congress. Many Democrats shuddered when President Clinton initially responded favorably to this, even saying he would consider working toward a constitutional amendment to guarantee a right to prayer in the public schools.[10]

Ten days after the election it was reported that Republicans in the House had distributed questionnaires to prospective staff members to make sure that anyone who was seeking a job from any House Republican agreed with a set of ideological positions consistent with the Gingrich agenda. Abortion should be illegal except in the case of rape. No affirmative action. Prayer should be allowed in schools. Homosexuals should be banned from serving in the military. No candidate for a staff position could agree with the proposition that "health care is a fundamental right." While members of Congress expect to hire staff members who are supportive of their positions, this kind of party litmus test was unheard of and indicated the degree of ideological fervor the new majority had brought to Washington.

The following week Senator Jesse Helms, Republican of North Carolina and soon to be chairman of the illustrious Senate Foreign Relations Committee, told an audience in his home state, "Clinton is not fit for the job as commander in chief." Later he said that Clinton "better have a bodyguard if he were to visit North Carolina."[11]

Republican leaders on the Budget Committee were beginning to put their plans in place as well. The House team announced that they would propose an end to some important entitlement programs under which an American was guaranteed benefits if he or she met certain eligibility standards—programs central to an adequate social safety net. Specifically the Republicans proposed to dismantle the national food stamp program, which provided food for 27 million people; to abolish the national school lunch program, which fed 25 million children a day; and to abolish the Women, Infants and Children program, which served 6.2 million Americans. The Republicans would achieve these ends by dramatically scaling back the funding for each of these programs and ending the legal entitlement to them. The reduced funds would be allocated in so-called block grants to the states. No longer would a pregnant woman, a schoolchild, or a poor family have a right to federal food assistance.

On November 28 the *New York Times* reported that Gingrich had said the House would vote on a constitutional amendment to require a balanced federal budget in mid-January: " 'It will be,' he said, 'our first smashing victory.' " The *Times* observed that this was "a safe political forecast." The newspaper interviewed Congressman Gerald Solomon, a Republican from upstate New York who had proposed a balanced budget earlier in the year. Solomon would be the new chairman of the Rules Committee, and he reflected on what a balanced budget would mean. Under his plan, federal spending on the environment would be cut by 44 percent, on agriculture by 72 percent, and on foreign aid and transportation by 30 percent. As Solomon put it, "It's painful as hell, but eventually you have to stop talking about it in the abstract and begin dealing with the details."[12]

While the Republicans were detailing the plans for their revolution, the disarray among Democrats became more apparent with each passing day. It was widely reported that many Democrats were not convinced that Clinton would in fact head the Democratic ticket in 1996. On November 27 Richard Berke wrote in the *New York Times*, "Three weeks after their top to bottom electoral wipe-out, Democrats remain uncertain over what to do next and virtually leaderless beyond a President who many in the party see as a big part of their problems. . . . Still shell-shocked, they cannot agree on what the party needs to do to make a comeback. And as Republicans grab attention with grand plans to retool government, Democrats seem ominously invisible, their leaders defeated or retired."[13] On December 8 a *Times Mirror* poll reported that Clinton trailed any generic Republican for president in 1996, and, significantly, two-thirds of Democrats wanted other Democrats to challenge Clinton for the nomination.[14]

The news coming out of the White House was not encouraging to those who hoped to resist the Republican agenda. On December 2 it was reported that President Clinton would ask Congress for $25 billion more in military spending, the largest increase in years and a direct response to Republican criticism that the military was underfunded. Coming out of a meeting with the new Republican leaders that same day, Clinton announced that he "wouldn't rule out more tax cuts for the middle class."[15] A week later the *New York Times* reported that Clinton was moving toward the Republicans and preparing his own agenda-setting speech, which would emphasize deep cuts in federal social spending and a restructured government.[16] On December 14 it was reported that Clinton was preparing to recommend eliminating housing programs: "The administration is trying to outmaneuver the Republicans by developing proposals that we would have expected to come from conservatives in the Congress. It's a preemptive strike."[17] The Republicans proposed to abolish the Department of Housing and Urban Development altogether. In short, talk coming out of the White House was all about preemptive strikes on the Republican issues and compromising with the new majority. There was very little talk of resistance—and, worse, no attempt to explain to the public what the radical Republican Contract would mean to average Americans.

Meanwhile Gingrich was moving relentlessly to consolidate his own authority in the new Congress. He was abolishing certain committees and creating new ones. Most important, to make sure that every chairman was committed to his agenda and loyal to his leadership, he was disregarding the tradition of awarding chairmanships based on seniority.

While Clinton talked about working with the Republicans, Gingrich stayed on the attack. On December 3 he said that up to one quarter of the White House staff had used drugs within the past four or five years.[18] On December 5 the Republicans formally elected Gingrich speaker of the House. He asserted, "It's not necessary to repeal programs; you just don't fund them."[19] Richard Armey was elected majority leader; he favored phasing out Social Security, replacing the graduated income tax with a flat tax, eliminating the Environmental Protection Agency, eliminating the minimum wage, repealing the Brady Bill (which required background checks on anyone purchasing firearms), and enacting a constitutional amendment for voluntary prayer in the schools.

Congressman Tom DeLay, from the suburbs of Houston, was elected Republican whip. He was a former pest control executive whose main passion was exterminating any form of government regulation. DeLay was also a skilled politician. He conceived the notorious "K Street Project," designed to cement a steady stream of campaign funding for the Republican Party and cut it off for the Democrats. Under the terms of the project, if any of the downtown trade associations or lobbying firms—major sources of PAC money and influence—hired top officials, they were supposed to clear their choices with DeLay to make sure they would be loyal to the Republican leadership. Those who hired people DeLay disliked were threatened with punishment when legislation in which they had an interest was considered.[20] DeLay also was the inspiration for innovative—and controversial—gerrymandering schemes in Texas and other states. Years later his hardball tactics backfired, and he was forced to resign after being indicted and later convicted for circumventing campaign fundraising rules, although the conviction was reversed on appeal.

With the Republicans proclaiming the death of liberalism, Gingrich taking the reins of power, the punditry announcing a political realignment, and even many Democrats desperately shifting to the right, it was an extremely difficult time for progressives who believed in the potential of government as a positive social force. Had our time passed? Were we destined to be in the minority for years to come? I thought Kennedy's victory in Massachusetts offered a way back. But there weren't many Democrats in Washington who saw things the way we did.

Chapter 5

PREPARING THE
RESISTANCE

GETTING THE SUBSTANCE

The first week after the election, Kennedy created a preliminary list of the policy and political experts and progressive advocates he hoped to see over the next month. He wanted to have ideas from as many sources as possible. He also wanted to shore up the morale of progressives and Democrats. Washington meetings with these experts were generally held at the senator's house high above the Potomac River in McLean, Virginia. If the meetings were in Boston, we would meet at a hotel, the Harvard Club, or the house of one of the guests. We called these sessions "issues dinners."

In my time with Kennedy, very few invited experts refused the chance to attend an issues dinner. Whether or not Kennedy knew the individual personally did not matter. If we thought he or she had something important to contribute to a discussion on a particular issue, we would simply call him or her up and extend an invitation. The senator used the dinners to generate new ideas, to test and develop arguments around existing ideas, and simply to build relationships with colleagues and policy experts.

When I first started working for Kennedy, we had issues dinners at his house as frequently as once a week. There were dinners on biomedical research with CEOs of some of the leading pharmaceutical companies in America, on health policy with former staff members and other leading health policy authorities, on drug abuse prevention, on the economics of the minimum wage, on research on early childhood development and education, and on the state of investment in science and technology. We held dinners with presidents of universities and other education policymakers, and with economists to examine broad trends or to focus specifically on tax policy, unemployment, or economic growth. Each year we had a dinner for the Democratic senators on the Labor Committee, and every other year, a dinner for both Republican and Democratic members of the Committee. We had smaller dinners with the ranking member, Senator Orrin Hatch, and his staff, and when Kassebaum became ranking member, with her and her staff. These were meetings to build personal relationships within the Committee and identify particular issues individual senators were interested in pursuing.

While these dinners had a serious purpose, they were also social gatherings marked by some lighter moments. One of the more colorful members of the Committee was eighty-nine-year-old Republican senator Strom Thurmond. He attended a bipartisan dinner of Committee members in 1991 and held forth in Kennedy's living room before a dozen senators of both parties on the secret of his longevity. He described his daily exercise routine: every morning before breakfast, forty minutes of pushups, lifting weights, jumping rope, and the rowing machine. Then he pantomimed his entire routine, concluding with his weight-lifting technique. I stood with a dozen senators watching their elderly colleague squat down, pick up an imaginary barbell, and grimace as he acted out the struggle to press it over his head.

The day I arrived in Washington, February 13, 1989, my first meeting with Kennedy as a member of his staff was at an issues dinner on the subject of national service. He and his staff had recruited six of the country's experts. Out of that dinner came the formulation of the first national service bill, which was ultimately enacted in 1990. This legislation was the forerunner to the National and Community Service Trust Act of 1993, which created President Clinton's AmeriCorps program.

Every issues dinner was arranged carefully by Kennedy himself. He was a serious and enthusiastic host who took a personal interest in the smallest details. He took particular care to ensure that the seating arrangement at the dining-room table would be conducive to productive conversation. After deciding on the guest list, he would select the menu. He personally decided whether to use the silverware and china he inherited from his mother. He also decided whether the guests were important enough to bring out his mother's silver epergne, which she had passed on to him. At the end of each branch of this centerpiece was a silver dish into which the senator put candies or other decorative or edible gifts for the guests.

On the day of an issues dinner, I would often find the senator alone at his desk, sketching the seating arrangement for the dinner that evening. It was important to decide whether, for example, the ranking Republican sat opposite Kennedy in the middle of the table or at one of the ends. When there were Republican and Democratic senators, should he alternate their seating? Should he put senators interested in health care at one end of the table? Should he put senators who knew each other together? Who would enjoy talking to whom? Who would benefit from talking to whom? When Kennedy arrived home on the evening of an issues dinner, just before the guests arrived, he would check the seating one more time and readjust the place cards if he had changed his mind.

The basic routine for the dinners themselves rarely varied. Guests would arrive at 7:00 and be led into the library for conversation and drinks. If a particular guest or group of guests hadn't been to the house before, the senator might lead a tour of the house to view some of the photographs and memorabilia of the Kennedy family and of President and Mrs. Kennedy, a handwritten poem from Jacqueline Kennedy to the senator, handmade Christmas gifts from one family member to another, and Senator Kennedy's oil paintings. At 8:00 the guests would be ushered into the dining room. As the soup was brought out, the senator would begin the discussion of the issue at hand with several questions he had prepared. He would start with the ranking guest of honor. If a particular dinner group consisted entirely of senators, the questions would be asked in order of seniority after the ranking member had been called upon. If the guests were not senators, the discussion would proceed in a less formal manner, with Kennedy asking questions depending on the precise expertise required. Discussions proceeded for upward of two hours. Between 9:30 and 10:00 everyone would adjourn to the living room for coffee and cookies. Usually a spirited conversation would continue until, at approximately 10:30, the guests would depart. I would stay behind briefly to go over what we had learned and to write up a "to do" list from the discussions. I would summarize the recommendations of the guests and the outcome of the discussion in a memo for the senator the next day. We would then follow up on each of the ideas that had been generated.

Given all the hours spent at these issues dinners, plus all Kennedy's other forms of preparation, policy briefings, policy memos, and books, it's no wonder that his substantive knowledge was legendary. His preparation for an extended debate on a major bill in which he had a special interest was unusual. First he read the bill, which was often hundreds of pages long. Typically he would ask the appropriate staff member to annotate the bill, pointing out and explaining key issues, and then he would review the annotated copy. As a result, he sometimes knew as much about the specific bill's language as the sponsor, sometimes more, and he used that knowledge effectively in floor debate.

The first issues dinner convened specifically to analyze the 1994 election results took place in Boston three weeks after the election, on the Sunday following Thanksgiving. Because he was concerned about the implications of the elections in a historical context, Kennedy invited the distinguished Columbia University historian Alan Brinkley, and Pulitzer prize–winning historian and author Doris Kearns Goodwin. In order to

move the discussion into matters of policy and political strategy, the senator also invited John Sasso, former chief of staff to Massachusetts governor Michael Dukakis, and Robert Kuttner, editor of the progressive
journal *American Prospect*. The senator's wife, Vicki, a trusted and percep-
tive advisor, and I made up the senator's contingent.

We assembled for dinner promptly at 7:00 in a small private dining
room at a hotel in downtown Boston. At 7:30 we all sat down for what
turned out to be an intense two and a half hours of dissecting what had
gone wrong for Democrats and what Kennedy needed to do to turn
things around.

The senator posed the first question as the discussion began: Where
do Democrats go from here, and what should our role be?

Doris Goodwin made several opening observations. The Democratic
Party was founded on fundamental values of family, patriotism, and religion. Somehow the Republicans had captured these themes and, moreover, had won the public debate on two big issues that affect people's
day-to-day lives: income and order. The Republicans had convinced the
public that they were the party that wanted people to keep their money
and to live in a disciplined society, while Democrats wanted to raise taxes
and were soft on crime. She suggested that Democrats needed to deal
with these issues more effectively. It didn't make it easier that the Republicans had mastered the art of communicating their message, whereas
the Democrats and the president had not.

"How do Democrats recapture these fundamental values?" asked
Kennedy. "How do we succeed in an environment where the Republicans
have monopolized the art of communication through their network of
talk shows? The audience for these talk shows are the very same working
families that should be the core of support for Democrats."

"There are two difficult realities facing Democrats as we look to the
future," Kuttner said, focusing on his central theme: the cause of working people and their families. "First, there is nothing that Congress is
likely to do that will address the anxiety that working people feel about
their future and the future of their children. Second, the Democrats in
Congress are not positioned to carry out an agenda, except in a defen-

sive posture. Senator Kennedy, you should take advantage of every single opportunity to rub the faces of the Republicans in the fact that Democratic programs would help working families and Republicans' proposals would not."

Brinkley said, "Perception is everything in public life, and the perception is that government is corrupted by money and that no one is able to do anything about it. The disparity between the public's perception and reality is greater than at any time in recent history. People don't seem to realize what government does for them. Maybe there is a way of clarifying that."

Sasso said that we should go back to our fundamental Democratic values. Democrats had to grab on to issues that were moving forward, like welfare reform, child care, and tax cuts, and turn these issues to our advantage. Democrats could redirect the Republican tax cut to favor working people rather than the wealthy by creating a tax credit for education and homeownership.

Doris Goodwin, still focused on communications, said she regretted that Democrats had not had the think tanks or foundations working to develop responses to these challenges.

Kuttner asserted, "The issue is living standards for working people. . . . We're for the working family, and they are not."

Brinkley agreed. "Working families now feel insecure." We needed to improve job training, education, and health care.

Sasso referred to the senator's reelection earlier that month. "In part, it was about strength and conviction. Leadership needs to be strong. We need to help the president be strong."

Brinkley was concerned that the president was afraid to fight. "What people find most troubling about Clinton is that they don't know if there's anything he'd go to the mat or fight to the death for."

Kennedy interjected that Clinton had taken on the National Rifle Association, something no president had done before, but he agreed with the overall point. "The beginning of the unraveling of Clinton's initiatives was the defeat of the investment and stimulus package in 1993. It was a modest $35 billion investment in education, research, and infrastructure. Republicans blocked it, and once they saw they could draw blood on this, they thought they could get away with attacking everything Clinton was for. Some Democrats deserted the president on that investment budget battle, so the Republicans got away with it. After that, school was out."

The discussion turned from developing Democratic themes to developing strategy. Brinkley reminded us that there were still a lot of Democrats in office; the Republicans held only very small majorities in the House and Senate. "Senator Kennedy's task is to keep the spirits of Democrats up," he argued. "The Democratic base is at a moment when it is dying to be energized."

Everyone at the table agreed that the central unknown was President Clinton. What was he going to fight for? What would he define as critical for the next couple of years?

At the end, the senator summarized the conclusions of the dinner: Democrats should not give up on previous efforts to improve the economic security of working Americans, to improve their health care, and to improve their schools. We should try to refocus, or retarget, tax cuts in ways that would help working people. Just as important, Democrats needed to reassociate themselves with working families on the level of values. On the strategic front, Democrats needed to urge Clinton to resist Republican extremism. We should work to put in place a Democratic infrastructure to develop ideas and messages for mass consumption, as the Republicans had been doing for years. Democrats should put the focus on the differences between them and Republicans, particularly how Republican proposals would favor the wealthy and not help working people. This outline turned out to be the foundation of Kennedy's strategy in the year ahead.

Kennedy held more than a dozen meetings in November and December with public opinion experts, historians, economists, and political figures. But we also had the business of the Senate to attend to.

THE NEW SENATE DEMOCRATIC LEADERSHIP

George Mitchell, who had led the Senate Democrats in the majority for six years, had chosen not to run for reelection in 1994, so there was no Democratic leader in the Senate. The Democrats remaining had to elect a new leader. Succeeding Mitchell was no easy task. Indeed it was hard to imagine how anyone could fill his shoes. Mitchell was an exceptional public figure, unquestionably among the most impressive leaders I observed in nine years in Washington. He first arrived in the Senate not by election but by appointment, in 1978, to fill the vacancy when Edmund Muskie left the Senate to become secretary of state under President Jimmy Carter.

I occasionally wondered whether Mitchell would ever have become a senator if he had not been appointed the first time around. He was then a federal judge and possibly too cerebral to successfully break into elective politics from the outside. But once he became a senator, he easily won reelection twice. He led by force of intellect and character. As a former U.S. attorney and federal judge, he was meticulous, brilliant in analyzing issues, a forceful advocate who understood subtleties and was able to explain complicated legislative issues in readily understandable terms. He could be a tenacious partisan but was always respectful of his Republican colleagues. Though a steadfast progressive, he could compromise when appropriate.

Early in 1994 Mitchell had rejected Clinton's offer of an appointment to the Supreme Court because he was committed to shepherding the president's universal health care legislation through the Senate. To leave that effort, he felt, would have left health care in the lurch. The regrettable outcome, of course, was that, despite Mitchell's best efforts, the health care initiative collapsed. Later in the year, he announced that he would retire from public office.

Veteran Democratic senator Jim Sasser of Tennessee announced that he would run to succeed Mitchell as leader. He had been the Budget Committee chairman, a veteran of years of jousting with Republicans over appropriations, civil rights, Medicare, and countless other issues, and was the choice of the Democratic establishment in the Senate. Sasser was very well liked by his colleagues as a genial, methodical, thoughtful legislator. He had a strong progressive bent but was willing to revise his positions as conservative forces in his home state of Tennessee began to gain in influence. He was a close friend of Kennedy, who was a strong supporter of his candidacy for leader.

Sasser was challenged by Tom Daschle, Mitchell's deputy leader and the cochairman of the Democratic Policy Committee. Daschle came from Aberdeen, South Dakota, and after serving in the Air Force, went to Washington in 1972 as a staff member for Senator James Abourezk. He was elected in 1978 to the House of Representatives (by only 139 votes) and was reelected four times before he ran successfully for the Senate in 1994 at age forty-seven. Only two years later he was selected by Mitchell as deputy leader. He had spent essentially his whole adult life in politics.

Daschle seemed younger and milder than he was in reality. His low-key manner belied fierce work habits and a tenacious commitment to many causes, particularly health care reform. During the health care debates of 1994, Mitchell designated him point person on the Senate floor for Democrats. During weeks of debate, Daschle was always present on the floor, strategizing how best to push ahead, deeply committed to winning what at first seemed an eminently achievable goal. Kennedy was greatly impressed by Daschle's work on health care, and it was during those weeks working together that Kennedy developed an admiration for and friendship with him.

Daschle's accessibility and lack of pretense were two of his greatest strengths. For weeks leading up to the health care debate, he met with staff members of other Democratic senators involved in the effort to coordinate the battle. His own staff referred to him as Tom, and he got to know staff members of other senators by their first names and worked very well with us. He had a special relationship with the staff in part because he had been a staffer himself. Daschle's honesty, earnestness, willingness to work hard, and humility were refreshing.

As it turned out, the race for minority leader wouldn't be between

Sasser and Daschle. Sasser himself was upset for reelection, one of the Democratic casualties of the 1994 elections, losing to Republican Bill Frist, a wealthy heart surgeon trained at Harvard Medical School and the son of the founder of Hospital Corporation of America, one of the largest for-profit health care providers in the country—a man who would years later become majority leader himself. With Sasser's defeat, it seemed that Daschle would have an easy walk into the job of Democratic leader, but there was uncertainty about his level of experience. Many senators just didn't know him well enough. So within days of the November election, Senator Christopher Dodd of Connecticut stepped into Sasser's place and promptly picked up the public support of most of Sasser's supporters.

Dodd had been a senator since 1980 after three terms in the House. He had built strong friendships in the Senate with many of the more senior members of the Democratic Caucus. His father, Tom Dodd, had been a senator, and Chris was schooled in the ways of the institution. He was an articulate, sharp, and tenacious liberal, but a practical one, who frequently kept the interests of the business community in Connecticut at the forefront of his priorities, even when those interests clashed with liberal orthodoxy. He was an excellent public speaker, a forceful advocate, and an unquestioned leader, particularly on issues involving children. He had been a chief sponsor of the 1990 Child Care Act and had been chairman of the children and families subcommittee of the Labor Committee for many years. He was also Kennedy's closest personal friend and political ally in the Senate.

The election was scheduled for December 2, and it appeared to be very close. There were forty-seven Democratic senators. The election would come down to one or two votes. The night before, Dodd believed he had it sewn up, 24–23. He had received a pledge from Carol Moseley Braun, who had been elected to the Senate from Illinois only two years before. But late in the evening before the vote, Dodd learned that her commitment wouldn't hold up. Moseley Braun had made no bones about the fact that she sought a position on the powerful Finance Committee. Daschle, who then held one of the coveted Finance positions, offered to step down and give his seat to her in return for her support. In the end she voted for Daschle, who won by one vote. Thus go elections in the Senate. Whether you win by a big margin or by one vote, you take the reins of power and all the perquisites that go with it, while the loser is left empty-handed. Having lost the leadership race, though, Dodd was selected in January as chairman of the Democratic National Committee, where he played a central role in Clinton's political recovery over the months leading to the November 1996 elections.

Because of their personal friendship, Kennedy's support for Dodd was never in question, despite his respect for Daschle. And Daschle did not resent Kennedy's vote for Dodd because he understood that Kennedy's loyalty to his old friend came first.

Once Daschle was elected leader, Kennedy could focus his attention on shaping the direction of the Democratic agenda for the new Congress. His first task was to make sure no irretrievable concessions were made to the new Republican majority. But he was equally committed to developing a progressive agenda for the party in the Senate and to executing an effective ongoing strategy to resist the most extreme elements of the Contract with America.

According to Senate tradition, on the opening day of a new Congress, the majority leader introduces five bills, numbered 1 through 5, and the minority leader introduces five bills, 6 through 10. These first bills are intended to lay out the priorities of each party for the members of the Senate and the public. They are messaging vehicles as much as legislative priorities. Kennedy set out to work with Daschle to make sure that the core Democratic issues of jobs, education, and health care were represented in the five Democratic priority bills. All the preparation for these bills had to be done by January 4, when Congress would be sworn in and the bills would be introduced.

There would, of course, be other bills beyond these ten that would be introduced on the first day of the new Congress and in the weeks immediately following. Kennedy would have his own legislative initiatives, so his staff needed to spend November and December drafting and negotiating those. For every bill, it was important to have a number of Democratic cosponsors and, if possible, support from the Republicans.

Much of the winter of 1994–95 was spent drafting and lining up supporters for these new bills.

Through our staff contacts we learned that Daschle was moving in
what we considered to be a safe direction with his legislative priorities—
not an aggressive working families agenda, no mention of education,
but nothing that gave up ground to the Republicans that could not be
recovered later. And since Kennedy hadn't supported Daschle and was
therefore not part of his inner circle, we had to avoid trying to assert too
much influence over Daschle's first decisions. There would be a Working
Americans Opportunity bill, which dealt with job training; an initiative
on health care; one on teen pregnancy and prevention; and a bill on
fiscal responsibility, which was in recognition of the popularity of deficit
reduction and was meant to be a counter to the Contract with America's
pledge to pass a balanced budget amendment. Finally, there was a bill
on congressional reform. This would show that the Democrats were sensitive to another one of the themes in the Contract: whether Congress
would be covered by the various regulations it enacted on private businesses. But Daschle was going to go further than the Republicans on this
issue; he was also going to propose dramatic reform of the campaign
financing system for congressional elections as well as lobbying and gift
restrictions.

Kennedy's strongest interest among these bills was the one on health
care, so he and I agreed we would make our first request to Daschle that
Kennedy be given a leading role in developing the health care initiative.
Kennedy had several conversations with Daschle about the leadership
agenda, and Daschle instructed his staff to work with Kennedy's staff on
the health care issues. By mid-December Kennedy was also well on his
way to working out a bipartisan health care reform bill with Republican
senator Kassebaum, the new chair of the Labor Committee.

Kennedy also volunteered to help with job training, in part because
the Labor Committee clearly had jurisdiction over this issue. Moreover
he wanted to keep an eye on Louisiana senator John Breaux, who was interested in job training and was much more conservative in his approach
to issues than Kennedy.

Immediately after becoming minority leader, Daschle appointed senators who had been his close allies in his victory over Dodd to newly created positions in what would be a group leadership model. It was important for Kennedy to work with each member of the leadership group as well as Daschle in developing the leadership strategy. Harry Reid, John Breaux, Barbara Mikulski, John Kerry, Bob Kerrey, and Byron Dorgan were given slots on the leadership team. Senator Reid is the Democratic majority leader today in part because he was an early supporter of Daschle's candidacy for leader in 1993, went on Daschle's leadership team in 1994, and became the majority whip for Daschle in 1999. When Daschle lost his reelection for senator in 2006, Reid was in line to become leader in 2007.

Senator Breaux had taken particular interest in job training issues, perhaps because he had been chairman of the Democratic Leadership Council, which for a decade had been the principal advocacy group and think tank for more conservative Democrats and the so-called New Democrat movement. In 1982, Kennedy had written one of the principal job training laws in partnership with then Republican senator and later vice president Dan Quayle. By 1994 Kennedy was for updating the job training structure by consolidating in one location an unwieldy number of separate federal job training programs, including career counseling, job search assistance, and performance evaluations of various programs. Breaux intended to introduce the Democratic Leadership Council's job training bill, which included streamlining and consolidating the job training system in many of the ways Kennedy had been urging. Because Breaux and the Democratic Leadership Council shared these goals, it was relatively easy to work with him on the content of the Working Americans Opportunity bill, which also included a voucher program for workers that was modeled on the GI Bill for college education.

THE LABOR COMMITTEE

Beyond working with the new Senate Democratic leadership, Kennedy lined up the Democratic members of the Labor Committee behind his agenda. Kennedy was always deeply involved in working with the Democratic leadership in the Senate on the important matter of which Democratic senators would serve on his committee. I was never clear on whether other Democratic committee chairmen took as much interest in which Democrats would go on to their committees as Kennedy did. But I soon learned that it was critically important to him that he be able to count on the votes of his Democratic colleagues on the committee. That way he wouldn't have to make major concessions to other Democrats on initiatives moving through the committee and could save the compromises to get the measure to the floor of the Senate.

There was a period during the Reagan presidency when a seat on the Labor Committee was not highly sought after by Democrats. Advancing a progressive social policy agenda in health, education, job training, and labor issues, the areas under the Committee's jurisdiction, seemed impossible. But starting in 1986 when the Democrats regained the majority in the Senate, continuing during the first Bush presidency, and particularly after Clinton's election, there began to be much more of a focus on social policy legislation, and the Labor Committee became ever more popular among Democrats. By 1992 the Committee's issues were clearly back in favor. It was therefore very important to Kennedy to have members on the committee who shared the core progressive, Democratic commitment to these issues. In an interesting contrast, many Republicans considered assignment to the Labor Committee an obligation rather than an opportunity.

Some moderate Republicans interested in social programs were attracted to the Labor Committee, including Jacob Javits of New York, Lowell Weicker of Connecticut, Robert Stafford of Vermont, Durenberger, Kassebaum, and Jeffords. Others joined for more idiosyncratic reasons. Senator John Warner, for example, once joined the Committee prior to his reelection campaign to demonstrate his interest in education and because he enjoyed working with his friend Kennedy. He later rotated off. Most conservative Republicans didn't want to have anything to do with the Committee. They didn't support Kennedy's expansive approach to the social programs in the Committee's jurisdiction (in fact they wanted to end them), but if they were true to their convictions and the Republican platform, they would end up having to vote against popular programs such as expanding educational opportunities, helping to meet the needs of children, and improving health care for women at risk of breast cancer. These votes could come back to haunt them the next time they faced reelection. In fact one of my jobs as staff director was to make their votes against our initiatives as difficult as possible by coming up with ways to frame the issues as motherhood and apple pie. Many Republicans left the Committee as soon as they gained sufficient seniority to substitute what, in their minds, was a more desirable assignment.

Such matters as the size of a committee are solely in the hands of the majority, and the Republicans decided to shrink the size of the Labor Committee from eleven for the majority and eight for the minority to nine and seven, respectively. The seven Democrats were Kennedy, Dodd, Mikulski, Tom Harkin of Iowa, Paul Simon of Illinois, Claiborne Pell of Rhode Island, and Paul Wellstone of Minnesota. Jeff Bingaman of New Mexico, who had been on the Committee in the previous Congress, had to step off in 1995 because of the reduced size. Of the other Democrats previously on the Committee, Wofford had been defeated, and Metzenbaum had retired.

Back in Washington after the Thanksgiving break, Kennedy called a meeting of the Democrats on the Labor Committee for November 29 to discuss the Democratic agenda in the new Republican Congress. We distributed an outline of the key political and substantive issues we intended to focus on: introducing a new health care bill, expanding job training, increasing the minimum wage, protecting against Republican labor law reform, supporting child care and immunizations, fighting against cuts in student aid, and protecting the national service program.

Even in the minority Kennedy's agenda was an activist one, though the Republicans now controlled the Committee agenda and could win every vote if they stuck together. But Kennedy had already decided that backing down was not the way to go. Joining him at the meeting in his office were Senators Metzenbaum, Dodd, Harkin, Bingaman, and Wellstone. They were part of the liberal wing of the Democratic Party in the Senate, but even they were surprised at Kennedy's optimism and his activist approach to the agenda.

Some of the senators remarked that they had never felt less comfortable plotting a course of action. It seemed they didn't believe the broad Kennedy agenda made sense. They wanted to take a cautious approach instead. Each was focused on narrow and specific areas of interest to them. Bingaman asked what the Committee's role would be in welfare reform. He wanted us to work with the Republicans on job training and child care. Metzenbaum was focused on labor issues; he suggested fights on striker replacement and use of child labor. Only Wellstone, the most liberal member of the Committee, seemed to agree with Kennedy's strategy. He recommended strong opposition to Republican initiatives starting in the Committee and working with media and interest groups. No other member of the Committee spoke in this meeting of across-the-board resistance to Republican extremism; no one thought a Democratic initiative to improve or increase the minimum wage had any chance. The collective recommendation to Kennedy was that we should take a cautious approach and wait for the Republicans to act, to see where they would try to go with Medicare and Medicaid and on the budget. Just wait and lay low until we could see the course the Republicans ultimately set. This lack of clear resolve, this uncertainty, this caution, even among the strong liberals on the Committee, was an ominous indicator of just how demoralized the Democrats were.

WORKING WITH THE REPUBLICANS

While Kennedy was beginning to work on Democrats to develop resistance to the Contract with America and to press his case for continuing to advance progressive legislation, he also began approaching Republican colleagues whom he hoped to persuade to join him in some of his initiatives. The first such meetings were with Kassebaum, the new chair of the Labor Committee, and the other Republicans on the Committee who were taking over as chairs of subcommittees on labor, health, education, and aging.

Kassebaum and Kennedy had known each other for many years. The daughter of Alf Landon, the Republican presidential candidate in 1936, Kassebaum was first elected to the Senate in 1978. She was thoughtful and widely respected. The fact that she and Kennedy both came from families with a political history gave them something in common. She was appointed to the Labor Committee soon after she arrived in the Senate, and by the time I arrived in 1989, she was the second Republican in seniority on the Committee after Orrin Hatch and was ranking Republican on the education subcommittee under Pell's chairmanship. As chairman of the full Committee, Kennedy had worked very closely with Pell on education matters and had ample opportunity to work with Kassebaum as well.

Education had historically been a bipartisan issue in the Committee, stretching back to an era when there were several moderate and liberal Republican members, including Javits, Stafford, and Weicker. These Republicans believed the federal government had a constructive role to play in education at the local level, particularly for schools with a large percentage of disadvantaged children, and they worked cooperatively with Democrats to advance that purpose. Kassebaum was in that tradition.

Through the early 1990s, the key education bills were worked out on a bipartisan basis and moved through the Senate, and ultimately the Congress, without acrimony. That, unfortunately, would change in the second year of the Clinton administration and especially after the Republican takeover of Congress. The new breed of conservative Republicans opposed any role for the federal government in elementary and secondary education. The new Republican majority was determined to eliminate the Department of Education, cut the federal investment in elementary and secondary education by a third, and scale back student loans dramatically. Since Kassebaum had never been comfortable with the right-wing Republican education agenda, Kennedy believed that she would continue the tradition of bipartisanship on education issues before the Committee, although it was likely that she would also be put in the position of implementing some of the Contract with America policies, even though she might not agree with them.

For many years Kassebaum and Kennedy both had offices in the south corridor of the Russell Senate Office Building across the hall from each other. This meant that as either of them was walking down the hall to his or her office they were likely to meet up with each other, particularly as they were both rushing to or returning from a vote on the Senate floor. This proximity created many chances for conversation and discussion about pending votes, matters on the Senate floor, and matters in the Committee. Personal relationships are deeply important for senators to be effective, as is respect for the Senate and its unwritten rules of conduct. Both Kassebaum and Kennedy honored this code: even if tempers flared, their arguments were not personal and misunderstandings would be mended promptly. Differences could be fierce, but agreements, when reached, had to be respected. A senator's word had to be a senator's bond.

While the slight, self-contained Kassebaum and the physically imposing, outgoing Kennedy were a study in contrasts, they shared some deep similarities beyond their common respect for the Senate and its institutions. Both were inherently cheerful, were eminently approachable by staff, took pleasure in the friendships they developed in the Senate, and trusted each other, despite their disagreements. When it was important for them to work something out, they would try, and more often than not they would succeed.

It was because Kennedy had taken the time over several decades to build relationships with other senators that it was possible, even in the minority, for him to build bipartisan coalitions and enact elements of his own agenda. Bipartisanship doesn't come naturally to many senators. Many come to Washington to hold off the other party, not accommodate it. But few things ever happen in the Senate without bipartisanship. Effective senators understand this—and none understood it better than Kennedy.

There are certainly examples of successful legislation that started out as purely partisan bills. But there are many more major bills in the Senate that pass because, from the outset, they are crafted with bipartisan support. In just the nine years that I worked with him, Kennedy enacted major legislation growing out of bipartisan initiatives with Senators Hatch, Dole, Danforth, Jeffords, Thurmond, Quayle, Durenberger, Kassebaum, John McCain, Lauch Faircloth, Thad Cochran, and Pete Domenici, among others. These senators spanned the ideological spectrum of the Republican Party, from the moderate Jeffords and Kassebaum to the conservative Hatch, Thurmond, and Faircloth.

The beauty of an early bipartisan alliance is that it provides at least some measure of instant credibility on both sides of the aisle. When Hatch and Kennedy signed on to a compromise, it gained instant credibility. They were so far apart on the conservative-liberal spectrum that when they agreed on a bill, it immediately had the potential for broad support. Hatch would sometimes joke that the only way they got together was that one of them must not have read the legislation. Hatch was a particularly desirable cosponsor because once he agreed to join with Kennedy on a piece of legislation, he was a tenacious advocate.

Some other Republicans with whom Kennedy cosponsored bills brought less with them in terms of their ability to attract Republican support. Jeffords, for example, was a cosponsor of the Kennedy-Clinton universal health care bill from the day it was first introduced in November 1993, but he brought no other Republicans with him then or in the months that followed, when the bill was debated in committee and ultimately on the floor. Kassebaum too was a very helpful cosponsor, and she and Kennedy worked naturally together on almost all the bills that came out of the Labor Committee during her tenure as chair. However, she was always under intense pressure from her Republican colleagues *not* to work with him on high-profile legislation.

Looking back over Kennedy's legislative record during the nine years I worked with him, the major successful bills, with the exception of the minimum wage increase and other labor issues, each had a Republican cosponsor. Hatch and Kennedy were the original cosponsors of several landmark AIDS care and research bills, including the Ryan White AIDS CARE bill. Hatch also was a cosponsor with Kennedy and Dodd of the 1990 Child Care Development Block Grant. This $1 billion-a-year program was the first major federal child care program since World War II that provided services for families not on welfare, and it was enacted with important standards for child care quality—standards that ultimately became a model for those adopted during the welfare reform debate of 1996. Hatch and Kennedy worked together as cosponsors of the Food and Drug Administration user fee bill and on several other bills involving regulation of pharmaceutical drugs. The User Fee Act was essential to the reform of the FDA and has been reauthorized every five years since it was originally passed in 1992.

The summer jobs initiative of 1992 was another major Hatch-Kennedy bill. Since it had been two years since their last major effort (the Ryan White bill), the senators thought it might be time for them to do another bill together. They agreed to have dinner with their staffs at Kennedy's house to figure out what the subject would be. I was there along with other Hatch and Kennedy health and education staffers; everything was set up as formally as if it were a typical issues dinner. The discussion was wide-ranging; each senator raised issues on which they might try to find common ground.

There had been youth and gang violence that summer in some inner-city areas, and when that came up in the discussion, someone said, "What about summer jobs?" President Bush had ratcheted back federal funding for summer jobs for at-risk youth. Like Kennedy, Hatch thought it was a bad idea to deny job and educational opportunities to kids who had few alternatives for staying out of trouble during the summer and had a tough time gaining work experience. They came up with the idea of an emergency supplemental appropriation to restore funding for the program. They left the dinner pledged to make it happen. And they did. The emergency supplemental passed in June with $600 million added to provide jobs for 300,000 young people.

The most important legislative achievement of the Hatch-Kennedy alliance was the Children's Health Insurance and Lower Deficit Act of

1997 (ultimately enacted as CHIP—the Child Health Insurance Program). On each of these initiatives it was always touch-and-go whether Hatch would come on board.

Dole and Hatch worked together with Democrats, led by Harkin and Kennedy, to enact the Americans with Disabilities Act. This landmark bill provided basic civil rights protections in housing, employment, and access to public facilities for over 40 million Americans. It took a strong bipartisan alliance to bring Bush to the point where he would sign the legislation.

Senator Danforth was the original sponsor with Kennedy of the 1991 Civil Rights Act, which restored rights eliminated when the Supreme Court overturned a series of civil rights cases in the 1980s, particularly involving employment discrimination. Danforth was both a lawyer and an Episcopal minister, with a deep commitment to the rights of minorities, and he was a tenacious ally during the months of debate and during the successful effort to bring the Bush administration on board and obtain the president's signature. Danforth had a long record on civil rights, so it was not surprising that Kennedy approached him to go along on the legislation or that Danforth agreed to work so hard to get it enacted.

With Faircloth and Thurmond, the initiatives were less broad in their scope. With Faircloth, the conservative Jesse Helms protégé from North Carolina, Kennedy drew up legislation to protect and rebuild southern African American churches destroyed by firebombs. With Thurmond, the legislation involved scientific research using fetal tissue, which was obtained from fetuses that had been aborted for other reasons. Thurmond, a strong antiabortion legislator, had always opposed such research, but in the late 1980s a daughter of his was diagnosed with juvenile diabetes. Fetal tissue transplantation research provided hope for discovery of new treatments for juvenile diabetes, as well as other diseases, and when this was brought to Thurmond's attention, he joined with Kennedy to enact legislation authorizing the National Institutes of Health to award grants for research using fetal tissue.

When Kennedy was developing a legislative idea, he always began by meeting one-on-one with Republican senators who were possible cosponsors. He unfailingly visited the senator in his or her office as a way of showing deference and respect, even if protocol suggested the senator come to Kennedy's office. The Kennedy staff did ample research on the Republican's record on the issue in question, and the senator was selected because there was some indication that he or she had a favorable attitude toward legislation in this area. Often Kennedy discussed possible Republican cosponsors with the public interest groups with whom he had been working on developing the legislation, and they, in turn, sought meetings with the Republican targets to assist Kennedy in his attempt to bring the Republicans along. At the end of the day, there were always many more meetings that didn't lead anywhere than there were Republicans cosponsoring a Kennedy bill. But when the strategy worked, the payoff was enormous.

A key ingredient in Kennedy's track record of bipartisan accomplishment was his tenacity. He worked assiduously at creating the building blocks of bipartisanship by maintaining strong personal relationships with Republican senators. Although he could disagree fiercely on the floor over the substance of a matter, he never personalized that disagreement or took it with him off the floor. He never forgot to send a note congratulating a senator for a particular achievement or to go out of his way to speak to another senator about an important event in that person's family life, or to thank a senator for a vote or a kindness on the floor. He often invited senators to his house for dinner or to play tennis. While Republican senators could disagree strongly with Kennedy's ideology, most of them enjoyed his company, trusted that he was a man of his word, and appreciated the respect he had for them as individuals and the attention he paid them on a personal level.

Kennedy's unique ability to hammer out agreements between parties with widely different interests and conflict-hardened positions extended beyond the Senate. One good example was his involvement in the national freight railroad strike of 1991, which threatened to bring the whole economy to a standstill. Two hundred thirty-five thousand workers had walked off the job, and production and distribution of the nation's coal, grain, autos, steel, and other key engines of the economy were in jeopardy. Commuter trains in the Northeast, which used the same tracks as the freight trains, were shutting down. Management, labor, and public officials seemed unable to talk together, and each was accusing the other of bad faith; the negotiations were going nowhere. Kennedy picked up the phone and called people high up in both labor and management. He had the clout and the relationships to bring them, as well as outside experts, to the table to hammer out a legislative solution acceptable to all sides. After a day and night of talking, he got everyone to agree to legislation which then quickly passed the House and the Senate and was signed by Bush in the middle of the night, ending the strike. Labor wasn't entirely happy, but they recognized that if they didn't follow Kennedy's lead, they were likely to end up with something a lot less favorable.

After the strike was settled, in a typical gesture, Kennedy purchased a wooden toy train, wrote a congratulatory note on it, and presented it to Sarah Fox, his top labor issues staffer, who had played a key role in the negotiations. She still has it displayed prominently in her living room.

So when Kassebaum prepared to take over the Labor Committee and Kennedy prepared to move down to the position of ranking minority member, I had every expectation that the relationship between the two would stay strong.

In the weeks after the November election, Kassebaum remained in Kansas, so the first contact Kennedy had with her was by telephone. Kassebaum initiated the call the week after the election, to discuss the new structure she was proposing for the Labor Committee. As chair, she could arrange matters as she chose. She would decide how the subcommittees were to be divided and what subject matter would fall within each. She told Kennedy she would maintain the children's, education, and aging subcommittees but that there was little interest among her Republican colleagues in having a labor subcommittee. She proposed instead an employment and productivity subcommittee, or perhaps a workforce subcommittee. This was, of course, purely a semantic matter. (I toyed with the idea of suggesting to her that we call it the "unions subcommittee," but thought better of it.) The same jurisdiction over labor issues existed whatever the subcommittee was named. The Republicans simply didn't want a subcommittee named for labor. To them *labor* meant the labor unions, which were not their political allies. When Jeffords was the Republican chairman four years later, he changed the name of the full committee as well, from Labor and Human Resources, to Health, Education, Labor, and Pensions. The change served several purposes: it emphasized health and education, which were the key areas of the Committee's activity; provided an appropriate acronym, HELP, by which the committee would come to be referred; and reduced the visibility of the word *labor.* In their phone call, Kassebaum and Kennedy also discussed matters for the staff to follow up on, including budget issues, office space issues, the number of members of the Committee and subcommittees, and the outline of a substantive agenda.

When Kassebaum did return to Washington, Kennedy arranged to meet with her to talk about the legislative agenda. Hanging on the wall of Kassebaum's office waiting room was a large map of the state of Kansas. Pins with colored heads were stuck into the map to mark all the places she had visited. There were several large oil paintings by Kansas artists, mostly portraying the Great Plains and Kansas cornfields. Kassebaum came out to greet us and invited us into her office. Susan Hattan, soon to take my place as staff director, and Ed Bolen, the chief counsel for the Republicans on the Committee, joined us in the meeting. Kassebaum promptly established that she was now in charge. She explained the new Committee structure of nine Republicans and seven Democrats. She would be consolidating the labor subcommittee and the employment and training subcommittee and transferring these subject matters to the full Committee. Health care would be retained at the full Committee. The 75 percent reduction in Kennedy's staff was consistent with the overall reduction Kassebaum was proposing for the Committee budget.

Kassebaum next discussed the job training legislation she hoped would become a bipartisan initiative and said that she hoped Kennedy would endorse her bill. She was going to schedule three hearings of three hours each on job training legislation for early January. In order to move hearings along, she would allow opening statements only by herself and Kennedy. The other senators would have to wait to give their statements until it was their time to question witnesses. This was a change; in the past each senator at the hearing had been allowed to give an opening statement. But often these statements extended the length of the hearings with little substantive benefit. Kassebaum had a tidy as well as take-charge approach to the proceedings.

Kassebaum then talked about her other priorities. She wanted to reauthorize the legislation supporting the National Endowments for the Arts and Humanities and to move other reauthorizations along quickly. She and Kennedy actually had a track record on protecting the NEA from Senator Helms and other conservatives who wanted to get rid of it entirely because it funded what they considered to be obscene artwork. To avoid government censorship, in 1990 Kassebaum and Kennedy included a provision in the reauthorization bill that any artist convicted of obscenity would have to return the funds from the NEA. That provision ensured that Kassebaum and Kennedy could say on the Senate floor that no government money would be used for the creation of obscene art, even though it was extremely unlikely that anyone would be convicted in a criminal obscenity case under these circumstances.

Kassebaum also wanted to be involved in child care legislation, welfare policy, and public health issues, particularly Medicaid. Kennedy raised the possibility of a bipartisan health care bill, and Kassebaum said she was prepared to work toward that end and directed her staff to continue meeting with the Kennedy staff.

The next Republican senator Kennedy met with was Jim Jeffords, the second in rank among Republicans on the Committee. Jeffords had been in Washington for eighteen years, starting as the single congressman from Vermont in 1975. He had made a reputation in Vermont for his low-key, unassuming, unpretentious approach to his work, as well as his flexible, moderate, almost liberal views. In his early years in Congress he slept in his office during the week to save money that otherwise would have been required to rent an apartment. This image of frugality stayed with him throughout his career in Congress.

In 1988 he was elected to the Senate to replace Robert Stafford, another progressive Republican who had served three terms. Jeffords was a

Republican in the tradition of Stafford and other senators such as Javits and Weicker—Republicans who worked with Kennedy on a whole range of education and health issues during their tenures on the Committee and who were more liberal than many Democrats serving in the Senate during that era.

Jeffords and Kennedy got along very well. While Democrats were in charge, Jeffords often crossed party lines to endorse Kennedy's progressive initiatives coming out of the Labor Committee. He had been a natural ally of Kennedy's during the health care debates—the only Republican to endorse the Clinton health plan. During the election campaign in 1994, Kennedy had actually slipped into southern Vermont from Massachusetts for a Jeffords public forum on education, an appearance that was widely seen as a gesture of support for Jeffords while he was engaged in his reelection bid. Jeffords repaid the favor later in the year, when he came down to be with Kennedy and Clinton at Framingham High School in Massachusetts for a bill-signing ceremony for the Elementary and Secondary Education Act.

Jeffords was a natural starting point for Kennedy in his effort to find Republican supporters for the initiatives on the minimum wage and health insurance reform. He had supported Kennedy's last effort in 1989 to raise the minimum wage as well as Kennedy's health care bill in 1993. The two talked, and Kennedy thought he made some progress on both issues. Jeffords warned Kennedy, however, that the struggle within the Republican Caucus between the moderates and the far right was intensifying. He told Kennedy that Dole had actually intervened to block aggressively right-wing Senators Phil Gramm of Texas and Trent Lott of Mississippi from obtaining seats on the Finance Committee, putting more senior and moderate Republicans on ahead of them.

Jeffords's concern was prophetic, but Dole's effort to hold off the right wing of the party and retain control of the Republican Caucus was not to succeed. In the leadership elections in December, Lott defeated (by one vote) Alan Simpson of Wyoming, a moderate and close Dole ally, for deputy leader of the Republicans, over Dole's strenuous opposition. Lott and his right-wing allies in the Republican-controlled Senate were waiting in the wings for Dole to give ground, or if not, to seize it from him.

When Kassebaum retired at the end of the 104th Congress, in 1996, Jeffords took over the chairmanship of the Committee and held that position until 2001, when he decided he could no longer stomach the positions he needed to take to accommodate his more and more uniformly right-wing Republican colleagues, who threatened to take away his chairmanship if he didn't toe the line. At that point he declared himself an Independent caucusing with the Democrats—flipping control of the Senate to the Democrats by a one-vote majority. After the switch, Jeffords gave the chairmanship of the HELP Committee back to his friend Kennedy and, in turn, was given the chair of the Environment and Public Works Committee. Unfortunately, the slim Democratic majority did not survive the 2002 elections. Jeffords retired in 2007 because of ill health.

MORE OUTREACH

Kennedy was continuing to have meetings and issues dinners with academics, historians, social scientists, economists, and individuals who were conducting public opinion polls on issues surrounding the election. As we prepared our affirmative agenda and particularly the health care initiatives, he wanted to follow up on where the public stood on health care after the 1994 defeat of the Clinton plan. So he met with Robert Blendon, an experienced analyst who teaches at the Harvard School of Public Health, and Mark Mellman, a leading Democratic strategist and pollster, who was to become an indispensable ally to the senator and the Democrats in the Senate during 1995 and 1996.

Blendon said his polls found that in 1994 people had become scared by too much health care reform all at once, and by 1995 their expectations for reform had been reduced. Middle-class voters, for instance, had become convinced that low-income groups would benefit from universal health care at their own expense. But health care was still a top issue for the public, and they did want government action. He said Democrats should push for programs to encourage employers to help employees obtain health care, and then in the future come back to an employer mandate to require employers to share the costs with their employees.

Kennedy raised a specific issue that had received bipartisan support in the Committee during the health care debates in 1994 and was addressed in both Democratic and Republican plans. People with insurance worried about "preexisting condition exclusions," which precluded coverage for conditions that existed prior to the commencement date of their policy. For example, if an individual had a heart condition before his or her insurance began, the new policy would not cover it. Kennedy wanted to do away with these exclusions. He mentioned two other areas, cutting down on health care fraud and expanding health insurance for children from working families, which he thought some Republicans might be sympathetic to. Kennedy's feeling was that if we could accomplish any of these, even in a Republican Congress, it would restore people's belief in the government's ability to act.

Mellman went beyond health care reform to say that our job was to reframe the discussion of taxes so that voters understood that Republican tax cuts meant tax cuts for the rich at the expense of the middle class and the poor. He also recommended reframing the discussion of the balanced budget so that the Republicans' budget cutting was associated with unwanted cuts to Medicare.

Kennedy was zeroing in on the economy, and on December 7 he convened another brainstorming session, a daylong meeting of economists at his office in Washington. He started the meeting by observing that over the previous two decades business profits were up by 14 percent, but wages for workers had been flat or had even fallen. "Shouldn't there be a way," he asked, "for Democrats to work on the system to make sure that some of these profits come to working families?"

George Perry, of the Brookings Institute, confirmed the senator's points: "Wages haven't grown for low-income groups in the newest recovery. It's very hard to know what to do about this. The tax side can only make a small difference." Robert Reischauer, about to become a resident fellow at Brookings, after having served as head of the Congressional Budget Office from 1989 to 1994, observed that dealing with the issue of wage inequality was difficult. Job training takes a long time to bear fruit. Because our own secondary education system hadn't met its responsibilities, prospects weren't looking good for high school drop-outs *or* graduates. Job training, tax cuts for working people, and keeping the economy strong were some ways to deal with the anxieties families were feeling.

Kennedy responded, "We need to get the president identified with job creation, with the strong economy and with cutting the deficit. His record in these areas has been outstanding." Reischauer agreed. In fact Clinton had brought the deficit down every year but was getting no credit for it. Reischauer believed the deficit would begin creeping up again by the year 2004, but he didn't think the world would come to an end if that happened, and he felt strongly that if we had to give up too much in investments in education and infrastructure to get the deficit down, it wouldn't be worth it. He did not think there was any deficit level that was inherently right or wrong.

Perry noted that the minimum wage increase would help to put money into people's pockets, and Reischauer added that when the mini-mum wage is raised, the wages of the workers above the minimum wage go up too.

Kennedy asked us to plan another dinner on the issue of social re-sponsibility: how we could encourage more Americans to be active in their communities and reengage them in the civic side of American life. We scheduled an evening dinner in Boston with Harvard professors Robert Coles and Michael Sandel. Sandel was a popular professor in the Government Department and author of several books on what he calls the civil society. Coles was a highly respected psychiatrist, teacher, and prolific author in the field of twentieth-century American social history and policy. He had spent years visiting and interviewing families in white working-class towns such as Woburn and Chelsea in Massachusetts.

Coles started with a summary of what he had found.

"These people are basically Democrats, but Republicans have gener-ated hate and resentment that distracts white working families from their economic vulnerability."

"Is there some way to make the point that ordinary people will lose from the Republican plan?" Kennedy asked.

Sandel: We've been presenting the Democratic agenda of the New Deal, but it was exhausted by 1960. It had largely succeeded, and another set of issues came to dominate our public policy. These issues involved values, community, and citizenship. Democrats have to figure out a way of speaking to these concerns, going beyond the New Deal issues of more or less government.

Kennedy: In my family, patriotism and the importance of family and of religion were assumed. Now the Republicans seem to have taken over these issues.

Sandel: Our emphasis as Democrats on individual rights and liberties has been tied too exclusively to individual rights. Our view of individual rights does not flow from a shared sense of community, of responsibility, of civic obligation, of citizenship. We have detached rights from obligations.

Kennedy: How can the Democratic Party begin to change the perception that it's lost touch on these old values—patriotism, religion, family?

Sandel: Democrats have to begin to emphasize the relationship between Democratic programs and these values. The Democrats' fight for job training, health care, and education should be couched in terms of rebuilding a sense of community. We are responsible to each other; the nation is a community.

Kennedy: What is the difference between perception and reality? What about those good old days, when the elderly and the minorities were solidly in the camp of the Democrats?

Coles: You have to go back to that past and remind people of the progress we have made. The Democratic Party led the battle for ending discrimination, for family and medical leave. Our society wouldn't be what it is if those battles hadn't been fought. Republicans are now talking about repealing these measures—Democrats have to remind people of this. Don't lose the focus on health,

education, and jobs, but present that litany unapologetically and
add the moral dimension and obligations that lie behind it. For
example, why shouldn't every college student have the responsibility to mentor one child?

There was a cadre of old friends and advisors to the senator, or to
his brothers before him, whom he had always relied on for advice. One
such friend was John Kenneth Galbraith, professor emeritus of economics at Harvard. In December the senator, Mrs. Kennedy, and I went to
meet with Professor Galbraith to hear his reaction to the election. It was
a memorable evening. Galbraith was eighty-six and going strong, inci-
sive and articulate, a venerable champion of progressive ideals whom
the senator had known for many years. He had first gone to Washington
during the New Deal, with President Roosevelt, and had served as ambassador to India during the Kennedy administration. He had written more
than a dozen books on economic policy. When the senator occasionally
invited him to Washington to testify, he was always one of the most pro-
vocative witnesses.

Galbraith lived just off the Harvard campus, on Professor's Row, in
a large, Victorian house. The inside was dimly lit, the furniture lived in,
unchanged, it appeared, for decades. It was evident that Galbraith was
suffering from a cold, and he made a point of apologizing that he hadn't
been able to meet at the senator's office. He took us to his first-floor
study and showed the senator a picture of the two of them, each thirty
years younger, taken during the Kennedy administration, and the galley
prints of his new book, *The Good Society*. Galbraith directed us to his living room, where Mrs. Galbraith brought tea and cookies, and Galbraith
started talking. He barely paused for the next hour.

"The problem is that only 38 percent of the eligible voters voted, so
the Republicans won with less than 20 percent of the vote. The essence
of Democratic success is to get people to vote, as they did in the Roosevelt era. There is no doubt about why we had a period of success. We
had a big turnout among low-income people. Those who aren't voting
today are those who most need the public services. It is the Republican

genius to get people to stay away from voting, to keep people who would vote against them from voting. With the southerners now taking over the Congress, this election was the revenge of the old Confederacy. . . .

"There's a big political division between the comfortable and the concerned. The Republicans' appeal to the middle class is a fraudulent way to release resources to the rich. The middle class will never see any gains from the Republicans. They didn't under Reagan. We need a minimum wage increase to ensure that the service industries aren't taking advantage of starvation wages. On welfare reform, let us begin by seeing that there are job opportunities. On job training, I don't put as much stock in this as others do. It's the last resort of a vacant liberal mind. Any tax reduction should be a credit for education; otherwise it will be so small, it will never be noticed, except by the rich. Republicans will give $500 to the middle class in order to get $500,000 for the rich. That is basic Republican doctrine. . . .

"I want to make a point in a slightly sardonic way. Don't take me too literally. We must come to understand the nature of government as a 'burden.' Government is not a burden when it is for the affluent—for defense, bailing out broken banks or the savings and loans. That is not a burden. Government only becomes a burden when it is for the poor people. It becomes a burden when it is food stamps or welfare that is involved. The burden is associated only with help to the poor, not help to the affluent. . . .

"We must have a basic safety net. In a rich society you cannot let people starve. We need a special proposal to deal with the great poverty in our biggest cities. . . .

"The Federal Reserve Bank has followed the policy of opposing inflation at the expense of higher unemployment figures. There's a big public lobby against inflation, but not a similar effort against unemployment. I would be for economic growth and some risk of inflation if that is an alternative to unemployment. We have to fight against what I call the pregnancy theory of inflation. You can't have a little inflation. I don't buy that. I'd keep interest rates down, encourage a high rate of growth, and take the risk of future inflation. . . .

"I'm willing to accept some continuation of the deficit. But there are two parts of the deficit. One part is the failure to pay for current needs. The second is the failure to invest, the purchase of long-term investments in transportation, for example. You can make a case for long-term investment because it will enhance incomes later. . . .

"The thrust toward internationalization of economic life is something we should not try to stop. I accept it. But we must have a strong emphasis on coordination of fiscal and social policy. We need to protect the workforce of high-wage countries from the low-wage countries. I've seen the cruelest form of child labor. Our social policies must connect with the new internationalism." And so it went, well into the evening.

There were other Kennedy issues dinners, briefings, meetings, and policy papers during December and early January. More academics, politicians, administration staff, historians, philosophers, and political allies participated, and many of the same themes and ideas were discussed.

Kennedy had solidified his thinking on the shape of the Democratic response to the Republican takeover. As he put it in meetings with the staff, "The election results were a mandate to make government work better, not to tear down government. In Massachusetts we won reelection on the theme of making government work for ordinary Americans. The direction of our campaign is the direction for Democrats in the country. We're beginning to hear what some Republicans want to do. We'll work with them on job training and education and health care. But there are some causes we're simply going to be relentless in fighting for, where the ordinary American working family won't be ignored at the expense of the rich. Capital gains versus middle-income tax cuts, for example.

"We're going to keep the recovery going, put some money into education, and gradually lift the incomes of working families. We're going to protect opportunity and not close the doors of higher education to middle-class working families and the poor. We're going to protect student aid. Not one cent from student aid—that's our symbolic line in the sand. We'll keep up the fight for health care. Good jobs should come with good health care. And we will not abandon the poor, as Robert Kennedy reminded us. The Democratic Party has always stood for community, for caring for others, for family, for patriotism, for morality—we will not cede these issues to the Republicans."

HOUSE DEMOCRATS

As Kennedy pointed out at our first meeting in November two days after the election, his real challenge was to work with his remaining Democratic colleagues in the Senate and the House to convince them that it was right substantively and politically to resist the Republican agenda. But Kennedy also wanted to convince his Democratic colleagues that it was still possible to move an affirmative Democratic agenda. Health care reform and an increase in the minimum wage were two initiatives he thought he could still steer through the Republican-controlled Congress.

As I said, Kennedy first worked with Daschle and the Democratic leadership in the Senate and with the members of the Labor Committee to urge resistance as well as to define an affirmative agenda for the Democrats; he was also determined to develop a strategy that Democratic House members would support. So he scheduled meetings in early December with the Democratic leaders of what was now the minority party in the Gingrich-controlled House.

There is generally much less contact between members of the House and members of the Senate than one might expect. The leaders of each party meet frequently with their counterparts in the other body to coordinate their general agendas and strategy, and senators serve on conference committees with House members to resolve the differences between versions of bills passed by the House and Senate. Conference committee deliberations, however, are usually concentrated into just a few meetings after staff have worked out most of the issues. Otherwise members of the House and Senate tend to go their separate ways. Members are busy with committee meetings, legislation on the floor, and their own constituent work. Matters are complicated by the fact that House members are typically in Washington only three days a week, usually returning home to their districts every weekend. So it was rare for a member of one body to visit or lobby members of the other.

But whatever the habits of other members, Kennedy felt that cultivating relationships with key House members was important. Whenever it seemed useful, he would head over to the House to meet with individual members. My first experience of this was on the national service bill in 1989 and 1990. A number of senators were interested in national service, particularly in putting together a pilot program for government support of community service programs. The national service idea was basically to create a domestic Peace Corps. But the House members were not as active, and once legislation had been put together in the Senate, it was necessary to light a fire under the House to generate companion legislation. So Kennedy identified Republicans and Democrats in the House who he thought would be interested. He began by assembling a list of members who had served in the Peace Corps.

Congressman Leon Panetta of California, a former Peace Corps volunteer who would later become Clinton's chief of staff, was a House leader on national service. Kennedy met with him and then went door to door in the House to meet with other prospects. The end result was that national service legislation was acted on in the House as well as the Senate and ultimately signed into law by President George H. W. Bush. This legislation was greatly expanded under Clinton into the AmeriCorps program.

The first meeting in the late fall of 1994 was with Michigan congressman David Bonior, who had been selected to become the second in command of the Democrats behind Minority Leader Dick Gephardt. Bonior was a sharp ex-seminarian with strong progressive views, and while Kennedy expected that Bonior would agree with his approach to the new legislative agenda, he wanted to learn what he could about Democratic plans in the House and how best he could help to shore up the progressive forces in the party.

The senator and I met with Bonior in his small office on the top floor, off a corridor above the old House chamber. Kennedy described the issues he had emphasized in his own reelection in Massachusetts. Bonior agreed: "Everything should be looked at in terms of how it will affect the working families, whose votes we lost in this last election." He made several other points. If there were going to be dramatic budget cuts, defense spending should be cut because it was not inherently popular. The whole theory that underpinned the defense budget was that we needed to be able to fight two major wars at the same time. Bonior said, "We need to reexamine that assumption." He thought we should come up with an alternative tax cut that would focus on people in the $30,000 to $70,000 income range, a cut that could be a populist alternative to what the Republicans were proposing, which primarily benefited the wealthy.

Bonior agreed with Kennedy that education, the minimum wage, and health care were all issues Democrats should continue to emphasize. He also agreed that a small initiative for seniors in the health care area was desirable, perhaps to include prescription drugs and better home health care in Medicare. And he agreed that Democrats needed to focus on fighting for working families: "How we are perceived as fighting for working people is critical. There have been workers who have been screwed by large employers. We have to be there visually for workers. We need a host of ideas to get ourselves back with those people who abandoned us at the polls."

A few days later, Kennedy went back to the House to meet with Congressman Vic Fazio of California, another member of the Democratic congressional leadership, but one who came from the more conservative Democratic Leadership Council side of the party. Fazio was still in shock about the elections. He seemed more passive and more resigned to the Republican control of the House than Bonior had been. But he agreed with the senator that we should work on a GI Bill for job training and perhaps try to make college costs tax-deductible for the middle class. Fazio was the first to mention immigration. Kennedy had been chairman of the Senate judiciary subcommittee on immigration. Fazio observed that the Republicans were likely to overreach and adopt excessively anti-immigrant programs. He talked about putting together a task force on immigration in the House and expected that there would be an opportunity for the task force and Kennedy to work together. It was a very cordial meeting, but Fazio did not convey the level of intensity that he and other Democrats in the House would need to be able to effectively resist the Republican tide.

Kennedy also asked to meet with his friend Barney Frank, the congressman from Massachusetts, who was well-known for his progressive views, quick wit, original voice, and sharp intellect. We had lunch with Frank in Kennedy's conference room in the Russell Building. As usual, Frank was full of ideas. He started right in expressing concern that the president would give away too much ground in his budget. "Why would we ever slice Medicare in our budget and neutralize the issue before the Republicans basically try to decimate the program? If the challenge is to reduce the deficit, why aren't we looking at more cuts to defense? Britain and France don't want our defense, so why don't we take them at their word? Why should we be prepared to fight two wars at once?

"The Republicans will come at us with all their initiatives, and we have to be better prepared than we have been before. We have to pick out the issues to poke holes in their public support. We shouldn't let them cut college education funding. When they try to zero out crime prevention and community development programs, they'll run into conflict from the mayors, even Republican mayors like Giuliani in New York and Riordan in Los Angeles. The Republicans are convinced that there are easy answers. The first thing for us to do is say, 'Okay—where are the easy answers?' Let's wait for the Republicans to come up with their answers, and then we can show how unpopular they are. Their budget will cut Medicare and charge students more for college education, and that won't fly."

Frank was convinced the ammunition would be there. Our job was to heighten attention to what the Republicans were doing, to explain it. Basically, he thought a waiting game was the best strategy—waiting for the Republican budget. In his view, we simply wanted to "bait the traps and wait to see what the Republicans do. We can come up with a better deficit reduction path and not take away anything that people want. We need to be prepared to document the harm the Republicans are going to cause. The worst thing we as Democrats could do is to cut a little here and a little there and basically neutralize all the issues."

He agreed with Kennedy that we should pull together a list of corporate tax expenditures and corporate welfare programs that we could offer up for budget cuts and deficit reduction. "We need to wait for the Republican budget and then make them vote on it. There will be many things they will try to do that just won't fly with the public. The biggest threat to this strategy is President Clinton. He puts out the first budget. We have to make sure that by cutting from all the places the Republicans are intending to cut—but just cutting less—he doesn't neutralize the power of these issues." Frank's point about Clinton and his budget echoed Kennedy's own thinking and turned out to be right on the money.

Kennedy also met with Dick Gephardt of Missouri, the majority leader, soon to be the minority leader. Kennedy and Gephardt had become close friends in recent years, a relationship that grew out of a shared commitment to issues such as health care and labor. Furthermore Gephardt had been particularly helpful to the senator's son Patrick in his election to the House that fall. When the senator sat down with Gephardt and several of his staff members in the latter's office in the Capitol, there was no need to persuade Gephardt about his goals. It was a question of what was possible and what the priorities ought to be.

Gephardt was uncertain of what the future held in the new Republican House. The vibes were not good so far, and there was no denying the basic fact that the Republicans were going to set the agenda. The rules in the House essentially gave complete control to the majority party, so long as it held its votes. There was no filibuster or other procedural device such as there was in the Senate to hold off the majority from any action it wished to take.

It was clear that Gephardt was sympathetic to Kennedy's strategy. But the majority leader was more preoccupied with protecting his members as best he could in the shift from Democratic to Republican control. The idea of developing a new Democratic affirmative agenda just at the point when Democrats were defeated and were about to lose control of the House was not paramount in Gephardt's thinking. He talked about ways to highlight the most extreme Republican measures and to build traction on these issues to resist them.

Kennedy agreed with Gephardt, but even more importantly, he began to speak with conviction about how, in this Republican Congress, he was convinced he could actually pass both health care and minimum wage legislation.

Chapter 6

THE STRUGGLE FOR THE
MIND OF THE PRESIDENT

WHAT WILL CLINTON DO?

Kennedy's contacts with members in the House and Senate in December 1994 were more his way of taking temperatures, shoring up Democrats, heading off any decisions that would later be irreversible, and laying the groundwork for January, than about persuading members to take a particular stand immediately. The situation with Clinton was different. In December the president would make major public pronouncements about his agenda, and he was preparing to deliver his January State of the Union speech. The most important target for the senator's strategy had to be Clinton, and persuading him to stick with the progressive agenda was Kennedy's greatest challenge. Without Clinton's support, the odds of defeating the most extreme measures of the Contract with America were greatly reduced. Clinton had the bully pulpit and the veto pen. If he used them to advance the cause of the Democratic resistance, it might

108

succeed. But if he tried to preempt the Republican agenda by moving to the right, giving ground on Medicare, Medicaid, education funding, tax cuts, or the environment, the Democratic opposition would be fatally wounded before it even began.

But how the president would use his tremendous persuasive powers was an open question. We did not know at the time just how badly shaken he and Hillary Clinton had been by the election results. But as they began to prepare for the president's own reelection campaign, they were contemplating a major change in direction. To help them think through their strategy, they privately sought advice from the Republican-leaning political consultant Dick Morris.

After Clinton had lost reelection for governor of Arkansas, Morris was involved in shaping the strategy that enabled him to win two years later in a conservative-leaning state. Morris had started out as a Democrat and originally met Clinton in the George McGovern presidential campaign. He had since moved increasingly to the right and had worked to help elect Republicans, including Trent Lott. He advised Clinton to move to the center and position himself as a New Democrat who offered a path away from Democratic orthodoxy—a third way between Republicans and traditional liberal Democrats in Congress and elsewhere. He urged Clinton to get out early with a balanced budget plan of his own that would align him solidly in the camp of cutting the deficit and make gestures toward the Republicans. For several months, Morris's role was kept secret—not just from us and the public but even from the rest of the White House staff. So when Kennedy set out on his mission to urge the president to draw clear lines in the sand against the Republican proposals, he was facing a tougher uphill climb than he knew.

The White House had announced that Clinton would be delivering a radio address before Christmas in which he would lay out his plans for the year ahead. Kennedy knew that it was vital to get to Clinton before he delivered that address.

Clinton had launched his presidency as a progressive, albeit one with a somewhat centrist, New Democrat slant. His first investment budget,

the so-called stimulus package in 1993, increased spending for education, research, and infrastructure, but the budget had been derailed by
Republicans and more than a few wavering Democrats. The health care
struggle of 1993 and 1994 had made Kennedy and the president close
allies. No one in Congress had a stronger track record on health care
than Kennedy, and no one in the Senate had worked more closely with
the Clintons in their effort to provide health care for all Americans. Even
when the senator had disagreed with the president, he expressed his disagreement in private, not in public.

Kennedy always felt the deepest respect for the Office of the Presidency. That attitude came from his family tradition of public service, and
particularly from his own experience of having a brother in the White
House. He also appreciated Clinton's affection for the Kennedy family.
In some ways, the president and the senator were soul mates—both were
larger-than-life characters; both loved politics, political combat, humor,
and argument.

PERSUADING THE PRESIDENT

Shortly after the election, the senator began planning for his meeting
with the president in which he planned to provide his own recommendations about the direction in which Clinton should steer the country.
Much of what Kennedy had us all working on during the last weeks of
November and early December was preparation for that meeting. He was
determined to persuade the president to stick to a progressive course
even in the face of the election results. The senator realized that if the
president backed off the Democratic agenda in his upcoming radio
speech to the nation, it would be tough to pull him back. So Kennedy
began shaping his arguments for the meeting before the content of the
radio address was set in stone.

The senator knew the basic themes he wanted to present to Clinton.
First, however, he would prepare for his meeting by talking to friends
and allies close to Clinton to ascertain what they were thinking, how they
were advising him, and to try out his themes. He met first with Alice

Rivlin, Clinton's director of the Office of Management and Budget (OMB). His first point to her was that the president's budget should be a benchmark that Democrats in Congress could use in a constructive way. Since the Republicans obviously would discard the president's budget in favor of their own, the budget was primarily a political document, which should emphasize the issues on which the Democrats would fight.

Second, education was a powerful issue for the country and for the Democrats. We should not lose the political high ground on education, he told Rivlin. "Keep your eye on Head Start and school reform and Chapter I funding for disadvantaged schools, job training, and School-to-Work." We should take the position that there should be "no cuts in student aid." Third, on health care: "Medicare cuts should not be used to provide tax cuts for the rich or for any purpose other than health care reform." And there ought to be incremental health care initiatives in the budget. Fourth, the big question was how to pay for middle-class tax cuts. Kennedy said finally, "Democrats need to mobilize our base."

Rivlin told the senator that the central discussion at the White House was about middle-class tax cuts and deficit reduction. Another area of concern was how to give governors more power over federal programs: whether, for instance, to leave block grants to the states in a new job training consolidation program.

Rivlin, a moderate, if not conservative, Democrat, was a reliable read on the attitude at the White House. Her comments did not sound promising. If she was right, the president was focusing on the Republicans' issues: tax cuts, spending reductions, and transferring power from the federal government back to the states.

The senator said to Rivlin, "Right now the president looks like he's trying to out-Republican the Republicans, and people won't buy it. You have to look at everything through the lens of working families. I'm not sure that's what the president is doing right now. He is struggling with how to pay for tax cuts. The president tried to cut corporate welfare, and the Economic Council and Wall Street went berserk and started calling to object. The president needs to come to grips with whose side he is on."

Rivlin responded, "It might be useful for you to give the president some very frank political reminders about the Carter administration, how President Carter moved to the center and left behind the core of the party. Remind the president he needs a symbolic budget, a defining budget. We understand the point that the president can't win unless his base is engaged. You, Senator Kennedy, can talk from the experience of rallying the base. . . . Talk to the president about your own campaign. That's where the president's head is. What worked in the campaign, and what didn't? The question is how you move the middle to you. Isn't the answer that the middle moved because you, Senator Kennedy, talked about the stuff they care about? Get on the political wavelength, and then the rest will fall into place with the president. Tell him, 'Here's what worked for me: jobs, education, and health care.' "

The senator next met with Leon Panetta, now the president's chief of staff. Kennedy's chief goal was to emphasize the "Don't cut Medicare" theme. "Take the high road on Medicare," he told Panetta. "Health care is still a priority. There are opportunities for insurance reform and expanding coverage for children. Focus on energizing the base. Lead with raising the minimum wage. Find savings to fund public programs. Don't hurt the poor by cutting Medicaid." There was nothing in Panetta's response with which the senator could not agree. He was buoyed.

Meetings at the staff level were not so encouraging. David Nexon, along with Clayton Spencer and Ellen Guiney, met with the OMB official in charge of education programs. Jack Lew, OMB associate director for legislative affairs and later Treasury secretary under President Obama, was also present. Remembering how the Republicans under Reagan had tried to cram the great bulk of their program into a single big budget reconciliation bill, Nexon started to explain that, in order to lay the groundwork for a veto of such a bill, the president's budget needed to draw strong distinctions between his position and what the Republicans would be proposing. Lew cut him off. "We're not talking about vetoes!" he exclaimed.

Kennedy wanted to meet with Clinton at least two days before his radio address. At that point, Clinton would be focusing intently on the content of the speech and would be revising and editing it right up to the end. Meeting with him too early would likely mean that the discussion was lost in the press of other conversations. But getting to him just when he was focusing on the speech was the right time.

We learned the radio address would be delivered on December 15. Accordingly, Kennedy's chief of staff, Paul Donovan, asked the White House to schedule a meeting with the senator on December 13. The meeting was put on the president's schedule.

For weeks our Labor Committee staff had been preparing background memos narrowing down the arguments for the meeting with the president and providing the necessary materials. We developed a detailed book with background on the budget, including sections on each of the specific budgetary issues about which we were most concerned, such as the middle-class tax cut and deficit reduction. We also provided memos on the four key areas in Kennedy's Committee: health care, education, children and families, and jobs. We added in all the recent *Washington Post* and *New York Times* articles on the president's decision-making process regarding the budget, the tax cut, and deficit reduction.

We had more conversations with people at the White House to try to understand the president's thinking. Liberals around the president were very concerned about the direction he seemed to be taking. They were particularly worried about his apparent emphasis on middle-class tax cuts. Harold Ickes, Clinton's deputy chief of staff, kept us posted on the timing of the president's decision on the budget, which would be late in December and early January.

A few days before December 13, I had a very disturbing conversation with Melanne Verveer, who was deputy chief of staff to Hillary Clinton and a longtime ally of progressive causes. She was very worried about where the Clintons would come out on the key budget issues. I suggested Kennedy talk to Verveer, and he told her what he had told others: "Right now it looks like the president is preparing to out-Republican the Republicans, but I just don't think people will buy it and it will never be enough. It will just move the center closer to the Republicans, and we'll end up worse than need be. All around the president there are people pushing the middle-class tax cut. They are good budgeters. They want to find the revenues for the tax cut, but they don't have good political ears. They will end up finding these revenues from programs that are supported by our Democratic base. They want to use cuts to health care and Medicare to fund the tax cut and even go beyond to reduce the deficit. But reducing the deficit doesn't have any political traction. The president should be looking at this through the lens of working Americans. How will these cuts affect ordinary American families? This is what the president has to come to grips with after the election. His budget is a political document. Whose side will he be on?"

As Rivlin had, Verveer advised the senator to talk very frankly and politically to the president. She also mentioned the Carter administration and the base. She told the senator, "You can't win if your base isn't engaged. The best way for you to influence the president's decisions is to talk from political experience."

From all these conversations with friends and allies in and around the White House we were convinced that the mind of the president was still not made up. There were many forces urging dramatic movement toward the Republicans. There were others urging him to hold the line. The unanswered question was where he would end up. So much of the future success of the Democratic resistance would hinge on that decision.

The stage was now set for the meeting with the president. Staff had several more briefings with the senator, and we kept sharpening the outline of key points. It went through many drafts. The outline was important because it would organize the presentation to the president and because it was likely that the senator would leave the outline with the president after the meeting. The time of the meeting kept changing, but it was finally set for 6:00 p.m. in the president's quarters. By midafternoon the outline was in final form. It had two sections:

THE OUTLINE

I.   Preliminary Points—The general strategy of my election can work for you.

    A.   Fighting for working families and demonstrating you are on their side in every conceivable way, at every opportunity.

Putting people first and contrasting our positions with Republican positions.

B. Key areas are education, job training, Medicare, health care and tax policy, minimum wage and protecting college financing.

C. Need to keep our base on our side. Unions, minorities, women, gays, education groups and the health community all worked like hell for me and helped the campaign enormously. Hard to head into 1996 without enthusiastic support of our base.

D. Pick out areas where Republicans are clearly extreme—orphanages, gag rule, food programs. Their harshness will not wear well over time.

II. Your Budget is a Political Document—The budget is a political document, not a policy statement. Accordingly, it should avoid making cuts in core programs like jobs and job training, education, and health care that would neutralize Democrats' ability to attack expected Republican cuts in these programs. Consider every proposal in terms of themes of whose side we are on. You may have to veto the Budget Reconciliation Bill if the Republicans pack their whole agenda into it as they did successfully in 1981. You need to have prepared a political case to justify the veto if necessary.

III. Four substantive points to demonstrate that Clinton and the Democrats are fighting for working families.

1. Education: Resist all cuts to student aid.

2. Health care: No Medicare cuts except for health reform. Health care is potentially still one of our best issues and we should propose a specific down payment plan and challenge the Republicans to pass it.

3. Job training: The Senator ran ads in his election featuring job training as the job component of our fighting for working families theme and it worked very well.

4.   We should pay for the middle-class tax cut for working families with incomes up to $75,000 and for some limited deficit
reduction by reducing corporate subsidies and tax expenditures, so-called corporate welfare.

We went over the outline one last time with the senator as darkness
set in. Then he and I got into his van for the drive down Pennsylvania
Avenue to the White House.

The waiting room to the West Wing was decorated with Christmas or-
naments, wreaths, and flowers. The room was known for its jar of M&Ms,
which sat on a table to the left of the door as you entered from outside.
A marine guard was responsible for keeping the jar full. A closet off the
entrance hall contained a box full of M&Ms; as the jar in the waiting
room got close to empty, the marine refilled it. I suspect many people
who came to see the president plotted how to get back and forth to the
M&M jar without appearing to be too greedy. I am one such person.

Pat Griffin, the president's director of legislative affairs, told us the
meeting had been moved to the residence in the East Wing and escorted
us there. Along the way, we were joined by Deputy Chief of Staff Ickes
and Chief of Staff Panetta. The president met us on the third floor and
took us to a large study decorated in the style of President Lincoln's era,
with overstuffed red chairs and couches and dark flowered upholstery.
Lincoln memorabilia were displayed throughout the room. The six of
us—the president, the senator, Panetta, Ickes, Griffin, and I—sat in a
circle of chairs and a sofa around a coffee table. Clinton was tall, strikingly handsome, welcoming, and relaxed.

We got right to business. The senator began his presentation, but the
president interrupted him. Apparently he had had advance warning of
what Kennedy had on his mind. "I take it you want us to stick with the
working family themes," Clinton said.

Now Kennedy interrupted: "Yes, the themes of my campaign basically identified us with working families. We laid the building blocks so I
could return to the Senate to continue the effort to strengthen security
for middle-class and working families. We need to identify certain power-

ful policy positions to symbolize this commitment." He kept going, not wanting to lose the floor. "First, on Medicare. No cuts to Medicare, except for new health care programs. And I hope you have a health care program in your State of the Union. The themes to work on are limiting exclusions for preexisting conditions and extending portability, improving coverage for children, temporary workers, and the elderly. There's a group of Republicans I'm talking to in the Senate who I think are going to go for this, so I hope you will."

On education, Kennedy urged, "No cuts to college aid."

Panetta jumped in: "Are there any education programs that can be cut?"

The senator said there might be some. "We'll get a list, but overall the money should be moved around, not cut. There are ways to help students with college aid, such as tax deductions for interest on loans and education savings bonds."

The president, not to be outdone, went even further than the senator. He raised the idea of total tax deductibility for all college expenses. "The Republicans are talking about capital gains tax cuts. Why don't we talk about targeted tax cuts for educational expenses? Won't that energize our groups?"

Before the senator could get to it, the president beat him to the punch and asked him about the minimum wage. "When they talk about indexing capital gains, why don't we talk about raising the minimum wage?"

Kennedy and Clinton went back and forth for over an hour. The senator made all the points in his outline, and there was little or no disagreement from the president or his staff on anything the senator said. We left the memo behind with Griffin and returned to the senator's van, where he dictated his recollection of the meeting into a tape recorder kept handy for such occasions. He used the tapes to jog his memory as he wrote his memoir, *True Compass*, and they will eventually be made available for historians.

Kennedy was pleased with the meeting. Clinton had been extremely friendly and had given him as much time as he needed. The president's key advisors had been present. Kennedy's argument had been clear and simple. The president took in everything he said and disagreed with nothing, even adding the idea of tax deductibility for college tuition. He implied that so-called targeted tax cuts for the middle class could be a Democratic response to the Republican drive to cut taxes overall. It was a social program in the form of a tax cut. Kennedy was impressed.

But then again, the president hadn't said he would follow our advice. And of course Clinton was famous for making people feel that he had heard what they said to him, and even agreed with them, but would then proceed in a different direction.

A MIDDLE-CLASS BILL OF RIGHTS

On December 15, the president gave his ten-minute radio address to the nation, his first important policy statement since the watershed election five weeks before. This was the speech that all our work had been geared toward. We felt we had done all we could; in fact, we would not do anything differently if we had to do it over. We all listened together in the senator's office, nervous but hopeful.

The president started by reviewing the economic situation. "For too long, too many Americans have worked longer for stagnant wages and less security. For two years we've pursued an economic strategy that has helped produce over five million jobs, but even though the economic statistics are moving up, most of our living standards aren't. We've got to change that. More jobs aren't enough; we have to raise incomes. Tonight I propose a middle-class bill of rights." He described four elements in this bill of rights: college tuition would be tax deductible; there would be a tax cut of up to $500 for the parents of each child under thirteen; tax-free individual retirement savings accounts would be expanded for the middle class; and participants in job training would be given the funds directly to pay for their choice among training programs. He said he would pay for these programs by reducing government spending in other areas, relying in particular on Vice President Gore's Reinventing Government initiatives.

He talked about cutting government and reducing government spending. "I know that some people want to cut the government blindly, and that's popular now, but I won't do it. I want a leaner, not a meaner, government that's back on the side of hardworking Americans." He said we needed lobbying reform and campaign finance reform more than ever because the special interests hadn't gone into hiding. He urged welfare reform and health care reform and promised to say more about each of these in his State of the Union address. His test for tax cuts: "Does an idea expand middle-class ideals and opportunities? Does it promote values like family, work, responsibility, and community? Does it contribute to strengthening the new economy?" He asserted, "We need to put aside the politics of personal destruction and demonization that has dominated too much of our debate. . . . We'll do a lot better job of meeting the challenges if we work together and find unity and strength in our diversity."

The newspapers reported that Clinton would outline a plan for tax breaks and for a middle-class bill of rights. The analysis was that he was moving to blunt the Republicans' tax-cutting message. But the difference between Clinton's and the Republicans' proposals was that each item of Clinton's middle-class bill of rights was targeted to the middle class and not to the wealthy or to business.

Phew! We felt we were still at the table. Kennedy was very pleased. The president had not talked about paying for tax cuts by cutting Medicare or Medicaid, as Kennedy had feared. And there was a strong commitment to education in the proposed tax deductions for college tuition. On the down side, there was no mention of the minimum wage or of a specific health care expansion. But the tone was right, and we all felt that at least no damage had been done. The president had not joined the Republican bandwagon. The battle for the president's mind was not lost.

In the week leading up to Christmas, the Republicans and their allies were moving full speed ahead with their plans. Rush Limbaugh, the right-wing radio talk show host, was invited to address a retreat for new Republican congressmen held in Baltimore on the weekend before the president's radio speech. Many of the members gave Limbaugh credit for their election success. But Limbaugh said, "The climate was there, this country has been conservative in its heart for the longest time. It didn't always vote that way, but it has now." He urged the freshmen congressmen to stay "rock ribbed, devoted, in almost a militant way to your principles." After Clinton's radio address, the Republicans praised him for proposing new tax cuts, but one after another said they would move much further and faster on cutting taxes and spending than he had proposed.

Kennedy left Washington for Cape Cod for Christmas week. When he came back to Washington to be sworn in for a sixth term in the Senate, he would be in the minority. But he and his staff were ready for 1995 to begin. The strategy was set. He had done what he could to rally the demoralized Democratic troops. The foundation was laid to resist the Republican juggernaut.

Chapter 7

ORRIN HATCH

RELATIONSHIP

When the Democrats lost the majority my world turned upside down. I even wondered whether there was any point in staying in Washington. But now, after all the meetings, especially the critical and successful meeting with the president, I was reenergized and reengaged. It was a time of crisis, and I couldn't abandon ship. I kept coming back to the importance of protecting the work we'd done on AIDS and other critical social issues we needed to save from the Gingrich budget cutters. And over the past five years my relationships with Kennedy and other senators and with staffers had grown stronger, enabling me to be effective in different ways.

Relationships were a vital part of the Senate experience, and Kennedy's relationship with Senator Orrin Hatch became one of the most productive bipartisan congressional partnerships in U.S. history. There may never have been two less likely allies: Hatch, the straitlaced, bone-thin, self-made, devout Mormon teetotaler and true-believing conservative from Utah, and Kennedy, the liberal, boisterous, fun-loving Irish Catholic from Massachusetts. But both believed that they were in the Senate to improve public policy. While tenacious, they shared a sense of humor, a love of music, and a willingness to compromise in order to make a deal. They understood the power that they brought to an issue when they joined forces and were always looking for common ground (except when Hatch was up for reelection and had to be more conservative and stay away from Kennedy). With Kennedy from the left and Hatch from the right, they were able to sweep up everyone in between. Hatch called me several times in 2009 and 2010, when Kennedy was very sick and then after his death, and said that if only Kennedy were still involved, they could have worked out a deal on health care.

Both cared about the personal side of their relationship. As a favor to Hatch, Kennedy supported Governor Mitt Romney's efforts to overcome public opposition to completing the steeple on the Mormon temple in Belmont, Massachusetts. Hatch came to Boston for Rose Kennedy's funeral, and when Hatch's mother died, Kennedy went to Salt Lake City for her funeral. Hatch assigned himself the role of stern critic of some of the personal transgressions in Kennedy's life, and Kennedy tolerated the scolding. Hatch enjoyed being known as Kennedy's friend, and he ended up helping to pass legislation that was often more liberal than conservative. Even though they disagreed fervently on most issues and frequently took opposite sides in important Senate debates, once they got off the floor their disagreements were put aside. I often saw them arguing in debate on the Senate floor (about the merits of the minimum wage, for example) loudly and derisively, and then when they accidentally met in the hallway afterward they would pat each other on the back, laugh, and chat about anything but the minimum wage.

Their relationship allowed them to reach agreement on bills that would never have become law without their mutual trust and willingness to work together. In 1990 Kennedy sought to amend the Taft-Hartley Act, which would be the first significant change to the law in twenty years, to allow employers to place money in a trust fund to be used by low-income workers for costs associated with renting or buying a home. A group of mostly immigrant members of Local 26 of the Hotel and Food Service Workers Union in Boston had already negotiated successfully to set up this kind of arrangement, but the law barred such payments. Hatch agreed to support this amendment, even though he normally would not have allowed Taft-Hartley to be reopened and amended without insisting on antilabor concessions. In return, Kennedy agreed to allow a special "Downwinders" compensation fund to be created for people who lived downwind of federal open-air nuclear tests in Utah, Arizona, and Nevada during the 1950s and 1960s and who had developed cancer as a result. Without Kennedy's support, Hatch had been unsuccessful in passing similar legislation.

As described in Chapter 5, their legacy on health care and other issues is extensive. From 1988 on, they jointly authored and cosponsored successful legislation in many areas: AIDS care and research, disabilities rights, Head Start expansion, summer jobs, the arts, food and drug laws, and in 1997 the life-saving Children's Health Insurance Program, under which more than seven million children receive health insurance.

"AH, THE POWER OF MUSIC"

A little-known ingredient of the Hatch-Kennedy relationship, and of mine with both of them, centered around a love of music. Kennedy had enjoyed music since he was a boy, sitting at the piano with his mother. She taught him her favorite songs, including "Sweet Adeline" and "Sweet Rosie O'Grady," and told him stories about her father, Honey Fitz, who was twice elected mayor of Boston. When she was a young girl, she campaigned with her father while he entertained crowds by singing, often calling on Rose to join in.

Kennedy had an untrained but strong bass-baritone singing voice and very good musical pitch. His larger-than-life personality helped him put over a song. His taste in music was eclectic, but he liked nothing more than standing around a piano and singing from the Broadway songbook or the Irish songs he had grown up with. One year, for his birthday, Vicki gave him a series of singing lessons with a teacher who came to their house. The sessions lasted for several months but were abandoned because the teacher emphasized Cole Porter songs, which Kennedy couldn't sing as well as the big Rodgers and Hammerstein and Lerner and Loewe romantic ballads. For another birthday, Vicki bought him a karaoke machine, but it never caught on. He had a neighbor in Washington, Steven "Spike" Karalekas, who played rock-n-roll on the piano, and Kennedy often invited him to his house to perform Chubby Checker and Fats Domino songs, which Kennedy joined in singing enthusiastically. Vicki loved these songs and knew all the words.

Hatch, too, loved music. He told me of his early memories growing up in Pittsburgh, where his parents, despite facing difficult economic circumstances, arranged for him to have a ticket to sit in the top balcony of Symphony Hall and listen to the Pittsburgh Symphony. For many years he has been writing lyrics for religious and patriotic songs and producing albums of these songs. He is an enthusiastic and energetic senator, but I sometimes felt his passion for song writing trumped all his other interests. His songs have been performed by many well-known artists and at important events. At George W. Bush's second inauguration, Hatch's "Heal Our Land," was sung by Santita Jackson, the daughter of the Reverend Jesse Jackson. In 1997 he wrote a song for Senator and Vicki Kennedy, "Souls in Love," for their wedding anniversary. He provided a copy of the song on a CD to the senator and they called him from their sailboat in Long Island Sound to tell him that they were celebrating their anniversary with his song.

In 1995 Kennedy discovered that I too liked music and had once sung on Broadway. From then on, music became a part of our life in the Senate, with and without Hatch. Kennedy first heard me sing one morning when, without any warning, he called me to his office. He was about to meet with Marvin Hamlisch, the composer of several shows, including *A Chorus Line*, who was in town to lobby for extending the copyright period for musical compositions. Kennedy, ever resourceful and always trying to make visitors feel at home, had arranged for a piano to be moved into his conference room at the Senate Russell Building, and after the discussion of copyright law, he asked Hamlisch to play it. He obliged, much to Kennedy's delight. Then Kennedy suggested to Hamlisch that I could sing while he provided the accompaniment. I resisted. Kennedy insisted. I gave in and started on one song from Hamlisch's musical *They're Playing Our Song* but couldn't remember the words and kept repeating only the title. Mercifully, Hamlisch stopped and suggested that I pick another song, any song for which I actually knew the words. I went with "The Girl That I Marry" from the musical *Annie Get Your Gun* by Irving Berlin, because I knew the words, having sung it to my wife at our wedding.

Hamlisch played with great fanfare. I sang along with full voice, attracting other staff members and curiosity seekers from up and down the hallway. Kennedy later gave me a picture of the performance, which he had endorsed with the inscription "Ah, the power of music" and which had been signed by Hamlisch. The photo showed Kennedy and his entire personal staff crowded into the room behind me, all grinning from ear to ear, especially Kennedy. After that, Kennedy took any opportunity to insist, often without warning and in spite of my reluctance, that I sing. A few days later, he saw Senator Kassebaum in the public hallway between their offices and had me sing "The Girl That I Marry" to her as tourists, staffers, and even the Capitol Police stopped to gape. Kassebaum, although obviously a little embarrassed, led the applause when I finished.

When Kennedy was asked by John Williams to conduct "Stars and Stripes Forever" with the Boston Pops at Symphony Hall during the Kennedy tribute at the 2004 Democratic Convention in Boston, he asked me to help him with his conducting moves. I wrote numbers and letters in the score to mark each refrain, and we practiced counting out the number of beats to help him look like he was actually conducting. He was particularly concerned that his arm gestures be in sync with the orchestra, especially at the last unexpected downbeat of the march. Much to both of our relief, he pulled it off beautifully at the performance. He did so well that he was later asked to conduct the march again at the Pops in Hyannis Port; at that performance he surprised us all when, at the two distinctive beats near the end, he wiggled his backside, then turned around and winked at the audience. He brought the house down.

Over the years, I watched him spend more and more of his rare free time on music. Many of his parties ended with his insisting that we all sing, and no one could turn him down. He was personally friendly with many Broadway musical stars, including Betty Comden, Marin Mazza, Kelli O'Hara, and Glenn Close, to mention a few who came to Boston or Washington to sing for him and Vicki. Audra McDowell and Brian Stokes Mitchell (seven Tonys between them) were part of the large group of stars honoring him the night he conducted the Pops during the 2004 convention. At a reception following the event, he insisted that I (zero Tonys) join him in singing with them. We sang together for over an hour in the presence of a big crowd that wouldn't leave. At a birthday party for him at the JFK Library he sang "Some Enchanted Evening" alone on the stage and there wasn't a dry eye in the place.

Kennedy only liked songs he knew well. When I asked what songs he wanted me to sing, he always requested the same ones: "On the Street Where You Live" by Lerner and Loewe and "Love Changes Everything" by Andrew Lloyd Webber. Sometimes I wondered if he valued my role as a singer more than my work as staff director. Sometimes the two over-lapped. My singing at his direction even played a role in closing the deal on the most important legislative action resulting from the Hatch-Kennedy partnership (which I describe in Chapter 22).

THE RYAN WHITE AIDS CARE BILL

A triumph of the Hatch-Kennedy partnership, and one of the key accomplishments we needed to protect from Gingrich and his cohorts, was the Ryan White AIDS CARE law. Many bills were enacted as a result of the Hatch-Kennedy cosponsorship, but few were as important as this one. And it was possible only because of a team effort by an unlikely group of Hatch and Kennedy staff members, who worked together as if the loyalty and friendship of Hatch and Kennedy were passed along to their staffs.

Today the Ryan White law receives almost unanimous support in

Congress every time it is up for reauthorization, which has happened four times since it was passed in 1990. It now generates over $2 billion a year toward care and medications for people with AIDS. Passing it the first time was touch-and-go, however, and funding it at the full amount took several years to accomplish.

By 1989 the AIDS epidemic was devastating poor and gay communities in America's largest cities and was beginning to spread into the heterosexual community, particularly among drug users. The disease was overwhelming the hospital systems. Although AIDS patients did not always require the full services of a hospital, they were too ill to take care of themselves. Without community or nursing care at home, they had no alternative but to remain in the hospital.

Addressing this crisis was an enormous challenge, but we had the right people for the job. Terry Beirn lived in New York and commuted to Washington to work as a consultant to the Labor Committee on health care and disability issues. For several years, he oversaw the programs of the American Foundation for AIDS Research (AmFAR), an organization at the forefront of the fight against the epidemic. Michael Iskowitz was a former legal services lawyer who also specialized in children's issues. In 1988 they worked with Kennedy and Hatch, who was then the ranking member of the Committee, to pass the Hope Act, which was designed to coordinate federal research on AIDS and HIV and was Congress's first comprehensive AIDS legislation.

Terry had a deep personal commitment to the issue that was profoundly moving to the few who knew about it. Shortly after I started work on the Committee in 1989, Terry came into my office and told me privately that he had been diagnosed with HIV in 1983. My first concern was for his health, but he assured me he was still feeling fine. I stared at him for a long moment with a mixture of awe and sympathy, not sure how to respond. But one thing was clear: he didn't want anyone's pity or any special treatment. He wanted money for AIDS programs. "Thanks for telling me," I said. "I admire your courage. We're going to do something about this."

In December 1989, at Terry's suggestion, Kennedy took a fact-finding trip across America to study the impact of what he called the twin epidemics of HIV and drug abuse on the hospital systems in New York, California, Missouri, and Georgia. The trip also focused on the plight of the uninsured, with a special emphasis on uninsured children, the difficulties faced by families needing long-term care, and the rising cost of health care. We ended up producing a book on what we found.[1]

The most dramatic findings were on the tremendous impact HIV and AIDS were having on the nation and on the health care system. The first stop was in New York City, where Terry arranged for Kennedy to visit the Bronx-Lebanon Hospital in the South Bronx, which had the greatest concentration of AIDS cases in the nation. While Bronx-Lebanon had what for the time was a model program, and the doctors and nurses caring for AIDS patients were extraordinarily dedicated, we were horrified by what we saw. The hospital system was breaking apart at the seams and was rendered incapable of delivering acceptable care to the legions of desperately ill AIDS patients. The emergency rooms were so overcrowded that patients were often unable to get timely or adequate care, and many were spending days on cots in the hallways. AIDS patients already occupied one out of ten hospital beds and stayed three times as long as other patients each time they were admitted. The New York City Health Department estimated that the city was facing an AIDS care bill of $7 billion over the next three years and that there were already 200,000 people in the city infected by the virus. If nothing was done, what was happening in New York City would soon be happening in the rest of the nation. Indeed, Kennedy found that the AIDS epidemic was beginning to have an impact even in rural Georgia. He came away from the tour convinced that action was essential, and he asked us to come up with a legislative response.

By 1989 the nation was eight and a half years into the AIDS epidemic, but the Reagan and Bush administrations had taken almost no action to help victims of this plague. Reagan did not even mention the word "AIDS" in public until the end of his two terms in office; then he did so in an exchange of correspondence and a personal meeting with Ryan White, a hemophiliac from Kokomo, Indiana. Ryan had contracted the

HIV virus from a blood transfusion and had been diagnosed with HIV in 1984, when he was thirteen.

After Kennedy's health care tour, we started to develop a strategy for an initiative to provide home health care, medication, and food to people with AIDS. The initiative would serve two vital purposes: AIDS patients could return to their homes and live with some dignity and independence as they struggled with the disease, and hospitals in the cities hardest hit by AIDS would be relieved of the unmanageable overcrowding they faced.

The question was how to enact such legislation when conservative Republicans, led by Jesse Helms, would fight so hard to stop it. Moreover, it was not clear the Bush administration would have anything to do with AIDS legislation, particularly if it called for spending federal money when the deficit was growing every year. To have any chance of success, we needed a Republican partner with unquestioned conservative bona fides. Hatch was the obvious candidate, especially given that he and Kennedy had worked together previously on the Hope Act. Kennedy approached Hatch for his assistance, and Hatch agreed. We were in business again.

Beirn and Iskowitz had an idea for legislation that Kennedy and I liked very much. It was taken for granted in Washington that when a natural disaster, such as a hurricane or a flood, hit a section of the country, causing devastation and financial loss to particular cities and communities, Congress and the federal government would immediately step in and provide emergency assistance and federal expertise. There was almost no limit to the funds that the Federal Emergency Management Agency would make available. The condition of the deficit at the time was irrelevant; all that was required was a declaration of a federal emergency. We reasoned that the AIDS epidemic was a health emergency that was devastating certain communities.

Beirn and Iskowitz developed an outline of legislation to provide emergency aid to the thirteen hardest hit cities. At Hatch's suggestion, they developed a section of the legislation to provide assistance to all states to care for patients with AIDS based on their share of the number of AIDS cases in the country. Beirn and Iskowitz had been thinking modestly, in the range of $50 million. They figured that we needed to start small, in view of the controversy sure to erupt around any legislation dealing with AIDS. Kennedy and I disagreed. If we were going to do it, we should do it right. We settled on $600 million, half for the hardest hit cities and half for the states, allocated based on the number of cases in each state. Hatch was an enthusiastic cosponsor from the beginning. Now we had to find a strategy for the uphill fight to get the legislation enacted.

It is almost impossible to get press coverage for the introduction of a bill unless the president is behind it or it is part of a scandal, and we needed press to pass this bill. So we decided to bring in a celebrity. The Washington press will usually cover celebrities, especially if the reason for their appearance is actually newsworthy. The obvious choice was Elizabeth Taylor. For many years she had been among the strongest public advocates for taking action on AIDS and had been particularly successful in fundraising for AIDS research. Beirn knew her from AmFAR; when he contacted her she agreed to speak at a hearing on March 6, 1990, at which the Hatch-Kennedy legislation would be introduced.

The hearing room that day was packed with senators, spectators, and Senate staff for what was announced as a 10:00 a.m. start time. It was a twelve-camera hearing, the most I had ever seen, and every senator on the Labor Committee had shown up and taken their seats on the dais.

Ten o'clock approached and Elizabeth Taylor had not yet arrived. Ten minutes passed, then thirty, then forty-five; everyone waited. Beirn and Iskowitz darted in and out of the hearing room, whispering to Hatch and Kennedy, "She's coming, we've been assured of it. She's just running late. It takes time for her to get started in the morning. She's really not a morning person." The overcrowded room got hotter and hotter.

Then, all of a sudden, the door from the hall swung open and Elizabeth Taylor, surrounded by a large entourage, swept in. She wore a fur jacket over a low-cut deep blue dress, with enormous diamonds on her left shoulder, dangling from both ears, and on her tiny left hand. She was smaller than I expected but incredibly elegant. Even at 11:00 a.m., early for a movie star, her dark hair was carefully styled, and she was as heavily made-up as if she were on a film set. Hatch and Kennedy rushed from their seats and competed to introduce her to each of the other senators.

At 11:30, ninety minutes after the scheduled start of the hearing, Taylor finally took her place at the witness table. Photographers rushed forward. Spectators stood up, if only for a glimpse of her. Radio and television announcers started live feeds. The senators and staff were delighted by the spectacle and all the press attention. This was far more glamorous than their usual hearings on such things as apprenticeships and job training. Then Kennedy banged his gavel with a ringmaster's flourish and called the hearing to order. "Senator Hatch and I are very pleased to be introducing the Comprehensive AIDS Resources Emergency Act, the 'AIDS CARE' bill," he boomed. "AIDS is a disaster that demands a response." Then he introduced Taylor.

"I'm here to congratulate you, Senator Kennedy, and you, Senator Hatch, for your introduction and bipartisan support of the AIDS CARE bill," she said. "AIDS is unmercifully killing people, people I know and love, and I suspect people you know and love. But, sadly, the darkest days of the AIDS crisis still lie ahead of us."

After she finished reading her statement, each of the senators had several minutes to provide supportive statements and ask her softball questions, which she handled easily, with style and warmth. Thirty minutes later she was gone, out into the hall and downstairs to her waiting limousine.

The introduction of the bill received considerable press, both on television and in newspapers, and suddenly the possibility of passing it did not seem so remote. After all, in Washington, if something doesn't happen in the press, it doesn't happen at all. By that standard, this hearing had really happened.

Beirn and Iskowitz mobilized grassroots support. Hatch and Kennedy began lining up a bipartisan group of cosponsors. We had more hearings in the Committee and then brought the legislation to an executive session of the Committee, where, on April 24, the bill was approved. Debate began on the Senate floor several weeks later.[2]

As expected, the prime opposition came from Senator Helms, who led the charge against it on the floor. Helms first became known to North Carolina voters as a TV and radio commentator whose on-air editorials expressed strong conservative viewpoints, "railing against [Martin Luther] King, 'Negro hoodlums,' the media, 'sex perverts,' and anyone on welfare."[3] After election to the Senate, he built a formidable conservative fundraising machine centered around his National Congressional Club. As the AIDS epidemic took off, Helms added gay people, or, as he put it, the "homosexual agenda," to the list of hot-button targets that would rouse his base of followers. He offered numerous amendments to our legislation and attempted to filibuster it. Never one for subtlety, he set out to make the debate about homosexuality and family values. He questioned legislative protections for individuals with HIV, saying, "90 percent of them caught the disease through unlawful conduct and warped 'lifestyles,'" and attacked the "homosexual movement" that supported them. "What began as a response to a public health emergency," he railed on the floor, "has become a battle for the transformation of the American value system."

To help counter this narrative, Beirn and Iskowitz had the idea of bringing Ryan White to Washington. Beirn knew Ryan because he had gone to Indiana to help him fight his dismissal from school as the result of his HIV status. Ryan had been to Washington before, when he and his mother met with President Reagan. Now, sadly, he was very ill, but he and his mother agreed to come back. His presence in Washington as the bill was being debated drew further media attention and spurred action in both the Senate and the House. He died before legislative action on the bill was completed, but his mother, Jeannie White, bravely returned to tell members of Congress that one of Ryan's last requests was that she urge them to pass the AIDS CARE bill.

In the final days before the vote, Hatch and Kennedy decided to rename the bill the Ryan White AIDS CARE bill. Jeannie White, Beirn, and Iskowitz, together with Hatch and Kennedy, were a formidable team of advocates. Mrs. White stood with Beirn outside the entrance to the Senate, greeting senators as they went onto the floor and imploring them to support the legislation. As votes on amendments were being taken,

Mrs. White went up to the gallery and looked down on the Senate floor below, well within view of senators making up their minds on how to vote.

On May 16 the bill won final passage in the Senate, and a month later passed the House. Both bodies approved the final conference language with only fifteen dissenting votes. President George H. W. Bush signed it into law on August 18. Due to the budget deficit, new government spending programs were very rare, but the Ryan White bill was one of them.

Today across the country, in cities and communities large and small, groups of health and social service providers, hospitals, community health centers, home health organizations, educators, and advocates supported by Ryan White Bill funding work to build networks of home-based care and medication for AIDS patients—increasingly important as more effective but expensive treatments have become available. Even in our era of hyperpartisanship, the Ryan White legislation has maintained near unanimous bipartisan support in both the House and the Senate. The program is a lifeline for HIV and AIDS patients, their families and friends, and for America's health care system. It is a truly powerful tribute to Terry Beirn that funding for the bill now exceeds $2 billion a year.

Terry got to see only the beginning. After the Ryan White Bill was enacted in 1990, everyone on the Committee gradually became aware of what a few others and I had known at the time of the bill, that for Terry the work on AIDS was a matter of life or death. Terry Beirn died of AIDS on July 16, 1991. Hatch and Kennedy held a memorial service for him in the Committee hearing room where Elizabeth Taylor had testified in support of the bill that Terry had done so much to create. Kennedy called Terry the "101st senator on AIDS" and said, "He probably accomplished more than all the other hundred together." Hatch added, "This country owes a great deal of gratitude to Terry, who was a large part of the AIDS effort."

Many of us on the Hatch, Kennedy, and Committee staffs had grown close working together on the bill. We formed a circle around the perimeter of the hearing room, holding hands and singing "That's What Friends Are For." Standing next to each other in the circle, holding hands and swaying to the music, Hatch and Kennedy led the singing.

Chapter 8

RALLYING THE DEMOCRATS

A SIXTH TERM

On January 4, 1995, the 104th Congress officially began as the newly elected and reelected members were sworn into office. Speaker of the House Newt Gingrich received the House gavel from Dick Gephardt. Bob Dole, the new majority leader, opened proceedings in the Senate. It was also a big day for the Kennedy family. Senator Kennedy was sworn in for a sixth term, and his son Patrick took the oath of office for his first term in the House of Representatives from Rhode Island.

The senator and his family and supporters gathered in the Senate Caucus Room to celebrate. Facing the third floor of the rotunda of the Russell Building and just around the corner from the senator's office, the Caucus Room was the scene of numerous historic hearings and held special memories for Kennedy as the place where his brothers John and Robert had each declared their presidential candidacies. After Kennedy died in August 2009, the Senate Caucus Room was renamed the Kennedy Caucus Room in honor of the three brothers.

As he stood at the podium surrounded by his wife, children, sisters, and members of his extended family, the senator spoke about working families and the defining values of the Democratic Party: decent jobs and schools, worker safety, care for the elderly, clean air. He said he looked forward to fighting for these values as the "fightingest senator from Massachusetts we've ever had." He cautioned that even as we celebrated his victory, we had work to do to protect the American people from what the Republicans had in mind for them. "Today must be remembered as the comeback day for the values we campaigned on in Massachusetts," he urged. "Let's get together and celebrate today, and tomorrow we fight together and win."

Then Kennedy introduced Vice President Gore, who was making the rounds at ceremonies for newly sworn-in Senate and House members. Gore said he'd never seen anyone campaign as well as the senator had in his fight for reelection. Looking around at the assembled members of the Kennedy clan, Gore teased, "The senator has really gotten into the message of working families." He said the senator understood, as did Franklin Roosevelt and John Kennedy, that the most important social program is an expanding economy. Before he left the podium, Gore pledged we'd see him reelected as vice president, a matter that was in considerable doubt after the 1994 Republican sweep.

THE NATIONAL PRESS CLUB SPEECH

Once sworn in, it was time for Kennedy to draw the battle lines for the Democratic resistance. Since the election, he had been planning to make a speech at the National Press Club in Washington. Once every few years he felt the time was ripe and what he had to say was important enough for a kind of Kennedy State of the Union speech. The Press Club was a good venue because virtually all the Washington journalists from publications large and small, famous and obscure, belonged, and a speech there was a signal of the importance of what he had to say.

Kennedy had essentially spent the two months since Election Day preparing for this speech, and he wanted it to have the maximum possible impact. When he stood up at the National Press Club podium on January 11 the house was packed. The speech was carried live on C-SPAN and covered by all the networks and major newspapers. Copies of it were sent by the new Senate Democratic minority leader, Tom Daschle, to all the Democratic senators, and by the House Democratic minority leader, Dick Gephardt, to all Democratic House members. The Democratic National Committee sent copies to all Democratic governors and members of the National Committee.

The speech began with a clarion call:

I come here as a Democrat. I reject such qualifiers as New Democrat or Old Democrat or Neo-Democrat. I am committed to the enduring principles of the Democratic Party, and I am proud of its great tradition of service to the people who are the heart and strength of this nation—working families and the middle class. . . .

I would have lost in Massachusetts if I had done what Democrats who were defeated in other parts of the country too often tried to do.

I ran as a Democrat in belief as well as name. This turned out to be not only right in principle—it was also the best politics.

Our issues, if we defend them, are popular. The working families in New Bedford, Fall River, Lowell, Lawrence, Springfield and Worcester in my state voted for me, and they have the same concerns as working families throughout the country.

The caricatures of us by the other side will be ineffective—as long as we vigorously oppose them and expose them, instead of sheepishly acquiescing in them. If Democrats run for cover, if we become pale carbon copies of the opposition and try to act like Republicans, we will lose—and deserve to lose. As I have said on other occasions, Democrats must be more than warmed-over Republicans. The last thing this country needs is two Republican parties.

If we fall for our opponents' tactics, if we listen to those who tell us to abandon health reform, or slash student loans and children's programs, or engage in a bidding war to see who can be the most anti-government or the most laissez-faire, we will have only ourselves to blame. As Democrats, we can win, but only if we stand for something.

The election last November was not a ratification of Republican solutions. By the narrowest of margins, they gained control of Congress. But less than 40 percent of eligible voters turned out on election day, and only slightly more than half of those—about 20 percent—cast ballots for Republicans. Some mandate!

To achieve victory in 1996, we must not repeat the mistakes of the past. We must make explicit to the American people our core values and beliefs which form the basis of our political philosophy and underlie our legislative proposals—specifically and most important, that we as Americans, with all our diversity, share a common purpose, a common sense of family, neighborhood, community, and country, of fairness, responsibility, and decency.

In this central battle for the minds and hearts of working Americans, heritage and history are on our side. Recall the great victorious battles of the past—for Social Security and Medicare, for the minimum wage and the rights of workers, for civil rights and equal rights, for protection of the environment, for a Head Start for every child and the education of all children regardless of their parents' income, for family and medical leave, for opportunity for women and a woman's right to choose. By any standard, these were extraordinary achievements. And all of them were won because they were sought and fought for by members of the Democratic Party.

My fundamental recommendation to the President is that he stay the course of change and do what he thinks is right. My advice to my fellow Democrats is that we work with the President for change—instead of seeking to change our principles, or distance ourselves from him.

He then presented the issues that he was going to highlight in the coming year—health care, education, job training, and the minimum wage—and ended with a flourish.

Let's renew our cause as Democrats. Let's hold our standard high and advance it proudly. Let's be who we are, and not pretend to be something else. And if we do, we will have a strong and winning case to take to the American people in this new Congress and in all the years ahead. The Republican majority will be a transient one, and the Democrats will be proud to be Democrats again.

In this speech to a nationwide audience, Kennedy announced a battle plan that he knew had to be popular with the public if it had any hope of being enacted under a Republican Congress. Conventional wisdom claims that nothing positive can get done by the minority party, but Kennedy felt sure that limited health care reform and a minimum wage increase met the test of popularity. Indeed polls taken throughout 1995 and 1996 confirmed that both were supported by over 75 percent of the public, including over 60 percent of registered Republicans. Having made the case, Kennedy got to work on both initiatives.

Chapter 9

THE FIGHT BEGINS

HEALTH CARE REFORM

Since 1969, when Kennedy introduced his first national health care legislation, he believed in comprehensive health care reform, and linked the drive for quality universal coverage with cost containment. Over the years his approach changed from the so-called single-payer national health plan, similar to Medicare, under which the government paid for provision of health care for all Americans, to the employer mandate, under which employers were required to provide quality, affordable health insurance to their employees and their employees' families, and public insurance would pick up the remaining uninsured. The shift was not because Kennedy thought one approach was better than another but because the political realities dictated that one seemed more achievable as time progressed.

The senator sometimes told a joke about his changing positions on the methods to achieve universal coverage while remaining steadfast to the goal. In the story, there are three candidates for the job of science teacher in a backwoods school deep in rural Louisiana. All three sit in an anteroom waiting to be interviewed by the school board. The first one summoned for his interview emerges looking downcast. The other two ask him what happened. He responds that he's been turned down for the job. A member of the board, he recounts, asked whether he believed the world was round or flat. "I told him I thought it was round, and the board members who thought it was flat blackballed me." The second candidate goes in to his interview and also comes out looking discouraged. Again, the other two ask him what happened. "I thought I'd learned from what happened to you," he says, referring to the first candidate. "So I said I thought the world was flat, and the ones who thought it was round blackballed me!"

The third candidate goes in for his interview. He comes out with a spring in his step and a smile on his face. "What happened?" the other two ask. "I got the job," he says. "When they asked me what I thought, I said that I could teach it round—or I could teach it flat!"

In the time between the collapse of the Clinton initiative for comprehensive health care reform and the 1994 elections, Kennedy altered his strategy on health care legislation. No longer would he insist on legislation that provided comprehensive, universal health care and cost containment all at once. Now he would return to piecemeal, or "incremental," health care reform, as it had been derisively referred to in the banner days of 1993.

As a starting point, the senator reviewed with his staff the elements that all the universal coverage bills had in common and should, in theory, be able to draw bipartisan support. The Democratic bills and their bipartisan competitors covered children, so we originally thought we would try to move a bill expanding health insurance coverage for children.

Kennedy met with a number of potential Republican cosponsors but was turned down. My old boss, Senator John Chafee of Rhode Island, seemed our best prospect. He was one of the leading child health advocates in Congress and the leader of the centrist effort to provide a meaningful alternative to the Democratic proposals on universal health care. But when Chafee told Kennedy that the new majority was going to be all about cutting programs and deficit reduction, and so expanding health insurance coverage for anyone was a nonstarter, Kennedy knew it was time to go back to the drawing board.

A feature that all past Democratic and Republican bills had in common was insurance reform, especially reforms addressing the problem of preexisting condition exclusions in insurance policies. These exclusions were a very real barrier to millions of Americans who wanted to change or leave a job. Half of all individuals with employment-based plans were subject to these exclusions, and the situation was worse for individual policies.[1] If workers with job-based coverage and health issues in their families wanted to change jobs, lost their jobs, or left to start their own business, they could find themselves unable to buy coverage that would cover them or their family members against the very illnesses for which they were most at risk. The resulting "job lock" was a barrier to labor mobility, stifled opportunities for individuals to advance, and exposed millions of Americans who had insurance to unacceptable risks if they became sick.

A related issue was that small businesses were often unable to obtain coverage if a single employee or family member of an employee had a health problem. Worse, whole sectors of small business were redlined out of coverage if they were thought to be engaged in occupations that attracted employees with higher than average health risks.[2]

Senator Kassebaum, the new chair of the Labor Committee, seemed the best possible partner for the portability approach. The Committee had held over forty-five hearings on health care reform during the twelve months leading up to its consideration of the Clinton bill in May 1994. Kassebaum had been the ranking Republican member of the Committee during this entire period. She and Kennedy sat next to each other on the dais during most of these hearings, listening to witnesses and comparing notes on problems and solutions in health care. In May 1994 the Committee held fifteen days of nearly daylong meetings in executive session, after which it reported to the Senate as a whole a universal health care bill growing out of the Clinton proposal. Kassebaum voted against the bill, but there were areas where compromises had been reached that she supported.

In 1994 there had been a clear consensus on addressing preexisting condition exclusions for people who had been continuously insured and on eliminating "job lock," as well as doing something about the special problems facing small business. In their telephone conversations and in meetings after the election, Kassebaum and Kennedy talked frequently about developing legislation to deal with these issues.

In the meantime, Kennedy began working on the political side of the effort, developing additional bipartisan support, lining up Democrats and recruiting Republicans, and also building support for the initiative among the advocacy groups in Washington and across the country. In his effort to recruit more Republicans he met with Senator Bob Bennett, who had been appointed by Dole to be chairman of the Republican Health Task Force, with Senator Jeffords, and others. There were frequent discussions with Democratic leader Daschle about including a prototype incremental health reform bill among Daschle's five priority bills, and with other Democrats about cosponsoring it. For many months at the end of 1994 and particularly at the beginning of 1995, Kassebaum and Kennedy and their staffs worked together on the substance of possible legislation and on building support for it, even before Kennedy's National Press Club speech on January 11.

MINIMUM WAGE

Kennedy had always been committed to increasing the minimum wage. Back in 1981 Congress raised it to $3.35 an hour, but the Reagan administration prevented any further raises over the next eight years. Many conservative Republicans opposed the very idea of a minimum wage, so it was not until 1989, under the "kinder and gentler administration" of George H. W. Bush, that Kennedy sensed the opportunity for a long overdue increase in the minimum wage. He made it his most important legislative priority, and by the fall of 1989 he had succeeded in striking a compromise with Bush and pushing an increase through Congress. Instead of the 50 cents a year for three years that he originally proposed, the senator settled for 90 cents over two years, bringing the minimum wage up to $4.25 by 1990.

Kennedy had held off introducing minimum wage legislation in the first days of the Clinton administration and did not revisit the issue throughout 1993 and 1994. The requirement that employers would contribute to the cost of the health insurance of their employees, the so-called employer mandate, was a central feature of the Clinton proposal, and the senator believed that adding an increase in the minimum wage on top of the employer mandate might interfere with the possibility of enacting health care reform. But by the beginning of 1995 there was no longer any reason to wait. He had made a pledge during the 1994 campaign in Massachusetts that he would go back to Washington after his reelection and fight once again to raise the minimum wage to a living wage. By then, due to inflation, the wage had fallen well below its historic level and still did not pay enough to lift a family of four above the poverty line.

So in January 1995, as the 104th Congress convened, Kennedy introduced his own minimum wage bill. Believing that anyone who works forty hours a week, fifty weeks a year, ought not to live in poverty, he introduced a proposal to increase the minimum wage 50 cents each year for three years, which would raise the wage to $5.75 an hour.

Activity around the minimum wage proposal, driven by Kennedy, was dramatic. He understood that the substance of the proposal needed to be fine-tuned and that there was much work to do on the politics of the bill. The White House was not convinced that a minimum wage increase had any chance of passing through a Republican-controlled Senate— and especially through the Gingrich-run House, where the Republican leaders wanted to abolish the minimum wage altogether. Conservative Democrats worried about the reaction of businesses in their districts employing low-wage workers. Kennedy also realized that the grassroots organizations that would support a minimum wage increase had to be reactivated.

The senator's first target for developing a consensus on the minimum wage was the Democratic leadership in the Senate and the House. He included references to the minimum wage in all his meetings in December with the leaders. He needed the president's support also, and the effort to get the president to include his support for the minimum wage in his State of the Union speech at the end of January was ongoing. Clinton had spoken somewhat positively about a minimum wage increase in the meeting with Kennedy in December, but there were many in the White House arguing that it was futile. It was Old, not New, Democrat, they believed—exactly the wrong message for the president to send. But Kennedy persisted. Whenever he spoke with anyone from the White House staff, he mentioned the minimum wage.

On January 22 Kennedy's 104-year-old mother, who had been in failing health for some time, died at the family house in Hyannis Port. For many years, Kennedy had returned to stay with his mother at every opportunity, sometimes alone and sometimes with his children and with Vicki. His mother was an important influence on him, the youngest of her ten children. I always believed that his sharp political ear, his high standards, and the unfailing respect that he showed public service and his colleagues came in part from his mother's influence.

The family held the funeral for Rose Kennedy on January 24 in St. Stephen's Church in the North End of Boston, blocks from where she had been born. It was a beautiful sunny day, cold but bright. A number of Kennedy's colleagues in the Senate, including Hatch and Ernest Hollings of South Carolina, attended the funeral. The entire Kennedy family was present, of course, having gathered at Hyannis Port in the days since Mrs. Kennedy's death.

On the morning of the funeral the family drove in a long procession from Cape Cod to Boston. Along the highways on the route, Massachusetts citizens stood by the road or on the bridges crossing the highways to watch the procession drive by, out of respect for Mrs. Kennedy. Many held signs thanking her for the example she had set with her life. The service itself was very moving. Mrs. Kennedy's surviving children, their children, and even her great-grandchildren walked or, in the case of infants, were carried behind her coffin up the aisle of the old New England church.

The evening Mrs. Kennedy died, Clinton called Kennedy to offer condolences. The president's State of the Union speech was only two days away. As the conversation was drawing to a close, the senator introduced the topic of the minimum wage increase. "Mr. President," he said, "you ought to say you're for it in your State of the Union. You ought to call on the Republicans to work on the amount." The president responded, "I think it's in."

Discussions over the next twenty-four hours between Kennedy and his staff and the White House turned to the amount of the increase. Kennedy preferred $1.50 over three years. His labor allies and others in the groups supporting an increase agreed. White House staff hinted that the president was inclined to support a 75-cent increase. We resisted. It was decided at the White House that there was no need for the president to refer to a specific amount in the State of the Union speech. The White House press effort around the speech highlighted the president's support for a minimum wage increase as one of his principal initiatives. The press reports stressed that Republican opposition would be fierce. Dick Armey, the new House majority leader, reiterated his opposition: "I will resist an increase in the minimum wage with every fiber of my being."[3]

On January 24 the president delivered his State of the Union address and, as predicted, opted for a statement in general support of the minimum wage increase rather than endorsing a specific amount.

A week after the State of the Union address, Kennedy returned from Hyannis Port to the Senate for the first time since the death of his mother. Daschle and Gephardt scheduled a breakfast meeting at 8:00 a.m. the next day for the joint Democratic leadership of the Senate and House to discuss the Democrats' agenda. Kennedy was invited to arrive at 8:30 a.m. to participate in the discussion of the minimum wage increase.

As with everything else on Capitol Hill, the majority party controls the congressional perks, including assignment of meeting rooms. Meeting rooms made available to the minority tend to be small, and this windowless room was packed. Members crowded around a large conference table; on one side sat Senator Daschle, and on the other Congressman Gephardt. Staffers were crushed together behind their members around the edge of the table and along the wall. As Kennedy entered and was shown to a seat at one end of the table, a senator was explaining that he didn't think it was a good idea for Democrats to be for an increase in the minimum wage at this time because, in view of the elections, it sent the wrong signal. It was "old" politics. It would only help the poor. It had no chance of success.

Kennedy's voice was an instrument of extraordinary range, stretching in volume from a whisper or a low murmur audible only to the ear at which it is aimed to a full-volume bassoon that can fill a convention hall without a microphone, and in tone, from hortatory, urging the audience on, to rowdy, as if on a roll with a joke, or, on occasion, angry. Having had barely enough time to take his seat, Kennedy unleashed a tirade on the subject of Democrats standing up for what they believed in. It seemed to me that he was still on edge, his emotions raw, from the week he had just been through after the loss of his mother. He clearly felt that everything he believed about the Democratic Party was on the line and that this was a moment of truth. All the Democratic leaders of Congress were gathered in one room, and this was his moment to make clear how he felt about the importance of the party fighting to raise the minimum wage. Democrats would either stand for their historic principles or, in the wake of the election, turn their backs on those principles and on the people who had supported Democrats for sixty years. It was as if all the meetings and discussions and strategizing since November 4 came down to this one moment.

"I can't believe what I'm hearing," he exploded. "If there is one cause the Democrats should stand for it is improving the wages of working people. If we are not going to fight for the wages of working people, who will fight for them? When the economy is thriving, and corporate profits are at an all-time high, and CEO salaries are hundreds of times what the average worker's is, who says we can't afford to increase the minimum wage by 50 cents an hour? It is unacceptable in America for anyone to work forty hours a week, fifty weeks a year, and still not be able to lift his family out of poverty. We can't do much about wages generally, but raising the minimum wage is one thing we can do. We know it works, it doesn't cost jobs, it helps women, who make up 65 percent of the minimum wage work force. Who are we afraid of? Is it the National Restaurant Association or the NFIB [National Federation of Independent Businesses, the principal small business lobby]? Isn't it better to raise wages of 10 million Americans than worry about a few restaurant owners in our districts? Eighty-five percent of the public supports raising the minimum wage. The minimum wage today is way below what it should be if it had kept pace with inflation since before the Reagan administration."

He was in full red-faced volume in this small room, as if he were addressing a crowd of ten thousand on the steps of the Capitol. "I can't believe what I'm hearing," he repeated. "The minimum wage will only help the poor, so we can't be for it? Well, if we won't fight for this cause, what will we ever fight for? If we won't stand with low-income Americans, who will? If we can't get behind a measure that has 85 percent popularity in the polls, then our heads aren't screwed on right. We can't be for it because it has no chance of success? Because the Republicans say there never should have been a minimum wage in the first place and they'll fight the increase with every fiber in their being? Well I say, bring on the fight! What better draws the distinction between us and the Republicans? I tell you if we fight for this issue we'll win it, and we'll win it in a Republican Congress. If we don't, we don't deserve to call ourselves Democrats!"

When he finished, there was a long silence, as if he had sucked the air out of the room. Senator Dick Durbin of Illinois was the first to speak up: "Well, I guess we now understand how Ted feels about this."

No one spoke in opposition. "Well, if we're going to do it, what level can we support?" asked a House member. Kennedy urged $1.50, an increase of 50 cents an hour for three years. Others suggested 75 cents over three years, at 25 cents a year.

Kennedy had a unique effect on his Democratic colleagues. They knew he was a fierce advocate and an exceptionally hard worker, that he was sincere and cared intently about the causes he fought for, that he was always well-prepared and thinking ahead, often of everyone else in the room. They liked his joviality and his commitment to the Senate. On the other hand, they thought he could go over the top. I felt that sometimes they wished he weren't there to hold their feet to the fire on progressive issues that they'd just as soon ignore. Or they thought his approach wouldn't work in their states, that he got away with being an outspoken progressive because he was from Massachusetts or because he was a Kennedy.

Recipients of a Kennedy harangue might believe that they were being talked down to, that Kennedy was being arrogant, that he thought he was always right, that he was belittling their intentions or questioning their conviction because they didn't feel exactly the way Kennedy did. But it had an effect. Listeners admired him and respected the fact that he hadn't surrendered his principles over thirty years in the Senate. They knew, in this case, that he would not give up until the minimum wage issue was brought front and center to the Democratic agenda. They knew they would have to deal with it one way or another, and they didn't want to be on the wrong side of the issue. Resentment at a passionate argument from Kennedy was always muted because members of Congress respected his sincerity and commitment. They knew when it was over, Kennedy could laugh at himself, give his adversary a friendly slap on the back, share a joke, or otherwise take away the personal sting. They knew he didn't act impulsively, and if his speech that morning in the caucus room was an exception it was also a window into his heart and into everything he believed the Democratic Party should stand for.

Kennedy's visit to the leadership meeting took less than half an hour. As the discussion about the size of the increase and how to go about reaching a consensus took over the room, the tension abated, and everybody began to relax. The camaraderie that had been missing among the Democrats returned. When the discussion on the minimum wage was finished, Kennedy got up from the table and left the room with a hearty laugh and a pat on the back from several members sitting by the door. The members agreed that they would meet again to try to reach an agreement on the level of increase the entire caucus could support.

Between the leadership breakfast meeting and the end of the week,

Kennedy contacted members of the House and Senate who were thought to be on the fence on the issue. He worked on the White House. He visited congressmen and senators in their offices. He kibitzed with senators on the floor during votes, telephoned each member of the Labor Committee, rallied staff—his own and staff of other senators—and met with labor groups and others in the minimum wage coalition.

We had called the minimum wage coalition back into existence in November 1994. This assemblage of church groups, civil rights groups, women's groups, children's groups, and labor, who all strongly supported the $1.50 increase, had last met in 1989, during the last successful initiative, also spearheaded by Kennedy, to raise the minimum wage. The senator knew that a $1.50 increase was not going to prevail with the White House or the Democratic leadership in Congress, and he was looking at compromises. One idea we had was simply to drop off the third year of the 50-cent increases, and turn it into a two-year increase of 50 cents a year, for a total of $1.00. The question was whether that compromise would be accepted by the leaders of the labor movement, who had already taken a strong position for an increase of $1.50. Kennedy met with AFL-CIO president Lane Kirkland and secretary-treasurer Tom Donahue, both of whom were longtime allies of his. Donahue in particular was a very close friend. Kennedy wanted to convince them that they should support 50-50 for two years. Then "we can come back and get another increase for the third year," he argued. Without support from labor, it would be almost impossible to pass a bill.

The minimum wage legislation showcased Kennedy at his best. He came down from his own preferred position to 50 cents a year for two years. At the same time he persuaded reluctant conservatives to go along with increasing the minimum wage, and then with increasing the amount they'd be willing to accept, from 25 cents a year to 50 cents a year. It was a perfect legislative compromise: those who sought the higher increase could take comfort in getting the first two years of a three-year plan; those who wanted a lower increase could point to a one-third reduction in the original proposal.

Kennedy was in close contact with Congressman Gephardt, who, like Kennedy, wanted to make sure the Democrats in the White House, House, and Senate were united on the issue. For Gephardt it was a question of what he could get the conservative Democrats in the House caucus to support. Speaking for conservatives in the Senate, Senator Breaux was now arguing for an increase in the amount of 50 cents for one year and 25 cents for the next.

A day after the meeting with the joint leadership, Kennedy met with Daschle to get a report on his conversations with the leadership and other Democrats in the Senate. Daschle made it clear that 50-50 was okay with him, but he thought that 50-25 was the best that the whole caucus would agree to. He had surveyed the other members of the Democratic leadership, and they too would only go to 75 cents, the level Breaux was comfortable with.

Later that day Kennedy went to the White House for a meeting on welfare reform, and the topic of the minimum wage came up. The senator talked with the president's staff members and then to the president, who told him, "I did what you asked me to do in the State of the Union, and 50-50 is okay with me." The president was now on board.

Kennedy then made the rounds of congressional Democrats. He told Daschle 50-50 was the lowest he would go. He talked to members of the House, who still weren't sold on 50-50. The House leadership still wanted to have a consistent position among all Democrats. Congressman David Bonior, a liberal, proposed 45-45, a masterful stroke because this was the amount that Congress had voted for in 1989 and that President George H. W. Bush had agreed to support. But Bonior was not hopeful that the conservative Democrats in the House or the Senate would go along.

Kennedy met again with the labor leaders Donahue and Kirkland. They were not enthusiastic about anything below $1.50. Donahue said, "Why should we go along if we're not getting anything in return? We haven't even been guaranteed that Breaux and the other conservative Democrats will support the 45-45."

Sarah Fox, Kennedy's chief labor policy staff member, advised him that there were reports coming out of the AFL-CIO building that Kirkland and Donahue might ultimately be persuaded to go below $1.50. Kennedy again called each of the eight Democrats on the Labor Committee, asking if they would accept 45-45. Then he went back to Daschle and Gephardt. He made the argument over and over again that 90 cents was the amount of increase that was negotiated with Bush in 1989. "We ought to be able to match that now," he urged. That level of increase was approved by a Republican president and supported by many Republicans in the House and Senate at that time. If a 90-cent increase was good in 1989, why isn't it just as good in 1995, when the minimum wage had once again fallen below its historic level in relation to the cost of living, the poverty level, and the average wage?

It looked as if everyone would fall in line behind 45-45, and the word went out to all the groups in the coalition that they should prepare to attend a press conference in the Russell Building, where it would be announced that a consensus had been reached among Democrats to propose a 90-cent increase at 45 cents each year for two years. Each group was urged to bring a written statement on the group's stationery endorsing the 45-45 increase. Democrats supporting the 45-45 increase were invited to attend a press conference to be held in the Rose Garden of the White House to announce that agreement had been reached among Democrats to support the increase.

On February 3, in the Rose Garden, the president, surrounded by Democrats, including Kennedy, announced that he was proposing a 90-cent increase in the minimum wage, from $4.25 to $5.15 an hour over two years. Although no Republicans attended the ceremony, it was an auspicious moment because Democrats across the spectrum had agreed to support the measure. It turned out to be a big moment in the resistance as well: the Democrats came together as a united force to lay down a marker against the Republican juggernaut. Few would have predicted then how far the minimum wage fight would lead and how successful it would turn out to be as a rallying point for the Democratic resurgence.

Later that morning, in a small room in the basement of the Russell Building, more than twenty-five groups in the minimum wage coalition arrived with their statements in support of the increase at 45-45. The press conference was hosted by the Women's Legal Defense Fund and the Leadership Conference on Civil Rights. The coalition put out its own press release and attached each of the statements from each of the groups. Someone from Kennedy's press office delivered these releases to the Congressional Press Gallery. The issue was joined.

What had seemed impossible just a month before had been achieved. The Democrats were united. The White House was on board. All our public interest allies had accepted the compromise, and announcements had been made at both ends of Pennsylvania Avenue. The conventional wisdom in Washington still maintained that the minimum wage increase had no chance in a Republican Congress. But the effort had begun.

Chapter 10

THE REPUBLICAN
ATTACK

While Kennedy and the Democrats were readying their counteroffensive, the Republicans were forging ahead with their legislative revolution. In the House, Speaker Gingrich and his new southern conservative leadership team, Texans Dick Armey and Tom DeLay, were riding high. Giddy with confidence and ambition in the wake of the Republican victory and impatient after decades of minority status, Gingrich claimed nothing less than a mandate to "reassert American civilization."[1] A former history professor, Gingrich saw himself as a transformative historical figure and was determined not only to carry out his pledge to pass his Contract with America in the first hundred days of the new Congress but to change the fundamental role of government in American life.

In the Senate, George Mitchell would be replaced as majority leader by Republican Bob Dole. Dole was a canny legislative strategist with a biting wit. While his views were generally quite conservative, he was a pragmatist by nature; he had been willing to compromise in the past and had even taken a leadership role on such causes as fairer treatment of the disabled and combating hunger.

Dole was determined to capture the 1996 Republican presidential nomination, putting him in a complicated position as 1995 began. He wanted to burnish his record of accomplishment in Congress, which would necessitate conciliation and compromise with Democrats. But he also needed to bolster his ideological credentials with the right wing of his party. In the 1988 primaries, Dole had been attacked from the right by George H. W. Bush, who labeled him a tax raiser and went on to win the nomination. This time Dole knew he had to protect his right flank against potential rivals, including Senator Phil Gramm, an aggressive conservative from Texas. Changes within the Republican Senate ranks also pulled Dole to the right. Conservatives Trent Lott and Don Nickles had been elected to the number two and three leadership positions in his caucus, and the 1994 elections produced eleven freshman Republicans, several of whom had been allies of Gingrich in the House. Committee chairmanships passed to some of the most conservative figures in politics, including Strom Thurmond (Armed Services) and Jesse Helms (Foreign Relations).

Given the continued slide to the right of the Republican Party in recent years, and the rise of the far-right Tea Party, it is easy to forget how truly radical the 1995–96 Republican agenda was—and how close they came to succeeding.

THE REPUBLICAN ATTACK ON GOVERNMENT SUPPORT FOR EDUCATION

Newt Gingrich often said that he envisioned America as an "opportunity society," yet the Republicans' agenda in the 104th Congress would have deprived millions of students of opportunity at all levels of education, from preschool through university. Just weeks after taking control, House Republicans voted to rescind $1.7 billion in already approved education funding that was built into the 1995 budgets of schools and universities across the country. This was just a warm-up. Shortly thereafter, the GOP budget resolution sent shockwaves by proposing to abolish the Department of Education (as well as the Departments of Commerce and Energy). The Contract with America had promised to "give parents greater control over education" but said nothing about abolishing the Department of Education.

In total, the GOP budget reduced funding for education programs by one-third, hitting hard at all levels of education. At least 350,000 children would have been dropped from Head Start, the preschool education program that helps children from poor families prepare for elementary school and provides services such as immunizations, health checkups, and nutrition. Some two million children in sixty thousand of the most financially distressed schools would have been affected by the Republican cuts to Title I of the Elementary and Secondary Education Assistance Act. Title I supports improving the math and reading skills of disadvantaged students and had helped to close the achievement gap between black and white children by 18 percent in math and 25 percent in reading. Twenty-three million students would have been affected by GOP cuts to the Safe and Drug-Free Schools program, which provides federal funds to schools for antidrug education and enforcement and to address drug abuse and violence through school safety, conflict resolution, and peer mediation programs. Four million American teenagers would be denied federally supported summer jobs. The GOP budget's elimination of the AmeriCorps National Service Program would have denied another four million students the opportunity to serve communities while earning money for college.

When it came to education, the new GOP's ideology trumped the pragmatic approach of the Republican-leaning business community, which understood the U.S. economy's need for a well-educated and adaptable labor force. The Business Roundtable, for example, urged support for the recently enacted Goals 2000: Educate America Initiative, which supported school reform and high education standards. Roundtable members proclaimed, "Education is an area within the federal budget where strategic investments must continue in order to assure that our children become productive workers and active members of society."[2] Despite this plea from an ally, the Republican budget eliminated funding for Goals 2000.

The federal programs that make college tuition more affordable also came under the GOP ax. The Republicans would have cut $10 billion in federal student loans over seven years. The Perkins Loan program providing subsidized loans to 150,000 low-income college students annually would have been eliminated. Interest rates on PLUS loans to parents struggling to pay their children's college tuition would have been raised, at a cost of up to $5,000 per family. President Clinton's direct lending program, which made unsubsidized student loans cheaper and easier to apply for, would have been rolled back, leaving banks offering risk-free (for the banks) federally guaranteed student loans without competition. Perhaps worst of all, the Republican budget cut Pell Grants by 40 percent, eliminating them entirely for more than one million students every year and reducing the amount of the grant for one million more.

For average Americans, the Republican animus toward federal support for education was hard to understand. Most Americans believe that education is a ticket to opportunity for individuals and an important ingredient for long-term prosperity for the country. As Kennedy said on the Senate floor, "Cutting education as we enter the information age is like cutting defense at the height of the Cold War." It was another area in which Republicans had misread their mandate.

THE REPUBLICAN ATTACK ON GOVERNMENT SUPPORT FOR HEALTH CARE

In 1995 the Republican wordsmiths claimed that their budget proposals would "save" Medicare, language that all House Republicans were urged to adopt in talking about the budget proposals when they held their annual retreat in early May. Polling had shown that when people were asked about cutting Medicare to balance the budget, they were strongly opposed. But when the question was posed as cutting Medicare to save the Medicare trust fund, the results were reversed.

In fact, the Republican proposal would have cut the program significantly and imposed the first steps in an ideological agenda of privatizing Medicare. The Republicans argued that they really weren't cutting Medicare, only reducing the anticipated growth of the program each year. They said that in order to secure the program's long-term solvency, they had to increase the amount seniors contributed by increasing premiums, copayments, and deductibles, and they needed to limit the cost of the services provided by reducing benefits. They also asserted that by cutting the budget they would force the administrators of Medicare to reduce payments to hospitals and crack down on fraud and abuse.

Although the Republicans wouldn't admit it at first, their cuts to Medicare would have dramatically increased costs for senior citizens. The bill reported by the House raised the share of the Part B premium (the part that pays for physician care) that the elderly would have to pay from 25 to 31.5 percent and started charging upper-income senior citizens an even higher premium—an overall increase of $60 billion in seniors' health cost burden.[3] The Senate bill reported by the Finance Committee not only raised the premium for the elderly, it added an increase in the Part B deductible. Together the two changes would have cost the elderly an additional $1,800 over the budget period—$3,600 per couple. The elderly who would have to pay the price of these reductions were an overwhelmingly low- and moderate-income group who already paid an average of one-fifth of their limited income for health care.[4] In addition, under the Senate plan, the eligibility age would have been gradually raised to sixty-seven—creating a devastating coverage gap for sixty-five- and sixty-six-year-olds. The Republican plan also substantially reduced the amount of Medicare reimbursements to hospitals and other providers. If enacted, they would have been the largest cuts in the program's history.

In provisions that were primarily designed not to save costs but to drive the underlying antigovernment agenda, the Republican proposal created the so-called Medicare + Choice program intended to eventually replace traditional Medicare with a private insurance system. Historically Medicare had covered enrollment in Health Management Organizations (HMOs) like the Kaiser Health Plan as an alternative to traditional Medicare. While the program was not restricted to nonprofit HMOs, in practice most HMOs fell into that class. In return for receiving Medicare funding for their Medicare enrollees, HMOs had to cover all the Medicare services, return any surplus payments to enrollees in the form of additional benefits, and accept payment at 95 percent of what Medicare would have paid for enrollment in the traditional program. (The 95 percent figure was based on the idea that HMOs were supposed to save money and the assumption that seniors enrolling in HMOs would be healthier than average and would therefore cost the program less.) Under the program the Republicans proposed, however, all kinds of private plans—not just HMOs—would become alternatives to traditional Medicare.

Medicare + Choice included complex changes in the way the formula for paying private plans was calculated, detaching it from the amounts paid under fee-for-service. While the new formula was complex, the Congressional Budget Office (CBO) estimated that enrollment in private options, which lacked many of Medicare's protections for beneficiaries, would double under the new plan.[5] Republicans hoped that private plans would ultimately displace Medicare altogether.[6] When a revised version of the proposal was adopted as part of the budget deal after the 1996 election, it was clear that Republicans wanted to stack the deck to make that happen: the GAO estimated that the private plans were paid an average of $1,000 more per enrollee than it would have cost to cover them under conventional Medicare.[7]

Part of the reason for the Republicans' Medicare cuts was simply to make their budget numbers add up, so they could get to a balanced budget at the same time they were proposing big tax cuts, but there was also an underlying ideological animus to America's second largest social insurance program and one of its most successful and beloved. Medicare was a real-world refutation of the right-wing antigovernment ideology that claimed large government programs—especially "entitlement" programs—were antithetical to liberty and opportunity.

In early 1995 Gingrich spoke at the inaugural meeting of the misnamed "Coalition to Save Medicare," which claimed its goal was to make Medicare available for future generations. A closer look at the Coalition, however, revealed that it was composed of for-profit insurance companies, who had nothing to gain from saving Medicare and everything to gain by chipping away at it. The slow demise of the Medicare program would have forced millions of seniors into managed care plans run by these same private insurance companies. Gingrich himself explained his cynical strategy: "Now, we didn't get rid of [Medicare] in round one because we don't think that's politically smart and we don't think that's the right way to go through a transition. But we believe it's going to wither on the vine."[8] In a speech to the American Conservative Union Dole said that during the debate over the establishment of Medicare in 1965, "I was there, fighting the fight, voting against Medicare because we knew it wouldn't work."[9] House Majority Leader Armey was on record with his opinion that Medicare had no place "in a free world."[10]

Republicans weren't so circumspect about Medicaid, however. Their budget *eliminated* Medicaid and replaced it with an underfunded block grant to the states. The block grant would have cut federal support for the health care of poor and disabled Americans by $182 billion, or almost 30 percent, over seven years. The Urban Institute estimated that 8 million Americans would have lost their Medicaid coverage, including 3.8 million children and 1.3 million disabled people.[11]

Beyond reducing funding for the program, the block grant structure would have eliminated a range of federal guarantees to ensure quality care and fair treatment for beneficiaries. For example, the Republican plan would have eliminated the guarantee of nursing home care for seniors. Under federal law, seniors are guaranteed that Medicaid will pay their nursing home bills after their own financial resources have been exhausted. Under the Republican plan, Medicaid would have been blockgranted, and states could decide whether or not to pay for costly nursing home care. The original version of the Republican bill would also have eliminated federal safeguards and allowed states to force the spouses and children of nursing home residents to exhaust their own savings to pay for the nursing home care of their spouse or parent. Many states had such laws on the books, but they were unenforceable due to requirements that the block grant would have repealed.

Among the harshest items in the original proposals were the provisions to eliminate federal standards for nursing homes. In 1987, responding to reports of widespread neglect and abuse in American nursing homes, Congress had passed and President Reagan had signed strict federal regulations for the care of nursing home patients. Since the Republican majority would not allow an official committee hearing on the issue, Kennedy held an extremely effective forum—a kind of unofficial hearing—where children of parents who had been tied to their beds and left unwashed for days, lying in urine-soaked sheets, suffering from bed sores due to lack of basic care, told their stories and pleaded that America not go back to the bad old days.

THE REPUBLICAN ATTACK ON THE LIVING STANDARDS OF WORKING AMERICANS

By the mid-1990s the wages of working Americans had been stagnant for two decades. The stock market was in the middle of an historic bull run, but the economic security of average working families was being steadily degraded by stagnant wages, corporate downsizing, mass layoffs, and an uncertain and often unfriendly global economy. At the heart of this story was the decline in the power and reach of organized labor. By 1994 only about 17 percent of workers were represented by unions—half the percentage of four decades before.

As if to turbo-charge these negative economic trends, the Republican 104th Congress launched a far-reaching offensive against unions and pro-worker policies. The assault began with a move to overturn Clinton's executive order denying federal contracts to companies that permanently replaced striking workers, which fundamentally weakened workers' ability to organize and exert economic power. Another early salvo in the Republicans' attack on unions was their attempt to attach a provision repealing the Davis-Bacon Act to a highway bill. Since the Great Depression Davis-Bacon had required that construction contractors receiving federal contracts pay their workers the prevailing wage in their communities.

The Republicans also moved to weaken regulation of pension funds. The budget reconciliation bill contained provisions that would have allowed corporations to withdraw "excess" money from their employees' pension funds—essentially a license to raid pension funds that were doing well because of investment gains and leave them unprotected against economic downturns. (Subsequent stock market collapses demonstrated why these dangers were real.) The original House-passed plan would have allowed corporations to withdraw from pension funds for any purpose the executives wished; the final bill required that any withdrawals be used for worker health and welfare programs. But since most corporations with pension funds already provided health plans for their workers, they could simply have replaced the money they already spent on health care with the looted pension money.

THE REPUBLICAN ATTACK ON THE POOR

The proposals to block grant and cut Medicaid and nutrition programs would have been devastating to low-income Americans' access to health care and food. The assault on cash assistance was laid out in the Contract with America and was included in various forms in a number of Republican proposals. The Contract prohibited welfare to mothers under eighteen years old and denied benefits for any additional children born to mothers already receiving welfare. During the development of this plan, conservatives proposed various time limits for welfare assistance; some said that families should receive benefits for only two years, while others wanted to limit the time to five years. Work requirements for receiving welfare were toughened. Some of the ideas in the Republican program were ultimately supported by many Democrats and the president in the welfare reform that was enacted eighteen months later. By then the proposals had been modified significantly, although not enough for Kennedy, Moynihan, and other liberals, who opposed the legislation on the grounds that children were not adequately protected.

To this day, Republicans tout the success of the 1996 welfare reform in promoting work and reducing the welfare rolls. However, other policies, not to mention the strong economy of the late 1990s, played a bigger role. Research has shown that expansion of the Earned Income Tax Credit (EITC) during the 1990s was the biggest factor in boosting employment among single mothers.[12] In 1995, however, the Republican budget proposed scaling back the EITC, effectively *raising* taxes on the working poor at the same time as it cut taxes for wealthy investors and corporations. The EITC, implemented by President Gerald Ford and expanded under Reagan and every president since, has been a centerpiece of bipartisan antipoverty policy for decades. The 1995 GOP budget, however, would have slashed $20 billion from the EITC, hitting working Americans on the edge of poverty with a tax increase of $332 in the first year of the plan alone.

SPECIAL INTERESTS AND THE REPUBLICAN CONGRESS

While the Republicans claimed a mandate from voters after the 1994 elections, it very quickly became clear that the special interests that had supported the Republican takeover would have unprecedented power and influence in the 104th Congress. The new majority moved quickly to reward its largest corporate financial contributors.

The Contract with America's ninth item, the so-called Job Creation and Wage Enhancement Act, pledged to do away with regulations that hampered small businesses and cost jobs. After the election, the Republicans began to draft legislation to streamline regulations and eliminate those that restricted small businesses unnecessarily and also to take broad steps toward seriously weakening the entire regulatory system. To give a few examples among many, these measures would have affected the government's ability to protect wetlands from development; punish companies that pollute the air and water; impose warning labels and other such consumer protections on pharmaceutical products; protect the safety of factories, laboratories, and other workplaces; and keep pesticides and other carcinogens out of food.

With the Republicans in the majority, zealous antigovernment conservatives proposed a "regulatory revolution." DeLay, who was so virulently opposed to government regulation that he likened the Environmental Protection Agency to the Gestapo, founded Project Relief, an ad hoc coalition of corporate lobbyists dedicated to dismantling federal regulations. Project Relief was composed of the representatives of business groups and corporations united in an effort to strip the federal government of the ability to regulate their business practices. DeLay and his deputies arranged for a "war room" for the Project Relief lobbyists just off the House floor.[13]

As the House deregulation package met resistance from Democrats and a few moderate Republicans in the Senate, Dole introduced his own regulatory reform bill, which was less extreme than what the House had passed but still a radical departure from decades of regulatory policy.

As 1995 progressed, Republicans in the House and Senate introduced bills ostensibly to "reform" but in reality to dismantle or even repeal the most important environmental protections on the books, including the Clean Water and Clean Air Acts, the Endangered Species Act, and the Superfund law, which funds the cleanup of toxic sites. The Republicans would have allowed corporate interests to plunder natural resources, such as the Arctic National Wildlife Refuge and Alaska's Tongass National Forest, authorizing oil and gas drilling and accelerated logging, respectively. The Republican Congress voted to cut the EPA's budget by one third, decimating its effectiveness in protecting the natural environment.

One Republican approach to the problem of too much red tape in agencies they didn't approve of was to tangle them up in more red tape. The underlying purpose was to paralyze federal agencies they didn't like. The theory was that if they could weaken the ability of these regulatory agencies to perform their required functions, over time public support would be undermined and the case for elimination of the agency in question would be strengthened.

Americans take for granted that they can eat food from the supermarket and take drugs from the pharmacy without fear that these products will poison and potentially kill them. Our system of federal regulation allows Americans to live, breathe, eat, and work under safe conditions. While there is a strong case for streamlining some regulations and making them more efficient, the leaders of the deregulation project in 1995 and 1996 were not interested in simply improving the responsiveness of the FDA, the EPA, the Occupational Safety and Health Administration (OSHA), and other vital agencies. The Republican Congress waged an assault on the protections that give us all the luxury of not having to worry that drinking a glass of water, eating a hamburger, or taking an antihistamine will harm us.

THE SOCIAL AGENDA OF THE REPUBLICAN PARTY

There was yet another component to the legislative program of the Republican Congress in 1995: carrying out the NRA's pro-gun agenda and responding to the rising power of the right-to-life movement based in the newly politicized evangelical churches. While pro-gun legislation was kept out of the Contract with America as too controversial, Gingrich had promised the pro-gun interest groups that he would attempt to repeal the ban on assault weapons, which had been passed by Congress and signed into law by Clinton in 1994.

In one breath, the Republicans claimed to be attempting to get the government out of people's lives; in another, however, they sought to involve the government heavily in a woman's right to choose whether and under what circumstances to have an abortion. Gingrich had excluded abortion-related issues from the Contract in order to avoid alienating pro-choice voters, but now that the Republicans were in power a series of measures were proposed to chip away at abortion rights. The House passed a bill removing the requirement that states fund Medicaid abortions for low-income women who had been the victims of rape and incest. Another bill would have eliminated federal funding for abortions for women in prison. Still another barred abortion funding for women covered by the federal employees' health insurance program. An amendment to one bill, proposed by Congressman Bob Dornan of California, would have prevented abortions from being performed in U.S. military medical facilities abroad.[14]

Cutting government support for education, job training, research, and health care was one thing. Cutting government protection of the environment, food and water, and workplace safety was something else. Imposing a divisive right-wing social agenda made the Republicans' agenda problematic for many Americans. Yet all this and more is what Republicans had in mind when they took control of Congress in January 1995.

Taken as a whole, the Republican agenda represented an attempt to write a new social contract, one that would have replaced the post–World War II consensus supporting federal responsibility for protecting the vulnerable, securing equal opportunity for all, and controlling the excesses of business with a different approach that viewed government as the enemy of freedom and opportunity.

This agenda was nothing short of a revolution, and in the early months of 1995 it appeared as if the ascendant Republicans might accomplish just what they set out to do.

Chapter 11

SENATE RULES

HOW THE SENATE WORKS

A straightforward description of the rules of the U.S. Senate (if such a thing were to exist) would suggest that nothing would ever get done. If a single senator decides to object to almost any action on the Senate floor for any reason, he or she can stop it in its tracks. And that single senator can do so even if every other senator supports going ahead. Sometimes there are ways around these kinds of roadblocks, but they are not quick or easy—and sometimes there are none.

It is essential both for enacting legislation and for resisting legislative initiatives in the Senate to understand the procedural rules. But focusing only on the Senate rules ignores the other equally important factor: the chemistry of the Senate. At any moment, the chemistry among the members, between the Senate and the press, and between the Senate and the country has a great deal to do with what happens on the Senate floor.

166

Senators need to get along with each other if they want to get anything done. They need to know how to compromise and to exchange favors. But the world they live in, although unique, is not an insular one. They respond to press coverage. They react to the mood in the country. They listen to interest groups with whom they have relationships. And they respond to the mood on the Senate floor—which can swing from belligerence and confrontation to lassitude and delay, or from impatience with debate to expeditious decision making, all in a matter of hours or even minutes.

Successful senators become masters of compromise, or "horse-trading." Very good senators also understand how the press and the mood of the country can shape prospects for success on the floor. And the most successful senators, like Kennedy, become masters of all the elements that drive action.

HORSE-TRADING

One of my favorite experiences with horse-trading involved the tireless and persistent conservative Jesse Helms. When Democrats were in the majority from 1987 to 1994, Helms was one of those Republican senators who most consistently obstructed Senate action. Personally genial and courtly, he reveled in the role of skunk at the Democratic legislative picnic. A master of using the rules of the Senate to get his way or at least force uncomfortable votes, Helms would go to the floor and object to almost any routine matter the Democrats were proposing, either to gain publicity for himself among conservatives and fuel his fundraising operation or drag out the Senate floor process. Or he would use his objection to hold out for an opportunity to horse-trade. He focused especially on obscenity and the arts, sexual orientation (or, as he would term it, "the homosexual agenda"), and civil rights ("racial preferences," in Helms-speak) and was relentless once he got started resisting a particular piece of legislation.

There was a way to deal with Helms, however, which I observed shortly after I arrived at my job in 1989. The Labor Committee had reported a string of small but vital health care bills to the floor, including such measures as immunizations for children, transplant regulations, and breast cancer funding. By August, when the Senate was preparing to adjourn for the summer recess, these bills had already passed the House and just needed approval by the full Senate to go to the president for his signature. Each had passed the Labor Committee with unanimous Republican and Democratic support, and we assumed there would be no difficulty moving them through the Senate, though there was not a lot of time to do so because of the pending adjournment.

After the bills were reported from the Labor Committee, notices were sent to the Democratic and Republican cloakrooms that we sought to pass the bills through the full Senate by unanimous consent. Under the usual procedures, the respective cloakroom staffs then notify all their senators of the Committee's request to determine if there are any objections. This process is called "hot-lining" in Senate parlance. I was informed that there was an objection from an unnamed Republican senator to moving the bills. It was Helms.

In the case of these health care bills, Helms was not interested in cooperating with the Labor Committee. Even though Hatch, the ranking Republican on the Committee, and other Republicans had supported these noncontroversial measures, Helms was determined to block them. So he was exercising his right to object, in the language of the Senate, to place a "hold" on these bills.

But this time, one Democratic senator was prepared for Helms's antics. Earlier in the year, President Bush had nominated a judge to a federal court in North Carolina. The judge was Helms's candidate for the bench; he had been found to be qualified by the American Bar Association, and Helms wanted the nomination confirmed by the Senate. When Bush nominated the judge, Senator Joe Biden, then the chairman of the Judiciary Committee, held up bringing the nomination to the floor, even though the judge had passed the required tests for confirmation. Biden knew that Helms wanted the judge confirmed, so he kept the nomination in reserve to use as a bargaining chip when Helms inevitably decided to obstruct another matter. At that point, Biden could not foresee what matter Helms would try to obstruct later in the year, but he knew from experience that there would be many. This horse-trading strategy worked with Helms only when he wanted something. Unfortunately, for the most part he didn't want anything other senators could give him, being generally more interested in blocking, obstructing, and forcing politically difficult votes than in getting anything done. When it came to this judge, however, there was something Helms wanted, and Biden was shrewd enough to realize this.

One August evening, as midnight approached and the Senate was preparing to adjourn, Kennedy and I were discussing what we would do about Helms's hold on the health bills. We spoke to Hatch and to Helms, but Helms refused to withdraw his hold, and Hatch couldn't get him to relent. Shortly after midnight, Kennedy asked Biden if he had any suggestions. Biden said that perhaps he could help. After he walked away we saw him talking to Helms, who was in the far corner of the Senate. When Biden returned, he asked Kennedy to provide him with a list of each of the health care bills that were being held by Helms. Biden would take the list to Helms and see if he could get him to back down.

I listed the eight bills on the back of an envelope that I had in my pocket and handed the list to Biden. We lost sight of where he went, but he must have found Helms because half an hour later he came back to Kennedy with the envelope. After each of the bills listed on the envelope was written "OK, JH." According to Biden, Helms had agreed to go along with approving the bills in return for Biden allowing Helms's judge to be approved that night as well. We took the envelope to the parliamentarian and the respective cloakrooms. The holds were lifted on the health care bills. They passed the Senate that very evening, and the president ultimately signed them into law.

Helms got his judge. The American people got improved health care. That's horse-trading in the Senate.

TUTORIALS ON SENATE PROCEDURE

Shortly after I arrived in the Senate, I realized I needed to master the body's parliamentary rules, or at a minimum understand the basics of Senate procedure, if I was to be effective in helping advance Kennedy's agenda. I arranged a series of tutorial sessions for our whole Committee staff. The training was done by the Congressional Research Service (CRS), an arm of the Congress staffed by career experts that provides nonpartisan research services to members of the House and Senate.

I asked senior staff members in the Senate who at CRS was the top expert on Senate rules and was told the best was Stan Boch. Senate rules were so complex and difficult to explain that it was vital to have Boch—and only Boch—conduct our tutorial. I contacted CRS, but Boch was on a travel detail to the Far East. It was unclear to me what an expert in Senate rules was doing traveling to the Far East—maybe studying the parliamentary rules of the Indian Congress. But I had been persuaded that only Boch would do, so I agreed to wait until he returned.

Weeks later Boch was back in Washington, and I scheduled a time for him to come to our Labor Committee offices for the tutorial. I remember these sessions well. Boch was a serious, brilliant analyst who had memorized two hundred years of Senate precedent and would attempt to summarize it all for a novice like me in several brief sessions. The first session was on the subject of the Byrd Rule, named, as I have discussed previously, after Senator Robert Byrd. The Byrd Rule was the place to start, Boch said, because it deals with what provisions are, or are not, "extraneous" on budget legislation. This was an especially important issue because a particular type of budget legislation—the reconciliation bill—is not subject to a filibuster and can pass the Senate with only fifty votes. For that reason, it is a vehicle for sweeping legislative change. President Reagan used it to move much of his conservative agenda in 1981, and it was the instrument President George W. Bush used to pass his massive 2001 tax cut. President Obama used it for health care in 2010. As we shall see, it also turned out to be a primary vehicle for Gingrich's right-wing revolution.

If a provision in a reconciliation bill is extraneous, it can be struck on a point of order; Boch looked at me over his wire-rim glasses and began to explain. "It is extraneous if it doesn't have any effect, or only incidental effect, on reducing or expanding the deficit. There are no absolute standards to apply on this determination, which raises the question of whether the Senate itself rather than the parliamentarian should make the decision about whether a provision is 'extraneous.'" Boch's opinion was that this point of order, which could be raised by any senator, should be submitted to the Senate for a decision on whether or not it was valid.

Boch then went on to explain "germaneness," which, he said, applied only to amendments. Being "extraneous" was different from being "not germane." The session on the Byrd Rule wrapped up. I felt that we had examined the issue of extraneousness in depth. If you don't understand, don't worry. I didn't either.

A week later, Boch returned for a second session, this time on amendments. He turned immediately to the issue of "degrees" as applied to amendments. An amendment that changes the text of a bill is a first-degree amendment. An amendment to a pending first-degree amendment (an amendment that has not yet been adopted or rejected) is a second-degree amendment.

There are perfecting and substitute amendments. A "perfecting" amendment may contain some change to the underlying text of either a bill or an amendment but not to its entirety. It is not a complete replacement. A "substitute," on the other hand, is a replacement for the entire text. The form of a perfecting amendment may come as an addition to a bill, as striking from a bill, or as striking and inserting.

Next, Boch said, is the question of what form of amendment has priority. He produced elaborate diagrams of first-degree amendments to insert, second-degree perfecting amendments to strike and insert, and second-degree substitutes both to the original and to a first-degree amendment. Then he noted that there could be a second-degree perfecting amendment to the first-degree amendment to strike and insert, whereupon the perfecting amendment has precedence over the motion to strike and insert. However, a motion to strike is not amendable, although you may amend the original text that is not to be stricken.

So it went through four sessions with CRS's and Washington's foremost expert on Senate procedure. Frankly, the whole experience was terrifying, because it proved to me that I would never master what was obviously critical information to have any success in enacting legislation.

In time I learned about the Senate by watching the floor, by receiving instructions from Kennedy, and by trial and error. The Democratic leader's floor staff, who were long serving and extremely professional, also provided expert and essential on-the-spot advice and counsel to Democratic senators and staff.

Four concepts are especially important to understand the rules that were to play an important role in Kennedy's attempts to move a legislative agenda in a Republican-controlled Congress and to keep the right-wing agenda from becoming law: the role of unanimous consent, the filibuster, the powers of the majority leader, and the rules governing amendments.

The basic proposition underlying all the Senate rules of procedure is that "unanimous consent," the consent of all members, is the normal route to taking virtually any action. If unanimous consent is not forthcoming, action is difficult, time-consuming, and often impractical. In the normal course of events, the Senate cannot convene without unanimous consent, cannot take up a matter for consideration on the floor, and cannot vote on an amendment. If a single senator objects, debate cannot be ended, legislation cannot be passed, final reports from the House cannot be taken up, nominations cannot be considered, budgets cannot be taken up, appropriations cannot be considered, and resolutions cannot be moved forward—at least not without great difficulty.

A senator wishing to exercise his or her right to object to a unanimous consent request used to have to announce the objection on the Senate floor, and then be prepared to engage in a filibuster, that is, to be recognized and then hold the floor by continuing to speak. In recent years senators have been allowed simply to lodge their objection and are not required to actually remain on the floor speaking hour after hour to maintain their filibuster. Senators are simply taken at their word that they would filibuster if required to do so, and the Senate goes forward with the process of breaking the filibuster as if the senator were speaking on the floor.

The only way to overcome an objection by a lone senator is to work through the elaborate procedure to break the filibuster, or, in Senate parlance, invoke "cloture." This process takes several days for each point of procedure that is objected to, and since a senator may object to each of the stages through which a measure needs to pass, he or she can take over the Senate and essentially preclude it from taking up any other business for up to two weeks.

This is how cloture works: On the first day, fifteen senators sign onto and file a cloture petition. Two days later, at the outset of Senate business, the petition becomes "ripe." At that point, the Senate votes on whether or not to invoke cloture and limit debate on the matter that is objected to. To succeed, a cloture petition requires an affirmative vote of three-fifths of senators, or sixty votes. If the cloture petition obtains the requisite sixty votes, there are then another thirty hours to debate the issue on which the single senator is objecting and on which cloture has been obtained. After the thirty hours, the issue is voted on. If there are other procedural steps through which the matter has to pass, this cloture procedure has to be repeated over and over again, taking up more Senate time until the process is finally completed and the measure itself can be acted on.

The power of a single senator to object to any Senate action is matched by the substantial power of the Senate majority leader. The members of the majority party, as the name implies, choose the majority leader. Even if a party is in the majority by only one senator, all the spoils and power of control flow to the majority party and, ultimately, to the majority leader. The majority leader sets the agenda, decides when the Senate will be in session, decides which measures will be brought to the floor for consideration, and decides whether those measures will actually get voted on (since he or she has the power to pull a bill from the floor as well as bring it up). Majority leaders also have the right of first recognition by the presiding officer, which gives them a critical lever for controlling the floor debate and the amendment process.

After the 1994 election, and after Senator Richard Shelby of Alabama switched from the Democratic to the Republican Party, the Republicans held fifty-three of the one hundred Senate seats. That majority, of course, was enough for them to install Bob Dole as majority leader.

Beyond the power of one senator to object and the power of the majority leader to control the agenda, there are numerous other rules adopted over time that govern every step the Senate takes. Each of these rules, in turn, has been interpreted over the years by the Senate parliamentarian and ultimately by votes of the members themselves. These rules and their subsequent interpretations result in a vast maze of practices, routines, habits, and customs that govern what the Senate does.

The rules just described are only the tip of the iceberg. The process of amending legislation, in particular, involves a complex set of Senate procedures (remember Boch's tutorial)—procedures that would turn out to be particularly critical in Kennedy's efforts to enact the minimum wage increase. The amendment process is often described in the Senate by reference to a tree with branches. The underlying legislation is the "trunk," and the "branches" are the amendments. As Boch explained, certain types of amendments are branches from the trunk; these are first-degree amendments of various kinds (remember the discussion of perfecting versus substitute amendments). Off each amendment branch are other branches, amendments to the amendments, the second-degree amendments. Thus, as each amendment is restricted to two degrees, the success of any given piece of legislation may lie in the ability of its proponents to anticipate and understand any potential amendment. Once all the permissible first- and second-degree amendments have been offered, the legislative tree is filled up, and no more amendments can be offered until one is voted on or withdrawn, thus opening up a new spot for a new amendment. So if a senator wishes to offer an amendment and ultimately bring it up for a vote, he or she has to find a spot on the trunk where a first-degree amendment is in order or a spot on a branch where a second-degree amendment can be offered. In turn, if a vote on an amendment is objected to, cloture must be invoked by obtaining sixty votes to move forward with the vote.

Passing progressive legislation or amendments appeared impossible for any Democrat at the beginning of 1995. Majority Leader Dole controlled what legislation would be brought to the floor, so unless irresistible political pressure was created, nothing he did not support would come before the Senate as a stand-alone bill. Because Dole enjoyed the right of first recognition, if he suspected an amendment he opposed would be offered, he had the power to fill the tree before any Democrat could be recognized. And if somehow both these hurdles could be surmounted, sixty votes would still be required to overcome cloture, which meant that at least thirteen Republicans would have to join with the forty-seven Democrats (assuming—a big assumption—that all the Democrats stuck together).

But Kennedy was undaunted, and he knew that for almost every power a Senate rule granted, there was a mitigating rule on the other side. While the rules provided Dole and the Republican majority lots of ways to frustrate the Democrats, they also provided Democrats with opportunities to resist measures proposed by Dole and the Republicans. Any Democrat could object to unanimous consent on any procedure, and the Republicans would have to gain cloture to override the objection, which would require picking up seven Democratic votes to gain the sixty votes necessary. While the majority leader has the formal power to control the floor and limit the minority's ability to offer amendments, the majority can't get a final vote on a bill without the minority's consent unless it can rustle up the necessary sixty votes needed to cut off debate. So ultimately the majority leader often has to allow votes on some of the minority amendments if he wants the minority to go along with allowing a vote on final passage.

How, why, and for what conceivable purpose could these rules ever have developed? Many books have been written about the development of Senate parliamentary rules. Suffice it to say that the Founding Fathers, deeply skeptical of governmental power, viewed the Senate, in George Washington's words, as the "saucer that cools the tea" of the legislation passed by the House. Consistent with that view, over time the Senate established an elaborate system of checks and balances to ensure that action was taken only after it had passed through a cumbersome set of gateways. In contrast, the House of Representatives is much more straightforward. There the majority rules. If the majority party can muster a majority by even one vote, a matter moves forward and the minority is helpless to object. But in the Senate the rules grant exceptional safeguards to the minority.

Although this description of Senate procedures may lead one to conclude that it is relatively easy for a single senator to obstruct or resist almost any piece of legislation, the reality is that personal chemistry among the senators often creates strong counterpressures on those seeking to object. Of course, skillful senators can also use such chemistry to enhance their positions.

Normally senators are reluctant to be seen as obstructing matters that appear to have broad support, and, over time, any senator who objects too often will come to be seen as uncooperative and resistant. He or she will be shunned by fellow senators and, most important, will forfeit any chance of moving his or her own bills through the Senate as others will use the occasion to retaliate by blocking his or her initiatives. Senators have judges they want confirmed, appropriations measures for their home states they want enacted, and pet causes to advance. They risk the chance of getting any of these things done if they are seen as being too obstructionist.

MEETINGS

All these procedural issues are analyzed and hashed over in advance and strategy gets set and worked out at meetings. Information learned at meetings is the currency of staff. Which meetings you attend, where you sit, and whether you speak is determined by your position in the Senate and what the Senate routine is for your position at that particular meeting. Members of the leadership group attend leadership meetings. Staff for leadership attend caucus meetings of all senators; staff for other senators do not, except when their senator is a central participant in the caucus discussion. Senators sit at tables in the center of the room; staff sit on chairs against the wall or stand crowded by the doors. Staff for ranking Democratic leaders on each committee run the meetings with the staff of other Democratic committee members to organize the Democratic position in the committee. And so it goes.

The way of life in the Senate is meetings: meetings of senators, meetings of staff, meetings between staff and senators, meetings between the leadership senators and their staffs, meetings of the Democratic Caucus with the leadership staff, committee meetings, meetings of staff on committees, briefing meetings of all possible configurations, meetings with interest groups, meetings, more meetings, and still more meetings.

There are fifteen committees in the Senate, each of which has a Republican and a Democratic staff headed up by a staff director, who is chosen by the chairman or ranking member. I had been staff director on the Committee on Labor and Human Resources for Kennedy when he was in the majority, and I was still staff director for Democrats, now in the minority, in 1995.

The most important meeting for Democratic staff directors is held every Monday morning while the Senate is in session to formulate basic strategy for the Democrats for the upcoming week. Invited to attend the meeting are representatives of the minority leader, Democratic floor staff (that is, the aides who manage the floor for the Democrats and run the Democratic cloakroom), representatives of the Democratic leader's team, key members of the White House legislative staff, and Democratic committee staff directors.

The meetings are used to review which bills will come up when and to communicate the Democratic leader's strategy for each bill, focusing primarily on the legislation that will be on the floor of the Senate that week. While the meetings are not really for decision making, it is possible to pick up the mood of other key Democrats from the comments made at the meeting by their staff directors or key staff members. One also learns something about White House strategy, although the White House staff attending these meetings are not the decision makers at the

White House. Since Clinton's election I had learned that White House positions were always in flux, so we had to work on many pressure points to influence its policies.

Information is power. In fact some aides at the White House would intentionally not inform us of key meetings and withhold other information because they felt compromise with the Republicans rather than confrontation was the right approach. So as we moved into the crucial struggle for the mind of the president, I sometimes felt that training as a CIA analyst would have been more useful than my law degree. But difficult as it was, we had to persevere in the never-ending search for information because the stakes were so high and key decision points were coming up fast.

Chapter 12

WILL THE DEMOCRATS UNITE?

In early 1995 the Democrats met to begin developing a game plan. Their mood was not encouraging, they were defeated and demoralized, and it was not at all clear that they could be rallied to resist. If the Democrats didn't show a reasonable degree of unity, even the best game plan and use of the Senate rules would only win a battle or two while ultimately losing the war.

After his close election as Democratic leader, Senator Daschle would play a key role in bringing the Democrats together. He moved quickly to appoint a leadership team of eight senators, who met every Tuesday morning to form the agenda and the plans for the week before the broader meeting of all Democrats at lunch. Daschle was tireless in his consultations and meetings with individual Democratic senators. He was hardworking, attentive to the needs of his colleagues, and unthreatening. His frank, open, unpretentious manner was a great asset. Members of the Democratic Caucus knew he was straightforward and committed to the best interests of the caucus as a whole. At the same time, though he came from South Dakota, a basically conservative and Republican-leaning state, his own personal views were deeply rooted in the progressive tradition, and he and Kennedy generally shared the same policy goals.

Kennedy's strategy for the Democratic resistance was now in place, even if other Democrats weren't yet ready to sign on to it. First, there was the defensive side. Democrats had to define what they stood for—and, equally important, what they stood against. Kennedy had laid down a marker in his speech in January: Democrats must stand for their historic commitment to improving jobs, education, and health care for working families. And he had made the rounds of all the key Democrats to take their temperature and advance his views.

While the battle for the president's mind was ongoing, at least Clinton had resisted moving dramatically toward the Republicans in his State of the Union speech or other public statements. Instead he had moved skillfully to co-opt some of the Republican positions. For example, he now supported targeted tax cuts for the middle class for college tuition, a $500 child credit, and he was prepared to introduce his own welfare reform bill, which, in his words, would "end welfare as we know it." In his budget, which he introduced on February 6, 1995, he made symbolic moves toward the Republicans by consolidating and eliminating some programs, with billions in associated savings. But he left untouched the key Democratic priorities that Kennedy identified: no cuts to education, no cuts to Medicare or Medicaid, no cuts to nutrition programs. And he didn't propose to balance the budget. Based on predictions from OMB and CBO, Clinton's budget projected deficits that were just short of $200 billion a year through 2005. The deficit wouldn't keep growing, but it was not going to be eliminated either.

Perhaps the president had taken Kennedy's advice at their December meeting that his budget should be a political document: if the Republicans were intent on eliminating the deficit, let them propose the cuts that would achieve it. Of course, no one foresaw how quickly the deficit would in fact be eliminated, partly through policy changes but primarily through the extraordinary economic growth that began in 1994 and 1995.

DRAWING THE BATTLE LINES ON MEDICARE

A central theme of the resistance would be a focus on Medicare. Although Medicare was never mentioned in the Contract with America, it would be virtually impossible to finance both a balanced budget and tax cuts—key Republican goals—without deep Medicare cuts. Kennedy had early on recognized this as a key Republican vulnerability.

Medicare, along with Social Security, was perhaps the most beloved and broadly supported of all government programs. It was absolutely critical to a dignified and comfortable life for the elderly and disabled. Nonetheless there were many Democrats who initially bought into the argument that Medicare needed to be drastically cut back in order to protect its solvency over the long haul, and therefore they resisted drawing a line in the sand over Medicare. Some even agreed with the Republicans that Medicare should be cut and the savings used to provide tax cuts. Developing a consensus among Democrats that defending Medicare was possibly the most powerful issue available to them would not come easily or quickly.

On January 30, 1995, Gingrich made a brief foray into the Medicare issue. At a speech to the American Hospital Association annual meeting in Washington, he declared that Medicare had to be revisited from the ground up. Every decision about Medicare, he said, would be made within the context of getting a balanced budget.[1] He seemed to be saying that cuts to Medicare would be used to balance the overall federal budget, and he certainly suggested that Republicans questioned the basic nature and structure of the program. The speaker's remarks offered the opportunity for Kennedy to throw down the gauntlet on Medicare, and seeing the opening, he immediately challenged the speaker. Kennedy went to the Senate floor on January 31, the day after Gingrich's speech, and warned that there would be a real battle if Gingrich had in mind major cuts to the Medicare program: "When Republicans in other years tried to break the promise of Social Security, senior citizens and their families all over this country told them that the answer was no. And the Congress responded. Today it is time to say to Newt Gingrich and his friends that when it comes to breaking the promise of Medicare, the answer is just as resounding and just as unequivocal. And once again the answer is no."

The first skirmish in the resistance to the Republican revolution was at hand. Threads of unity were emerging among Democrats around specific themes, but there was still a long way to go. Republicans had just begun to try to enact the Contract with America. Where the Republican revolution would lead, no one could predict, but most bets among Washington observers were that it would succeed.

REPUBLICANS ATTEMPT TO TAKE BACK FUNDS ALREADY APPROPRIATED

In late February, after the initial skirmish over Medicare, a second opportunity for the Democratic resistance presented itself. As the Republicans' budget-cutting strategy in the House became clear, the Democratic staff directors began to plan their counterattack. We had learned that the Republicans intended to jump the gun on their budget cuts by not waiting for the budget for the following year but actually trying to take away (rescind) funds that had already been appropriated and distributed from the prior year's budget.

Each year some emergency spending requirement comes up that requires an emergency supplemental appropriations bill. Emergencies are usually natural disasters like floods, earthquakes, or hurricanes, or unforeseen defense expenditures, such as deploying troops in Bosnia or South Korea. These are expenses that are not anticipated, and new funds must be appropriated for them. In 1990, during a budget summit involving President Bush and the Democratic leaders of Congress, all parties agreed with the principle that emergency spending bills would be paid for outside the existing budget. Funds that had already been appropriated and allocated for existing needs would not be rescinded to cover emergencies. This agreement codified an approach to emergency appropriations that had been observed on a bipartisan basis for many years: since emergencies were, by definition, unforeseen, they should not be funded by taking away appropriations for regular budget needs.

Republicans in the House planned to show early on just how tough they would be on cutting social programs. They knew that cuts in the annual budget would not take place until the new fiscal year, which began on October 1, 1995, but in their zeal for change they wanted to show results immediately. So they set out to rescind funds for fiscal year 1995 that had already been appropriated by legislation enacted by Congress and signed by the president in 1994. The emergency spending bill that would provide disaster relief in forty states became an opening wedge for their broader agenda. Not only did they demand that the money appropriated in the emergency spending bill be offset by cuts to existing appropriations, but they also added an extra $9 billion in cuts beyond what was needed to offset the disaster spending.

The rescissions included extensive cuts to education programs, including Head Start, school lunches, aid to disadvantaged school districts, funds for the Safe and Drug-Free Schools program, technology in the schools, and teacher training programs. Teachers who had already been hired for the year would have to be laid off in the middle of the year, students dropped from their school lunch programs, Head Start enrollment scaled back, and new computers that had already been ordered canceled. In addition, environmental protection initiatives would be scaled back, funds for crime prevention eliminated, college aid cut, nutritional programs for women and infant children cut, and aid to farmers and for job training reduced. The House Republicans were certainly not shy about an early start on their antigovernment agenda.

Earlier in February, as soon as he learned about the Republican rescissions strategy, Kennedy responded. He told me that it was essential to shape what was clearly going to be an ongoing debate about budget priorities. In this case, the issue was not just budget priorities going forward but honoring commitments already made.

Kennedy first talked to other Democratic members of the Labor Committee about his concerns to obtain their support. He then requested a meeting of Democratic members of the Committee with the Senate Democratic leadership to discuss strategy for resisting the Republican rescissions bill. On February 14 Labor Committee senators Kennedy, Harkin, Mikulski, and Dodd met, joined by Daschle, Reid, and others on the Democratic Senate leadership team. Kennedy proposed organizing a resistance to the rescissions bill in the Senate. He also noted that Senate Democrats needed to confer with the White House, perhaps with Chief of Staff Leon Panetta, to agree on a joint strategy regarding the bill. Obviously resistance would not work if the White House did not back us up.

Senator Harkin spoke next. Harkin is a consistent, tough-minded, articulate progressive. He was two-thirds of the way through his second term in the Senate, having been reelected in 1990, the first Democratic senator from Iowa to be reelected in decades. He was someone Kennedy could count on to put up a spirited attack against Republican extremist ideas. Until the 1994 election, Harkin had been chairman of the Appropriations subcommittee that handled funds for health, human services, labor, and education, so the Republicans were now trying to rescind funds that had been appropriated under his watch. He said he would oppose any rescissions that would cut domestic spending or shift domestic funds to military spending. (Clinton's initial request for disaster relief funding had also included a request for $2.6 billion in additional defense spending. The Republicans raised that to $3.4 billion.) There was no resistance to this from the other senators, and though nothing had been decided, a discussion had begun.

A week later, at the Democratic staff directors meeting, staff for a number of moderate senators finally agreed that at the very least any spending needs for defense should be paid for only out of the defense budget. But there was still no consensus on whether to resist cuts to social programs, and there was no focus on what the Democratic message on this legislation would be.

Two days later Kennedy and Daschle attended another meeting to discuss the Democratic response to the rescissions bill. This time members of the Budget and Appropriations Committee were present. Senator Daniel Inouye of Hawaii, a veteran of over thirty years in the Senate and the ranking member on the defense appropriations subcommittee, indicated that he would be working to make sure that any extra defense spending would be offset by cuts to the defense budget and not by cuts to domestic programs. But that still left the problem of offsetting the emergency spending and the deeper cuts the Republicans proposed as a down payment on their overall agenda.

Senator Bingaman, a member of the Labor Committee in 1993–94, argued that whatever happened in the rescissions bill would be a precedent for the rest of the year. We had to be clear now that we would not allow cuts to domestic social programs to pay for additional defense spending, and that it was equally dangerous to require that emergency supplemental spending be offset with domestic cuts. Allowing Republicans to hold hostage all domestic programs when disasters occurred and emergency funding was called for would be a very bad precedent.

Senator Byrd was second in seniority only to Senator Thurmond. He was the ranking member of the Appropriations Committee and the leading parliamentary expert in the Senate. He had been the Democratic majority and minority leader before he stepped down in 1988 and was replaced by Senator Mitchell. He was immensely powerful in the Senate and unmatched in his knowledge and control of the federal appropriations process. When Kennedy and I visited West Virginia to campaign for Al Gore during the 2000 election, Kennedy commented that half the highways and buildings in West Virginia seemed to be named for Byrd: the Robert C. Byrd Academic and Technology Center, the Robert C. Byrd Expressway, the Robert C. Byrd Federal Correctional Institution, the Robert C. Byrd Health and Wellness Center, the Robert C. Byrd Library (in Wheeling), the Robert C. Byrd Library (in Morgantown), the Robert C. Byrd Industrial Park, the Robert C. Byrd Visitor Center at Harpers Ferry, and even the Robert C. Byrd Green Bank Telescope. A complete list of West Virginia projects named after Byrd would go on for several pages. There are even nine federal projects in West Virginia named after his wife, Emma Ora Byrd. Within two years of his chairmanship of the Senate Appropriations Committee, Byrd had surpassed his announced five-year goal of making sure more than $1 billion in federal funds was sent back to West Virginia. He has been quoted as saying in 2002, "West Virginia has always had four friends: God Almighty, Sears Roebuck, Carter's Liver Pills, and Robert C. Byrd."

Senator Byrd was a unique personality. His parents both died when he was very young, and he was raised by an aunt and uncle. He went to a one-room schoolhouse, taught himself to read, and became a remarkably knowledgeable scholar on literature, history, and particularly the classics. He had written extensively on the history and procedural rules of the Senate. He often went to the floor and spoke without notes for hours at a time, reciting Senate history, linking it to the Romans and the Greeks, to Shakespeare, and to other philosophers and writers. His commitment to the institution of the Senate was unequaled. He was the great orator of the Senate when I arrived in 1989, albeit in a nineteenth-century style, from a time before television and teleprompters. Byrd was feared but respected, ridiculed in some circles for his sentimentality, his grandiosity, and his reverence for the Senate, but deeply admired in others. Although he had ousted Kennedy from his position as majority whip in 1977, Kennedy was among his admirers, and he had one of the closest relationships with Byrd of any of the members of the Senate.

I recall one impressive moment in their relationship. Kennedy was at a dinner with the author and historian David McCullough in 1992, where McCullough spoke passionately of the Longfellow House in Cambridge, Massachusetts. General George Washington was based there during the early days of the Revolutionary War and it subsequently became the residence of the poet Henry Wadsworth Longfellow in the nineteenth century. McCullough told Kennedy it was one of the most important historical houses in the United States and was in a terrible state of disrepair.

It held papers from the Revolutionary War and from Longfellow's time, but there was no climate control or manner of keeping the papers or the house safe. McCullough was very concerned about the house and its contents.

Kennedy went back to Washington determined to get the funds for the preservation of the Longfellow House from the Appropriations Committee, chaired by Byrd. To impress Byrd, Kennedy spent several days memorizing Longfellow's poem "The Midnight Ride of Paul Revere." When he was ready he set up a meeting in Byrd's ornate Senate office in the Capitol building. Since Kennedy thought that Byrd would be more receptive to him if they met alone, I was not present at the recitation. However, Kennedy reported that he made it through the whole poem and thought it had gone well. Sure enough, money was appropriated for the Longfellow House to be taken over by the National Park Service and restored to properly safeguard its valuable contents. Would the funds have been found if Kennedy had just asked for them? I do not know, but I am sure that Byrd was impressed with the effort and passion that went into Kennedy's presentation and request to save this historic national treasure.

As chairman of the Appropriations Committee that had presided over the funding decisions of 1994, Byrd now made it clear that we should not cut domestic programs to offset emergency expenses or pay for additional defense needs. Doing so violated the agreement from the 1990 budget compromise. He hoped that the president would be persuaded to veto one of the Republicans' budget-cutting bills to show that he supported protecting necessary domestic programs. He also believed that some Republicans were also opposed to rescinding already appropriated funds. Byrd hoped that Republican senator Mark Hatfield of Oregon would not go along, a hope based on the fact that Hatfield, the new chairman of the Appropriations Committee, was a moderate Republican who was pragmatic and frequently progressive in outlook—clearly not a soldier in Gingrich's Republican revolution. Byrd argued that we needed a united Democratic Caucus because with over forty votes, we could stop anything. He said that somebody had to break the back of the Contract with America. If the president picked the right place to veto something, he could begin to slow the momentum from the Republican House.

Meanwhile, on February 22, as the Republicans celebrated the fiftieth day of controlling Congress, President Clinton came to the Capitol to meet with Democrats to draw attention to the strategy of exposing the harshness of Republican proposals in the Contract. As House Minority Leader Gephardt said, "The fact is the Contract with America does absolutely nothing to address the problems most Americans face in their daily lives—good jobs, affordable health care, access to quality education, and a rising standard of living."

The next day Kennedy went to the floor and announced the introduction of the Child Care Consolidation and Investment Act of 1995, which provided additional funds for child care and built on his 1990 legislation. It was an occasion for him to hammer on the callousness of intended Republican budget cuts. He pointed out that House Republican cuts amounted to a 20 percent reduction in child care over the next five years and coined the phrase "Home Alone," the title of a popular movie, to describe the Republican child care plan.

At the staff directors meeting on February 28, John Hilley, then Daschle's policy director, said that based on his discussions with the White House, the administration agreed in principle that we shouldn't cut domestic spending to pay for defense and also opposed the idea of offsetting emergencies with cuts of appropriated funds because it violated the agreement of the 1990 budget summit compromise. That sounded good, but then Hilley added that, while the principle was right, it was "bad politics" for Democrats not to offset, or pay for, emergency or additional defense spending requirements. It wouldn't do for Democrats in the current climate simply to fund the emergency relief programs and cover the costs of doing so in the next year's budget, as had been agreed in the 1990 budget summit. Apparently principle might need to go by the wayside.

This was not a good sign; it meant that the White House and certain Democrats might not stand firm on the issue. If the minority leader's policy chief thought it was "bad politics" for Democrats to oppose cuts to already appropriated funds to pay for emergencies, what did that suggest some members of the Democratic Caucus were telling Daschle? Other staff directors asked Hilley whether the administration was prepared to veto a Republican rescissions bill. Without the president, the Democrats had limited leverage with the Republicans. Hilley responded that there were three or four areas in the Republican proposal that involved callous and extreme cuts, but opposing the cuts sounded like an "Old Democrat" message, so they were trying to reframe it.

During the week of February 28 the Republicans in the House completed work on their antiregulatory measures, bills that would temporarily suspend most new regulations and tie up proposed new rules on health, safety, and the environment in a morass of preconditions. This deregulation measure would provide another opportunity for sharp criticism of the Republican revolution. But that same week, the Democrats in the Senate suffered another blow when Ben Nighthorse Campbell of Colorado switched to the Republican Party, leaving only forty-six Democratic members.

The Republicans in the House also moved to make it more difficult for consumers to sue corporations for damages in injury cases. On March 7 the House Agriculture Committee, supported by Republican leadership, decimated the food stamp program by cutting over $16 billion over five years and removing the individual entitlement. It was now to be a block grant to the states.

Though Democrats sensed the need for a resistance strategy, there was still no agreement on that strategy, and no one yet knew whether the president would take a stand. Regardless, Kennedy pressed ahead.

THE BALANCED BUDGET CONSTITUTIONAL AMENDMENT

Every Tuesday the Senate goes into adjournment from 12:30 to 2:00 while the two parties hold their respective luncheon caucus meetings for all their members in reception rooms just off the Senate floor—the larger Mansfield Room, which is off the corridor along the south side of the Senate, for the majority; the smaller Lyndon B. Johnson Room, off the Senate lobby, for the minority. These weekly lunches are part of the Senate routine, and senators make it a point to attend.

The meetings are private—only senators and leadership staff generally attend—and are the key forum for considering strategy on issues coming to the floor and longer-term issues. Because Tuesday caucuses usually have the broadest attendance of any event during the week, it is a Senate ritual for reporters to gather at the doorways to question senators as they come and go. Such encounters are often impromptu press conferences.

At the March 1 Democratic Caucus lunch, senators discussed the pending balanced budget amendment to the U.S. Constitution, which was coming over to the Senate from the House. This measure would provide a critical early test of Democrats' willingness to resist a central item in the Contract with America. Because it was a constitutional amendment, Republicans needed sixty-seven votes to prevail. But Democrats were deeply split.

A constitutional amendment requiring a balanced budget would be strongly opposed by most Democratic progressives, who viewed it as a disaster because it would require such drastic cuts to domestic programs. From the point of broad economic policy, most economists, conservative and liberal, believed that the government should run a deficit when the economy is faltering rather than being locked into a balanced budget that could intensify an economic downturn.

But defeating it would be difficult because most Democrats thought it was not a good issue on which the whole caucus should stake out ground against the Republicans. Polls generally showed that the public supported a balanced budget amendment, and at least a dozen Democratic senators were already on record as supporting such an amendment, if not the specific version the Republicans proposed. A marker of how divided the Democrats were on strategy was the suggestion by one senator that Democrats let Republicans pass all the legislation they wanted in the first several months of the session! His reasoning was that ultimately the Republican actions would backfire against them once the public saw how harmful the new laws were.

The vote was held on the balanced budget amendment the next day, March 2. It failed—by one vote. A number of Democratic senators found ways to rationalize voting against it despite having previously endorsed the idea, and Republican senator Hatfield defied immense pressure from within his own caucus to cast a courageous deciding vote against the amendment.

Neither at the March 1 caucus lunch nor at the staff directors meeting a week later was a strategy agreed upon for the rescissions bill. At the staff directors meeting we learned that the Republicans in the Senate labor, health, and education appropriations subcommittee were engaged in preparatory work on the rescissions bill. It would be passed through committee the following week and come to the floor of the Senate in mid-March, following final action in the House. We were waiting to see exactly what shape the Senate cuts would take before we prepared our response. It looked like the cuts to the anticrime program had been dropped and some money had been restored for summer jobs, but education and housing programs were still slashed dramatically. Time was short, and a strategy still had to be devised.

DEFENDING AMERICAN WORKERS FROM GOP ATTACKS

As the rescissions bill moved through the Appropriations Committee, another fight loomed on the Senate floor. For years Republicans had stuck with their business allies in attempting to preserve the right of a business to replace its striking workers, and then keep the strikebreakers in their jobs permanently. Although the right to strike is protected by law, the value of that right shrinks dramatically if a worker risks being permanently displaced. Employers relied on a footnote to a Supreme Court opinion that allowed them to permanently replace strikers even as the nation's labor laws gave workers the right to strike.

Though the footnote appeared in a Supreme Court opinion in 1938 (*National Labor Relations Board v. Mackay*), employers had not used it until the 1980s, when Reagan replaced striking air traffic controllers. Since then it had become much more common for employers to permanently replace striking workers. Democrats and their labor allies felt that the abuse of the provision significantly tipped the balance against labor as it entered negotiations with employers over working conditions and wages.

After Democrats won the Senate back in 1986, and particularly after Bush replaced Reagan, efforts were made in the Senate to close the loophole created by the footnote. Proposed legislation filed in 1989 allowed employers to hire temporary workers during a strike but prohibited them from permanently depriving striking workers of their jobs after the strike was over. Although Democrats controlled the Senate from 1986 to 1992, they were never able to muster the sixty votes required to overcome a Republican filibuster against closing this loophole.

When Clinton was elected president he vowed to work with labor and its allies to remedy the situation. In 1994 he issued an executive order that made it a condition for any business seeking contracts with the government to agree not to permanently replace striking workers. The Republicans and their business allies cried foul, asserting that it was beyond the power of the president to issue such an executive order, and challenged the order in the courts. In 1995, at the urging of business, Republicans set their sights on repealing Clinton's executive order as one of their first agenda items in the Senate. On March 14, Senator Kassebaum, on her first foray to the Senate floor as chair of the Labor Committee, brought a proposal to rescind the president's executive order. Since the measure had been moved through the Labor Committee several weeks earlier, Kennedy and other Democrats had already seized that opportunity to go to the floor and use the striker replacement issue as yet another front for the Democratic resistance.

FOCUSING ON WORKING FAMILIES

By mid-March, Democrats had begun to focus their resistance. The first item was Republican cuts to Medicare, although in response to Gingrich's comments rather than a specific Republican proposal to cut the program, which would not emerge until May, when the House budget resolution was reported from committee. The second item was the House rescissions bill, although the shape of the strategy had yet to be determined. And the third item was the striker replacement issue, which was an opportunity for Democrats to frame resistance to the Republican agenda in terms of who was standing up for working Americans.

In the current political landscape, articulating a sound-bite-ready description of your priorities can be an important first step in obtaining public support for an initiative and ultimately getting legislation passed. In 1995 the focus for Democrats was on protecting programs benefiting low- and middle-income Americans. The question was how to describe that priority in the most appealing way possible. This problem had been vexing Democratic senators and staff members for several years. There was "the middle class." That wasn't bad, because most Americans consider themselves middle class. But some were uncomfortable with that label, because America is supposed to be a classless society. In fact when Democrats stood up against tax cuts for the wealthy paid for by program cuts for everyone else, the Republicans would accuse us of class warfare. Moreover there seemed to be broad resentment among many low- and moderate-income families against welfare recipients who seemed to be getting a free ride while they themselves were struggling to make ends meet while working very hard. The Republicans had tried to tap that resentment in their Contract with America and to identify a broad range of government programs with handouts to the "undeserving" poor. We needed a label that would reinforce the public sense of our commitment to work and family—two values that the Democratic Party has always stood for—against Republican attempts to appropriate them, dating as far back as Richard Nixon's presidency. So when it came time to identify who Democrats were fighting for, the phrase *working families* came into vogue.

Kennedy first started using the term at the beginning of 1991, when he was organizing hearings in the Labor Committee to set the agenda for the year ahead on jobs, education, and health care for average American families struggling in the economic recession. The Gulf War was under way, and President Bush was riding high in the popularity polls. The conventional wisdom was that he would be invincible in the 1992 election. But Kennedy saw an opening, which he seized upon in hearings and major speeches, including at George Washington University and the U.S. Conference of Mayors in January and February. The message was that Bush was ignoring domestic problems and the needs of average Americans at home, while all his focus was on the war in the Persian Gulf. When the troops came home, Kennedy asked, what would they return to? In the face of the recession, would there be jobs for them? Would their families have health care? What would be the condition of their children's schools? Initially we alternated between referring to *middle-class families*, *middle- and low-income families*, and *working families*. Ultimately we settled on *working families*. We felt that advocating for working families connoted both that we were concerned about parents, children, and family values—not just individuals—and that we were focusing on hardworking Americans who deserved any help the government could offer.

Over time *working families* became the description of choice for Democrats. Indeed Kennedy's mantra in his 1994 campaign was "Working families—jobs, education, and health care." The working families theme would become a central organizing device for the Democratic resistance to the Republican Contract with America.

As the striker replacement vote drew near, Kennedy recruited allies such as Cardinal John O'Connor, archbishop of New York. In an op-ed piece in the *New York Times* Cardinal O'Connor wrote, "In my judgment, [the right to permanently replace striking workers] can make a charade of collective bargaining and a mockery of the right to strike."

The damage that the Republican agenda would do to working families was, as Kennedy had hoped, beginning to emerge as a central theme for the Democratic resistance. On March 15 Dole scheduled the striker replacement issue for debate on the Senate floor. Kennedy connected the striker replacement bill to the broader concerns of working families. "Working families," he said, "are hurting. Yet, the new Republican majority is advancing an agenda which is an assault on working families." He went on to link the striker replacement bill to cuts in college scholarships and loan programs, in day care, in the school lunch program, and in summer jobs. And in a preview of the broader debate to come, he contrasted the assault on social programs benefiting American families to the Republican tax cuts: "Only yesterday the [House] Ways and Means Committee gave tax breaks to the wealthiest individuals and corporations in the country by voting to lower the capital gains tax and effectively eliminate the minimum tax on corporations. 'No,' they say. 'It's just a coincidence that we are providing all of these tax breaks to the rich at the same time we are making all these cuts to programs for working families.' Come on.

"This," he declared, "is the first battle."

As the debate continued, Kennedy introduced the topic of the minimum wage, proposing a sense of the Senate resolution saying it should be increased. He said, "The broader issue at stake is really the standard of living for working families." Personalizing the issue, he described the plight of David Dow and his wife, who had testified at a forum Kennedy had held on the issue a week before:

> Both of them effectively make the minimum wage. Both of them work hard. They have a child. These are people that are playing by the rules. These are people that want to work, honor work, have a pride in work, want to go to school, or are trying to go to school. He is paying back $80 a month in student loans with the money he makes at the minimum wage because he wants to keep ahead so he can go back to school, but he wonders when that tide is going to take over, when it is going to push him under.
>
> Aren't we talking about providing these people, who have a wonderful opportunity as parents to love and adore their children, with

> a real opportunity to spend time with their children? Don't we have
> some responsibility to make sure that we are going to be attendant to
> their needs to care for their children?

This speech on the Senate floor was representative of speeches Kennedy made almost every day during 1995 as the Democratic resistance to the Republican Contract with America was taking shape. It demonstrated several aspects of his strategy: focus the issues on working families, highlight the specific consequences of the Republican legislative initiatives, and bring the issues back to the level of real people and how they are affected by what the Gingrich-led Republicans were trying to do.

The debate on striker replacement continued for several days. Kennedy objected to allowing a vote on final passage of legislation to repeal the president's executive order, effectively filibustering the measure. To prevail on the matter, Dole needed to file a cloture petition and gain sixty votes to end the filibuster. When the vote was held on March 15, Republicans mustered fifty-eight votes—two short. Kennedy had held all but five Democrats. Hours later Dole announced that he would withdraw the Republican bill from the floor. The Democrats had narrowly won the first two skirmishes of the war to come.

While Democrats were holding their own in the Senate, the Republicans in the House were rolling along. On March 16 they completed enactment of their version of the rescissions bill, eliminating over $17 billion in funding already appropriated in 1994 by Congress for domestic programs.

WILL THE DEMOCRATS TAKE A STAND ON EDUCATION CUTS?

The Democrats' next major stand in the Senate would be against this rescissions initiative. The resistance was picking up other allies. On March 19 Democratic senator Jay Rockefeller of West Virginia and a group of children's advocates held a rally on the steps of the Capitol. The theme of the rally was "Pick on someone your own size," and the message was that draconian Republican cuts would hurt children. That same day Hillary Clinton weighed in for the first time since the November elections with her own take on the Republican revolution. She said she would work on critical social programs and focus attention on Republican spending cuts, which she said were designed only to finance tax breaks for the very rich.

In spite of Mrs. Clinton's position, there was still uncertainty about where the Clinton administration stood. Down Pennsylvania Avenue, at the White House, the president was moving in the direction of the Republicans on the rescissions issue. He was proposing both covering the costs of the emergency spending by appropriations cuts and going beyond, to a total level of $13 billion in cuts, still short of the $17 billion the Republicans had approved in the House but nevertheless movement toward their position. He proposed rescissions at NASA, the Interior Department, the Small Business Administration, and the Federal Emergency Management Agency. Just two years earlier, in 1993, as his first legislative initiative, he had proposed a new investment and stimulus package of $35 billion for transportation, infrastructure, and other investments to strengthen the U.S. economy. Now he was negotiating with Republicans to cut billions of dollars from already appropriated funds that didn't need to be cut under the rules agreed upon in the Bush budget agreement.

Every other Wednesday the ranking members of the committees in the Senate met at lunch. On March 17 the Democratic committee leaders talked about how to respond to the rescissions package but still reached no consensus. Kennedy had asked the Labor Committee staff to draw up a list of the likely cuts to education and health programs that would be required if cuts of the magnitude Republicans had proposed were passed. We were armed with this ammunition for the staff directors meeting on March 20, as Democratic staff from the Appropriations Committee outlined the cuts in the rescissions bill that the Republicans had forced through the Committee. The bill included significant cuts to aid to disadvantaged elementary and secondary schools and most other education programs.

By now Kennedy had met with the Labor Committee and with Minority Leader Daschle several times on how Democrats should respond to the Republican agenda. There had been several caucus lunches, a ranking members lunch, and more meetings, but the Democrats still hadn't agreed on a unified strategy to resist the Republican cuts. There was considerable ambivalence within the caucus about how broadly Democrats should resist and even whether Democrats should resist at all. Ten Democrats, led by liberal senator Paul Simon of Illinois, had voted with the Republicans to enact a balanced budget amendment, and the Democrats who had opposed the amendment were being accused of resisting a balanced budget. Now, only a week later, many Democrats argued, how could they resist Republican cuts to pay for the so-called emergency appropriations?

Making matters worse, as the rescissions bill was coming to the floor, Republicans were planning a week of celebrations to mark the completion of the first hundred days of their revolution.

With the debate on the rescissions bill looming, Democratic Policy Committee director Ron Klain called a meeting in Daschle's conference room of some of the staff members who had been most active on the rescissions issue. Klain was a superman among Senate staffers. He was only thirty-five, but his career since his days at Yale Law School had included being a clerk on the Supreme Court, staff director for Senator Biden on the Judiciary Committee, and chief of staff in the Department of Justice to Attorney General Janet Reno. When Democrats lost the majority in the Senate, Klain returned to the Senate as chief of staff for Daschle on the Democratic Policy Committee, and after a year with Daschle he moved to the White House to become chief of staff to Vice President Gore (a role he was to repeat for Vice President Biden in the Obama administration). He had the capacity to be a tough-minded progressive, and we thought he had the potential for becoming a strong ally for those determined to resist the Republican juggernaut. But we weren't sure; he was more pragmatic than he was ideological. What we did know was that he was smart, politically savvy, and excellent at bringing people together and organizing positions.

Also attending the meeting was Jim English, longtime staff director for Senator Byrd on the Appropriations Committee. English was middle-aged, congenial, extremely cautious, precise, and authoritative, with an encyclopedic knowledge of the complex process of appropriations bills. If Senate rules are arcane, appropriations and budget practices are almost impenetrable. English consolidated and enhanced his power by holding his cards close to his vest and relying on technical budget jargon to leave others in the dark. It was rare for other staffers to argue with him. He always knew more than they did, and when they wanted to get something done on the Appropriations Committee, it was essential to have English as an ally. If he wasn't, they didn't succeed.

English did exactly what his boss, Senator Byrd, wanted, but he did it with a flourish and a sense of authority. Though Byrd was opposed to the rescissions, he and English were not inclined to organize a caucus-wide resistance, nor to put together a strategy on how best to convey the message that Democrats would not stand for dismantling core social programs.

John Hilley was also present at the meeting. Hilley was the most powerful staff member in the Senate, working for Daschle as he had for Mitchell. He had been an economics professor at Lafayette University in Pennsylvania before coming to the Senate to work on the Budget Committee under Senator Sasser. He spoke authoritatively, but less about Senate appropriations and budget procedure (although he was familiar with these) than about economic policy and strategy. Hilley was extremely smart but intensely pragmatic rather than ideological. He was looking for another job and had expected to go with his former boss when Mitchell was appointed commissioner of Major League Baseball, but the appointment hadn't happened. We didn't think of Hilley as an ally. As he saw it, Democrats simply weren't going to stomach resistance to Republican budget cuts so soon after the 1994 elections and just after the balanced budget amendment had been defeated. And at some level, as a Budget Committee veteran, the idea of balancing the budget probably had a certain visceral appeal for him.

Prior to the meeting, Kennedy met with his staff for one more strategy session on the rescissions bill. Carey Parker, the senator's longtime legislative director and the closest thing the senator had to an alter ego on policy, reminded us that the Republican strategy was a shell game. Their strategy was not really about emergency spending or more money for defense; it was about tax cuts they wanted to grant the wealthy and their ideological agenda of degrading the government's role in society. Kennedy suggested we focus on education, perhaps to start rallying Democrats by proposing an amendment that simply restored education funding. That suggestion was to become the basis for the Democratic strategy in the Senate. We took it to the meeting with Klain.

Klain began the meeting by saying we needed a critique of the Republicans' first hundred days, focusing on who the winners were under the Contract (big corporations and special interests feeding on tax loopholes) and the losers (children and working families). This critique was to be rolled out the following week as the hundred-day anniversary of the Republican takeover of Congress approached.

Klain then turned to the rescissions bill. Nothing had been cut from overall defense spending. The great bulk of the cuts came from domestic social programs, and billions of dollars would be added to the defense budget. Hilley turned to the Democratic strategy on the floor, emphasizing that we needed to show we were supportive of the idea of scaling back government. Klain obliquely pushed back, saying we needed to get "a little definition" for Democrats. Clayton Spencer, Kennedy's education staff director, and I added that we needed to establish what Democrats were fighting for, namely education and protecting children.

Klain quickly picked up on the theme. "Winning isn't the objective," he said. "In the House the rhetoric has been mean—slash and burn. Here, we need it to be about what we Democrats are fighting for. Let's spotlight a few specific items from all Republican states to show how they are protecting their own spending and just cutting spending that goes to education and children."

Hilley said, "We need to demonstrate that we are for cutting too. But let's focus our cuts on projects that go to Republican states. We could offer amendments to eliminate specific items that go to those states. That way we can get Democrats to support us. We're for cutting too." Hilley was still proposing a defensive agenda: showing we could cut as well as the Republicans.

As Kennedy had suggested, Spencer and I proposed an amendment simply to restore education funding and funding for children's programs. There was skepticism around the table about whether we could get Democrats to support restoring funding—even for education—but Kennedy's staff was asked to put together a list of those programs that we thought were politically popular, that Democratic senators would be willing to support, and that would provide a contrast with the Republicans.

The battle within the Democratic Party about how to respond was now joined, and the budget conservatives and liberals were each making their case. That afternoon we put together a list of programs to be restored: Drug-Free Schools, student aid, Head Start, the Women, Infants, and Children nutrition program, school reform, and national service. As events developed then and in the years since, it seems obvious that education is a powerful issue, one around which everyone would rally. But it was not so obvious in March 1995. Then the momentum was with the Republicans for cutting everything; they were even planning to eliminate the Department of Education. Protecting education spending was not a given. Some Senate Democrats thought Kennedy was suggesting drawing the lines around education because education programs were in his Committee. Why not rally around infrastructure—highways or bridges or housing?

Kennedy spoke with Daschle to urge him to go along with a strategy to restore education cuts to the rescissions bill. Education, Kennedy argued, was the right issue upon which Democrats should take a stand. We met again with Hilley a day later to go over the list. He hoped we could turn the list into an amendment to restore some of the cuts that Daschle and the Democratic leadership would offer. He appeared now to be on board with the strategy. Daschle too was ready to go along. The question was whether he could get moderate and conservative Democrats to enlist.

We had crossed an important bridge. We had a chance of an amendment to restore education funding being offered by the Democratic leadership, not just by Kennedy and the liberal Democrats on the Labor Committee. Later that day we went back to Klain to talk about the strategy. He said there was little enthusiasm for the strategy among moderates in the party, but we should press ahead with putting together an amendment for Daschle to offer.

Meanwhile Republicans in the Senate were preparing for the showdown over the rescissions bill. Majority Leader Dole made it clear that he would continue to support the cuts in the House rescissions bill and that he also favored the elimination of the Department of Education as well as the Departments of Commerce, Energy, and Housing and Urban Development. His proposal was identical to that made by House Republicans a month earlier.

By the last week in March the Senate was preparing to bring the rescissions bill to the floor, but Democrats still did not have consensus on the strategy to oppose it, despite Kennedy's and Daschle's work to develop an amendment to restore cuts to education and children's programs. On March 24 the Senate Appropriations Committee voted to cut $13.5 billion from the budget—more than twice as much as was needed to pay for emergency funding.

But off the Senate floor, the effort continued. Members of Kennedy's and Daschle's staffs worked with Byrd's staff to put together the amendment to restore education funds. They scanned the programs that the Republicans proposed to cut, picking out those that were the most popular. Daschle asked his leadership team to persuade the moderates to support the amendment. Kennedy lined up speakers from the liberal wing of the party and began talking to moderate Republican senators who might well support the effort to restore education funding. This group of Republican targets, which had always supported education funding, was small and tended to be from the Northeast: Olympia Snowe and Susan Collins from Maine, Arlen Specter from Pennsylvania, and Chafee and Jeffords. We needed at least four Republicans and all forty-six Democrats to carry the amendment. Kennedy enlisted every Democratic member of the Labor Committee to talk to these Republican targets.

Daschle thought he had an agreement with Dole to allow him to offer the amendment to restore education funds on March 30. Kennedy and his allies worked feverishly behind the scenes to line up Democratic votes for the amendment, as well as the four Republican votes needed to pass it. But that morning, when we expected to debate the Daschle amendment, Dole put off the day of reckoning by temporarily setting aside the rescissions bill and bringing up an unrelated matter involving U.S. government guarantees for financial assistance for Mexico. The debate on the Mexican issue droned on all day, precluding any chance to discuss the Daschle amendment.

Kennedy told me, "It's apparent Senator Dole is worried about the vote. He does not want us to debate and vote on the education amendment because he's not sure he can win it. Several of the moderate Republican senators must have told Senator Dole that they will vote against him to restore the education funding. He does not want to have another defeat on the floor. After losing the balanced budget vote, he can't afford to be defeated again, particularly as the House is winding up its first hundred days with a blaze of legislative activity." This was another example of Kennedy's understanding of the chemistry that was happening on the Senate floor.

Senators waited on the floor to debate the Daschle amendment late into the night on March 30. Finally, Senator Packwood, who was managing the bill on the floor, said that the Senate would stay in all that night, all the next night, and even into Saturday to finish the rescissions bill.

Dole agreed to allow Daschle to offer his amendment at 10:00 the next morning. So on March 31, Daschle, Kennedy, and other Democrats who had been scheduled to speak on the subject of the Daschle amendment came to the floor at 10:00 a.m. for the debate. Daschle offered the amendment, but immediately Dole arranged to file a first-degree and then a second-degree amendment, filling up the amendment tree and blocking Senate consideration of the Daschle amendment. Daschle and his cosponsors were not even allowed to speak in favor of the amendment, as the Senate went into a quorum call to avoid debate.

At noon Dole came to the floor and announced that he was again setting aside the rescissions bill and turning to a conference report on an unrelated matter. There would be no chance to debate and vote on the amendment.

But once again Dole provided Kennedy with an opening. The conference report that Dole brought to the floor for debate as a substitute for the rescissions bill provided tax breaks for the self-employed by allowing them to deduct 25 percent of their health insurance costs from their earnings, a proposal that was supported by members of both parties. But the conference report left out one important provision that the Senate had included in the version of the bill it had previously passed: a provision to eliminate a tax loophole for the rich so specialized that it did not benefit even the average billionaire, just the small number of billionaires who had renounced their U.S. citizenship in order to reduce their taxes. We called it the "Benedict Arnold tax loophole," after the infamous traitor. The loophole allowed an individual to renounce his U.S. citizenship, move his residence out of the country, and escape paying taxes on capital gains accrued before he left the country. Eliminating this loophole would save the Treasury $3.6 billion over five years, and a bill to do so had passed the Senate unanimously. But the House had refused to go along with the Senate, and the conference report on the self-employed tax deduction bill had restored the Benedict Arnold tax loophole.

This decision handed the Democrats another opportunity to highlight Republican priorities, and Kennedy jumped right on it. By putting a conference report on the floor that included the Benedict Arnold tax loophole, the Republicans were attempting to restore a $3.6 billion tax cut for unpatriotic billionaires at the same time they were insisting on cutting $1.3 billion from children's programs, the amount the Daschle amendment would restore. Kennedy had a field day on the floor for several hours. He was followed by Senator Simon and other Democrats who picked up on the same juxtaposition.

The Senate Democratic Policy Committee, which puts out "talking points" almost daily to help Democrats focus their message, put out a special weekend edition on March 31 entitled "GOP Blocks Votes to End

Tax Loophole for Billionaires and on Democratic Amendment to Protect Education." It read, in part:

> Today in the Senate, Republicans delayed emergency funds for California disaster relief and on the tax deduction for health care expenses of the self-employed. Why? The Republicans put off Senate action on these measures to avoid voting on Democratic proposals to end a tax loophole for billionaires and to protect more than one million children from cuts to education, nutrition and housing.
>
> We Democrats believe that education for our children should not be cut while billionaire Benedict Arnolds are allowed to escape taxation. Why won't the GOP let the Senate vote on these proposals?

Democrats now had a simple message. Some of them reveled in it.

On April 3, Senator Dole still couldn't let the education amendment come to a vote because he hadn't figured out how to handle it. On April 4, in an attempt to avoid voting on the Daschle amendment, he filed a cloture petition to cut off debate on the rescissions bill; under the rules the petition would be voted on two days later. If it passed, under the arcane rules of the Senate, the Daschle amendment would no longer be "germane" and would automatically be withdrawn.

After filing his cloture petition, Dole approached Kennedy and Daschle to discuss a compromise. He indicated that he would restore some of the funding to education and children's programs. He obviously didn't have the votes to defeat the Daschle amendment or to invoke cloture while it was pending, and he wouldn't bring the amendment to the floor if there was a chance that he would lose it.

Dole was in a bind at this point. He had arranged to announce his candidacy for president on April 10, the beginning of the Easter recess. But before he made his announcement he was determined to finish the rescissions bill in order to enhance his image as the majority leader in Washington who got things done, who was willing to cut the budget but who could also find the funds to provide emergency aid for California.

He couldn't lose a key vote on budget cuts, as he had lost the balanced budget amendment, in the days before he announced his presidential bid.

Both sides were now fully engaged in a public relations competition. While the Republicans in the House were heralding their completion of all ten items in the Contract with America within the first hundred days of the new Congress, Kennedy and other Democrats were unremitting on the Senate floor, attacking Republican priorities. Off the floor, Democrats were equally active in spreading their message. At the staff directors meeting on April 3, Daschle's staff laid out the schedule for the week of the hundredth day after the Republican takeover of Congress. There was to be a press conference with Daschle, Gephardt, and Democratic governors on April 4 condemning some of the Republican policies. On April 5 Daschle would give a speech on the "winners and losers" of the Republican legislative agenda. While Republicans were celebrating on the steps of the Capitol, Vice President Gore planned to speak about winners and losers under the Republican plan. To top it off, the president was going to be in Dallas on April 7 to wrap up the week by further driving home the winners and losers message, and he would mention that Democrats were fighting for education.

As the last week before the Easter recess began, Dole essentially conceded that he would lose the vote on the Daschle amendment. So he made several proposals to Daschle. He would restore between $500 million and $700 million in education funds cut by the rescissions bill. Daschle brought the proposal to Kennedy. Staffs examined it and analyzed which programs Dole was offering to reinstate. We concluded that $700 million wasn't enough. Dole bit the bullet and proposed restoring $800 million. After consulting with Kennedy, Daschle accepted the proposal. Dole could now avoid a vote that he knew he would lose. He could pass the rescissions bill and the emergency supplemental appropriations it included before he began the Senate recess and formally announced his presidential candidacy.

The deal, however, was contingent upon approval by both party caucuses. Daschle called a meeting of Democratic senators for April 6. It was now nine days after Dole had first introduced the rescissions bill, which he had expected to push through the Senate in no more than one or two days. Instead his plan had run into a Democratic roadblock led by Kennedy and Daschle. Together with the defeat of the balanced budget amendment and the Republican failure to override a Kennedy filibuster on labor's permanent striker replacement issue, the successful effort by Democrats to restore education funding to the rescissions bill represented the first signs of life for the Democratic resistance. Moreover the Democrats, led by Kennedy, had begun to give definition to the Republican agenda: tax breaks for the rich juxtaposed against cuts to programs for working families and particularly for education and children. Now the Democrats were meeting to discuss what they had achieved.

The proposed compromise restored $800 million for education. It represented a real victory, but nothing in the Senate is easy. Senator Mikulski, the ranking Democrat on the veterans and housing appropriations subcommittee, was concerned that housing programs were bankrolling the emergency supplemental spending bill. Others worried about their own priorities or felt the deal did not restore enough funding.

Kennedy interrupted: "We are hearing frustration in this room because the dollars cut from housing and veterans programs and even education programs—although some of them will be restored under the Daschle compromise—are already being spent in tax reductions for the rich in the House. But it is a good compromise that will restore funding already appropriated for education programs."

Senator Kerry pointed to the difficult reality of our situation: "If there aren't forty-one Democratic senators to vote against ending the filibuster on the emergency bill, then we don't have any negotiating strength to do better than what Senator Daschle has already achieved. Without forty-one votes we are in a no-deal situation." Recognizing this reality, other senators spoke in favor of the compromise. Senator Reid summed up the emerging consensus: "We should declare victory and talk about what we have restored."

After the caucus meeting the Senate reconvened. Kennedy and Daschle went to the floor again to discuss the Benedict Arnold loophole and the amendment to restore education funds. The first vote was on the Kennedy sense of the Senate Resolution to eliminate the Benedict Arnold loophole. Said Kennedy, "By voting for this resolution, we can give a clear, resounding message to the members of the Finance Committee so this egregious loophole will be closed at the next possible opportunity." At 3:05 p.m. the vote was held; it passed 96–4. John Kyle of Arizona, Connie Mack of Florida, Larry Craig of Idaho, and Phil Gramm of Texas were the only members voting against it. Next Dole offered a revised emergency spending bill that restored $800 million for education and children's programs. The Senate voted 99–0 to pass it.

REACTIONS TO THE FIRST HUNDRED DAYS OF THE REPUBLICAN REVOLUTION

On April 5 the House of Representatives approved what for Republicans was the crown jewel of the Contract with America and the last of the ten bills to implement it: a $189 billion tax cut over five years. On April 7 Gingrich spoke to the nation about the first hundred days of the Republican revolution. "Last September, the House Republicans signed a Contract with America," he said. "We signed this contract and made some promises to you and to ourselves. You elected us and for the last ninety-three days we have been keeping our word. With your help we are bringing about real change. We voted on every item in the Contract, but while we have done a lot, this Contract has never been about curing all the ills of the nation. One hundred days can't overturn a neglected decade."[2]

President Clinton was in Dallas and responded to Gingrich. It wasn't a full-blown attack. The president accepted the Republican position that the "voters [had spoken out] and demanded bold changes in the way we govern and the policies we pursue," although he said that demand for bold change was expressed in *both* his election in 1992 and the 1994 election. He described the House Republicans as "passing a series of bold initiatives" in their first hundred days and suggested his task was to temper and moderate those initiatives rather than reverse them. "In the next hundred days and beyond, the President has to . . . sift through the rhetoric and decide what is really best for America. In making these decisions, it is absolutely vital that we keep alive the spirit and momentum of change, but the momentum must not carry us so far that we betray our legacy of compassion, decency, and common sense."

Clinton used his strongest words to date in describing some of the Republican proposals, calling the Republican tax cut "a fantasy." "We have to choose," he said. "Do you want a tax cut for the wealthy or the middle class?" The House welfare reform bill was "weak on work and tough on kids." He would veto the House bills that repealed the ban on assault weapons, placed limits on lawsuits in product liability cases, and undermined protection of the environment. And he hadn't "forgotten the need to reform health care."[3]

So the first hundred days of the Republican takeover had passed. The main actors—Clinton, Gingrich, Dole, and Kennedy—had staked out their ground. Clinton was beginning to find his voice after the dark days of November and December. He wanted to work with the Republicans where he could, but not on the most extreme measures, such as the cuts to education. And he would not accept tax cuts skewed to the rich. Gingrich had passed all the elements of the Contract in the House, but they were extreme and, as it turned out, not very popular. Dole had gotten nowhere in the Senate with *any* of these measures and had lost the balanced budget amendment. He couldn't move regulatory reform because it was stalled by a filibuster over the antilabor provisions his colleagues were trying to impose. And the budget rescissions passed by the House had to be scaled back substantially in the Senate. Kennedy had laid the foundation for the attack on the Republican revolution, and he had quietly and methodically done the same for his own initiatives—the increase in the minimum wage and reforming health care—that would become the affirmative part of the Democratic resistance.

The day before the hundredth day, Education Secretary Richard Riley called Kennedy's office; the senator was out of Washington for the recess, so the secretary asked to speak to me. "Please get word to the senator about how much we appreciate what he did on the education fight," Riley said. "He led the fight, we won, and everyone agrees it was the right thing to do." Even though not every Democrat was on board and even though some of the critical elements hadn't been agreed to by the Democratic Caucus or the president, the shape of the resistance was emerging.

Chapter 13

THE CAPITOL, THE SENATE, AND THE CITY OF WASHINGTON

THE CAPITOL BUILDING: "THE NATIONAL SYMBOL OF THE DEMOCRATIC PROCESS"

After six years as a Senate staffer, I knew the Capitol and its surroundings intimately, and the majestic building had come to have a very special meaning for me. It was more than a physical structure. It stood for public service, history, and the permanent truths of U.S. representative government. By the Easter recess in April 1995, I had begun to get used to Congress being under the control of the Republicans and had adjusted to our new role as defenders of Democratic principles rather than primarily makers of new policies.

Regardless of who controlled the Senate, the Capitol remained the center of my life in Washington. Senator Byrd and Congresswoman Lindy Boggs, in their brief architectural history of the Capitol building, write that it is "the national symbol of the democratic process." I went there every day when I needed to go to the Senate floor, to meet with members of Daschle's staff, to confer with Kennedy in his Senate hideaway, to attend a press conference in a Capitol meeting room, to buttonhole senators as they came and went from the floor for votes, to meet with lobbyists, and to negotiate conference agreements with Republicans and members of the House.

The building itself was a source of endless fascination, and over time I learned something of its history. Three of our Founding Fathers who became president were involved to varying degrees in the design of the Federal City and its buildings. In 1791 President George Washington appointed a commission that initially selected the French-born architect Pierre L'Enfant, the man who created the magnificent street plan for the City of Washington. He was fired in 1792 because of delays in completing the Capitol design and because his headstrong ways had created enemies. In 1793 Washington accepted the design of amateur architect Dr. William Thorton for the small first Capitol building so that it would be ready by 1800.

A new board led by Thomas Jefferson chose the accomplished British-born architect Benjamin Latrobe, who together with Jefferson designed the southeast wing for the House of Representatives and completely rebuilt a new north wing, putting the Senate level with the House on the second, or principal, floor. The building was badly damaged by fires set by British troops in 1814.

In 1817 Latrobe departed, and President James Monroe and the board selected Charles Bulfinch, a distinguished architect from Boston who had designed the Massachusetts State House. He designed a modest rectangular building with a copper-covered wooden dome resembling an inverted teacup. The central space under the dome was the Great Rotunda, and on the south side of the Rotunda was a large ceremonial meeting hall for the House of Representatives. To the north was the original Senate chamber, a relatively dark room with windows opening only to the east. Desks enough for two senators each from approximately thirty states were crowded onto the floor of the chamber, facing an immense throne-like construction, where the vice president would preside over debates. Above the throne was a vast replica of an American eagle, and the throne itself was draped in deep red velvet curtains. The grandeur of this throne seemed more fitting for a European monarch than for the presiding officer of the upper chamber of the first modern democratic republic, but perhaps it represented the Founders' conception of the Senate as a body filled with an aristocracy of talent, if not of birth. Ringing the semicircular back end of the room was a narrow balcony where spectators could observe the debates below.

In the basement of the Capitol building, underneath the old Senate chamber, was another room, the same size and shape as the Senate chamber but with a very low ceiling. This was the meeting place for the Supreme Court. Originally the seats for the nine justices were along a table to the east end of the room, and tables for counsel who would argue before the Court were arrayed facing the judges. The physical space suggests that, when the building was designed, the Supreme Court was not expected to be an equal third branch of the government; the Senate and House were the centerpieces of the Capitol, while the Supreme Court was relegated to the basement. It took Chief Justice John Marshall and years of Court decisions establishing the power of the Court to interpret the Constitution and overrule legislation passed by Congress or actions of the executive branch to establish the Court as an equal third branch. By 1850 the Supreme Court had moved to its own impressive building to the east of the Capitol, across 1st Street.

By the 1850s the Congress and its workload had outgrown the space available in the original Capitol, and plans were made to add two new wings—one to the north to hold a new Senate chamber and one to the south for the House. Ringing these chambers would be numerous offices and ceremonial spaces. The Supreme Court briefly occupied the old Senate chamber, and the old House chamber became part of the ceremonial Hall of Statues. The current magnificent dome was also constructed when the wings were added, although work was postponed during the height of the Civil War.

Both the old Senate chamber and the original Supreme Court chamber have been restored and are visited by tourists, and the old Senate chamber has been used for ceremonial occasions and for when the Senate needs absolute secrecy for its proceedings; for example, the entire Senate crowded into its old chamber in 1999 to discuss procedures for the upcoming impeachment trial of President Clinton. The debate over procedure was heated and rancorous and appeared likely to be resolved strictly on partisan lines—making what was already a national embarrassment even worse. But an unlikely pair, hard-edged conservative Phil Gramm and Ted Kennedy, stepped outside the historic room and developed a compromise that secured the support of all one hundred senators.

THE CONTEMPORARY SENATE

The center of my life in the Capitol was the new Senate chamber. Constructed at the time of the Civil War, it is a large, relatively plain rectangular room. Desks for individual senators, looking like desks for schoolchildren in the nineteenth century, are arrayed in a semicircle facing the elevated seat of the Senate president. The floor is slightly raked so that the desks in the back are higher than the desks in the front row. A representation of the Senate chamber has been constructed and can be visited at the Edward M. Kennedy Institute for the Senate, next to the JFK Presidential Library in Boston.

In front of the Senate president's desk and below that front row of senators' desks is an open space, the "well," where senators often mingle during votes. Their votes are recorded at a desk in the well, in front of and below the Senate president's desk. Against the wall behind the senators' desks are rows of benches where staff members sit.

Desks of Democratic senators are to the right as one looks out from the Senate president's chair, and desks for Republicans are to the left. The desks designated for Republican and Democratic senators are moved from side to side of the aisle to reflect the changing partisan balance that results from the most recent election. Just off the Senate floor, behind the Republican side of the room, is the Republican cloakroom, and behind the Democrats' side is the Democratic cloakroom. The cloakroom is where senators retreat when they want to have conversations with colleagues from their own party.

I was always in a state of wonder when I was actually working on the Senate floor. Access was guarded very carefully. If you didn't have the proper credentials, you simply could not get on the floor. Occasionally, during a Senate recess, I brought visitors to the floor by taking them to the Democratic cloakroom or through the lobbying room in order to show them Kennedy's desk. I would open the top to show them copies of old speeches and Senate rules. If I pulled out the drawer and moved the papers out of the way, the signature of John F. Kennedy was visible, scratched in the wood. It has been the tradition of senators down through history to scratch their names in the wood of the drawers of their desks when they left the Senate, and Senator Kennedy had chosen to use his brother's desk. Only senators are allowed to sit at these desks. When Carey Parker, Kennedy's long-serving legislative director, first went to the floor as a new staffer in 1968, he was unaware of the rule and plopped down in Kennedy's chair. When Kennedy snapped, "Get out of that chair," Carey, thoroughly flustered, sprang to his feet, and the senator continued, deadpan, "That's my chair. My father bought it for me, and no one else gets to sit in it!" Then he broke into a broad grin.

Being on the floor of the Senate when it is in session is a memorable experience. Staff members are not allowed into the well. Instead they sit on benches at the rear of the chamber or on small, low chairs next to the desk of whatever senator is speaking or waiting to speak on the floor. The placement of these chairs enables the staff member to hand briefing papers and other materials to the senator as he or she prepares a statement and allows the senator to consult with the staff member during debates.

Sitting next to a senator who is engaged in a heated debate brings a combination of pleasure at being involved and anxiety that the senator will turn to you with a pressing question that you can't answer. Staff members are silent bit players on the C-SPAN telecasts of the floor debate; they are often included in the picture of the senator addressing the floor—not because the senator intended for staff members to appear in the picture but because it is often impossible to get the senator in the picture and not the staff member as well. There are different theories about the proper demeanor for staff members in this position. Should they look with admiration as their senator speaks (the dutiful spouse pose)? Should they be deeply engaged in thumbing through papers, occupied in assisting the senator with important points he or she is making during the debate (the essential advisor stance)? Or should they sit blankly, staring straight ahead, to emphasize that the senator is the star player and totally able to carry the debate on his or her own (nonessential prop effect)?

Kennedy staffers often had an additional role—chart master. The charts were large, about 4'x3'. They were produced—overnight if necessary—by the Senate printing office according to our instructions, which usually called for simple messages or graphs, a primitive form of Powerpoint. Kennedy was a pioneer in the use of charts in Senate floor speeches. The charts served several purposes: they were visual illustrations of the senator's arguments (positioned near him, they stayed in the C-SPAN camera shot); they also served as mnemonics to help structure his remarks when he spoke extemporaneously, which he preferred to do during floor debates. When the senator spoke repeatedly on the same topic—like the minimum wage—the number of charts would grow and grow. Others used charts, but Kennedy used them more extensively than any other senator. A staffer would carry many charts to the floor and spend his or her time feverishly anticipating which chart to display, while ducking in and out of the camera's view. The charts were also used to present enlarged photographs. A famous example was a blown-up picture of a foot that had been severely burned and scarred by a cosmetic that had not been approved by the FDA.

Usually only one staffer at a time can sit beside a senator. Remaining staff are relegated to chairs behind the rail in the back corners, Republicans on one side, and Democrats on the other. At the beginning of my tenure, there were large, soft leather chairs and couches at the back of the Senate utilized by senators and staff alike. But when television was introduced on the Senate floor, Senator Byrd thought the image of staff members sprawled out on leather furniture was not consistent with the dignity of the Senate. The comfortable chairs were replaced by backless wooden benches with rather thin red velvet padding on the seats, and a railing was put in front of the benches, ostensibly to cover women's legs but also perhaps to emphasize that the staff were not senators but an entirely separate and inferior species.

For important bills involving many senators, staff would be packed along the bench behind the rail like athletes waiting to be summoned by the coach. When their senator came up to the rail, the appropriate staff members leaped to attention from the bench. The goal is for staff to be at the rail so the senator does not have to wait, which means you rush to get up as soon as you see your senator coming back to the rail. Heaven forbid you ever get there early when the senator actually wants to talk to another staffer; then you would need to slink back to your spot on the bench as another staff member answered the call. Except when they are conversing directly with their senators, staff are required to remain seated on the bench. Senate door-keeping staff are constantly monitoring their conduct, keeping them seated, keeping their conversations to a minimum and to a whisper, and closing the floor when the bench becomes too crowded.

The voting process in the Senate is steeped in tradition. Each senator must actually be present on the floor to cast a vote. Since there are as many as ten to twenty votes in a given day, senators are constantly traveling to the Capitol from their offices and from hearing rooms sprinkled around the Senate office buildings.

When a vote is taken, one of the clerks seated below the Senate president's chair calls out the name of each senator alphabetically. Senators often have no idea which bill or amendment is under consideration. They go immediately to the well, where the floor staffs are seated at a small table directly below the clerk and the parliamentarian. The floor staff for each side prepares descriptions of every amendment and keeps a running tally of the votes. As senators arrive on the floor, they first study the statement of the amendment provided by their party's floor staff, then look to see how their colleagues have voted already, and in due course cast their vote by approaching the well and whispering, by calling out "Yay" or "Nay," or by catching the eye of the clerk and indicating their vote with a thumbs-up or thumbs-down. At the end of the reading of the names, the clerk reads off all the votes: "Voting in the affirmative—Mr. Akaka, Mr. Baucus, Mr. Biden. . . . Voting in the negative—Mr. Abraham, Mr. Ashcroft, Mr. Bennett. . . ."

The rules allow senators to change their vote after it has been cast, as long as the voting is still open. In close votes, lots of cajoling goes on, usually in the area of the well. The leaders of each party can be seen in feverish discussions with individual senators prior to their casting their vote. The floor manager for the bill also engages in discussions with individual senators about the matter on which they are being asked to vote. One of the jobs of staff members is to keep them advised of the upcoming votes and to let them know the staff recommendation on how they should vote. Most often senators simply vote with their party, but there are many issues on which they break ranks, and there are also many issues on which the party simply doesn't have a position. When elections are approaching, senators in a tight race will sometimes withhold their vote until the outcome is clear. If their vote will make no difference, they usually have the approval of the party leadership to vote with the side that will help them with their constituency, no matter what the party position is.

It is during these votes that the senators conduct much of their most important business. We would always give Kennedy a folder of cards indicating which senator he should try to meet on the floor and have a discussion with, either to get support for a piece of legislation or to plan some activity that the senators would advance in cooperation with each other. There were also cards with talking points for individual senators, which Kennedy often left with them as a summary of the points he'd made and the action requested.

Kennedy was very dedicated to the job of kibitzing with individual senators and used his time on the floor extremely productively. He would wait at his desk, looking at the prime entry area to the Senate off the elevators, and when he spotted a senator with whom he needed to talk, he would pounce. If it was a complicated matter or one that he wanted to discuss in private, he would bring the senator over to any open desk, sit next to his colleague and discuss the matter while the vote was going on.

During a vote, there is often much hilarity and joshing. Most senators enjoy each other's company. They have particular friends among their colleagues, and they always look forward to a good laugh or a good discussion when they see the senators on the floor waiting for or during a vote. Kennedy kept his desk in the back row so that he could easily slip off the floor without being noticed and so that he was not the focal point of attention in the front row.

He had great fun sitting next to Senators Dale Bumpers and Bill Bradley. Senator Dodd, his great friend, was seated just below. From the back row he had easy access to staff, to the cloakroom, and to telephones, and despite his seniority it never occurred to him to move forward.

Except for voting, senators come to the floor only if they intend to participate personally in the debate, which usually means that during a run-of-the-mill debate there are only a few senators on the floor. The television cameras are arranged to focus directly on the senator who is speaking or, when a vote is going on, to focus on the area of the well and the Senate president's desk and chair. At no time during a debate do the TV cameras pan across the chamber. If they did, most times they would show that it was virtually empty. I was always greatly amused to watch senators standing at their desks with a microphone on their lapel gesticulating as if their colleagues were rapt in attention, packed into the chamber. "My brother, my sister, my colleague from so-and-so," senators would declaim with arms waving to the nearly empty chamber, as if across the room was that very colleague, listening intently, preparing to respond at any moment. The audience at home would never know the chamber was empty, and perhaps that was not entirely misleading, because senators occasionally listened to the debates back in their offices.

The exception to this rule of the generally empty chamber is in the later hours of debate on a big bill, when successive amendments are voted on within a relatively short period of time—so that there is no reason for members to go back to their offices—and there is typically lively debate between proponents and opponents. It is at these times that the Senate truly comes alive, particularly if it is nighttime, when there are no competing hearings, schedules are open, and members are most relaxed.

In the corner of the Senate on the Democratic side is a large desk with a phone. Senators can use the phone as long as they speak very quietly. A drawer in the desk is filled with hard candy, candy kisses, and other bite-size sweets. Senators with a sweet tooth or needing a shot of energy are constantly walking over to look for candy. They occasionally leave cash in the drawer, which the cloakroom staff use to replenish the candy. David Nexon was one of the few staffers bold or hungry enough to dip into the senators' candy jar. He'd been around long enough and was well enough liked by the senators and floor staff that they generally turned a blind eye to this breach of decorum.

Just off the floor, guarding the entrances, are the Capitol Police and other Senate staff who check the credentials of everybody before they enter the floor. Clustered off the floor and throughout the Senate wing are the offices of the secretary of the Senate, the sergeant at arms, and functionaries who run the finances, the proceedings, and the daily activities of the Senate, forming something of a community unto themselves.

The area of the Ohio clock, just outside the senators' only entrance on the south side of the floor, is famous in Senate lore for a number of reasons, not least because a group called the Armed Resistance Unit placed a bomb there in 1983 to protest U.S. military involvement in Lebanon and Grenada. When the bomb went off, it shattered the face of the clock, blew off the door of Majority Leader Byrd's office, and punched a large hole in the wall of the Republican cloakroom. Fortunately, the bomb went off at 10:38 p.m., when the area was deserted. The area under the Ohio clock is also famous among Senate reporters as the scene of regular press availabilities for the two party leaders and many impromptu press conferences of other senators.

Along the walls around the area of the Ohio clock are arrayed busts and portraits, primarily vice presidents of the United States. In 1994 there were busts of Vice Presidents Ford, Rockefeller, Mondale, and Bush. There was no bust of Spiro Agnew, who resigned as vice president under Nixon as part of a plea bargain with the U.S. Attorney's Office in Maryland. He had been investigated for accepting envelopes stuffed with cash bribes—payoffs for awarding public building contracts while he was Baltimore County executive and later Maryland's governor. He even accepted payoffs for previous conduct after becoming vice president. Nixon appointed Gerald Ford to succeed Agnew, and, of course, Ford ultimately became president himself when Nixon was forced to resign as a result of the Watergate investigations.

Shortly after Republicans took control of the Congress in 1995, I learned that a committee of Republicans had commissioned a bust of Agnew and that it would be installed in the vice presidents' gallery. I remember thinking that I should tape an envelope filled with cash to the bust. In any event, the Agnew bust was installed, despite the fact that he resigned in disgrace.

Hideaways are private offices hidden throughout the Capitol building that are assigned to members of the Senate, largely on the basis of seniority. They give senators a convenient place to work or meet when they want to stay close to the floor. Tucked away off back corridors, they are almost impossible for an outsider to find.

Kennedy had a plum hideaway on the third floor of the Capitol, behind an unmarked door next to a narrow corridor leading to the Senate library. The room was small, probably ten feet by twenty. It had a fireplace, which was directly above Dole's fireplace on the floor below, and Kennedy used to joke that if he ever needed to get Dole's attention he could block up the chimney and smoke him out of his office. The British allegedly used the fireplace in 1812 to light the torches with which they set the White House on fire. I don't know if the story is true, but the senator told it to almost everyone who visited him in the hideaway.

The room was painted dark green and featured portraits and memorabilia of the Kennedy family. There were pictures of Kennedy with his children, a newspaper clipping from the *Providence Journal* from the day his son Patrick was elected to Congress, and several extraordinary portraits. Over the fireplace was a portrait of the senator's oldest brother, Joseph P. Kennedy, who was killed in World War II, and over the sofa was a portrait of his grandfather, "Honey Fitz." On the desk were pictures of the senator with President John Kennedy and with Attorney General Robert Kennedy.

A significant attraction of the Kennedy hideaway was the view from one of its windows down the Mall, past the National Gallery and the Air and Space Museum, to the Washington Monument, the Lincoln Memorial, Arlington National Cemetery, and the Robert E. Lee house, rising on the hill beyond the cemetery in the distance. The senator enjoyed this room because it was absolutely private and very convenient for meetings when he needed to be ready to return quickly to the Senate floor for a speech, a debate, or a vote. It was around the corner from the press gallery, so we also used it for briefings and meetings prior to press conferences.

Because of his relationship with Senator Kennedy, the hideaway had a special meaning for Senator Hatch, and he was pleased that his seniority in the Senate allowed him to claim it after the senator's death.

THE CITY

Beyond the Capitol and the grounds and offices surrounding it lies the city of Washington. The experience of living and working in the city was a central factor in my life. I would take visitors first to the Jefferson Memorial and then to the Lincoln Memorial. One can understand American history by reading the inscriptions carved on these two memorials. On the Jefferson Memorial, Jefferson's words from the Declaration of Independence proclaim the idealism and hope of the founders of the United States: "We hold these truths to be self-evident: that all men are created equal; that they are endowed by their Creator with certain inalienable rights; that among these are the right to life, liberty, and the pursuit of happiness."

Then we would climb the great stairs leading to the statue of Lincoln and the temple in which it sits. On the left-hand wall is inscribed the Gettysburg Address: "Four score and seven years ago, our fathers brought forth on this continent, a new nation, conceived in Liberty, and dedicated to the proposition that all men are created equal." Lincoln's words speak to the difficulty of achieving the idealistic goals set out by Jefferson. To Lincoln, Jefferson's "self-evident" truth was only a proposition, a matter being put to the test by the great Civil War and still to be proven. Lincoln acknowledged that there was still some doubt whether America could live up to the high ideals Jefferson had set for it. That struggle to reach those ideals has been the great struggle of America, the unfinished business of the country.

Chapter 14

EXPOSING THE REPUBLICAN BUDGET BEFORE LABOR DAY

The first four months of 1995 had been tumultuous, but the months that followed were more crucial. The president had been persuaded not to give away too much ground in his first budget, but how he would ultimately respond to the Republican challenge was not yet known. We had put the Republicans on the political defensive over the cuts in their rescissions bill, but the fight over the bill had not ended. And the rescissions bill was just the curtain-raiser for the main act: the regular appropriations for fiscal year 1996. While the ten legislative items in the Contract with America had cleared the House, Senate action on most was still pending. The struggle over Medicare and other entitlements, tax cuts, and the deficit had not even really begun. We were still a long way from a government shutdown, but the threat was starting to loom.

THE BUDGET AND APPROPRIATIONS PROCESS

Through the Easter recess, the struggle against the Republican agenda had been a two-front war against the legislation growing out of the Contract with America and the Republican rescissions bill. Kennedy and others had also sought to link the Republicans' plans to cut taxes and balance the budget simultaneously to a pending assault on Medicare, but absent specific Republican proposals, it was hard to get traction on this issue.

In May, however, the full scope of the Republican budget proposals began to emerge, and Kennedy once again pressed the Democrats to unite in a forceful response. To follow the chain of events that culminated in the two government shutdowns—the so-called train wreck that ultimately derailed the Republican revolution—a short digression to explain the mechanics of the budget process might be helpful.

Three types of legislation related to the budget played a significant part in the process leading to the shutdown: the budget resolution, the appropriations bills, and the budget reconciliation bill. The budget resolution began to shape the debate, but the actual shutdown was the result of a prolonged clash over two types of legislation: the annual appropriations bills and the so-called "reconciliation" bill. Had the Republicans been successful in forcing the president to sign reconciliation and appropriations bills to their liking—or even achieving a compromise that acceded to a significant share of their budgetary and other demands—the revolution would have had a very different ending.

The budget resolution is a blueprint of how the government will raise and spend money over the next year and for a specified number of years to follow. It is normally passed in the spring and is subject to special rules: debate is limited, so it can't be filibustered, and the types of amendments are also limited. While the budget resolution is important, it does not have the force of law. It is not subject to presidential signature or veto, and it is only a self-imposed guide for congressional action. By including amounts by which Medicare was assumed to be cut and taxes were to be reduced, the budget resolution began the linkage of the two issues, but actual legislation to make specific changes to Medicare and to the tax laws still had to be passed by Congress and signed by the president.

The two types of budget-related bills that do have the force of law are the appropriations bills and the reconciliation bill. Broadly speaking, these also relate to three types of programs: discretionary programs, mandatory ("entitlement") programs, and revenue programs (taxes). Discretionary programs are subject to year-to-year appropriations of funds. If no funds are appropriated for the year, the program, even if authorized by law, can't operate because the government has no authority to spend funds to run it. The total amount of appropriations is capped by the budget resolution, but the appropriations committees decide how to allocate money within that cap. And the cap can be ignored by Congress if it chooses. In a mechanical sense, it was the failure of the Congress to pass the needed appropriations bills into law that caused the government shutdown.

Funding is automatic for mandatory programs. For example, Medicare is an entitlement program. Every individual meeting certain conditions is eligible to receive health benefits spelled out in the law and to have those benefits paid for by the government. That entitlement is not subject to the appropriations process, and changes in benefits, eligibility, or payments to providers have to be made by changes to the Medicare law itself. The same is true of the taxes collected by the government. If taxes are to be cut—by lowering the rate on capital gains, for example—a specific change in the law needs to be made.

Congress can make changes to entitlement programs or the tax laws at any time by passing legislation. But the reconciliation bill, which can be authorized only by the budget resolution, offers a much easier route to making these changes than the normal legislative process. The budget resolution may include reconciliation instructions—changes to mandatory spending or revenue targets—to committees in each house of Congress with jurisdiction over mandatory spending or revenue. The committees are then supposed to report back specific program changes to achieve those goals. The committees' reported legislative changes are then packaged into the full reconciliation bill that goes to the floor of the two houses for action. If there are differences between the bills passed by each house, a conference committee resolves the differences and the conference report then goes to each house for passage and transmittal to the president. The advantages of a reconciliation bill—or its defects, if you are opposed to it—are that it can't be filibustered, it can be passed by a simple majority of the Senate, and amendments are subject to strict limitations.

Unlike the appropriations bills, the government doesn't shut down if a reconciliation bill doesn't pass. In fact failure to pass a reconciliation bill has no consequence except that the changes to entitlement programs and taxes contained in the bill are not made. But because the reconciliation bill was the vehicle for such a large share of the fundamental changes to government the Republicans hoped to accomplish, the Republican strategy called for using the threat of a government shutdown as a lever to force the president into a "grand bargain" to accept not only their draconian cuts to discretionary programs but their tax cuts and assault on Medicare and Medicaid as well.

RALLYING DEMOCRATS TO PROTECT MEDICARE: MAY 1995

One issue that Republicans did not emphasize during the first hundred days was the fate of Medicare. Medicare was not even mentioned in the Contract with America.

Kennedy and some of the leading Democratic pollsters, particularly Mark Mellman, believed that the Republicans were most vulnerable on what their budget-cutting strategy would do to senior citizens and to the Medicare services upon which they relied. The Republican tax cut of over $200 billion, coupled with their pledge to balance the budget, was well understood in Washington—but not in the country at large—to mean large cuts to Medicare. The question was how to translate that into a powerful issue that senior citizens and the rest of the country would understand.

By the time the House and Senate adjourned for the Easter recess, Democrats had shown that by sticking together and focusing on a specific issue they could succeed at least in stalling the Republican juggernaut. This strategy had worked with education and protecting striking workers, but there was no consensus yet among Democrats on what should be the next place to push back. Considering the central place that Medicare would eventually have in the Democratic resistance—it was the issue that ultimately hurt the Republicans more than any other—it may be surprising that for the first several months of 1995, many Democrats and the White House had not even settled on a strategy to resist the large cuts to Medicare that we knew the Republicans were going to propose and the fundamental changes they hoped would cause the program to "wither on the vine," in Gingrich's words. We had at least preserved our ability to fight back, however, because the president had not conceded any key ground in the budget he presented in February.

Gingrich made it official on May 7, announcing that cuts to Medicare would be included in the Republican budget resolution: $283 billion in cuts were assumed in the House budget resolution, which passed the House on May 18; $250 billion in the Senate, which passed on May 25. The final budget resolution agreed to by the conference committee and passed by the Congress on June 29 provided for $270 billion in Medicare cuts and $245 billion in tax cuts. On *Meet the Press*, Gingrich said the cuts wouldn't affect seniors because the Republican plan would encourage recipients to enter into less expensive health plans and reduce waste and fraud. What he didn't say was that the only way the Republicans could finance their tax cuts and still get to a balanced budget was through big cuts to Medicare.

Beyond the need to finance their tax cuts, the Republican leadership harbored a special animus toward Medicare as a huge, popular, and effective program that by its very existence seemed to rebuke their antigovernment ideology. (Although Gingrich had indeed said his goal was to have Medicare "wither on the vine," he subsequently claimed he was talking about the Health Care Financing Administration—the agency that administered Medicare—rather than the program itself.)

Republican leaders were well aware that Medicare could be a political minefield. In the same way that Gingrich had honed the language in the Contract for maximum political appeal, he counseled Republicans not to use "cut" and "Medicare" in the same sentence. Republicans should speak of "saving Medicare" because the program cuts they were proposing would postpone the projected date at which the Medicare trust fund would run out of money. By the same token, Medicare cuts were not cuts; they were reductions in the rate of growth. Republican proposals to open the program more broadly to private insurance companies and pay them higher rates were to be described as expanding people's options rather than transforming the program.

Technically these arguments were not entirely false. The Medicare cuts were reductions from baseline or current law spending. This is the spending that would occur without any changes in the law as the result of medical care cost inflation and increased program enrollment. This is the way cuts have historically been measured. So the Republican cuts would not reduce spending below the 1995 level, but they would be cuts in the normal use of the term in Washington. More importantly, not only would they mean fewer resources for doctors and hospitals to care for Medicare beneficiaries, but the Republican plan would have imposed significantly greater financial burdens on seniors already struggling to pay medical costs that Medicare didn't fully cover.

It is also true that the Medicare Part A trust fund—the part of the program that pays for hospital care—was projected to run out of money at some point, 2002 under the annual projections at that time by the Medicare program trustees. But the trustees' report had projected early bankruptcy for the program a number of times in the past, and the projections had proved erroneous or Congress had taken steps to make sure bankruptcy didn't occur. In fact, two decades after the Republican predictions of bankruptcy, the Trust Fund is still paying the promised benefits and still solvent. Moreover, Part B of the program—the part that pays for physician care and other outpatient services—is financed by a combination of general revenues and beneficiary premiums and can't ever become bankrupt. But the Republican cuts were directed at both parts of the program.

Finally, the changes the Republicans proposed to open the program up more broadly to private insurance plans were based on the argument that private plans could deliver care less expensively than Medicare and beneficiaries would choose to join them, eventually eliminating the traditional program. But the Republicans tried to stack the deck in favor of the private plans, and enrollees in private plans would have lost key protections that beneficiaries enjoyed under traditional Medicare, such as prohibitions against providers charging them more than their insurance would pay. And if enough providers dropped out of Medicare to participate in private plans, Medicare would no longer be a realistic alternative for beneficiaries.

So the Republican arguments were tenuous at best.

The Republican raid on Medicare became an especially powerful issue for Democrats. Not only did Medicare enjoy broad and deep popular support, as the political war over the Gingrich revolution was to unfold, the rough symmetry between the $245 billion in tax cuts and the $270 billion in Medicare cuts became a huge political vulnerability—one of the biggest mistakes the Republicans would make. Democrats now had a giant opening to argue that not only were the Republican cuts to Medicare cruel and unfair; Republicans were carrying out this wrongheaded policy in order to fund tax breaks for the wealthy.

In early May I met with Ron Klain to discuss organizing the Democratic resistance around Medicare. Klain had already been thinking along the same lines. He advised that we make clear to the public how Medicare cuts would affect each senior citizen. He also said we needed to engage hospitals in the fight, since hospitals received the largest share of Medicare spending and it was unlikely that the Republican targets for cutting could be hit without taking a significant chunk out of hospital revenues.

We had to address the argument that Medicare would be bankrupt by 2002 if we didn't adopt the Republican program. And we had to distinguish between the different components of Medicare, since, as noted earlier, the whole solvency issue was irrelevant to Part B.

When Republicans returned to their districts during the Easter recess, they heard from constituents that Medicare cuts were not popular. In Washington, Gingrich tried to obtain a commitment from President Clinton for a bipartisan effort to restructure Medicare. Clinton asserted that Republicans had to first establish how deep the proposed cuts would be. Gingrich replied, "We are going to put Medicare into a separate box. Every penny saved in Medicare should go to Medicare. It should not be entangled in the budget debate." Of course, for budget purposes, everything is fungible. Gingrich wanted to shift the onus for the attack on Medicare away from the Republican Party by getting the president to agree, in advance, that the program needed to be cut and restructured, but the president was too canny to oblige, at least at that early stage.

The Senate came back into session after the Easter recess on April 25. The Republicans kept moving forward with their effort to roll back government regulations in the areas of the environment, health, and worker safety. Despite vocal Democratic opposition, Hatch moved Dole's so-called "regulatory reform" bill through the Judiciary Committee. The bill would tie up federal agencies seeking to issue rules to protect workers, consumers, or the environment in a mass of red tape; repeal prohibition of cancer-causing chemicals in processed foods; eliminate certain environmental regulations; and scale back rules on occupational safety and health. Republicans had given free rein to the lobbyists from the corporations to write the laws that would deregulate their industries.

At the staff meeting on April 24, Democrats struggled to shape their message. Mellman briefed us on the results of his recent poll, which indicated that the public perceived the Democratic Party as a failure. Even if the Democrats believed in the right thing, they couldn't get it done. People weren't following what was happening with the Contract with America, didn't yet fully understand its substance, and thought the Republicans should be given a chance. The poll showed that people believed the Republicans were for the rich and the Democrats for the poor, but no one was on the side of the average person.

In more encouraging news, however, the poll showed that many thought the Republican budget cuts were going too far too fast, that the budget deficit and deficit reduction were more important than tax cuts, and that while the public wanted to deal with the budget deficit, specific cuts weren't popular. Either way, though, the public didn't think Democrats were capable of cutting spending.

The public wanted education funding protected and particularly liked the idea of tax deductibility for college loans. Medicare was "off limits"; there simply should not be cuts to services or increases in copayments or deductibles. There was a strong public reaction against lobbyists and big corporations taking advantage of the tax code and having special access to legislation. The poll showed that people believed the economy was getting better, but they worried about their jobs being moved overseas by big corporations. They thought the current tax system wasn't fair, and they wanted tax credits for education, children, and housing. They trusted the Democrats more on education and Medicare, and the Republicans more on the economy and budget cutting.

Mellman advised the Democrats to form an agenda that protected working people against greedy corporations, a message along the lines of "I won't let this go through because we need to protect the middle class against the Republican propensity to give to the greedy rich and greedy corporations. Democrats should fight against greed and to protect jobs from overseas slave labor, to strengthen education and health care, worker protections, and the minimum wage."

On May 4 the White House held a conference on aging and used the occasion to raise the issue of Medicare. Clinton asserted, "I will not support proposals to slash these programs, to undermine their integrity, to pay for tax cuts for people who are well off." The contours of the Medicare debate were being defined.[1]

THE STRUGGLE OVER THE RESCISSIONS
BILL FINALLY ENDS: MAY 1995

The Republicans finally passed the rescissions bill on May 17, and President Clinton promptly vetoed it. As Kennedy had advised, he focused on the education cuts. These cuts were deeper than the compromise reached in the Senate as a result of negotiations in the conference committee.

The president's decision to veto the bill was complicated by the fact that there had been a bipartisan negotiation in the conference committee and nine Senate Democrats had signed the conference report. Kennedy had helped strengthen the president's spine by rounding up enough pledges from Senate Democrats to assure the White House that the veto would not be overridden. A revised bill finally passed on July 17 and was signed by the president on July 27. The final bill restored funds for education, job training, child care, and the environment, but large cuts remained in many other areas.

THE NEXT BATTLE OVER EDUCATION: MAY 1995

Despite the beating they were taking over the cuts to education in the rescissions bill, Republicans hadn't learned their lesson about the power of the education issue. So when they began to move the budget resolution for fiscal year 1996 through the House and Senate, it still included large reductions in federal education spending. Members of the House and Senate, including Dole, were still advocating the elimination of the Department of Education.

Kennedy arranged a meeting of White House, Department of Education, and congressional staff to talk about the proposed education cuts. Everyone agreed that there would be no unilateral disarming on the issue. Democrats would not allow student debt for college to be increased. We would continue to emphasize that Republicans were cutting education to pay for tax cuts for the rich. We would not accept limiting access to college or cutting back on dollars for schools. We would not make it more difficult for the children of working families to succeed in school and college. We would not turn our backs on America's future. It was a very simple theme, and we would say it over and over again: We would not abandon education to pay for tax cuts to the rich.

When Kennedy picked up this theme in a speech on the floor on May 10, Senator Chafee also happened to be on the floor, so it fell to him to respond. In the 1960s Chafee was a reform-minded, liberal Republican governor of Rhode Island. In fact, as I described earlier, I had campaigned for him myself and actually managed one of his campaigns after I graduated from law school. In 1972 he had been elected to the Senate. As a moderate Republican, he must have been more uncomfortable with each passing year as he had to cast votes in agreement with conservative Republicans. On education, abortion, legal services, the environment, and a whole series of other progressive issues, he and Kennedy thought alike, and Chafee could usually be counted on to vote with the Democrats.

By 1971 and 1972, I was far enough away from Rhode Island and firm enough in my dislike of President Nixon's policy on the Vietnam War that I registered in New York City as a Democrat, and, needless to say, that is what I have been ever since. I suspect Senator Chafee had wondered sometimes if he too should have been a Democrat. But I have always had a connection and friendship with Senator Chafee, so I felt a particular familiarity with both participants in discussions or debates between him and Senator Kennedy.

Despite Chafee's and Kennedy's similar views on many issues and their genuine liking for each other, there was a certain uneasiness in their relationship. It was competitive, and they both seemed to enjoy directing barbed remarks to each other. Harvard (Kennedy) versus Yale (Chafee). Irish versus Yankee. Two New England senators, Democrat versus Republican. Kennedy's son Patrick had been elected to Congress from Rhode Island in October 1994, and Chafee undoubtedly saw him as a political rival, possibly even a future opponent for the Senate.

When Chafee died in 1999, he was replaced by his son, Lincoln Chafee, who was appointed to the seat by the Republican governor Lincoln Almond. Before following his father into politics, Lincoln Chafee worked as a farrier. He was a moderate Republican and a somewhat shy man who did not mingle with the more right-wing members of his party. They did not talk to him while he was waiting between votes on the floor, so he was often sitting alone at his desk. After several months, I discovered that Kennedy would frequently wander over and sit next to him on the Republican side of the aisle and talk to him. I suspect Kennedy knew how he must have felt and reached out to him as a kindness. After Lincoln Chafee lost his Senate seat, he restarted his political career in Rhode Island and was elected governor in 2010 as an Independent. He later became a Democrat.

I remember John Chafee coming to Kennedy's office to talk about health care in 1993 and 1994. He was very interested in some of the mementos that Kennedy collected and had on display. One was an antique rake used by cranberry workers to rake cranberries from a bog. It was a heavy wooden box with an open bottom and a handle with a row of long needle-like fingers protruding along the edge of the opening. The berry pickers would drag the rake underneath the cranberry bushes, scraping the berries into the box when the rake was pulled up. It would have been hard, backbreaking labor. Chafee admired the rake and inquired about it. "That's what your ancestors had mine working with in the cranberry bogs," Kennedy joked. They both laughed, Chafee a bit uneasily.

Back on the Senate floor, Chafee felt bound to defend the Republicans against Kennedy's attacks. He tried to turn the question of the education cuts around by talking about the need to balance the budget and the failure of the Democrats to come up with an alternative. He said, "I do not believe we can continue on the [deficit] path we are on, which consists of sending the bills to our children. I think it is immoral."

Kennedy shot back that it was hard to understand how we were protecting our children when we were increasing the indebtedness of students going on to higher education by 25 or 30 percent. He described the Republican concern with balancing the budget as hypocritical when they refused to look at cutting corporate welfare and had refused to support the deficit cuts included in Clinton's economic program.

THE BUDGET RESOLUTION CONFERENCE REPORT FINALLY PASSES: JUNE 1995

After a month of negotiations, the Republicans in the House and Senate finally resolved their differences over the budget resolution. The conference report was adopted by both houses on June 19. It largely split the difference between the two and left the basic structure of the original House proposal intact. It provided for very large cuts in domestic programs, an increase for defense, and a big tax cut, with a projected balanced budget in seven years. As noted earlier, the Medicare cut was set at $270 billion and the tax cut at $245 billion.

As the spring of 1995 turned into summer, people around the country began to take notice of the cuts to popular programs proposed by the Republicans. Public interest groups started to mobilize in Washington to oppose the cuts. The American Hospital Association and other providers, as well as advocates for veterans, the elderly, farmers, and education all rallied to complain about the impacts of the cuts. It appeared to us that the resistance was finally building at the grassroots.

THE CLASH OVER APPROPRIATIONS HEATS UP

Normally the appropriations bills percolate through the committees to the Senate floor one at a time in June and July so that they can go to conference and be completed well in advance of October 1, the beginning of the new fiscal year to which they apply. As the Republicans' budget resolution completed its journey through the Congress, the appropriations bills were beginning to move as well.

When the Senate reconvened after the July 4 recess, Kennedy's staff was briefed on the initial Republican proposals for cuts to the labor, health, and human services appropriations bill. This bill included virtually all the programs under the Labor Committee's jurisdiction. The proposed cuts were staggering: nearly 25 percent across the board; $9 billion would be struck from appropriated education programs. The proposed levels amounted to the most draconian cuts that education programs had seen at any time in our history. But a final resolution to the appropriations process was a long way off.

ASSAULT ON FOOD SAFETY AND ENVIRONMENTAL REGULATIONS

Meanwhile Kennedy and some other Senate Democrats were beginning to establish a new front for the resistance. Over the July 4 recess, the *New York Times* reported, "Congress is moving to revamp the rules on food safety."[2] These initiatives would turn out to be disastrous for the Republicans. The proposed new rules would have reduced inspection of meat, scaled back measures intended to improve testing of seafood, eliminated the Delaney Clause (which forbids adding carcinogens to foods) without substituting an alternative standard, allowed pesticides that could contain carcinogens to continue to be used in foods, and delayed certain regulations that protect children from lead poisoning. David Kessler, the head of the FDA, who had originally been appointed by President Bush and was retained by President Clinton, said, "These proposals are an assault on forty years of consumer protection."[3] The antiregulatory provisions would turn out to be an easy target for Democrats and those who were looking for ways to expose the extremism of the Republican revolution.

A new Gallup poll for CNN was published on July 13, showing that for the first time since June 1994, Democrats had pulled even with Republicans on the question of whether Americans would prefer a Republican or a Democrat for Congress in 1996. In November 1994 the Republicans had been up in the polls by 5 percent.

The debate on deregulation continued on the Senate floor. Senators Barbara Boxer and Patty Murray joined Kennedy in discussing the dangers of eliminating protections that assured mammogram safety. Kennedy talked about undoing worker safety standards. A provision in the Republicans' deregulation bill would have stopped cleanups at hundreds of toxic waste sites across the country. In the first Senate vote on environmental issues since they took control, Republicans defeated an amendment eliminating the provision.

The assault on environmental regulation was well under way—and not only through the deregulation bill. During the week of July 18, Republicans moved ahead on their appropriations bills. They used the process to propose revoking nearly twenty environmental laws and to restrict enforcement of statutes like the Clean Air and Clean Water Acts.

For days the debate on the deregulation bill continued on the Senate floor, and Democrats turned their attention to worker safety protections. This time Kennedy focused on the proposed elimination of protections for mine workers under the Mine Safety and Health Act and the scaling back of OSHA. He detailed some of the improvements that had been made in workplace safety that would be weakened or eliminated under the Republican plan: cotton dust standards which had prevented brown lung disease among textile workers, standards relating to lead poisoning which had saved thousands of lives in lead smelting and battery manufacturing plants, safety management standards to prevent chemical explosions, and so-called lockout and tagout standards to reduce injuries from potentially dangerous electric-powered equipment.

In the House on July 17 Republicans attempted to take up legislation that would place additional restraints on environmental regulations. They wanted to scale back the Clean Water and Endangered Species Acts, reduce grazing fees, scale back protections against pesticides, escalate harvesting of timber in national forests, limit regulation of and reduce royalties for mining on public property, and eliminate provisions to hold businesses responsible for cleaning up hazardous waste sites they had created.

In the Senate on July 18, the Democrats successfully blocked cutting off debate and moving to passage of the deregulation bill. Senator Dole got only forty-eight votes to close off debate on the bill and move to final passage, twelve votes short of the required sixty votes. On the floor with Kennedy, I began to feel that the momentum might be beginning to turn in our favor.

ASSAULT ON MEDICARE

Kennedy, Daschle, and other senators held a press conference on July 19 to refocus attention on the Medicare issue. Daschle warned that under the Republican budget, seniors would pay more and get less: "Medicare is a trust fund, not a slush fund for tax cuts for the rich." Kennedy added, "The Republicans are planning a funeral for Medicare." Harkin said, "Republicans would not save Medicare; they would destroy it." Senator Bob Graham of Florida called the cuts to Medicare "a stealth bomber coming at seniors."

But while congressional Democrats were raising the stakes on the Medicare cuts, the president seemed to be moving in the opposite direction. In an address from the oval office on June 13, Clinton had announced a program to balance the budget in ten years. His new budget was not terribly detailed, but it cut Medicare by about $125 billion, a little less than half of what the Republicans were proposing. The cuts were supposed to come without cutting benefits—meaning, presumably, that they would all come from reductions in provider payments.

There seemed to have been two motivations behind the president's move. First, he felt that the balanced budget was a powerful issue. If he could co-opt it, the Republicans would have lost the major item they were fighting for that the public broadly supported. Second, the president wanted to be a leader, not just a naysayer, and he felt putting out his own balanced budget proposal that moved toward the Republican position was a better stage-setter for negotiations than simply talking about all the things he didn't like about the Republican proposal. Whatever his motivations, congressional Democrats were furious, and a number criticized the president directly. Kennedy knew that public criticism of the president was counterproductive, but, like other Democrats, he felt that the administration shouldn't have surrendered the high ground on Medicare, and he was concerned that they might be abandoning the effort to make clear to the public what was actually at stake in the Republican revolution.

When we heard from our sources at the White House that Clinton was about to offer his own balanced budget proposal, Kennedy tried to reach him to persuade him to hold off. But the budget hawks, knowing that Kennedy was exceptionally persuasive with the president, tried to use their influence over Clinton's schedule to block a meeting. Kennedy, however, was not to be deterred, so he asked us to check Clinton's schedule ourselves. It turned out Clinton was going to be at a big public ceremony on the White House lawn to swear in new police officers from all over the country. The ceremony was designed to highlight Clinton's anticrime package, which had funded 100,000 new police officers nationwide. Kennedy learned there would be a contingent of troopers from Massachusetts at the ceremony, so he arranged to attend and sit in the front row. When Clinton saw him, he would not be able to avoid talking to him, and then Kennedy would be able to make his pitch. As predicted, after the speech Clinton asked Kennedy to walk back across the lawn with him, and they then spent forty-five minutes alone together in the Oval Office, while Clinton's staff cooled their heels just outside.

Afterward Kennedy told me that he didn't think he had had much success. Although Clinton had agreed to postpone the announcement for a week, Kennedy felt the president had basically made up his mind, and that turned out to be the case.

There were other occasions when Kennedy used the strategy of getting in to see Clinton at a critical time when he thought he would have the most influence. For example, Kennedy had been supporting Stephen Breyer, a former staff member on the Judiciary Committee, for Clinton's first appointment to the Supreme Court. We thought Breyer had a good chance with Clinton, but he didn't get the appointment. Instead it went to Ruth Bader Ginsburg, supported by Moynihan. We learned afterward that Moynihan had met with Clinton right before the appointment and that may have helped tip the scales. Kennedy vowed at the time that if he ever wanted anything from Clinton, he would see Clinton personally just before he made the decision.

A year later, when there was another vacancy on the Supreme Court, Kennedy was once again advocating for Breyer. He told me he wanted to know when Clinton would actually be making his decision. When we had this figured out, Kennedy told me, to "Find out what Clinton's schedule is, and see if there is a way I can get in to see him." We investigated through the White House scheduling office, and it turned out that Clinton was giving a speech to a group of educators at the Hyatt Hotel on Capitol Hill, so Kennedy got himself invited to speak as well. He gave his big stump speech on education, and then Clinton arrived, surprised to see Kennedy and to hear the audience giving him a standing ovation. When Clinton's speech was over, Kennedy followed him into the hall and spoke to him about Breyer's candidacy: "I hope it's going to be Breyer; he's the right guy." Clinton did end up nominating Breyer. Shrewd, relentless, and strategic, Kennedy never left any promising stone unturned that might help him achieve his goals.

In late July the administration held a briefing for Senate staff members on the president's position on Medicare. In the days leading up to the briefing, there had been considerable backdoor lobbying of the White House by congressional Democrats urging a strong position on resisting the Republican Medicare cuts. In part the administration wanted to show that they meant what they said when they claimed that introducing their alternative budget with Medicare cuts sufficient to shore up the Medicare trust fund would free the president to attack the Republicans for their much larger cuts. At least some in the administration now seized the opportunity to do just that. It was as if the harder they attacked the Republicans for their deep Medicare cuts, the more it vindicated the president's strategy of offering his own balanced budget plan and his own more limited cuts.

Meanwhile, in what appeared to be a lonely bipartisan step amid the partisan tumult, Senator Kassebaum came to the floor on July 21 together with Kennedy and urged the reauthorization of the Ryan White AIDS CARE Act. Some brave Republicans were going forward with the business of reauthorizing legislation that provided vital lifelines for people who couldn't help themselves. By the time the Ryan White bill reauthorization was ready to pass the Senate, it had over sixty-five cosponsors.

THE BUDGET DEBATE INTENSIFIES

The thirtieth anniversary of Medicare, which fell on July 30, provided an opportunity for Democrats to attack Republicans again over their $270 billion cuts to Medicare and to continue to link the cuts to the tax breaks the Republicans sought for wealthy Americans. As the day approached, Democrats across the country began to sharpen their message. House and Senate Democrats on key committees sent out talking points to their constituents, highlighting stories in the *Washington Post* and the *New York Times* asserting that the proposed cuts would mean increased costs to seniors. Moreover, they argued, Republican plans would force seniors into HMOs, and seniors' ability to choose their own doctors would be limited.

Polling confirmed that the issue was really taking hold with the public. As the anniversary date approached, Mark Mellman held another briefing for Democratic staff members and described the public reaction to the Medicare debate. The Democrats were almost thirty points ahead among Americans over fifty. Three-quarters of Americans believed that Republicans were breaking the promise not to cut Medicare. "The public isn't interested in balancing the budget if it means cutting Medicare dramatically," he said. According to Mellman, Democrats needed to repeat the argument that the Republicans were cutting Medicare not to ensure the solvency of the Medicare trust fund but because they wanted to provide tax breaks for the wealthy. He urged Democrats to use their own wordsmithing power and talk about "tax breaks," not "tax cuts."

In the week leading up to the Medicare anniversary, the Senate Democratic Policy Committee released background information on the Republican plan. On July 25 Democrats held a national Medicare birthday celebration in the Cannon Caucus Room, attended by President Clinton, Vice President Gore, House and Senate Democratic leaders, and members of the House who had been in the Congress in 1965 when Medicare was enacted. The room was packed with seniors and other Medicare supporters, and the enthusiasm for the cause of protecting Medicare was enormous. The Democrats highlighted statements from Republicans denigrating Medicare and pointed out that thirty years earlier, on July 28,

1965, 57 percent of Senate Republicans had voted against creation of the program. Now 100 percent of Senate Republicans voted to raid the Medicare program in order to give new tax breaks to the wealthy.

President Clinton used his radio address on July 29 to focus on the Republican plans to cut Medicare. He invited his stepfather, Richard Kelley, and his mother-in-law, Dorothy Rodham, to join him in the Oval Office for the address, in which he said, "We do need to protect Medicare from going bankrupt, but we don't have to bankrupt older Americans to do it."

House Democrats revealed that the Republican-sponsored Coalition to Save Medicare, which the Republicans were advertising as a "collection of grassroots organizations interested in preserving, protecting, and strengthening Medicare," was, as we've described, made up of the insurance companies that would benefit as Medicare recipients were forced into privately run managed care. On the floor of the Senate, Kennedy asserted that the Coalition was "an unholy alliance that offered the insurance industry the chance to get its hands on Medicare and earn vast additional profits at the expense of senior citizens." He placed into the *Congressional Record* an analysis of the Coalition's goals, which concluded that the benefits that selected corporations would receive from the proposed tax breaks would total $148.5 billion over seven years. This included the repeal of the corporate alternative minimum tax, which cost $22.1 billion over seven years, $47.8 billion in increased write-offs and deductions, and $78.6 billion in capital gains tax breaks. The report also listed the campaign contributions made to Republicans by the members of the Coalition. Kennedy added a study his own office had prepared showing that if the Republican effort to move seniors from conventional Medicare into private insurance succeeded, insurance company premium revenue would increase by $1.2 trillion over the next seven years and profits could increase by as much as $75 billion.

The Republicans were mobilizing to fight back. Frank Luntz, the Republican pollster who took credit for developing the Contract with America, was telling the Republicans that Medicare was a make-or-break issue, that they needed to make the case that they were saving Medicare from going bankrupt, that they weren't cutting it but simply slowing its growth. In July they sent out talking points to their members on how to deal with the Medicare issue during the August recess. The message—focusing on the projected insolvency of the Medicare Hospital Insurance Trust Fund—was that Republicans promised to "preserve, protect, and improve the program." But it would be a hard sell, since the bottom line was that they were trying to cut the program by $270 billion.

On July 30 Democrats again used the occasion of Medicare's thirtieth birthday to keep up the drumbeat, gathering with seniors and other Americans in Independence, Missouri, at the site where President Lyndon Johnson, with former president Harry Truman at his side, first signed Medicare into law, to celebrate the success of Medicare and highlight the threat to it posed by the Republican budget.

Democrats had found their issue. They were united on the message, and the public, according to the polls, was overwhelmingly on their side.

MORE EXAMPLES OF REPUBLICAN EXTREMISM

In addition to Medicare, other matters were starting to advance through the legislative process, each of which would prove immensely unpopular and contribute to the collapse of the Republican agenda.

On August 1 the Republicans passed legislation in the House to limit the enforcement activity of the Environmental Protection Agency. The *New York Times* reported that the provisions included in the bill would "prohibit the agency from spending any money next year to regulate commercial development in wetlands, air pollution from refineries, water pollution from city sewers, pesticides in foods and the like."[4]

Next the labor, health, and human services appropriations bill moved through the House. It cut low-income heating assistance, eliminated fifty thousand children from Head Start and 12 million meals from nutrition programs for senior citizens, and slashed funds for Safe and Drug-Free Schools by 60 percent and School-to-Work by 25 percent.

As the Republican budget-cutting program moved through the committees, education continued to be a major battleground, receiving almost as much attention as Medicare. Kennedy's office opened a website for college students to transmit stories about their need for student aid and how the proposed Republican cuts would hurt them. He went to the floor and put into the record a summary of over 1,500 of these statements from students, organized by state: stories of students who would not be able to go to college or would be forced to drop out because they could not afford the tuition without the help of student loans.

On another front, Dole rejected Democratic efforts to compromise on the deregulation legislation.

As the August recess began, back in Atlanta, Speaker Gingrich, in keeping with the Republicans' plan to defend their position on Medicare, scheduled a meeting to discuss Medicare changes. The event was sponsored by one of the Washington foundations that make up the conservative infrastructure, the Congressional Institute. John Lewis, a Democratic congressman from Atlanta, tried to attend the meeting, along with a hundred union members who had also been invited. When Gingrich learned that there would be a debate with Lewis and union members about Medicare, he slipped out of the building, leaving by a back elevator. In the afternoon, after Lewis left, Gingrich returned and declared, "In an Administration whose capacity for truth is highly limited, their recent effort to scare senior citizens, I think, is among the most despicable I have seen, and it is patently false."[5]

I had several conversations with former staff members and friends of Kennedy in Massachusetts and elsewhere, asking how we were doing. What is the right position for the senator? Are we making a difference? One of the people I spoke with was Paul Kirk. Paul was worried about whether Clinton would show sufficient resolve and leadership. "It seems like there is too much political calibration. We have to lay out on the menu the differences between the parties. How hypocritical that the Republicans, the party of law and order, would repeal the ban on assault weapons. Why would we give up on investing in the future in people, in kids, in health?

"Let's compare our priorities with theirs. There is a cogent argument for continuing the fight to make life better for Americans. The Republican opposition makes it easier to wage this fight, because they can't help themselves from going too far. When the Republican crowd is so insensitive and mean-spirited, you need a clear and compelling voice out there to make the case against them. That's Senator Kennedy's role, and that's how he's performing."

We used the recess to line up our strategy for the fall, when the moment of truth would occur, starting with the areas where the Republicans would try to roll back government programs under the jurisdiction of our committee.

Chapter 15

THE SENATE RETURNS TO THE BUDGET AFTER LABOR DAY

When the Senate reconvened in September, Daschle called a meeting with Rockefeller and Kennedy to discuss the Senate's Medicare strategy. Daschle was under intense pressure from the moderates to come up with a Democratic Senate proposal to cut Medicare. He wanted Rockefeller and Kennedy to help him develop cuts that would be acceptable to the liberal wing and still preserve the Democratic message. "The Republicans have convinced the press that the Medicare system is broken," he said, "but they don't need $270 billion to fix it. That's too big a cut. . . . What should we be suggesting? Shouldn't we come up with $89 billion in cuts so that we can be for something? We need to coordinate this effort with the White House and the House."

Rockefeller responded, "It's easy to identify $89 billion in cuts which can solve any problem for the Medicare trust fund through the year 2005.

I'll propose a plan for $89 billion in the Finance Committee and it will be voted down. We can make some policy improvements to Medicare. For a long-term solution we should have a Medicare Commission, with seniors and actuaries, like we did with Social Security in the 1980s, to take care of the trust fund for the years to come."

Daschle believed that a Medicare Commission would be the wrong remedy at the wrong time—in effect, suggesting that Republicans were right when they said Medicare was broken. "That's not our first-tier issue. We have to educate people about the issue of the $270 billion cuts the Republicans are proposing. We need to devise ways of breaking through. We need a big message project. How are we going to create a message strategy?"

Kennedy thought it was still premature for the Senate Democrats to propose any cuts. "This is the number one issue for Clinton and for Democrats. Ultimately we may need an alternative, but we need to keep the focus on the Republicans' proposal as long as we can. If we have a plan for cuts ourselves, it's more difficult to put into sharp relief our differences with the Republicans. We should put focus and attention on *their* cuts. We should take the position that there will be no increases in costs to beneficiaries. If you have to have a plan, hold it for now. We need to keep focusing on this issue and dragging it out so the public has a chance to understand it."

When the Senate came back into session after Labor Day, it was faced with a major distraction before it could get back to the debate on welfare and Medicare. The Senate Ethics Committee had voted unanimously, 6–0, to recommend the expulsion of Senator Bob Packwood of Oregon, the chairman of the Finance Committee, for engaging in a pattern of repeated sexual misconduct, obstructing the Ethics Committee's investigation by altering evidence, and soliciting job opportunities for his ex-wife from individuals who had business before the Finance Committee. Inexplicably, Senator Dole thought it would be all right if Packwood continued wielding his vast power on the Finance Committee even after the unanimous vote by the Ethics Committee. But Dole did not get away with this preferential treatment for his friend. When he and Packwood saw that this approach wouldn't fly they agreed that Packwood would no longer vote in the Senate and would leave within three weeks. Regardless of his personal failings, Packwood was a moderate Republican and an effective chairman. In contrast, his replacement, William Roth of Delaware, was a true believer in tax cuts as the overriding goal of government policy.

With the Packwood matter out of the way, the Senate turned back to the welfare reform bill. Many Democrats, led by Moynihan, were deeply upset by what they viewed as the harshness of the legislation, but Clinton was for it, as were a majority of Senate Democrats. Unlike defending working families, defending dependent poor families was widely regarded—probably correctly—as a political loser. So there was little likelihood the bill could be held off.

There were, however, important ways the bill might be improved, one of which was to restore the funds for child care. Kennedy went to the floor with Dodd to support an amendment to restore child care funds and to recap the history of this issue in the development of the welfare bill in the Senate. He reminded senators that he had labeled the first welfare bill earlier in the year the Dole "Home Alone" bill. It required parents to work but did nothing about child care. Then came the sequel, as he put it: "Home Alone II." Republican leaders sought to address the need for child care by exempting mothers with babies under the age of one from the work requirement. "But once you reach the age of one, they said, you're old enough to care for yourself. You do not need child care. You are on your own. This is the 'Home Alone by two' bill." This, Kennedy said, was "a continuing nightmare for the mothers of preschoolers and school-age children, who had to face the choice of leaving their children home alone or losing their benefits and livelihood." He contrasted the Republicans' willingness to cut assistance for poor children with their failure to address "corporate welfare"—undeserved tax breaks for large, wealthy businesses.

Dodd and Kennedy offered an amendment to include $6 billion for child care in the welfare bill. The amendment required that the money be taken out of the $424 billion in corporate tax breaks. On September 11 Republicans defeated it, 50–48. By the end of the week, however, with growing concern among moderate members of the Republican Caucus about their "Home Alone vote," Democrats had worked out a compromise with Dole that would add the child care funds, which Kennedy and Dodd had proposed, to the bill.

With that compromise, Daschle indicated that he would reluctantly vote for the welfare bill. In his radio address over the weekend, the president said that the compromises on the welfare bill brought it closer to his plan, although he still did not say that he would sign the bill.

On September 19 the Senate approved the welfare bill. Kennedy joined Moynihan, Bradley, and other Democrats in criticizing the legislation. Moynihan said, "I hope the president will veto this bill. It's sure as hell cruel in the lives of American children." Kennedy excoriated the Republicans for their misplaced priorities: "The Republican majority has already shown that it is willing to spend money when the cause is important enough to them. When the Republican majority wanted to preserve a $1.5 billion tax loophole for American billionaires who renounce their U.S. citizenship, they found the money to preserve it. When the Republican majority wanted to increase defense spending $6.5 billion more than the Defense Department requested for this year, they found the money to fund it. When the Republican majority want to give the wealthy a $245 billion tax break, they will find the money to fund it. But now, when asked to reform welfare and create a genuine system to help America's 10 million children living in poverty, the Republican majority tells those children: 'Sorry, check returned, insufficient funds.'

"I say to my colleagues: Can you look into the eyes of a poor child in America and say, 'This is the best hope for your future'? I cannot, and that is why I must vote no." The bill passed 87–12.

As the welfare debate continued in the Senate, Gingrich and the Republicans in the House announced that they would finally reveal the details of their plan to cut Medicare by $270 billion. Kennedy went on the attack: "We are not talking about senior citizens paying a few dollars more for Medicare. Under the Republican plan, senior citizens will be asked to pay thousands of dollars more for Medicare in order to fund a tax cut for wealthy Americans."

PREPARING FOR THE SHOWDOWN ON THE BUDGET

At the staff directors meeting on September 11, representatives of the administration discussed the president's strategy as the budget crisis loomed and the end of the fiscal year (September 30) approached without either an appropriations bill or a continuing resolution. (A continuing resolution is a measure to keep the government open while Congress completes work on regular appropriations bills. Usually it extends programs for which regular appropriations have not been passed at the previous year's funding level. The continuing resolution can be short term, a matter of days or weeks, or long term, six months or more.) One week later Senate staffers were told that the president would be stepping up his travel around the coutry in order to emphasize the Democrats' message on Medicare and Medicaid. He would be in Pennsylvania, Florida, Colorado, and California.

Rhetoric heated up as the deadline to fund the government approached. On September 12 Speaker Gingrich, Majority Leader Dole, and other Republican congressional leaders had gone to the White House to meet with Clinton to talk about the budget. Gingrich came out of the meeting to say, "If there is any way we can work together in a mature way we are going to cooperate." But, he added, "there is not going to be a compromise on the Republican drive to balance the budget in seven years." The Republican political analyst Kevin Phillips published polls from late August that showed the public strongly opposed the Republican cuts to Medicare.

The next day, Senator Kassebaum, on behalf of the Labor Committee, proposed her plan to meet the deficit reduction targets allocated to the Committee under the budget resolution. The plan would have cut student loans by a total of $10 billion, in part by adding a 2 percent charge to colleges and universities on all federal loans their students received. This plan was widely denounced by universities, their representatives, and the ranking Democrat on the committee, Senator Kennedy. Keeping up his attack on Republican tax cuts, he said, "The Republican Congress has no business picking the pockets of students and working families to pay for tax cuts for the rich."

On September 16 the president weighed in again on the Republicans' Medicare proposal: "Their plan would increase premiums and other costs for senior citizens. It would reduce doctor choice. It would force many doctors to stop serving seniors altogether. It threatens to put rural hospitals and urban hospitals out of business. Brick by brick, it would dismantle Medicare as we know it."[1] He contrasted the Republican proposal to his own more moderate plan to cut $124 billion from Medicare and $54 billion from Medicaid over seven years. House Minority Leader Gephardt said of the president's plan, "I think even that is too much."[2]

Republicans in the House and Senate simultaneously completed their conference report on the appropriations bill funding environmental programs. It cut funding for the Interior Department 8 percent and scaled back or eliminated numerous provisions protecting the environment, including protections under the Endangered Species Act, the Mining Act, the National Park Service's role in managing the Mohave Desert, the National Biological Service, grazing regulations, logging, and conservation programs financing home insulation for the poor. It even prohibited the Interior Department from issuing new standards for energy efficiency in appliances such as refrigerators and air conditioners.

On September 22 the *New York Times* reported that Gingrich threatened to hold hostage an increase in the federal debt limit as a means of forcing Clinton to accept the Republicans' budget plans. If Gingrich carried out his threat, the United States would default on its debt for the first time in its history. He was also threatening the president with shutting down the government if he didn't accept their budget, with its unprecedented cuts to education, Medicare, Medicaid, and children's programs, its restrictions on government actions to protect the environment, food safety, worker safety, and the myriad other radical changes in government policy.[3] Veterans of the Washington scene had never seen anything like it.

However, the Republicans were way behind in completing their work. By September 25, less than one week before the beginning of the new fiscal year, they still had not passed any of the thirteen appropriations bills needed to keep the government running. John Hilley told the staff directors, "Message is the key. The Republican budget is extreme. Our plan to save the Medicare trust fund saves $89 billion. That is the responsible position. Democrats are for a balanced budget in the mainstream way. The president may try to sign some of the appropriations bills after fixing them. But some high-profile bills are simply not fixable and will be vetoed. We want a clean, quick continuing resolution to head off any form of government shutdown.

"The appropriations bills will come to the floor later this week or next week. We want to focus our message so we'll have time for only three to four amendments. Since we're likely to lose the amendments, we want to make sure they are our best message amendments. If we pass a continuing resolution and the Republicans keep working on the appropriations bills, they may get the reconciliation bill to the White House by the end of October or early November. If the reconciliation bill is not satisfactory to the president, he will veto it. Then, he hopes, a deal will be possible with the Republicans on both appropriations and the reconciliation bill."

In addition to emphasizing the scale of the cuts, Democrats in the Senate also attacked the Republicans for ramming through the cuts and their Medicare restructuring proposals without hearings. The Democratic talking points were "Republicans refuse to hold public hearings on their Medicare proposal and are preparing to push their extreme proposal through Congress before seniors can understand its potential consequences." Republicans had held twenty-four days of hearings on Whitewater and eleven days of hearings on Waco—but not a single day on cuts to Medicare.

The following week, Republicans opened another legislative front that would ultimately boomerang against them. They proposed the stiffest new curbs on immigration in decades. These proposals would restrict automatic entry into the United States for relatives of immigrants and make it more difficult for foreigners to gain political asylum and for U.S. citizens to sponsor immigrants. And they reduced by almost half the number of legal immigrants allowed into the country each year.

On September 28 the labor, health and human services appropriations bill came to the floor. Democrats had a field day attacking it. Almost one quarter of the schools participating in the federal school reform program would lose their federal funds. Head Start would be cut by $132 million. Safe and Drug-Free Schools would be cut in 97 percent of communities. And the list went on. Beyond the program cuts, the bill also revived the anti-union provisions that had failed to pass earlier in the year on rehiring striking workers and paying prevailing wages for firms receiving federal contracts. "This bill deserves to be defeated," Kennedy said on the floor. "It is an unconscionable attack on the dreams and aspirations of millions of working families across the country and on their hopes for the future."

Having failed to enact any appropriations bills or the budget, Republicans rushed through a short-term continuing resolution to keep spending going into the new fiscal year, but at a lower level than the previous year.

The next appropriations bill on the floor was the funding for the Commerce, Justice, and State Departments, which was debated on September 29. Kennedy went to the floor to focus attention on the drastic reduction in support for the federal Legal Services Program. As he put it, the program had received bipartisan support for decades, and it would now be cut by more than a third for 1996.

Together with other Democratic leaders, Kennedy and Daschle met again with the representatives of the health care advocacy groups. What had they done since the last meeting with Kennedy four months ago? The American Hospital Association representatives had been less than forceful in their advocacy, perhaps fearing Republican retribution. They were primarily concerned about where the cuts would be allocated: would they come from the hospitals or from the beneficiaries? They cared much less about cuts to beneficiaries. While opposing the cuts affecting their members, the AHA supported a provision of the Republican bill to allow doctors and hospitals to join in provider-sponsored networks to compete with insurance companies in providing care, and spent much of its energy trying to keep that provision in the bill rather than keeping its focus on defeating the whole proposal. The AARP was less than strident in its criticism. The American Medical Association complained that the Medicare spending reductions in the Senate Finance Committee proposal were "too much, too fast." A day later, however, the AMA changed its mind, indicating that it would now support the Republican plan in the House because it had received assurances that the cuts to physicians would be less than they originally appeared—presumably at the expense of senior citizens, other providers, or both.

On October 3 the president issued the first of his vetoes of Republican appropriations bills. It was a small appropriations bill in comparison to the larger bills that had yet to be completed, providing $2.2 billion for the administrative expenses of Congress. The veto was a warning shot: the president said he didn't think Congress should take care of its own business before it took care of the people's business. Since the rest of the government hadn't received permanent appropriations, he didn't see why Congress should.

Keeping up his criticism of the Republican Medicare cuts, on October 5 Kennedy held a forum in the Senate Caucus Room, where he and other Democrats heard from the AARP, the American College of Physicians, and a coalition of businesses that provided health insurance benefits to workers. The same week, Republicans once again left themselves open to attack by constructing their block-grant proposal for Medicaid in a way that effectively repealed federal standards for safety and care of seniors in nursing homes. As noted, these standards were enacted ten years earlier in reaction to highly publicized instances of unsanitary and unsafe conditions in nursing homes.

On October 9 Senator Sam Nunn became the eighth Democrat of fifteen up for reelection in 1996 to announce his retirement—a bad omen for the upcoming elections unless Democrats could turn the Republican revolution into a potent issue to defeat Republicans.

During the week of October 9, the Republicans brought a job training bill to the floor that would have eliminated the Job Corps program. But by the end of the day, Democrats had mustered enough support for Job Corps that they were able to reinstate the funding.

On October 12 Democrats picked up on another proposal by the Republicans that would come back to haunt them; this involved financial responsibility for the Medicaid-funded nursing home care of married beneficiaries. As described earlier, in block-granting the program, the House Republican Medicaid plan would have had the effect of repealing a law originally championed by Senators Kennedy, Mikulski, and Mitchell and signed by President Reagan to protect spouses from having to give up, or "spend down," everything they had (their car, their home, and their savings) in order for their sick spouse to become eligible to receive nursing home care financed by Medicaid. These provisions were called "spousal impoverishment protections." As the Democratic talking points noted, "It would be callous for Congress to bring back the days when the price of nursing home care for a loved one meant the loss of a family home and the loss of one's life savings."

By October 12 the polling data on Medicare showed the issue was hurting the Republicans even more. Over 80 percent of all Americans, including wealthy Americans, opposed cutting the future costs of Medicare to pay for a tax cut.

THE SEARCH FOR ONE "BIG IDEA"

On October 16, in preparation for the pending budget impasse, Kennedy invited several political consultants to his home to discuss the Democratic strategy. (The final House reconciliation bill was finally introduced the next day.) These discussions revealed that the party still wasn't unified on whether to fight back against the Republican revolution or make a deal. This division reflected the president's own divided mind and the ongoing argument within the White House. Kennedy, however, was looking ahead. He believed Democrats were on firm ground in opposing the Republican revolution and standing up for their traditional values but that they ultimately needed a clearer agenda of their own.

Kennedy insisted that he and our liberal allies needed to do everything possible to strengthen the president's resolve, to show him that the best way to close down the Republican revolution was to stand our ground in opposition to it. Democrats had to stand for progressive change, what his close friend and political strategist Bob Shrum called "the big idea." All the work that had been done over the summer to highlight the extreme measures proposed by the Republicans for Medicare, nursing homes, education, and the environment had helped educate the public. But we still needed a dramatic event that would be a tipping point.

Robert Reischauer, former director of the Congressional Budget Office, a moderate Democrat and cautious Washington insider, was sometimes at odds with Kennedy and Senate liberals. He said that Republicans had to pass the reconciliation bill they'd been promising to pass all year so that they could say they had done what they said they would do. He expected the president would veto the bill because the tax cuts were too large. Then negotiations would start between the White House and the Republicans in mid-December. Reischauer predicted that in December the president would want a budget bill. Once he vetoed the first bill, he would have the high ground, and he would then want to show that he could make a deal.

Barney Frank, who later became chairman of the House Banking Committee and one of the two chief architects of the Dodd-Frank financial reform bill, said Clinton would end up signing a reconciliation bill, but under protest, and would make it the theme for 1996 that he went along with this terrible budget in order to keep the government from closing down. Whether or not this worked in the election, the country would be left with a terrible set of policies.

Robert Shapiro was a former Moynihan staffer then with the centrist Democratic Leadership Council and the Progressive Policy Institute, its think tank arm. He said the worst outcome for Democrats and for the economy would be to have no reconciliation bill. That would confirm to the American people the truth about Washington gridlock. Shapiro thought we needed to focus on the cuts the country didn't like, but that we also needed to show that we had our own cuts, our own ability to re-structure government, and our own way to reform the health care system.

Celinda Lake, a distinguished Democratic pollster, advocated for a strong stance against the Republicans; she believed in it, and her polls told her it would work. She said it was clear the Republicans were going too far. Democrats had to make the Medicare cuts understandable and contrast them to the tax cuts. Everything looks best for the Democrats when contrasted to the tax cuts, she said. We had to emphasize what the Republicans were cutting: not only Medicare, college loans, and school lunches but also small business loans and inspectors for the Envi-ronmental Protection Administration. The problem for Democrats was that 90 percent of the voters didn't know what the Democratic plan was, whereas 60 percent of the voters knew that the Republican plan was to reduce the deficit and reduce taxes.

Days later Kennedy assembled another group of strategists to focus on what the next big idea for the Democrats might look like. Jeff Faux, director of the Economic Policy Institute and one of the leading liberal economists in Washington, opened the discussion. "Forty percent of the problem is the income and wages issue. The other 60 percent of the problem is that the distribution of income has gotten much worse. If you take a high school graduate today, who was earning $20,000 before, he should be at $31,000 if his wages had grown as they did in the years before 1973. Instead he is actually at $13,000 a year. Before 1973, if you made the typical income you had enough savings so that you could sur-vive for three and a half months without any income before you went bankrupt. Now you can only last two weeks before you have to sell off your house to live. Anxiety is there for middle-class Americans because their savings are gone. This reversal for the middle class has occurred while in the last decade profits have been going up for corporations and are at the highest they've been in twenty-five years."

Tom Glynn, deputy secretary of labor, was a liberal ally of Kennedy's from Massachusetts, a shrewd pragmatist, and a defender of the administration's position as seen through the eyes of Labor Secretary Robert Reich. He made similar points: "Most of the indicators are up—productivity, stocks, et cetera, but wages are continuing to stagnate. We have the anomaly of layoffs being profitable for companies after mergers. We used to say layoffs were a product of economic distress." He suggested some ideas: "Is there a federal role in regulating mergers and acquisitions regarding employment? What about a training tax? What about gains sharing and tax incentives for employee stock option plans? We need to get a handle on the pension issue."

Mark Mellman, the Democratic pollster, speaking from a "purely political perspective," reported that individuals were feeling squeezed. A majority felt their income was falling behind the cost of living. They wanted more dollars in their pockets. The Republicans' plan to cut taxes was a one-step process that was simple to understand, whereas education and training were a four-step process and may or may not affect their incomes. Yes, education and training mattered, but the public didn't see it as a direct help to them in terms of their wages. Another problem was time. More and more people were working more and more hours, and it was their perception that they had less and less time for their families. The big idea we had to move toward was "when the average worker does better, the economy does better."

Bob Shrum responded that people don't ask for diagnoses, they look for solutions. As far as he was concerned it was "wages, wages, wages," not "jobs, jobs, jobs. People are profoundly unhappy. They are not feeling the economic recovery. We need to have legislation, to fight for it and maybe lose it, but take it to the country. We need a big economic idea."

Tom Donilon, Shrum's quieter consultant colleague, said there was growing anger at corporate America and it was a rhetorical battle that we were not engaging in. Yes, people had to take personal responsibility for their lives, but so did corporate America. There was an implied contract between workers and employers that had been broken. Now they didn't get a raise; instead they could lose their jobs. We needed to create a rhetorical battle and force Republicans to take tough votes that would show they weren't on the side of middle-class Americans. Shrum asserted that if Kennedy didn't put out a story about what the problem was and pose a clear solution, we couldn't win. We couldn't run as the party of status quo. Presidents Roosevelt, Truman, and Kennedy had their story and they told it. Now the story was: "My company is screwing me. Isn't anyone going to stick up for me? We are going to fight for you."

Mellman turned the discussion back to the immediate issues. He said the political climate had improved as a result of what we had done. Tax breaks for the wealthy, screwing up nursing homes, cutting Medicare—these messages were beginning to work for Democrats. Congressional Democrats were five points ahead of the Republicans, and every day we made a little bit more of the case. That was the result of three months debating Medicare. "Once every day we have to talk about it," he said. "That's what it takes to break through to the public."

Mellman's comments echoed advice that Theresa Bourgeois, Kennedy's canny Labor Committee press secretary, had given him. When Kennedy complained that he was getting bored with using the same talking points over and over again, she said, "Senator, repetition is key to breaking through with the public. You need to repeat those points until you think that if you have to say them one more time you are going to throw up. Then you say them again."

CONTINUING CONCERNS ABOUT THE PRESIDENT

While Kennedy and the progressives were thinking about their strategic responses to the Republicans and their big ideas for the country, there were signs from the White House that President Clinton was waffling about taking a hard line on the budget. There was more talk and speculation about an alleged White House "triangulation" strategy—a plan for the president to enhance his own political standing by taking a "statesmanlike" position in between but above both the Republicans *and* the Democrats. The rumors about this strategy had first surfaced in July, when, over the objection of congressional Democrats, Clinton had proposed his alternative budget, moving a considerable distance toward the Republican position. On October 13 the press reported that Clinton was truly committed to the triangulation strategy and was preparing to walk away from the Democrats in Congress.

Pat Griffin, the president's chief legislative aide, was dispatched to the staff directors meeting to calm the congressional Democrats. He said he was upset by the triangulation stories: "It is a royal disaster at every level. The triangulation characterization is not part of our script; it is not intended. It is not part of our strategy. It doesn't work. How can we keep moving forward? How can we apologize? The proof will be whether we act right in the next challenge ahead of us. We need to work together."

John Hilley presented the current budget situation. If we used Congressional Budget Office numbers to balance the budget, we couldn't get there in seven years with the limited scale of the president's cuts. The estimates provided by the Office of Management and Budget, which are more favorable to the president, would get us there in seven years. This was the first I'd heard about the dispute between the CBO and OMB estimates, but they would become a central part of the discussion in the weeks ahead.

At an October 30 staff directors meeting, while the Republicans were managing their conference committees and working out the differences between the House and Senate, Daschle's staff urged Democratic senators to stick with the message, to keep it up and to amplify it: "The Republican budget is extreme. It deserves a veto. The president is doing the right thing." Then Hilley said quietly that Democrats had to think about what their position would be after the president vetoed the initial bill. There would be negotiations, so what was the Democratic alternative? We had to come up with a deal that a majority of Democrats could vote for. Democratic senators needed to agree to the principle of a balanced budget by a certain date. But they would also need to support the principle that every committee and every area had to contribute. Hilley's comments were ominous for those of us who wanted the Democrats and the president to maintain a hard line against the Republicans, a strategy we believed was succeeding.

Griffin made a plea to the staff directors: "The president's radio address on Saturday was very strong. The Republicans are hitting us hard. They are setting up unmeetable conditions. You guys in the Senate have to give us cover. We need the folks on the Hill to say we are doing the right thing at the White House. The Republicans haven't backed off their Medicare cuts or tax cuts. The pressure is growing on the White House to get into the fray and cut more. The criticism is growing that our budget is out of balance by CBO standards."

President Clinton continued to send out mixed signals. At a fundraiser in Houston on October 17, he made a remark that worried Democratic strategists who wanted him to take a strong stand against the Republicans: "Probably there are people in this room still mad at me about that budget [his first budget, in 1993] because you think I raised your taxes too much. It might surprise you to know that I think I raised them too much too."[4]

To a member, Democrats in Congress had stuck with the president in 1993 on the budget. Many who had lost their seats in the 1994 election believed it was because of that vote. Congressional Democrats were furious with the president as Washington headed into the endgame of the titanic struggle with the Republicans over the budget.

Chapter 16

THE FIRST TRAIN WRECK

THE REPUBLICAN BUDGET FINALLY
COMES TO THE SENATE FLOOR

The president may have been waffling, but the Republicans were not. On October 19 House Republicans voted to approve their Medicare bill, complete with $270 billion in cuts. The bill was brought up separately from the rest of the reconciliation bill in a futile attempt to separate the Medicare cuts from tax cuts, even though the two bills would have to be merged later. The remainder of the reconciliation bill passed the House a week later.

The president continued to send mixed signals. His June proposal to balance the budget in ten years had infuriated congressional Democrats. Now he said it was possible that he and Republicans could balance the budget in seven years, which would require even deeper cuts. It was the first time he had indicated that he might accept the Republicans' seven-

263

year timetable. Congressional Democrats who wanted a strong position from the president had new reason to worry about his resolve.

When the Senate started voting on its version of the reconciliation bill on October 26, Democrats were ready with the key amendments they planned to offer during the fifty hours allocated to pass the bill. The debate on Medicare rolled on, with Kennedy, Rockefeller, Wellstone, Boxer—Democrat after Democrat—coming to the floor to attack the Republican plans to cut Medicare. The *New York Times* published a poll that day showing that by more than 2 to 1 the American public rejected significant cuts to Medicare even for the purpose of balancing the budget.[1]

The Republican reconciliation bill would block-grant Medicaid and cut it by some 30 percent over time. Kennedy said, "The Republicans basically pull the rug from under the children of America. Why are we doing it? To provide tax breaks for the wealthiest corporations, companies, and individuals in this country." The elimination of spousal impoverishment protections and nursing home quality standards were also highlighted.

Later in the day Kennedy was back on the floor to offer an amendment to restore funds for student loans cut by the Republicans. His amendment would have removed the Republicans' new student loan tax and eliminated increased interest rates on the parent-student loan program. Kennedy's speech was one of his strongest to date. His voice rising, he declaimed, "Republicans are being found guilty beyond a reasonable doubt of hurting senior citizens on Medicare; guilty of hurting helpless elderly patients in nursing homes; guilty of punishing innocent children on welfare; guilty of closing college doors to the sons and daughters of working families; guilty of pandering to polluters and endangering the environment; guilty of massive giveaways to powerful special interest groups; guilty of taxing low-income workers; guilty of taxing hard-pressed college students—all to give tax breaks to millionaires. I say, Shame on the Republicans for using their majority power to hurt the vast majority of Americans. This bill will be dead on arrival at the White House, and we ought to bury it right here in the Senate."

Early on October 28 the reconciliation bill passed the Senate by a vote of 52–47. Everyone involved interpreted the debate as a critical clash over the direction of the U.S. government. Dole said, "This is the most historic moment in my memory in the Congress of the United States." Daschle called it "a tragic day and a historic day." Most Democrats left the floor immediately after voting, not wanting to witness the Republican triumph. Kennedy, however, watched to the end. In his view, this was a historic moment, albeit one he hoped to make transitory.

President Clinton swung back on the offensive in his Saturday radio address, telling Republicans, "Back off your cuts in the vital areas of Medicare and Medicaid, the gutting of our commitment to education, the ravaging of our environment or raising taxes on working people. Back off your cuts in these vital areas. Until you do there is nothing for us to talk about."

THE PUBLIC SUPPORTS A VETO

By October 31 Republicans still hadn't passed eleven of the thirteen appropriations bills for the fiscal year that began on October 1. On November 1 Republican leaders went to the White House and had a private two-hour discussion with President Clinton. It was reported that they got nowhere. Democrats touted a poll on that same day from the *Wall Street Journal* showing that 61 percent of the American people wanted Clinton to veto the Republican budget, and 73 percent preferred smaller Medicare and education cuts and balancing the budget over ten years instead of seven.

On November 2 Democrats were back on the floor attacking the reconciliation bill. With more time to analyze details of the bill, Kennedy highlighted benefits to the special interests: the pharmaceutical industry would no longer be required to provide discounts to Medicaid programs; the American Medical Association, in return for its support of the cuts in Medicare, would get weaker antifraud and conflict-of-interest rules and would be allowed to issue supplemental bills to patients above the amount that Medicare reimburses (called "balance billing"); the nursing home industry would gain provisions eliminating federal nursing home standards.

The debate in Washington was back at fever pitch. The president moved from one position to the next: one day he was strongly critical of the Republicans and their agenda; the next he said he wanted to work with them to reach a balanced budget on their seven-year terms. Perhaps the vacillation was a masterful strategy: keep the Republicans guessing, appear reasonable and presidential to the public. That would have been fine if we weren't so concerned about where he would end up. We still believed it strengthened our hand for the ultimate negotiations to clearly identify our differences from the Republicans and continue to expose the extremism and harshness of their proposals.

KENNEDY VERSUS DOLE ON *MEET THE PRESS*

The Sunday morning television talk shows are a Washington institution. The top two shows in 1995 were *Meet the Press* on NBC, hosted by Tim Russert, and *This Week with Cokie Roberts and Sam Donaldson* on ABC. They were an hour long each. CBS's *Face the Nation*, hosted by Bob Schieffer, was a half-hour long. There were also weekend interview shows on CNN and Fox and a slew of other shows that had guests from the Washington political scene.

Some politicians loved to be on these shows and were on them almost every weekend. Orrin Hatch on the Republican side and Daniel Patrick Moynihan on the Democratic side come to mind as two who rarely turned down an invitation. Washington strategists believed the shows were a very good way to get a particular message out because there was likely to be little other news on a Sunday. News shows on Sunday night and newspapers on Monday morning had to report something, so the weekend shows were attractive venues.

Although he was invited regularly, Senator Kennedy was one of those politicians who normally did not accept invitations to appear on the Sunday shows. He was often out of Washington in Hyannis Port or in Boston on the weekend, and it was not as easy to tape the shows from outside of Washington. When he was in Washington he preferred to spend the time with his family, go to church on Sunday morning, and generally relax and regroup for the week. He had two young stepchildren, and there was normal family activity to tend to. And when the senator did decide to appear, he wanted to be sure he was fully briefed and prepared—a time-consuming process. But occasionally the opportunity to appear on a Sunday show was irresistible.

In late October, Tim Russert called to invite Kennedy to appear on his show on November 3. Russert told the senator that the other guest that day would be Bob Dole. It would be a good opportunity for Kennedy to highlight his views on the Republican budget and other aspects of the Republican agenda. There would be extra attention focused on *Meet the Press* that day since Dole was the Senate majority leader and the leading candidate for the Republican nomination for president in the election that would occur almost exactly one year later. Kennedy and Dole, two giants from their parties. What a great match-up. Kennedy accepted.

Meet the Press ran ads in major newspapers:

TED KENNEDY AND BOB DOLE FACE OFF

The Liberal Democrat from Massachusetts and the Conservative Republican from Kansas tackle tough questions on Medicare, taxes and the role of government.

Why read about it on Monday when you can see it on Sunday? *Meet the Press* with Tim Russert celebrating forty-eight years.

Because the audience for this appearance would probably be larger than the normal Sunday morning audience and since the reporters who covered the presidential campaigns would be watching, as would the reporters who covered Congress, Kennedy decided to spend even more than the usual time preparing for his appearance. Early in the week, he called some of his staff together to discuss the themes he wanted to focus on. He asked us to check with our advisors to get ideas for points to make during the show.

Mark Mellman said that Medicare was the issue on which to focus. He suggested Kennedy start with Dole's statement a week earlier that he was proud to have opposed Medicare in 1965 because he knew it wouldn't work.

Kennedy knew that he would be asked how he felt about President Clinton. Paul Kirk suggested the senator should be very clear that although the president hadn't yet reflected the follow-through and resolve on the issue of the budget that people may have wanted, Kennedy was certain that perception would dissolve when the president vetoed the budget. "Clinton himself had in fact acknowledged that there hadn't been the appearance of resolve and consistency, but now we were really into the crunch time. The budget is a statement of values, a strategy. Priorities on the Republican side go beyond balancing the budget. They seem to be harsh. We are now at the Rubicon. The president needs to stand up, show resolve and veto the bill."

Ranny Cooper, the senator's former chief of staff, said that what was important was what people would take away from the show: the distinction Kennedy had drawn between Democrats and Republicans. "Here's our view of the world and here is their view," she said. "The reason the senator is appearing is to take a stand and to draw a line between us and them. We don't want the headline to be the differences between Kennedy and the president. So the senator might say, 'I note from my brother's experience that it is difficult to second-guess what it is like to sit in the president's chair.' Be careful what you say about the president because if you say more than that, the takeaway will be you are criticizing the president. You should say, 'I am not here to discuss whatever differences I may have with the president. I am here to discuss how mean-spirited the Republican budget is.'"

Michael Powell, Senator Dodd's chief of staff, said, "Russert will paint Kennedy as the ultimate liberal. He is going to be tough because he is always tougher on Democrats. Senator Kennedy should constantly get back to the message. This show is about political positioning. The American people didn't vote for what the Republicans are trying to give them. It is a lie that there is a need to make draconian cuts to Medicare. The country is rebelling against the Republican budget."

When the Senate finally adjourned in October 1994, Kennedy faced a tough fight against Mitt Romney. © *Brooks Kraft/Sygma/Corbis*

Kennedy worked hard to address the needs of Massachusetts fishermen over the years. As described in the opening chapter, Nick spent Election Day 1994 in Gloucester. © *Michael Dwyer/Associated Press*

On the morning of November 8, 1994, Kennedy waits his turn to vote at his home precinct in Hyannis at the West Elementary School.

© *Tom Landers/The Boston Globe via Getty Images*

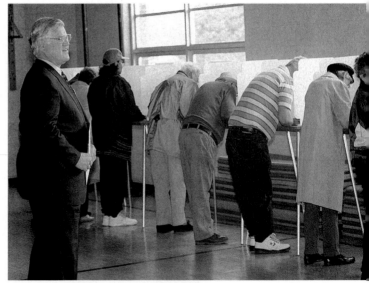

TV news flashes the results of the Kennedy-Romney contest on election night. Kennedy had come back from behind to score a landslide victory.

© *Jason Reed/Reuters/Corbis*

With Vicki by his side, an ebullient Kennedy addresses supporters after his victory speech on November 10, 1994. © *Pat Greenhouse/The Boston Globe via Getty Images*

Portrait of the Labor Committee membership circa 1993 in the President's Room off the Senate floor. Seated, from left: Claiborne Pell (D, RI), Tom Harkin (D, IA), Strom Thurmond (R, SC), Chris Dodd (D, CT), David Durenberger (R, MN); standing: Nick, Harris Wofford (D, PA), Barbara Mikulski (D, MD), James Jeffords (R, VT), Howard Metzenbaum (D, OH), Kennedy, Orrin Hatch (R, UT), Nancy Kassebaum (R, KS), Jeff Bingaman (D, NM), Susan Hattan (Republican committee staff director), Dan Coats (D, IN), Paul Simon (D, IL). *Courtesy of Senate Photographer Office*

Portrait of the Democratic Committee staff circa 1993. Nick is seated in the front center with David to his right. *Courtesy of Senate Photographer Office*

Kennedy presides at a Labor Committee hearing on health care. © *John Duricka/Associated Press*

Senators Kassebaum and Kennedy and their staff confer during the Labor Committee markup of the Clinton universal health bill on May 18, 1994. Susan Hattan is standing at the far left, next to Nick and Ron Weich. David is seated behind Senator Kennedy.

© *John Duricka/Associated Press*

Nick and Hillary Clinton in her office after a strategy meeting on health care. *Courtesy of the White House*

Boston Globe photo of Kennedy, Elizabeth Taylor, and Orrin Hatch, with an inscription by Senator Kennedy to Senator Hatch. Taylor's testimony before the Labor Committee in support of the Ryan White Act generated tremendous press and helped move the Ryan White AIDS Care Act forward. © *John Duricka/Associated Press, courtesy of Senator Orrin Hatch*

THE BOSTON GLOBE • WEDNESDAY, MARCH 7, 1990

AP PHOTO

SEEKING AIDS FUNDING – *Sen. Edward M. Kennedy, Elizabeth Taylor and Sen. Orrin Hatch, a Utah Republican, promote a bill introduced yesterday that would provide $600 million to help care for AIDS victims. Half of the money would go to 13 large cities, including Boston.*

Meeting at the oval office June 10, 1993, after the signing ceremony for legislation eliminating the ban on NIH-funded fetal tissue research. From left: Nick; Senator Kennedy; Dr. Van Dunn and Michael Iskowitz, both senior Kennedy staff on the Labor Committee; President Clinton; Robyn Lipner, a staffer for Senator Brock Adams (D-Washington); Marty Ross, M.D., on the Republican staff of the Labor Committee; Walter Broadnax, deputy secretary of Health and Human Services; and Jerry Kleppner, assistant secretary for legislation at Health and Human Services. *Courtesy of the White House*

Republican candidates pose on the Capitol steps for the signing ceremony of Newt Gingrich's "Contract with America" in September 1994. © *Ira Schwarz/Reuters/Corbis*

Kennedy and Nick confer with Clinton, Chief of Staff Leon Panetta, Deputy Chief of Staff Harold Ickes, and Director of Legislative Affairs Pat Griffin on December 13, 1994. The meeting took place in Clinton's private study, the Treaty Room in the family quarters. The room was decorated by the Clintons in the Victorian style of the Lincoln era.

Courtesy of the White House

Kennedy addresses a minimum wage rally of union workers on the steps of the Capitol. © *Michael Williamson/The Washington Post via Getty Images*

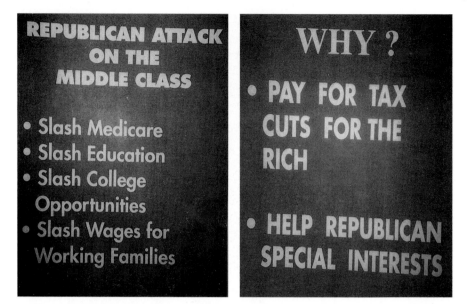

An example of the charts Kennedy used when he spoke every week on the floor in 1995. Visible behind him on CSPAN, they served as another way to remind viewers of the intended Republican cuts.

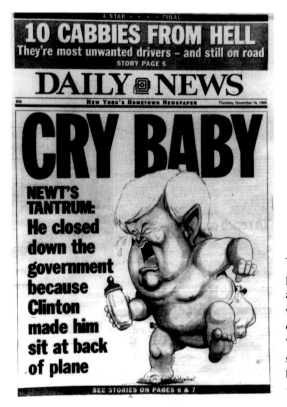

The November 16, 1995, front page of the *New York Daily News* after Gingrich claimed that the vetoed debt limit extension and continuing resolution bills were "tougher" because Clinton had snubbed him on the plane ride back from the Rabin funeral.

The New York Daily News/Associated Press

Dole leaves the Senate after his resignation speech. Kennedy's fight for the minimum wage had made a shambles of Dole's plan to campaign based on his accomplishments as majority leader. © *Richard Ellis/AFP/Getty Images*

Gingrich makes a point to a skeptical-looking Clinton, Lott, and Gephardt during ne-gotiations over the second government shutdown. © *David Hume Kennerly/Getty Images*

On July 28, 2004, Brian Stokes Mitchell joined Kennedy and Nick in the lower level of Symphony Hall following a tribute concert held for Senator Kennedy during the Democratic National Convention.

© *Tom Fitzsimmons*

Audra McDonald joined the group. Kennedy loved a chance to sing, especially with Broadway stars.

© *Tom Fitzsimmons*

Ted and Vicki with their Portuguese water dogs, Splash and Sunny.

© *Nancy Kaszerman/ZUMA/Corbis*

Kennedy conducts the Boston Pops. *© Charles Krupa/Associated Press*

As staff applauds, Nick finishes with a flourish after singing with Marvin Hamlisch.
© Alan Porter, Focused Images

The east front of the Capitol building with the original dome designed by Charles Bulfinch. The Bulfinch dome was replaced when the modern Capitol building was constructed during the 1850s. *Daguerreotype by John Plumbe, 1846. Courtesy of Library of Congress*

The old Senate Chamber. *Courtesy of U.S. Senate Commission on Art*

Kennedy's "hideaway" office in the Capitol, just off the Senate floor. The table is an old rudder from Kennedy's sailboat that his children had made into a table for him. David is seated at the lower right. © *Ron Sachs/CNP/Corbis*

To Nick. a great day and a great victory for health reform. Well done!
Ted Kennedy
aug/96

Kennedy celebrates signing the conference report on the Kassebaum-Kennedy insurance reform legislation, August 1996. Seated from left: Carey Parker; Nick; Lauren Ewers Polite, David's deputy on the health staff; Kennedy; David; and Dennis Kelleher. *Courtesy of the author*

Kennedy and Hatch together in Hatch's office on February 10, 1994. As was typical for negotiations between the two, they sat side by side facing the staff. *Courtesy of Senator Orrin Hatch*

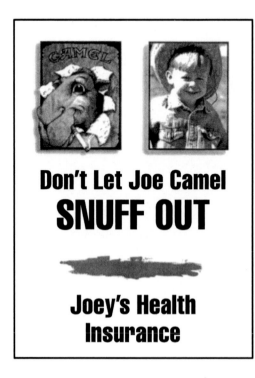

The Joey vs. Joe Camel ad for CHIP had different versions, but was always topped by a picture of the two symbolic antagonists—a child versus the cartoon symbol of a giant tobacco brand. *Courtesy of the Children's Defense Fund on behalf of the Campaign for Child Health Now Coalition*

Kennedy and his son, Congressman Patrick Kennedy, on the podium of American University in Washington, D.C., on January 28, 2008, when Kennedy announced his endorsement of Obama.

© *Mike Theiler/Reuters/Corbis*

A cartoon about Hatch and Kennedy and their child health insurance bill. It appeared in the *Salt Lake Tribune* in 1997.

Kennedy, Nick, and Vicki on Kennedy's sailboat, the *Maya.*

Courtesy of the author

Nick sings one of Senator Kennedy's favorite songs, "Love Changes Everything," at the memorial service held at the John F. Kennedy Library on August 28, 2009. © *C-SPAN*

Current and former Senate staff and friends gathered on the Senate steps at the Capitol on August 29, 2009, to pay tribute to Senator Kennedy as his hearse passed by the Senate on its way to Arlington National Cemetery." *©Pool/Mark Wilson/Getty Images North America/Corbis*

On Friday night we met with Kennedy at his house to prepare for Sunday morning. We ran through the possible questions Russert might ask and Kennedy tried out his answers:

On the president's Republican advisor, Dick Morris: "Don't ask me about Dick Morris. Medicare is more important than Dick Morris. This might not be the answer you want, but it is the answer you are going to get."

On President Clinton: "If I am asked about President Clinton being someone who changes his positions, I am not going to criticize the president, but look, if you want to talk about someone who changes his position, look at Senator Dole. Earlier in his career he was for civil rights and voting rights, now he is against affirmative action. Earlier he was for breaking the glass ceiling for women. Now he is against it. Earlier he was for the Americans with Disabilities Act. Now he is for blocking new regulations to implement the Act. He is the master of changing positions, not just in rhetoric, but in reality. Oh, there is one issue he has never changed on, and that is Medicare. He has always been against it. . . .

"The best way to advance the values of the Democratic Party is to reelect President Clinton. No one should run against him. . . .

"I think President Clinton has been a better president than he has been a politician. He stood firm on affirmative action, gun control, the economy, and foreign policy. He has taken tough positions. It is unfair to criticize him for not having taken tough positions."

On running against President Carter: "I stood up for some very basic principles. I had big differences with him on health care, but he and I have stood together many times since then."

On Colin Powell running for president: "He'll make his own decision. Frankly, from the things he has said, he sounds more like a Democrat than a Republican.

"Everyone in the Republican race has been pushed to the right. I worked with Senator Dole on affirmative action and the Americans with Disabilities Act. Dole's whole campaign is a campaign against his record in the Senate. The whole Republican Party is forcing people to run against their own views."

On the debt limit: "Republicans have the responsibility to pass it. The debt limit should not be a political football."

On Medicare: "The president should veto any bill that threatens Medicare, and I will vote against any budget that destroys Medicare."

On negotiations between the president and the Republicans: "It's always useful to talk, but the president needs to stand up on fundamental principles. No draconian cuts to Medicare to pay for tax breaks for the rich. Don't slam the doors of college on middle-class families, do not abolish the Department of Education, and don't cut funding to the schools. Protect children and the environment.

"The Medicare battle is all about whether government will serve the interests of the many or the privileged. This has been the enduring struggle in American politics. Going back to the beginning of the Democratic Party we stood for serving average Americans, not just the privileged. These are enduring ideas on which Democrats have always won elections, and on which they will win in 1996. We are in favor of better jobs and wages, health care, and education. I make no apologies for these values."

Aren't you just with the status quo? "I have fought for years for fundamental change. During the years I have been in the Senate the changes I have fought for have had a profound effect. Voting rights, trucking deregulation, airline deregulation, minimum wage, student loans, health care, doing something about the stagnation of the standard of living and of earnings. Republicans simply want to cut taxes for the wealthy and cut programs for the middle class to pay for it."

On Saturday, November 2, we were back at the senator's house for another few hours of preparing for the show. We left confident that he was ready to take on Dole and would do so very effectively. He would make the case against the Republican budget, and we hoped that would have some effect on President Clinton. He reminded us of what his brother Robert had said about these Sunday morning shows: "You decide what you want to say and go in there and say it no matter what the questions are." There were three parts to the message the senator wanted to convey:

1. He is not there to criticize the president. The president will stand tall against the Republican budget.
2. The main issues that differentiate Democrats and Republicans are Medicare, education, tax breaks for the rich, the environment, and campaign finance.
3. Senator Dole has changed his positions on many issues over the years. Republicans are much too tight with the special interests and their programs are much too extreme to be accepted by the American people.

When I got home my daughter, Kate Lowenstein, phoned. She was crying. Yitzhak Rabin had been shot and killed. I was horrified. Rabin, the prime minister of Israel, was an irreplaceable leader who had kept Israel together while he negotiated peace with the Palestinians. His death posed a significant threat to the future of peace in the Middle East.

It was a small matter in comparison to the scale of the tragedy in Israel, but there was now the question of *Meet the Press*. Shouldn't the Kennedy-Dole program be scrapped in favor of a tribute to Rabin? We talked to Russert, who said that they were going forward with the show as planned and that he would have a tribute to Rabin in the beginning of the hour and then interview the Israeli ambassador prior to turning to the Kennedy-Dole segment.

The next morning at 7:30 we met the senator for coffee at his house before the show and then headed to the NBC studios in D.C. The building was nondescript. We walked down a long corridor to a waiting room, called the green room, where muffins, stale bagels, coffee, orange juice, and a plate of fruit were laid out. A TV was tuned to NBC. We mingled with the other guests and made small talk with Russert. The senator was shown to a small makeup room nearby and then escorted to the studio itself, which is a large open room with the set installed in the middle of the space. It has none of the grandeur that one sees when one watches the show from home. Selected guests and tourists were invited to sit as a live audience in the studio.

While waiting for their segment to begin, Kennedy and Dole listened to the tribute to Rabin and the discussion with the Israeli ambassador. Dole was interviewed next. David Broder, the distinguished *Washington Post* reporter and one of the panel of interviewers, asked him about his vote against Medicare in 1965. Dole tried to explain by claiming that he supported "Eldercare," a voluntary program that was means-tested. He believed Medicare "hasn't worked very well." It was a "fair idea but has cost a great deal of money." With Medicare there needed to be "fundamental change," more choice and other options. Dole finished by saying that he and Kennedy were "good friends" but with "different philosophies."

After a commercial break it was Kennedy's turn. He began by expressing his condolences to the Rabin family and called Rabin "a real hero for the peace process," which, Kennedy asserted, would continue. Then he turned to the Republicans' Medicare cuts. He made the point that the cuts would raise premiums and undermine the quality of care and were going to pay for tax cuts for the wealthy. When the panelists asked Kennedy about welfare, he responded that while he disagreed with the president on welfare, Clinton had offered great leadership in many areas, such as creating millions of jobs. As expected, Kennedy was asked about Dick Morris, and responded, "People aren't concerned with Dick Morris. They are interested in Medicare and student loans." He went on to discuss the Republican budget, corporate welfare, defense spending, and other issues. He accused the Republicans of being for the special interests and said that the Democratic Party was needed more today than at any time in the past twenty-five years. The discussion turned to the 1996 presidential race, and Kennedy predicted that it would be a Dole-Clinton race with Clinton winning. We were delighted with his performance and believed he had effectively made all the points he wanted to get across.

When the taping was completed, we accompanied the senator back to his house. He had made the decision to attend Rabin's funeral in Israel. A plane was provided by the White House to fly U.S. senators and members of Congress to Israel. Kennedy was in a hurry because the plane was to leave Andrews Air Force Base only a few hours after the taping. His son, Congressman Patrick Kennedy, had decided to go with him to Israel; the two of them would be the representatives of the Kennedy family.

As we stood in the senator's kitchen, he asked Patrick, me, and others who had been with him at the studio if there were some special gift he should take to Mrs. Rabin. We thought of roses or traditional Kennedy mementos. Vicki inquired about tradition at a Jewish funeral. I said that at the end of the funeral mourners go to the grave and put soil on top of the coffin. We had an idea: could the senator take a small amount of soil from the Kennedy graves at Arlington and place it in Rabin's grave? That would be a powerful gesture of solidarity between Americans and Israelis and a gesture from the Kennedy family, which, it went without saying, had experienced the tragedy and horror of assassinations.

At that point there was only a short amount of time to get to the cemetery and then to Andrews in time to catch the flight. We agreed I would drive Patrick to Arlington and we would meet up with the senator on his way to the air force base. The only problem we faced was being arrested for defacing a public monument, but hopefully we could talk our way out of that. We broke all speed records getting to the cemetery, drove past the guards and the ticket office, past the crowds lined up to visit, all the way up to the JFK gravesite. Patrick jumped out of the car and hustled past unsuspecting tourists with the trowel and paper bags we had brought from the senator's house hidden under his coat. From a dirt patch twenty feet behind the grave he filled the two small brown bags with soil, and with one last glance over his shoulder, jumped back into my car. Inside of five minutes we were rushing down to meet the senator, who was waiting at the arranged rendezvous for the trip to Andrews. He arrived just in time for the flight, two small bags of very important soil stowed safely in his carry-on bags.

The gift of soil from the Kennedy grave to Mrs. Rabin and the act of transferring the soil to Rabin's grave was covered extensively in both the

Israeli and U.S. press. We hoped that this small gesture of solidarity with Rabin and the Israeli people from the Kennedys showed America's deep grief and respect.

THE GOVERNMENT SHUTDOWN APPROACHES

At the staff directors meeting on November 6, Daschle's staff reported on the meeting held at the White House the previous week between the president and Democratic and Republican congressional leaders. The president was the strongest Daschle had ever seen him, telling the Republicans, "I have gone the extra mile to understand your priorities, but I ran to protect health care, education, and jobs. These are my priorities. I'd just as soon Bob Dole have this job as be blackmailed." Steve Ricchetti, one of the president's aides, said the meeting had gotten very personal. The Republicans accused the president of calling them extremists, to which the president responded, "I've expressed my priorities and you have made no movement." It was very intense, direct, and blunt.

The continuing resolution was to expire at midnight on November 13, when the government would shut down for the second time if the funds were not approved. Meanwhile the White House and Democratic leaders in Congress were scheduling events to highlight the budget issues. A Tuesday event would focus on how children would be hurt under the Republican budget. Busloads of seniors had been invited to the White House for a rally on Wednesday to protest the Medicare cuts. Later in the week, we had events focusing on jobs and investments in research and development, and then on Republican proposals to undermine the private pension system.

Shortly after returning from the Rabin funeral, Daschle told Kennedy that on the plane back from Israel Dole had told him that Gingrich wanted a deal on the budget more than anyone. According to Dole, Gingrich wanted to show that he was the speaker who could get things done. The Republicans would be willing to go down to $124 billion in Medicare cuts and $70 billion in Medicaid cuts. They would restore the EITC. They needed some sort of a tax cut. They'd use OMB figures and save a little bit of money on Social Security and other programs by cutting back the consumer price index, which was the benchmark for automatic increases in these programs each year. Dole believed that Clinton would take Republican direction on the substance of the cuts to Medicare because the message from Clinton was to get a deal. Dole's conversation with Daschle turned out to be far from an accurate description of what would actually happen and showed the disconnect between Dole and the House Republicans.

During the week of November 6, the debate over the budget continued. As the Republicans negotiated among themselves to resolve the differences between the reconciliation bills passed by the House and Senate, Democrats criticized them for meeting in secret. On November 7, Election Day in several states, Democrats rebounded from the disastrous elections of 1994, unseating the Republican governor of Kentucky and holding off expected Republican gains in state legislatures in Virginia, New Jersey, Maine, and Mississippi. The next day, Colin Powell announced he would not run for the Republican presidential nomination. His decision eliminated what might have been Dole's and then Clinton's strongest opponent. On November 8 the Republican House passed a resolution to allow the government to continue spending money through December 1, and the extension of the debt limit advanced to the floor. Democrats went back to the Senate floor each day all week long to attack the Republicans on their Medicare proposals, particularly on the increases in the premiums seniors would be responsible for paying.

On November 9 Democrats received news that they greeted with considerable glee. Frank Luntz, the Republican pollster credited with putting together the Contract with America, revealed that in fact the Contract had been developed based on research on the most effective packaging, not the intensive polling research on policies Republicans had previously claimed.[2]

Democrats pointed to a new set of polls that showed them running six points ahead of Republicans for the upcoming congressional elections. The polls also found that 57 percent of Americans thought the Republican budget went too far and 62 percent believed Medicare would be jeopardized by the Republican budget. Meanwhile Gingrich's popularity was at an all time low: 56 percent of the public had an unfavorable opinion of the speaker. By a margin of 60 to 33 percent, the public thought the president should veto a Republican budget intended to balance the federal budget in seven years, cut taxes, and cut the rate of spending on programs like Medicare and Medicaid. In fact 75 percent opposed cutting the rate of spending on Medicare, 66 percent opposed cutting the rate of spending on Medicaid, 74 percent opposed cutting student college loans, and 53 percent opposed reducing the EITC for the working poor.

There did not appear to be any agreement between the Republicans and the president on the budget, and the press began reporting on what a shutdown would involve. Passport offices closed. Veterans' benefit checks withheld. Smithsonian Museums in Washington and national parks and monuments across the country closed. Federal court civil cases postponed. Social Security applications not processed. Another train wreck appeared likely.

The president wanted to meet with the Republicans to talk about the budget, but the Republicans refused to include congressional Democrats in their budget meetings. On November 11 Clinton and Dole talked on the phone, but it was apparent that no progress was made. Dole claimed the president had said in effect, "Get lost." The president asked his chief of staff, Leon Panetta, to meet with the Republican and Democratic congressional leaders that afternoon. "But," he said, "I will not allow them to impose new immediate cuts in Medicare, education, and the environment as a condition of keeping the government open."

The Republicans' debt limit extension and continuing resolution to keep the government open were moving through the House and Senate, but they found it impossible to resist adding legislative provisions (known as "riders") that they knew would be unacceptable to the president. These included a limit on the Treasury Department's power to avoid a default if a debt limit were to be reached in the future, a version of the deregulation bill, a bill limiting habeas corpus rights, and a provision requiring the president to accept a seven-year balanced budget based on CBO scoring.[3] Reaching a balanced budget through the CBO rather than the OMB, which was controlled by the president, was more difficult because its scoring was based on higher spending projections and lower revenue projections. So a balanced budget under CBO scoring would require much deeper cuts in spending. The shorter amount of time in which to reach balance would also make the necessary cuts deeper than under the president's ten-year budget.

One rider to the continuing resolution turned out to be a huge tactical mistake for the Republicans. Their reconciliation bill proposed to set the enrollee premium for Medicare Part B at 31.5 percent of projected program costs each year, an increase of more than one quarter over existing law and a large additional burden for seniors. The Republicans had been told that if the premium increase were not legislated right away—without waiting for the reconciliation bill to pass—it would be impossible to program the government computers in time to make the change for 1996. Republican staff warned that attaching the change to the continuing resolution was political dynamite; in effect, the Republicans would be shutting down the government in order to force senior citizens to pay more for Medicare. But the leadership didn't listen. Medicare cuts were central to their program, and they were going to push ahead.

The stage was set. If the president refused to accept the Republican proposals by end of the day on November 13, the government would shut down.

First, the Republicans passed and sent a debt limit extension to the president, who vetoed the bill, as he said he would, because the riders obligated the government to pass the Republican congressional budget plan. Clinton described what he saw as the Republican endgame:

> Last spring, Speaker Gingrich said that he and his new Republican
> congressional majority would force me, the congressional Democrats,
> and the American people to accept their budget and their Contract
> by bringing about a crisis in the fall, by shutting down the government

and pushing America into default unless I accepted their extreme proposals. In this way, the congressional Republicans sought to get around the United States Constitution, which gives the president the power to veto measures not in the public interest.

In recent days, Congress has chosen the path of confrontation. It is not in the national interest, but it is exactly what they said they would do last spring.

I know the American people want us to balance the budget with common sense and without bitterness, to drop the extreme proposals and get to work. Congress should take the sensible step of passing the legislation necessary to keep the government open and to have America meet its financial obligations. . . . This is not the time or place for them to backdoor their budget proposals. It is not the right thing to do. I can not and will not accept it.[4]

On the floor, Kennedy was offering motions to instruct the conferees on the reconciliation bill to drop giveaways to the pharmaceutical industry and to maintain federal nursing home standards.

Meanwhile the Republicans and Democrats continued their argument over the level of funding in the continuing resolution that would allow the government to remain open for a few days at a time. The Republicans were trying to use each continuing resolution to further ratchet down funding levels.

At the staff directors meeting on November 13, the day the continuing resolution was due to expire, the president's legislative advisor, Steve Ricchetti, reported that the shutdown appeared inevitable. The president's veto of the Republican debt limit extension was carried live on CNN. Over the weekend, feeling pressure to meet with the Republicans, Clinton said he would meet if they took Medicare cuts off the table. The White House was particularly worried about the debt limit. The longer the delay in approving the extension, the more interest rates would go up. Congressional Democrats and the White House continued their strategy of staging an event a day to expose the extreme measures in the

Republican program and the recklessness of shutting down the government to try to force the president to accept it.

Later in the day, John Hilley briefed Democratic staff on the status of the negotiations with the president. He said that the meetings at the White House over the weekend had produced no results. Republicans in the Senate wanted to drop the riders from the continuing resolution and the debt limit, but Gingrich refused. They wanted to lock in a seven-year balanced budget using their budget numbers from the CBO, but that would lock in their priorities, not the president's. On the debt limit Hilley said the Treasury had come up with ways to get through the month but couldn't get past the point when it would need to send out Social Security checks in early December. The Republicans would finish their reconciliation bill that week and send it to the president. He intended to veto it immediately. Hilley repeated that it was critical that the Democrats stay on message. "The Republicans are going to try to turn the debate into 'they are for balancing the budget; we aren't.' We can't let them shift the ground. They have an extreme budget, which the American people reject by almost three to one. We have a slower and more reasonable approach to balance. Theirs is an extreme agenda that the public has rejected. They have reverted to political blackmail. We won't let them hold us hostage to their priorities."

Following Hilley, Mark Mellman said that we were winning this debate by a twenty-point margin. The people were blaming Republicans for the cuts and for this crisis. It doesn't matter if the budget is balanced in seven, eight, nine, or ten years, he said, the message should be that the Republicans are shutting down the government. They are risking the credit of the United States, all to cut Medicare, cut education, and roll back environmental protections. These are radical tactics. We need to be on the offensive and focus on the irresponsibility of shutting down the government to force their extreme agenda.

THE SHUTDOWN BEGINS

Clinton vetoed the Republican debt limit extension and continuing resolution, and on the next day, November 14, the shutdown began. The *Washington Post* published a poll showing that two-thirds of the American public blamed the Republicans.

The following day Gingrich made a bad situation for the Republicans worse. He complained that President Clinton had snubbed him on the way back from the Rabin funeral by not calling him to the front of Air Force One for a private chat and then making him and Dole leave the plane by the rear ramp with other members of Congress. He claimed the spending bill that the president vetoed was "tougher" because of this snub. In response the *New York Daily News* ran a widely circulated front-page cartoon of Gingrich dressed in a diaper and holding a baby bottle with the caption "Cry baby Newt's tantrum: he closed down the government because Clinton made him sit at the back of the plane." The episode played in the media for days.

The day before the Gingrich outburst, the Senate Democratic Caucus met with members of the president's cabinet. Senator Jack Reed of Rhode Island opened by asking the cabinet members to tell the president to hang tough: "Don't let the Republicans take away your Medicare." Senator Dodd reviewed the elections of the previous Tuesday. Looking at the lowercase races, as he put it, the Democrats had done very well. In Mississippi, where we used Medicare ads, we won in the legislature. In Virginia we were outspent two to one in the legislature, but we held our own. In New Jersey we had an overwhelming victory for Democrats. In Maine we regained the state legislature. In Staten Island, Charleston, South Carolina, Macon, Georgia, and Washington State we did well. "Newt Gingrich has given us a lift. We are on the right track," Dodd said. "We are talking about the issues that cause people to vote for Democrats."

Daschle said that Dole would be bringing the conference report on the budget reconciliation bill to the Senate floor on Thursday. The conference report represented the agreement worked out between House and Senate Republicans that they planned to pass in both houses and send to the president. Daschle promised that the Senate Democratic Caucus would be well organized to get the message out. There would be a staff meeting every morning during the crisis. He also reported on a meeting at the White House the previous day, just before the shutdown: "After the president vetoed the debt limit bill on November 13, Gingrich and the Democratic congressional leaders went to the White House at 10:00 p.m. Gingrich was as confrontational and noncooperative as I had ever seen him. He said, 'I won't even schedule the debt limit or the continuing resolution for the foreseeable future.' But then, after his one-and-a-half-hour diatribe, Gingrich told the meeting we should all go out and say it was a constructive meeting."

Daschle told us: "The president was very good. Medicare was hardly discussed. Now the Republicans are saying the president has to agree to a seven-year budget with Congressional Budget Office numbers. But we can't be tied down that way. Seven years is not doable with such large tax breaks. The agreement to a seven-year budget is premature. The CBO numbers are by far the most conservative of all the economists' numbers. Their growth predictions are very low. At the meeting we agreed to keep talking." Daschle added that it was premature to predict how long Gingrich would hold out. "He has no desire to negotiate an agreement on anything other than his own terms."

Senator Jim Exon, the Democratic ranking member on the Budget Committee, reported on a second meeting of the budget committees held earlier that morning. "I expected that we would go in and come up with a compromise, but the Republicans rejected a twenty-four-hour debt limit and continuing resolution. They don't care about sending people home. The Republican House members are so tied to this strategy that the leaders can't agree to anything unless they get unanimous approval from all the Republicans."

Treasury Secretary Robert Rubin pointed out that without a debt limit extension, the government would default. "By borrowing from the Thrift Fund and the Civil Service Retirement Fund we could get to December 1. This is coercive pressure on the president to get him to sign a reconciliation bill. The president is not going to do what they want him to do. Even the threat of default will be seen in the international markets for years to come. This is a very serious business for the country."

Senator Howell Heflin of Alabama reminded the group that the Republicans were talking about a continuing resolution that would cut 40 percent of the budget. "We should make some hay on a 40 percent cut on veterans, a 40 percent cut on food stamps, a 40 percent cut on the space program."

Dodd suggested that Daschle go out on the Senate floor on an hourly basis and repeatedly offer a clean continuing resolution that would keep the government funded on a day-to-day basis. The Republicans would object, and that would show who was responsible for the shutdown. The caucus agreed that Daschle would offer a clean resolution on the debt limit and a continuing resolution that afternoon. He would also reiterate the point that the Democrats wanted to reform Medicare but would not ask seniors to take the kind of hit the Republicans were proposing and that no one else was being asked to take. Finally, Daschle would make clear that the Democrats were all for a balanced budget.

Democratic staff members met again with Hilley and Mellman. A new continuing resolution had come over from the House. As Heflin had said, it provided a 40 percent cut in health, education, commerce, housing, veterans, and labor programs. The Democratic Caucus was united that they should counteroffer with a clean continuing resolution lasting until December 22 with the funding formula from the first continuing resolution, which was 95 percent of the previous year's spending. Hopefully, we would have a continuing resolution to take us beyond the weekend, when the Republicans would send up their reconciliation bill conference report and the president would veto it.

Hilley emphasized, "The debate must not be seen as being about whether we are for a balanced budget or whether we are for a seven-year, eight-year, nine-year, or ten-year balanced budget. It's about not cutting Medicare to pay for tax breaks for the rich." Mellman added that the CBO was off by $100 billion that year and we shouldn't fall for a debate over whether we were using CBO or other numbers. He reiterated, "This is a political battle, not a substantive one. Our message should be, one: the Republicans are using radical tactics in pursuit of an extreme agenda, two: this is a premeditated plot that was hatched many months ago to shut down the government to force the Democrats to accept Republican cuts to Medicare, and three: Gingrich is acting out of personal pique; he said his 'seven years' was an intuition. It's a hunch and a grudge. That's what is motivating Gingrich."

Kennedy met with other Democratic senators to discuss their strategy when the reconciliation conference report came to the floor. Daschle outlined a possible substitute budget: a Democratic proposal for a seven-year balanced budget using CBO figures. Some of the conservative and moderate Democratic senators said they felt compelled to support a budget that would meet these tests, and Daschle was trying to come up with a Democratic alternative.

Kennedy and Senator Paul Sarbanes resisted. "Look at the figures. There is a $500 billion difference between CBO figures and a balanced budget over seven years and our previous position. We are talking about $500 billion more in cuts to get to a seven-year balanced budget." They urged senators to get the figures; otherwise it would be the end of day care, education, public health, and other priorities for which the Democrats stand.

But some liberal senators, including Russ Feingold, joined the moderates, saying they had been for a balanced budget and they couldn't vote against this proposal. "Why aren't we getting a proposal from the president?" Senator Graham asked. Senator Simon, who led the fight for the balanced budget amendment on the Democratic side, said he would have to vote for it. Senator Kent Conrad of North Dakota said we wouldn't have any Democratic programs left if we accepted the CBO figures, particularly if we went along with the tax cut.

Senator Dodd pointed out that the Democrats had told the president he hadn't been firm enough. If on the first night that Clinton stood up to the Republicans, the Senate Democratic Caucus split with him, it would be a major loss. "We must stick together." Senator Biden thought the Republican assault on Medicare had permanently harmed them. "We should stay with Daschle." Senator Wendell Ford said that we should stick with the president. The situation had turned around dramatically: the public was now with the president.

At the end of the meeting it was apparent that Daschle's substitute budget would hold 85 to 95 percent of the Democratic senators, although not Sarbanes or Kennedy, and avoid defections to the Republicans.

The long-anticipated train wreck had finally occurred. Those who thought the Republicans would never shut down the government and threaten its ability to honor its commitment to pay its debts were proven wrong. And those who said the president wouldn't dare veto the Republican bill and doubted he would have the stomach for a full-scale fight over the Republican budget were also wrong. But the final outcome of the fight and the president's willingness to stay firm were still very much an open question.

Chapter 17

THE SECOND
TRAIN WRECK

In the end, the first government shutdown lasted for only six days, from November 15 to 21. After considerable thrashing around and disagreement within the House Republican Caucus and between House and Senate Republicans, the House Republicans were able to pass a short-term continuing resolution that funded the government for six days and by its terms demanded the president agree to the goal of a budget that balanced over seven years based on CBO scoring. The continuing resolution passed 277–151, with the support of forty-eight Democrats worried about appearing to be opposed to a balanced budget. This got the House within striking distance of the number of votes they would need to override a veto.

Worried about the possibility of an override, the White House negotiators made concessions to the Republicans—concessions that they portrayed to concerned liberal Democrats as essentially meaningless. These included nonbinding language committing both sides to try to achieve a balanced budget within seven years using CBO scoring, after CBO consulted with outside experts on economic assumptions. The Democrats insisted on language that required the balanced budget to "protect future generations, ensure Medicare solvency, reform welfare, and provide adequate funding for Medicaid, education, agriculture, national defense, veterans, and the environment [and] that adopt tax policies to help working families and to stimulate future economic growth."

Both sides claimed victory, but Panetta, the president's chief of staff, much to the consternation of the Republicans, almost immediately asserted that the seven-year target was only a goal and that a balanced budget might take eight or nine years.[1]

After the passage of the continuing resolution, negotiations were resumed, but no agreement was reached. The discussions were marked by considerable acrimony, each side believing the other was negotiating in bad faith. Dole wanted to avoid another government shutdown regardless of whether an agreement had been achieved, but conservative Republicans made that difficult by demanding that Clinton offer his own seven-year, CBO-scored balanced budget as a precondition for negotiations.

THE SECOND SHUTDOWN BEGINS

With the failure to agree on a budget or pass a continuing resolution, the government shut down for a second time at one minute past midnight on December 16. The following Monday, over 250,000 federal workers were put on furlough.

On December 19 the president vetoed two Republican appropriations bills, for housing and environmental protection. The next day he vetoed another, for the departments of State, Justice, and Commerce. Still no appropriations for Health and Human Services or Education.

With the government shut down, the discussions among Democrats at the staff level and with members of the cabinet and White House,

House and Senate, went on and on, with more and more intensity day after day, at more and more meetings. There was a distinct split within the Democratic Caucus, although it was largely concealed from public view. Moderate and conservative Democrats insisted that we needed to offer the Republicans something to meet them halfway, to negotiate a compromise and end the shutdown. Kennedy and the liberals argued that any "compromise" the Republicans would accept would force Democrats to give up fundamental principles and that we were winning the war of public opinion every day the shutdown continued. It would be both substantively wrong and politically foolish to meet the Republicans anywhere near halfway.

Following developments was a full-time job. A working group of the moderate Democratic House and Senate members met during the week to talk about corporate welfare and the inflation adjustment to Social Security. Although Social Security benefits are indexed to inflation so that they do not lose purchasing power over time, some economists argued that the way the consumer price index (CPI) was computed overstated actual inflation; they proposed a technical adjustment that would have significantly reduced benefits over the long run. This idea had gained some traction, although other economists thought the CPI actually understated the impact of inflation on the elderly, and the professionals at the Bureau of Labor Statistics had declined to adopt the proposed change. Ultimately we were able to develop a strong Democratic consensus that the CPI should not be reduced.

A task force on tax entitlements was established. There was some support for proposals that would save $84 billion, but some of the cuts would be highly controversial. There was also some support for an across-the-board cut in corporate tax entitlements. But Treasury would not recommend any of this.

Kennedy and other members of Congress met with White House staff, including George Stephanopoulos, senior White House advisor on policy and strategy; Laura Tyson, chair of the Council of Economic Advisors; Chris Jennings, White House senior health policy advisor; Panetta, and Rivlin. We were informed that President Clinton was going to call

Dole to tell him we had a CBO budget that balanced in seven years, but he wanted to know what Republicans were going to do about Medicare and Medicaid. Clinton was going to urge Dole to let a continuing resolution go through. Panetta said, "The president's now up to $124 billion in Medicare cuts, $65 billion in Medicaid cuts. He's got almost $50 billion in corporate welfare cuts." He asked for a reaction. Predictably, it was, as Yogi Berra would say, "déjà vu all over again," with congressional Democrats all over the map.

> Congressman Dave Obey, a fiery liberal: "There's fewer discretionary dollars than the Republican bill has. I can't support it. I'll leave Congress rather than support it."
>
> Congressman Benjamin Cardin, a respected pragmatist: "It's a good proposal."
>
> Congressman Charles Stenholm, a leading Blue Dog: "We've got to have something out there we can vote for."
>
> Kennedy: "What about more cuts to corporate welfare and defense?"
>
> Congressman Robert Matsui and Congresswoman Barbara Kennelly: "We don't want to be tax-and-spend."
>
> Senator Simon: "Reconsider CPI cuts."

Senators Conrad, Kerry, and Wellstone were concerned that if we put out this new position of further concessions we would still be forced to make a compromise.

Kennedy met with Labor Secretary Reich, who told him, "We're making progress on corporate welfare. Get congressional Democrats to keep the heat on the Treasury Department."

I talked to Tom O'Donnell in Gephardt's office, who said, "The president is out of his mind [to offer a new budget proposal]. We should stick to our guns. It's foolish to put the president in the room with the Republicans."

Laura Petrou of Daschle's staff sent an email to Democratic staff in the budget group: "Dole, Gingrich and the president have agreed to a CR [continuing resolution]. DeLay and Armey have trashed it and said no CR unless the president hands down a CBO, seven-year scored budget plan. . . . Dole says this is not his blowup; it is the House Republicans' blowup. We have unanimous Democratic support for the Democratic Senate plan. Senator Daschle is negotiating for the caucus. Our message on the budget: a balanced budget is possible, the Democrats have moved, but we are still protecting our priorities. On the shutdown: we should isolate Gingrich. The government should be open. Veterans' checks are not being processed. Parks are closed. Loans aren't happening for students. We should take a clean CR and pass it. The Republicans are in disarray."

We met with Stan Greenberg, one of the president's pollsters, who said, "There's a troubling development. The president does not know whom to meet with among Republicans. He's talked twice with Dole, but House Republicans don't agree with Dole. We don't know whom to trust. Gingrich turned down a framework agreement."

On December 19 a full-page ad appeared in the *New York Times* and *Washington Post* paid for by the CEOs of a number of America's largest corporations, including Xerox, Goldman Sachs, the Equitable Companies, the Blackstone Group, and the Business Roundtable, who were urging congressional leaders and the president to reach agreement on a balanced budget. It seemed the highest hypocrisy: business CEOs speaking out in favor of balancing the budget but not including any contributions by their companies—effectively letting working people, the poor, and the elderly bear the pain. "Without a balanced budget the party's over, no matter which party you are," the ad stated. The CEOs called for a balanced budget within seven years and for the leaders to "have everything on the table, including long-term entitlement programs as well as the size and shape of any tax cut."

I suggested Kennedy write back to the CEOs. He liked the idea and wrote an open letter pointing out that the CEOs were asserting that every form of spending should be on the table. He asked whether their large corporations would be willing to accept a reduction in their tax entitlements and corporate subsidies. As the letter said, "Surely if elderly couples depending on Medicare and with an average income of less than $17,000 a year would be required by the Republican plan to pay an additional $2,500 in Medicare premiums to balance the budget over the next seven years, corporations could be asked to contribute their fair share. If four million children would lose their health care and five million senior citizens and disabled Americans would lose their Medicaid protection to balance the budget, corporations could be asked to bear their fair share. Surely if education funding would be cut by 30 percent, and millions of college students would have the cost of their student loans increased to a point where they may no longer be able to afford college, corporations could be asked to bear their fair share."

He proposed that since the Republican plan would provide a reduction of 17 percent in the federal budget over the next seven years, the corporate leaders should agree to a 17 percent reduction in tax subsidies for corporations and wealthy Americans. If the 17 percent reduction were applied to only one quarter of tax expenditures, it would save $170 billion, more than enough to balance the budget in even fewer than seven years. He urged the CEOs to appoint a task force to review tax entitlements and put together a proposal that would lead to the corporations bearing their fair share of budget reductions. He sent the letter to the six principal cosigners of the advertisement. He heard nothing back from any of them.

KENNEDY RALLIES THE ADVOCACY GROUPS

On December 19 President Clinton, Dole, and Gingrich met at the White House. Clinton described a number of different ways they could structure the negotiations, although none involved his presenting his own CBO-scored, seven-year balanced budget. Dole and Gingrich agreed that there would be more face-to-face talks and that they would personally become involved in negotiating an agreement on the budget while allowing the government to reopen.

But back on December 15 the Republican leadership had told Gingrich that the Republican Caucus wouldn't go for a continuing resolution unless Clinton offered a budget that would be balanced in seven years by CBO scoring. Now the full Republican Caucus went even further. When Gingrich reported on his White House meeting, the group consensus was that there should be no continuing resolution until there was an actual budget agreement that achieved the Republican goals. Gingrich had created a Frankenstein. The new Republican majority was so committed to its policy goals that it was willing not only to shut down the government but to keep it shut down until they got their way.

That consensus was formalized the next day. The House Republican Conference adopted a resolution refusing to reopen the government until a budget deal had been reached. It was a demonstration of how ideological they were and how out of touch with the wishes of the American people.

President Clinton called the collapse of the agreement to restart negotiations "a very troubling development. The most extreme members of the House of Representatives rejected that agreement. These Republicans want to force the government to stay closed until I accept their deep and harmful cuts."[2]

As the shutdown continued, Kennedy and his staff began a new round of meetings with the public interest advocacy groups. First he met with representatives of all the Washington education associations to talk about what the cuts to education would mean. Processing of twelve to fifteen thousand student loans per day would be stopped. Processing of a hundred thousand student aid forms would be stopped. Eligibility for additional students would be discontinued.

Joel Packer of the National Education Association declared that education could not operate under those terms. Greg Keeley of the Coalition for Education Funding said, "The continuing resolution is a disaster for us." Gerry Morris of the American Federation of Teachers pointed out, "There's a 23 percent cut on the House Republican side for K to 12 education. Particularly in urban areas this will hurt. The president needs to save the education initiative." Terry Hartle, in charge of government relations for the American Council on Education, speaking for the independent colleges and universities, stated flatly, "The 10 percent cap on direct lending is impossible."

Then Kennedy met again with representatives of senior groups. John

Rother of the AARP told him, "Our number one priority is to keep the guarantee on Medicaid. The direct financial hit on beneficiaries has thrown up a big cloud on the whole budget. Senator Moynihan had a press conference this morning calling for a 1 percent CPI reduction. Over ten years the average Social Security recipient will lose $5,000 by such a reduction. And the biggest hit is on the lowest income seniors." Steve Petroulus of the National Council of Senior Citizens added, "Senator Kennedy's letter to the corporations is touching a major nerve. It all comes back to equality. We oppose Medicare cuts. We found the soul of the party and the president is not going to win unless we get the serious cuts out." Mike Rogers said, "The budget hurts the older people through the Older Americans Act: Heating assistance, Meals on Wheels, nursing home standards, home care."

There were more discussions between the Republicans and the White House in the week leading up to Christmas but like those before them they went nowhere, and the budget talks were suspended. Both sides put out their spin on the reasons for the breakdown. Gingrich and Dole held a joint press conference at which Dole said, "We think we moved a long way. Everyone has been attentive for fifty hours, but we're not getting there so we are going to recess for one week. The American people want a balanced budget and they are looking to us to get a balanced budget with CBO numbers." Gingrich added, "We're trying hard to get a balanced budget. We hope we will see something decisive out of the White House, but now is a good time to take a deep pause and let things evolve a bit. That's why we're not characterizing the negotiations." Dole piped up, "But of course we're available any time. There are wide differences right now."

Clinton responded, "We've arrived at a point where all sides have agreed on enough cuts to balance the budget. We made progress today. The balanced budget is within reach." The president sounded optimistic. "We need to clarify the areas of agreement, but we'll recess until next Wednesday. We're protecting Medicare and Medicaid, the Earned Income Tax Credit, children and the environment. I want to do this. We've already cut the deficit in half. Whether it's ten years or seven years. The budget put forward by Senator Daschle balances in seven years."

THE SHUTDOWN CONTINUES

It was now the week before Christmas, and the U.S. government was shut down for the second time. It had been almost one month since November 21, when President Clinton had conceded to the Republicans that he would agree to a seven-year balanced budget using CBO numbers, and Republicans had said they agreed that the budget deal would protect the president's priorities in the area of Medicare, Medicaid, education, and the environment—which I referred to as the M-squared, E-squared Democratic priorities (M2E2). At that point, the congressional leaders and the president had agreed to a continuing resolution that would keep the government open until Friday, December 15 at midnight. But after the president's concession, for three weeks there had been essentially no meaningful negotiations. Republicans had not come forward with new proposals to protect Medicare, Medicaid, education, and the environment. Instead, they were waiting for new economic assumptions from the CBO, which they finally received on December 13 or 14. During this period, President Clinton had provided a new proposal for a balanced budget in seven years, which protected his priorities, but Republicans dismissed it out of hand because it was still not based on CBO scoring and did not grant them the policy changes they wanted.

By the end of the week, talks had resumed but there was no progress to report. Over the holidays, each day Democrats in the Senate offered to pass legislation to reopen the government, but Senate Republicans blocked the Democratic effort on behalf of the House Republican Caucus. As Christmas approached, President Clinton was hopeful that talks were showing progress, but there was still a sixty-seven-page list of disagreements between the two sides. Members left Washington for the Christmas holiday not expecting to come back until after the New Year. The government remained closed.

With the benefit of hindsight, it is clear that the Republicans made an immense miscalculation. They believed the American people fundamentally supported their vision of a smaller government with sharply curtailed responsibilities. According to Republicans, the shutdown was the result of the president's stubborn refusal to accept this vision, and when the American people blamed him for the shutdown his resistance would crumble. They also thought that most people would barely notice a temporary shutdown. But they were wrong on both counts.

More than one million Americans felt the impact of the shutdown directly: 28,000 seniors and workers were unable to apply for Social Security or disability benefits; 200,000 Americans got no answer when they called Social Security's help line; more than 7,000 American veterans were unable to file compensation, pension, and education benefit claims; 75,000 Americans could not get passports; 700 recruits were unable to enlist in the armed forces—the list went on.

Two shutdowns made the situation particularly vivid for people across the country. In the East, the National Gallery of Art had been drawing record attendance for its exhibition of an unprecedented collection of paintings by the seventeenth-century Dutch artist Johannes Vermeer. Its exhibition included twenty-five of his thirty-five surviving paintings. The exhibition was wildly popular. Crowds began lining up at 4 a.m. in the cold and rain to wait for tickets. Tens of thousands of other tickets had been distributed months before the exhibition even opened. These fastidious, serene paintings of the Dutch middle class in their homes captured the imaginations of thousands of Americans, but, because of the shutdown, the exhibit closed its doors. In the West, the Grand Canyon National Park and all the other national parks were closed. Visitors who had hoped for months to travel to the Grand Canyon to explore its breathtaking scenery had to call off their plans.

Except that they are each in their own way remarkable, it would be hard to find a greater contrast than between small, quiet paintings of everyday Dutch life in the seventeenth century and the vast, wild, timeless vistas of the national parks. But neither would have been available to the American people without an expansive view of government responsibilities—in one case to preserve vast stretches of America for public enjoyment rather than private gain; in the other to maintain a world-class free museum.

The number of Americans who actually had to cancel visits to the national parks because of the shutdown was probably small, and the number who lost their chance to see the Vermeer exhibit even smaller. But more than 200 million Americans visit the national parks every year, and tens of millions of Americans and their children visit museums every year. The National Gallery of Art hosted four million visitors annually all by itself. The public reaction to even the temporary loss of access to these national assets seemed to validate a view of the role of government that the Republican revolution denied.

On December 29 Gingrich said House Republicans would not agree to any temporary continuing resolution to reopen the government until the budget had been agreed on, reaffirming the earlier Republican conference resolution.

On January 3 Republicans in the House approved a resolution to bring all 200,000 furloughed federal employees back to work immediately, but they would be working without pay. This rather bizarre proposal was a reaction to criticism that federal employees who were not working could expect back pay when a settlement was reached. From the Republican point of view, the spectacle of government employees being paid for not working was almost a caricature of their worst visions of government. The plan had little hope of passing both branches.

On January 4 House Republican leaders once more seemed to be on the verge of acquiescing and reopening the government until March 15 to give more time for negotiations, but the freshman Republican congressmen revolted again.

On January 5, day nineteen of the shutdown, Republicans in the Senate agreed to reopen the government, but House Republicans refused to go along. The fallout from the government shutdown began to affect the private sector, as Christmas came and went and 1996 began.

Returning from Cape Cod, where he had spent the Christmas and New Year's holidays, Kennedy met with Senators Daschle and Dorgan.

Daschle said that Republicans would now make a deal on Medicare at $124 billion in cuts, in line with the president's figure. Dorgan reported, "Republicans will reduce their tax cuts to $185 billion, but the difficulties on the details on policy will be as difficult as the money. As far as I am concerned, the quicker these negotiations break down, the better. The people who most want a deal are Clinton and Gingrich. The Republicans are still cutting twice as much as the Democrats on health care."

REPUBLICANS SUDDENLY CHANGE COURSE

On January 5, while still refusing to go along with the Senate Republican proposal to simply reopen the government, the House Republicans abruptly changed course. It was now clear to Gingrich and most of his leadership team that they were holding a losing hand: the public was blaming them for the government shutdown and the failure of Congress to reach a budget agreement, and they weren't forcing Clinton into an agreement that would meet their goals.

The House passed two continuing resolutions to expire on January 26. The first sent federal workers back to their jobs but did not fund their agency activities, an attempt to answer the criticism that federal workers were effectively being paid for staying home (although, with no funding to operate their agencies, it was unclear what they would do when they got to work). The second stated that if Clinton proposed a balanced budget using CBO numbers, a full continuing resolution would go into effect. This second continuing resolution opened the door to reopening the government.

On January 6 President Clinton offered a budget that met the terms of the second continuing resolution, noting, "You can balance the budget and still provide adequate protection for Medicare, Medicaid, education, and the environment, and provide tax relief for working families." John Kasich, the Republican budget chairman in the House, responded that the difference between the Clinton plan and the Republican proposal was vast: "We've got an incredible gulf between the two proposals and frankly we've got a long, long way to go." But CBO said the new budget—which was based on the Daschle budget and was actually more protective of Democratic priorities in many areas than Clinton's original ten-year balanced budget—balanced, and that was enough to get the government reopened until the end of January.

The *Washington Post*/ABC poll of January 9 provided an interesting finding that indicated how Clinton might fare against Dole, his likely Republican opponent. While the government was shut down, both the Republicans and Clinton lost approval. When it reopened, Clinton's numbers went back up, while the Republicans stayed down or fell even further: 75 percent of Americans thought the government shutdown was a "bad thing"; 50 percent thought the fault for the shutdown belonged to the GOP, while only 27 percent blamed Clinton.

On January 10 the Republican leadership and the White House met again and agreed to break off the talks. Although the official description was that the talks had "recessed" for a week, the Republicans, at least, were done. Dole viewed the talks as fruitless and a distraction from his presidential campaign. Gingrich had concluded that Republicans were losing the war of public opinion and no deal was going to get done. He could not move far enough toward the Democrats to reach a deal without infuriating his caucus, even if he had been inclined to do so.

On January 14 Kasich announced that Republicans had now agreed to extend the debt limit and raise the debt ceiling. "My sense is you don't want to mess around with defaulting here in the United States." On the budget, he noted that the parties were still "universes apart."[3]

On January 17 Republican leaders made the end of the negotiations official, informing the White House that they would not resume discussions. By the next day, however, Republicans hadn't agreed on what steps to take to extend the debt limit or even keep the government open after the continuing resolution expired.

Although the Republicans had thrown in the towel, the president apparently hadn't. On January 18 I talked again to Tom O'Donnell, Gephardt's chief of staff, and once again he was nervous about the president's resolve. "Clinton is talking again about moving on Medicare. Gep-hardt met with him yesterday. He asked how high we could go without raising premiums. The president wants a deal."

Mellman reported to the Democratic staff on poll numbers: "We were caught off guard by a poll that shows the president was down during the shutdown, but the evidence is clear. It's a temporary phenomenon dur-ing the shutdown; the numbers bounced back. Democrats are up 50–27 as of January 7 on whose fault the shutdown was. The president is back to where he was over Senator Dole. On substance 68 percent are opposed to slowing the rate of growth of Medicare to balance the budget; 82 per-cent are opposed to cutting education to balance the budget. Our mes-sage is different than it previously was. The Democrats have proven we can balance the budget in seven years while protecting Medicare, educa-tion, and reducing taxes. Republicans want to cut Medicare, Medicaid, and education to pay for tax cuts rather than have a balanced budget. The State of the Union will be next Wednesday. We're planning for a clean continuing resolution [meaning all programs would be extended] through March 15, but we have to be ready for a targeted continuing resolution [which would fund some targeted programs less than others], if the Republicans insist on it."

By January 21 the Republicans were halfway through the first Con-gress of their revolution, and the *New York Times* ran a report card on where their major legislative initiatives stood. In the lead story, Adam Clymer summarized the status of the GOP revolution: "The Republican revolution is stalled on Capitol Hill, blocked by an ideological appetite bigger than its majorities can fulfill, by an unexpectedly determined Democratic opposition, and by the public's resistance to sacrifice."[4] Of the original ten items in the Contract with America, portions of only three had been passed into law: the Congressional Accountability Act, which tightened congressional ethics rules; limits on unfunded man-dates; and restrictions on securities litigation.[5] None of these was cen-tral to the Republican revolution's vision of a remade America. And of course, the sweeping cuts and restructuring of entitlements, the tax cuts, and the achievement of a balanced budget—all central to Republican goals—were mired in the vetoed reconciliation bill and the failed budget negotiations.

Congressman Armey, contradicting the position taken earlier in the week by Congressman Kasich, declared that the debt limit extension would be held up in order to put additional pressure on President Clinton to negotiate, suggesting that the Republican Caucus was still not resigned to giving up, even if Gingrich was.

On January 23 two new polls, from *Washington Post*/ABC and *New York Times*/CBS, showed Democrats leading Republicans, if the election were on that day, by 52–43 and 47–40, respectively. These were dramatic shifts from a year before.

As the State of the Union address neared, congressional Democrats were still worried that the White House and the president might make a deal with the Republicans on the budget that the Democrats would not like. They were worried about losing the political message and the political edge they had earned over the course of the year, and particularly over the government shutdown.

On January 22 Steve Ricchetti of the White House legislative staff and Gene Sperling of the White House Economic Council came to the Hill to talk to key Democratic staff about the State of the Union to be delivered the following day. Sperling was well-known to the Democrats and their staff and had a hand in the drafting of the State of the Union. Their goal was to make sure the Democrats in Congress were unified in supporting the president. Ricchetti was worried about the reception the speech would receive on the floor and in the press availability afterward. He said, "We need to show common identity, a common sense of purpose from all Democrats. We have to be unified in support for the speech. We don't want to let the zealots on the other side become the story as they attack us."

Sperling referred to the president's tendency to change his mind about the text of his speeches. "We have five days and one car ride to go, but the basic structure is staying together. The speech will set up popular themes for next year. It will set out different challenges to the country—shared responsibility, economic security, education, crime. And in each area the president will suggest how he would address these issues. There will be the theme of realistic optimism.

"It's an uplifting speech, challenging people beyond the budget. He wants to connect with broader themes in a way that fits with our budget message. The speech will show our commitment to a balanced budget but that we are for progress and for moving on to other things. He will say, 'No one is ever shutting the government down or defaulting again. No one should threaten default to get his or her way. It's unthinkable to hold the country hostage to get their way.' The president will not want to be seen as partisan. He wants to keep on the high ground."

THE BUDGET DEBATE ENDS

Meanwhile the Kennedy staff was following the appropriations developments on a daily basis. Jim English, of Senator Byrd's staff, told us on January 23 that Chairman Hatfield's staffers were talking about a continuing resolution through March 15, with funding set at the lower of the House or Senate appropriations bills but a floor of 75 percent of the previous year's spending. However, some programs might be targeted, either to be eliminated or to get funding above the 75 percent level.

That day Kennedy went to the floor to observe that the continuing resolutions that were keeping the government open were having devastating effects, particularly on education, because they effectively authorized only 75 percent of the prior year's funding. He pointed out that schools and colleges needed to plan for the following school year, which began in the fall, and now they could do so only on the assumption that they would take a 25 percent cut in their federal appropriations. This meant teachers being laid off, schools being closed, students being deprived of student loans.

The day of the State of the Union arrived on January 23. The President made headlines, surprising us all with what appeared to be a lurch to the right, when he declared, "The era of big government is over."

For at least a decade afterward Democrats had to live with that phrase every time the budget was debated. But the substantive emphasis in the speech was on reopening negotiations to reach a balanced budget that would meet the challenges of security for working families, health care, education and training, crime prevention, and preservation of the environment. Dole gave the reply to the president's speech, which was widely criticized as nasty and failing to offer an uplifting message.

The next day Republicans changed their minds again on the debt limit. Now they would extend it, but only until March 15.

The House Republicans and the White House agreed on a measure to continue the reopening of the government for forty-five days, thus averting a third federal shutdown. Kennedy noted, "This is the fourth temporary funding measure for the fiscal year, and it's taking a terrible toll, particularly in the area of education. Uncertainty simply won't work when you're planning school budgets." On February 1 a new group of conservative Democrats and moderate Republicans from the House and Senate began meeting to reach a compromise budget. The "Mainstream Coalition" was back at work.

Except for the continuing fight over appropriation levels, the debate over the radical Republican budget was essentially over. Members of Congress began to look beyond the budget impasse to move forward with new legislative initiatives and to begin to define the agenda for the presidential election year. Dole was out campaigning in New Hampshire. He was being challenged by Pat Buchanan and a handful of other right-wing Republicans. No budget compromise had been reached. The Republicans were relying on stopgap spending resolutions to keep the government open. The steam was running out of their passion for brinksmanship over shutting down the government. Ultimately there would be further skirmishes into March about possible shutdowns and refusals to extend the debt limit, but the Republican resolve had evaporated. Democrats worked to restore funding and enforcement authority at the EPA and other programs, with some success. On March 13 Republicans reversed course on education, agreeing to restore funding that Democrats had been seeking so that schools could plan for the year beginning in the fall of 1996.

In mid-March the Republicans had to pass another one-week extension of the continuing resolution. There was more thrashing, but the focus had now shifted. Republicans had lost ground in public opinion; they were way behind in terms of voters' preference for congressional elections in the fall. President Clinton's approval rating was up in the mid-fifties for the first time in several years, and the focus of the Republican revolution had shifted. Now the questions were who would win the primaries for the presidential election, what issues would drive those primary elections, and just how successful would the Democrats be in actually passing some of their prized initiatives for health care and the minimum wage as the 1996 legislative year unfolded?

The budget struggle that had occupied Congress for more than a year was now essentially over. Gingrich and Luntz's Contract seemed to me to be rapidly becoming history. Eventually the president and the Republicans agreed to compromised appropriations bills in all areas of government. The issues of entitlement cuts, taxes, and a balanced budget were postponed until after the election, when, as it turned out, the thriving economy provided all the additional funding necessary to bridge the gap between the two sides.

All in all, Democrats came out way ahead after this long, contentious, difficult year. The Republicans were blamed for the government shutdown. Their belief that the public would support the shutdown and their broader agenda turned out to be fundamentally wrong. They had lost big. And any Democrat who did not see how to defeat the radical right was not paying attention.

It is clear that both the substance of the Republican revolution and the Republican tactics had backfired. The Republicans were tarred with extremism, with recklessness, with irrational and threatening conduct. They were the party that had no compassion. That is why George W. Bush had to run as a "compassionate conservative" in 2000 if he wanted to stand a chance of beating Al Gore. And the Republicans alienated large numbers of Americans from constituencies across the spectrum of the nation—women, minorities, immigrants, environmentalists, union families, senior citizens, anyone trying to keep their loved ones in safe nursing homes, young Americans trying to figure out how to finance their college education.

Another consequence of the budget struggle was that President Clinton reclaimed a favorable approval level with the American people, and Senator Dole and the Republican leadership saw their ratings fall through the floor. From the shutdown on, the likelihood that Dole would ever beat Clinton in the election was slim indeed, and more was to happen in Congress in 1996 that would further reduce that likelihood.

But in November of 1994, none of this had been clear, and the Republicans had a real chance of transforming American government with their extreme agenda. Democrats were divided and demoralized, and President Clinton's reaction to the party's devastating defeat was still unknown.

After some initial waffling, the president made no major concessions either in his first budget or in his public statements. But there was always uncertainty about where he would come out. His genuine commitment to progressive causes seemed to be at continual war with his desire to end the policy gridlock by making a deal and his varying assessments of what different strategies would mean to the future of his presidency and the 1996 campaign. He was surrounded by a White House staff who seemed to represent his own divided state of mind—a staff with fluid factions wavering between a strategy for reaching an agreement with the Republicans and achieving a balanced budget even if it meant deeper cuts than the congressional Democrats could tolerate, and those who saw the political and substantive advantage in holding the line to protect vital programs for working families.

Things were not much clearer in Congress. There were moderate and conservative Democrats in the Senate and Blue Dog Democrats in the House. They would have reached a budget agreement with the Republicans within days of the initial proposal, and that budget would have been very close to what the Republicans originally sought. More broadly, a significant number of Democrats worried about seeming too intransigent, too unwilling to compromise, too much the captives of liberal causes and interests that the public might see as outdated and insufficiently committed to a balanced budget. As noted earlier, as late as January 6, when the budget talks were on life support and the Democrats had clearly won the war of public opinion, forty-seven House Democrats signed a Republican letter saying they would support $168 billion in Medicare cuts.

So Daschle and Gephardt constantly juggled warring factions within their caucuses. Often it seemed that the easiest course of resistance would have been to concede and sign on to a Republican-style balanced budget agreement. Fortunately, a handful of Democratic progressive activists in the Senate, led by Kennedy and supported by Daschle, and a larger group of progressives in the House, encouraged by Gephardt and Bonior, mounted an ultimately successful war against any balanced budget agreement that would violate Democratic values and priorities.

The campaign was complicated by the fact that no one in this progressive band of senators and congressmen could ever know exactly what was going on with the negotiations between the White House and the Republicans or indeed in discussions between Democratic moderates and conservatives, the White House, and Republicans. So it became a daily effort to shore up the president and the progressive staff members in the White House and to try to undercut or work around the White House staffers who sought a budget deal to show that the president could in fact deliver and work with the new Republican Congress.

Everyone in this band of progressives had his or her special duties. Senators went to the floor to attack the Republican proposals. They met day after day with interest groups who were their strongest allies against extreme budget cuts. Staff members bird-dogged every White House staff member and the staff of all congressional leaders on a daily, if not hourly, basis to find out what they could about where things stood and what was happening in the discussions behind closed doors and to provide ammunition to shore up their negotiating positions if they were wobbling. These strategic efforts went on for almost eight months.

At each point when the president was faced with a decision about moving toward the Republican position, there was always the possibility that he would do so, even if it meant pulling the rug out from under the congressional Democrats. After all, his advisor Dick Morris had coined the phrase "triangulation" as the president's strategy to separate himself as a third force from the Democrats in Congress.

Every time a decision was approaching, the progressive troops swung into action, circling the White House and making targeted strikes at like-minded White House staffers, and ultimately at the president himself. Many times the president took steps the progressives did not agree with. The first alternative budget, which proposed much larger cuts to Medicare than the progressives would have liked, in their view blurred the differences between the Democratic and Republican budgets. The decision to go with a seven-year budget, the decision to accept what turned out to be wildly conservative budget estimates and economic projections by the CBO, the giving ground on Medicare cuts—were all unnerving at the time. But at the end of the day, the president stood firm for core Democratic programs and beliefs—and that was what ultimately mattered.

We never believed the president needed the cover of his own balanced budget to win the political battle against the Republicans. And we worried that offering any cuts would blur the distinction between Democrats and Republicans and turn the argument into one over arithmetic rather than the direction of government. But the public supported a balanced budget, if not the policies the Republicans proposed to get there. And when the crunch finally came around the government shutdown, perhaps the president felt more comfortable taking a hard line because of the steps he had taken to show that he too supported a balanced budget.

At the beginning of the year, none of the Washington insiders would have predicted that American politics would end up where they did a year later. The Republican revolution seemed an irresistible force backed by majorities in both houses of Congress and by what appeared to be a monopoly on energy and commitment. Democrats and progressives, by contrast, were dispirited and floundering. Kennedy's early, personal, and tireless leadership was crucial in rallying the demoralized Democrats and bucking up the president. Without Kennedy's vision, hard work, and strategic insight, the Republican revolution might have had a very different ending.

In the end, Kennedy's agenda of fighting for working families in the areas of jobs, education, and health care—the same agenda on which he had won reelection in 1994 while other Democrats were losing as they moved to the right—had carried the day. The central focus on no cuts to Medicare and Medicaid to pay for tax cuts for the rich, not one cent cut from student aid and other education programs, and protection of the environment—my M squared, E squared mantra—became the banners under which Democrats and the president ultimately stood together. These, more than any other issues, broke through to the American people and demonstrated the extremism of the Republican agenda.

There were other heroes on the progressive side, in the White House and in Congress. I have always suspected that Hillary Clinton played a critical role in advising the president to stand firm. The Democrats could not have been successful without Daschle's willingness to let Kennedy and his allies in on the decision making, his own essential commitment to their position, and his ability to find common ground for the caucus. In the House, of course, Minority Leader Gephardt had much less leverage because he simply was in no position to stop anything the Republicans threw at him. But he kept the drumbeat going throughout the year. In many ways it was because of his leadership that House members first confronted the extreme Republican proposals, exposed them, and brought them to the attention of the American people. And in retrospect, he was able to maintain a surprising degree of unity in his diverse caucus.

The story of resisting the Republican revolution now returns to the presidential election of 1996 and to the titanic struggle in the Senate between Senator Dole and Senator Kennedy. But first, Kennedy, who had been searching for that new "big idea," announced it in a major speech in February.

Chapter 18

A NEW "BIG IDEA"

HOW TO MAKE THE RISING
TIDE LIFT MORE BOATS

Kennedy began 1996 preparing for his annual agenda-setting speech, which he would give at the Center for National Policy on February 8. We were working to develop proposals around themes and ideas the senator had settled on during meetings over the previous several months with advisors and policy experts. We thought we had found the new "big idea" that Bob Shrum said we needed and that we now had a story we could tell the American people. Looking back today from the vantage point of almost two decades, it is clear that the problem Kennedy defined in 1996 has only become more serious and that the American dream can be re-captured for tens of millions of working families only if the political will is found to implement effective solutions.

I was excited about helping to develop this new agenda. It responded to what I had heard from families in Gloucester during Kennedy's reelection campaign sixteen months earlier. The speech would deal with the economic insecurity of working families and focus on steps that could be taken to improve stagnant wages and close the income gap between the rich and everyone else. Perhaps more important than the specific policy proposals was the goal of trying to refocus attention on the withering of the American dream and away from the "government is the enemy, balance the budget at all costs" focus of the past year.

Kennedy, Carey Parker, Bob Shrum, and I met to discuss the speech and think about the overriding "big idea" and possible titles. "Economic Growth and Shared Responsibility"—too dull. "Life in the '90s: Working Harder and Earning Less"—too negative. "How to Close the Widening Economic Divide: A New American Dilemma"—too cumbersome. "Getting America Moving Again in the '90s"—a cliché and too vague. "The Rising Tide: How to Make It Lift More Boats." This one made the point exactly, was an apt metaphor, and hearkened back to President Kennedy's famous statement about the importance of a growing economy, "A rising tide lifts all boats." That statement was true in the 1960s, but it was true no longer—and hadn't been for the past quarter century.

Several days before the speech, we had a bit of a setback. It's not as widely noted as other aspects of politicians' work in Washington, but competitiveness among the big players, especially when it involves credit for big ideas, is very intense. Secretary of Labor Robert Reich had been practically a lone voice within the cabinet preaching the idea that the economy, although doing well in many respects, was not working as well as it should for working families. He had an idea to provide tax advantages to corporations that treated their workers well, avoided layoffs, and provided adequate benefits. This was almost exactly the same idea Kennedy had planned to unveil in his speech. When he heard that Kennedy was preparing his speech, Reich quickly jumped in ahead. On February 6, two days before Kennedy was to give his speech, Reich gave a speech at the George Washington University Business School in which he called for two tax rates for corporations. He'd beaten the senator to the punch—and it was no accident. Reich undoubtedly thought he owned the idea and wanted to be sure he got credit for it.

Kennedy was a bit disappointed but good-humored about it. He liked Reich, saw him as his strongest progressive ally in the cabinet, and understood that Reich was as competitive as he. And maybe Reich's endorsement of the two-tier corporate tax idea would cause observers to take it more seriously.

On February 8 the senator gave his speech "The Rising Tide Should Lift More Boats" to the Center for National Policy. The audience was a mix of progressive activists, friends, and journalists. He began, "By most indicators, the economy is doing well." The stock market is high, and unemployment and inflation are at relative lows. But "those appearances are deceiving." America's great prosperity is "uneven, uncertain, and inequitable."

> All is not well in the American economic house, because all is not well in the homes of too many American workers and their families.
>
> Americans are working more and earning less. Their standard of living is stagnant or sinking. They have been forced deeper into debt and they have less to spend. . . . President Kennedy said that a rising tide must lift all boats. And for the golden decades after World War II, that was true. But today's rising tide is lifting only some of the boats—primarily the yachts.

This income inequality was "economically unjustified, socially dangerous, historically unprecedented, and morally unacceptable."

Kennedy asserted that economic issues are inseparable from values. He criticized leaders who talked about "family values" without addressing the fundamental economic unfairness that undercut those very values. "The V Chip [a technology championed by the White House to give parents more control over TV viewing by their children] makes sense," he argued, "but it is no substitute for college loans. It will not buy clothing or food. It will not give working families a sense of hope. We have no chance of restoring values if we don't improve the lives of working Americans."

He then laid out his response to what he called the "quiet depression" facing working families. In Kennedy's strategy, the business sector, the individual, and government each had a role to play. "Government does have a role to play as the agent of our common concerns and the expression of our shared values. The era of big government may be over, but a return to the era of no government is no answer." He outlined ten principles to increase economic security and economic justice. They included making the Federal Reserve "more aggressive in permitting and encouraging economic growth" and a two-tier corporate tax rate rewarding companies that create American jobs, avoid layoffs, and pay adequate wages. Other principles were using antitrust laws to restrain mergers and acquisitions that cause workers to be laid off, strengthening unions, investing in education and training, and making research a priority. Finally, he called for improving the income and benefits of working Americans by raising the minimum wage and making health insurance portable from job to job.

He concluded by emphasizing the importance of the work ahead:

> We are coming to the close of what has been called the "American Century." It has been an extraordinary era in which we have conquered imperialism, fascism, and communism abroad. We have wrestled with racism, sexism, poverty, depression, crime, and other enemies within. . . . We can and must end the income gap in America. It will require a new Progressive era. We can and must restore true progress in America. That is our duty as progressives. That is the defining mission of the Democratic Party. And, in my view, that is the only way we can win—and the only way we will deserve to win—in 1996.

The speech was widely viewed as a major success and an important contribution to the debate on the income gap and wage inequality. All the major newspapers covered the speech, noting that what Kennedy said in past annual speeches had been extremely influential among progressive Democrats. The press was particularly impressed with the specific list of initiatives and ideas Kennedy offered.

The administration, however, was not going to endorse Kennedy's overall theme. It was an election year, and they believed it was better politics to emphasize the recovery and strength of the economy under Clinton, not the economic difficulties working Americans continued to face.

THE REPUBLICAN PRESIDENTIAL PRIMARIES

Republicans' attention in February and March 1996 was on the presidential campaign. Dole won the Iowa caucuses on February 13, but Pat Buchanan, whose populist, antibusiness, pro-worker message was taking hold, finished a surprisingly close second. Dole left for New Hampshire the next day and adopted Buchanan's theme: "Corporate profits are setting records and so are layoffs. The bond market finished a spectacular year. But the real average hourly wage is 5 percent lower than it was a decade ago." Buchanan stormed through New Hampshire, attacking corporations that laid off workers, championing economic nationalism, and blaming the international economy and free trade for the woes of the American worker.

New Hampshire held its primary on February 20, and Buchanan was the shocking victor over Dole, Lamar Alexander, and Steve Forbes. Three days later, in one of the surprisingly frank offhand remarks that had become something of a signature for him, Dole said, "I didn't realize that jobs and trade and what makes America work would become a big issue in the last few days of the campaign."[1] He was referring specifically to the New Hampshire campaign, but his remarks suggested naïveté, indeed cluelessness about the whole set of economic issues that were driving the Buchanan campaign. These issues became the subject of intense debate among Democrats and others across the country. Magazine after magazine and newspaper after newspaper ran feature stories on the layoffs of workers and the dissatisfaction and concern they were feeling as they watched their job security disappear. Ironically, Buchanan was echoing the Kennedy message, and now even Dole was beginning to pick up on it.

Steve Forbes won the primary in Arizona, which threw the Republicans into further chaos, but Dole won the primary in South Carolina. Then he won in New York, Florida, Texas, Tennessee, Mississippi, Oklahoma, and Oregon. In each case, he won by a 2 to 1 margin. The press declared him a virtual lock for the nomination, but he faced a seemingly impossible predicament: his campaign had run out of funds and would not receive another infusion of public funding until after the convention. He'd wrapped up the nomination, but he had no money left to advertise or organize a national campaign for the general election.

What Dole did have, however, was his position as majority leader of the Senate. Normally only the Capitol Hill reporters write about Congress, and their stories rarely lead the news. During a presidential campaign, however, the press needs to report on what the nominees are doing every day, and more often than not these are front-page stories. So now we had not only the congressional press corps but also the presidential press corps descending on the Senate. The Senate was truly in the spotlight.

Meanwhile the reputation of the Republican Congress was in free fall. Congress still hadn't passed appropriations bills to keep the government running for the year, and the government was still operating on temporary continuing resolutions. Democrats were pounding away on the fact that the Contract with America had failed. Republicans had passed almost no bills and were engaged in blocking popular initiatives, such as health care reform and the minimum wage increase.

Kevin Phillips, the conservative political analyst, wrote, "Clinton knows he's got a fat target in his sights: virtually as fat as the Capitol Hill target Republicans had in their sites in the Autumn of 1994. The public implosion of the Contract with America, which had stalled for months until its credibility finally ran out in January and February, has been in the works for a long time, according to the survey results we've been seeing for a year. As we've noted, these polls show the most rapid reversal of a new Congress's credibility in the polls' records." Phillips largely attributed Dole's poor prospects to "the albatross of an unpopular Republican Congress."

The House Republicans were experiencing the collapse of their popular support. Gingrich now had the highest unfavorable rating of any politician in America, and he and his Republican troops in the House were desperately trying to retool their message and figure out where their agenda was headed. Senate Republicans were still trying to figure out how to deal with the extremists in the House and were content to let their leader set their agenda.

House Democrats were looking forward to the elections in November in anticipation of winning the House back. Their model was the campaign of 1948, when President Truman ran a winning campaign against a "do-nothing" Republican Congress and the Democrats regained control of the House, which they had lost two years earlier. The House Democratic leadership wouldn't say it publicly, but they hoped that no legislation would pass. They would advocate for bills like the minimum wage increase and health insurance regulation, but at least in the spring of 1996 they never anticipated that House Republicans would agree. So they kept feeding talking points to their members on the extreme do-nothing Republican Congress.

The White House, of course, single-mindedly focused on the presidential election. This focus was clearly evident in a meeting that I attended with key presidential aides and Democratic Senate staff members on March 26. George Stephanopoulos and other senior White House staff came to the Capitol to urge us to keep Dole busy on the Senate floor. Stephanopoulos hoped that over the next four months, while the Congress was in session, Dole could be tied down on the floor rather than out campaigning. Democratic senators should go to the floor to question him and force him to respond on the spot. "Make him seem to be the 'legislator-in-chief,' responding to pressures from his party, responding to questions from the press, generally bogged down in the muddle and gridlock on the floor," Stephanopoulos told us. "Create votes on new issues each week that will cause Dole to take unpopular positions. Make him vote on assault weapons, where he'll have to vote to repeal the assault weapons ban. Make him vote on family and medical leave again and again. Dole has only a small amount of money left, so he's stuck in the Senate. Let Dole be Dole. Smoke him out, from April 15 to the end of July. Don't let up on him."

Dole himself wanted to be seen as the master of the legislative process, the man who could make Washington work, the strategist and powerful leader who could take the edge off the extremism of the Republican House members but press forward with an essentially conservative agenda. This didn't seem to us to be a winning agenda that spoke to the central concerns of most Americans. But it was Dole's opportunity to show that he was, as he put it, "a doer, not a talker."[2]

Kennedy, however, was not focused on Dole or his campaign. Unlike the House Democrats, he was focused on getting legislation enacted, and the two initiatives that were his priorities were the minimum wage increase and health insurance reform.

The stage was set for a monumental collision on the Senate floor. On one side, Dole was determined to control the agenda and use his performance on the Senate floor as the centerpiece of his strategy for his presidential campaign. On the other, Kennedy was focused on enacting a minimum wage increase and health insurance reform. Little did we know that these two legislative efforts, moving along separate tracks during 1995, would turn out to have a pivotal role in the outcome of the 1996 presidential election. They would embarrass Dole, undercut his central claim of effective leadership, expose the warring forces within the Republican Party in Washington, symbolize the collapse of the Republican Contract with America, and ultimately lead to Dole's ignominious departure not only from his position as Senate majority leader but from the Senate itself.

TRYING TO MARKET THE "BIG IDEA" OVER WHITE HOUSE OBJECTIONS

The day after Dole's surprising loss in the New Hampshire primary, Clinton and various members of Congress and the cabinet gathered in the Roosevelt Room at the White House at an event to establish a hotline for child abuse. I was there with Kennedy when he and the president talked.

"What did you think about the New Hampshire vote?" asked Clinton. "You know Buchanan is opposed to cuts in Medicare and the Veterans' Administration. I heard about your talk, but I haven't read it. Growth policy makes a lot of sense. The president of United Technologies is outlining what corporations should be doing. We've got to do something more."

Kennedy told the president he had planned to do an event the next week with Felix Rohatyn, a leading New York investment banker who also happened to be a progressive Democrat, the labor leader John Sweeney, and probably Robert Reich. Clinton ignored this and continued, "We really need a growth policy. Harkin wants Greenspan [chairman of the Federal Reserve] to go. I'm leery about taking this step."

Back in the Senate, the Democrats, led by the ranking members and Daschle's leadership team, were holding events and daylong seminars on stagnant wages, the income gap, education, seniors, and child care. Kennedy talked to Robert Reich at the White House about the wage gap. "We don't have support at the Treasury to take up the issue," Reich said, but he thought there was a vacuum waiting to be filled.

Kennedy scheduled an issues dinner in his Senate hideaway, still trying to come up with legislation based on his February speech—the idea that a week's work ought to provide a living wage and adequate health care, as well as different ideas for structuring the tax code to reward corporations that treated their workers well. Shrum, who had been at the meeting, called back the next day to say that we should make this an issue of security: "lost job security, lost income security, lost health security, and lost retirement security." He liked the two-tier tax structure. He wanted to strengthen pensions and argued that this was the time for Kennedy to travel around the country, meeting with displaced workers, holding forums, and showcasing his policy ideas for encouraging corporations to act responsibly toward their workers.

We met with Gerry Shea, right hand to John Sweeney at the AFL-CIO, who described the "America Needs a Raise" campaign. There were twenty-five targeted congressional districts in which the AFL-CIO had placed campaign organizers who would concentrate on wages, pensions, and health care portability. Shea urged us not to move too quickly to the "correct" solution, but rather to foster discussion on the problem, and then develop solutions over the course of the next year. Gephardt's chief economic advisor ran a task force for the Democratic leadership in the House and Senate that met every week on these issues. By March 20 the group had come up with a draft of a Democratic agenda based in part on Kennedy's speech, and they were ready to release the document.

But the document was never released, and the press conferences were never held to announce the program. Events overtook intentions. The White House had been keeping its eye on the group, had viewed the document, and now responded negatively to releasing it. Why, the White House asked, would we want to highlight the fact that workers were not doing well and were feeling insecure when there was a presidential election in eight months and Clinton needed to run on his success in getting the economy moving?

As Shea had signaled, labor wasn't ready to go forward either. Their idea for 1996 was to identify the problem and then study the solutions. They felt they had enough to run on without giving the Republicans a new Democratic agenda to attack. Meanwhile, Buchanan had been winning Republican primaries by attacking corporations. Is that where we wanted to be? With Buchanan? So while individual members spoke about it, highlighting the wage gap and the income gap and developing an exhaustive agenda to deal with those issues drifted to the back burner. There was no overt decision not to emphasize these issues—the campaign to elevate them just faded away.

That's how Washington works sometimes. Original ideas that would change the whole structure of the economy, drafted by leading members of the party, don't see the light of day because they don't fit politically. To make something fly in Washington you have to have both the right idea and the right moment. In this case, the inside game just wasn't going to work at this particular moment; given the way they perceived the dynamics of the election, we weren't going to have the White House or labor or enough others in the party with us.

By the spring it was clear that there was to be no broad new Democratic House and Senate public campaign built around the wage and income gap issues or the changes to the tax code and corporate securities law on which we had been working for months. The work put into these ideas paid off, however, because out of those discussions grew a new Democratic congressional agenda focusing on economic security for working families, put together by the House and Senate leadership. While not as bold or imaginative as the program Kennedy had outlined in his speech, that agenda did bring back traditional Democratic themes.

Indeed, by March 1996 the Democratic Caucus had come full-circle back to the message from Kennedy's 1994 reelection campaign. After all the pulling and tugging, the huffing and puffing, the advertisements, the threats, the shutdowns, the mainstream, the middle ground, the coalitions, and the Blue Dogs, Democrats were back where Kennedy would have had them start: with working families. The Democrats called it "Families First," and it had four main components: health, education, jobs, and retirement.

For the first two months of 1996, the Senate and House had basically been out of session, with Dole campaigning in the primary states. When the Senate came back in session at the beginning of March, Dole was ready to move forward with his strategy of showing that he could rise above the partisanship and bickering and lead the Senate to get things done. But lying in wait, not for Dole but to advance his own Democratic legislative agenda, was Kennedy. For several months the presidential campaign of 1996 was between Bob Dole as majority leader of the Republicans in the Senate and Ted Kennedy as de facto quarterback for a Democratic agenda that just a few short months before no one thought was possible.

Chapter 19

LAYING THE
GROUNDWORK

THE MINIMUM WAGE INCREASE

The Democratic members and staff of the Labor Committee held a week-end retreat in the spring of 1995. Although most of the effort went into developing our defensive agenda, there was also an affirmative agenda. No one on the outside would have given us a chance of getting any of it done, but we had to try. This year our fight was to pass Kassebaum-Kennedy and increase the minimum wage.

I've described Kennedy's herculean efforts to pull together minimum wage supporters behind the 90-cent increase. The actual legislation was introduced by Kennedy and Daschle, with the president's support, in March 1995, only three months into the new Congress. Now the task was to get the bill passed over the intense Republican opposition we knew was coming.

We began our campaign by focusing, as always, on three elements:

substance, politics, and the press. Arguments needed to be tested. The case against the legislation needed to be analyzed. Answers had to be crafted to meet each of the arguments against the bill. Opponents argued that an increase in the minimum wage would cost jobs, but all the research the staff had done showed that employment had actually gone up after previous minimum wage increases. Kennedy wanted to know how an increase would affect different segments of the community: women, children, minorities, immigrants, working people, union members, individuals earning more than the minimum wage.

The grassroots campaign, or the "outside game," to raise the minimum wage posed some special challenges. There are organizations whose staff wake up every day thinking about how to protect education funding or Medicare or how to strengthen civil rights or women's rights, but there was nothing comparable for the minimum wage. Every time there was a new minimum wage fight on the horizon, Kennedy had to assemble a coalition of existing groups and persuade them that the minimum wage should become an important part of their agenda. In the late fall of 1994 and the early months of 1995, while Kennedy was working to bring Democrats together around an increase in the minimum wage of an agreed-upon amount, he was also reconvening the ad hoc coalition that had dissolved after the last increase in 1989.

To get as many groups as possible to join the coalition we held weekly meetings, usually in the anteroom of the Labor Committee hearing room in the Senate Dirksen Building. Every Monday morning throughout 1995 and 1996 we met with the coalition members to plan strategy, coordinate the grassroots activity, and keep track of the vote count. At each meeting the core group would be encouraged to recruit additional members of Congress and groups to join and were asked to set up meetings in Washington and also in the members' districts.

Our message was always the same: Raising the minimum wage was the right thing to do both substantively and politically. Democrats were united behind a 90-cent increase, and it was important to mobilize them against the Republicans. At each Monday meeting, participants would describe their contacts with senators and congressmen and staff the week before. Over time we would put together all the data we had on each member, what that member was saying about the issue, and whether he or she was committed or we had additional persuading to do.

Meanwhile Kennedy and other senators were working one-on-one with other key members of Congress to obtain their support. Once the critical work had been done to get an agreement on the 90-cent increase, Kennedy again went door-to-door in the Senate and the House talking to Democratic members to get their commitment to vote for the increase and to hear their advice on when and how to make it happen. It was unusual for a senator to take on the task of meeting with members of the House on a particular piece of legislation, but it was Kennedy's trademark to leave no stone unturned.

These two efforts—the grassroots effort of the coalition and direct member-to-member contacts by Kennedy and others—were key elements of the inside and outside games.

The third part of the overall effort was the public relations strategy. We needed to create both public awareness of the minimum wage campaign and a sense among members that this was an issue of concern to voters. There were several pieces to this, including creating different kinds of events in Washington to attract attention to the issue. We had press conferences attended by key sponsors of the legislation, representatives of the Clinton administration, cabinet officers whenever possible, and members of the minimum wage campaign steering committee. We often invited House members as well as senators. We tried to bring in "real people"—individuals from across the country whose stories were compelling and who were willing to tell them to provide the human side of the need for an increase in the minimum wage. When Democrats controlled the Senate we could schedule hearings whenever we chose, on whatever topics we chose; we could invite whatever witnesses we wished, and the Committee would pay for their transportation. Now we didn't control the hearings—the topics, the dates, or the witnesses—so we had to replace hearings with forums, rallies, and press conferences.

The press we generated kept the issue alive and building in 1995 and helped bring us to a crescendo in 1996. We had an opening press conference in the Labor Committee hearing room in March 1995, then in April we held a minimum wage forum in the grand, ceremonial Senate Caucus Room. There were events in the Capitol, on the Capitol steps, and outside in the Senate Swamp, a patch of ground in front of the Senate side of the East Front of the Capitol that was often used for press events. We brought people earning the minimum wage, workers above the minimum wage whose wages would probably also be bumped up if the minimum wage were to be bumped up, small businesses supporting the increase, economists making the case for it, advocates from all the different public interest groups who supported it, and union members to testify, to lobby, and to meet the press.

John Sweeney was a key ally. He had a particular interest in health care issues, in part because his union represented many nurses and hospital workers. He and Kennedy worked together and got to know each other well around the issue of health care in the early 1990s and particularly during the Clinton health care effort in 1993 and 1994. When Sweeney defeated Tom Donahue and became leader of the AFL-CIO in October 1995, one of the first things he did was settle on "America Needs a Raise" as the organizing message for his campaign to increase union membership, strengthen unions, and raise the minimum wage. By 1996 red, white, blue, yellow, and green "America Needs a Raise" posters were an integral part of all the progressive rallies and marches in Washington and across the country. One of our biggest rallies was held on the vast west steps of the Capitol in the spring of 1996, where, in September 1994, Gingrich had held his kickoff rally and signing ceremony for the Contract. Now worker after worker stepped to the microphone on a sweaty, hot day, with a vast "America Needs a Raise" banner draped behind the stage and the Capitol and its huge dome in the background. These events drew press and kept the message alive.

Simultaneously with the events in Washington, the groups were organizing public relations campaigns all over the country. They were writing op-ed pieces, calling talk shows, meeting with editorial boards, writing letters to the editor, and creating the grassroots support that ultimately moves votes in Congress. Progressives are usually no match for conservatives when it comes to marketing campaigns for issues, but on the minimum wage increase the progressives did very well. It made sense to average Americans of all income levels that it was not fair for someone to work hard forty hours a week, fifty-two weeks a year and still not earn enough to lift his or her family out of poverty. Polls showed the public supported the minimum wage increase by 75 percent or more, and the combined force of the grassroots lobbying, the inside and outside games, and the steady public relations blitz, fueled by press conferences, hearings, rallies, and one-on-one meetings with the press corps, created powerful momentum.

The biggest microphone in all of Washington of course belongs to the president, and his support of the minimum wage increase, from his State of the Union speech in 1995 through its enactment in 1996, was vital. Each time he spoke on the issue the press wrote about it. The unity among Democrats, the coalition and their groups, labor, and the coordinated message campaign from the White House worked spectacularly.

In addition to building the substantive arguments, mobilizing the grassroots, and pushing the public relations campaign, the challenge in 1995 was to pin down Democratic support. Being in the minority we needed close to unanimous support among Democrats in the Senate to put real pressure on Republicans. And we needed at least fourteen Republicans to overcome a filibuster.

There was one Republican who supported the legislation from the outset, Senator Jim Jeffords of Vermont. The Vermont minimum wage was already above $5.15, and there was no question that he would be for an increase. But no other Republican jumped on immediately, and therefore our initial task, before we tried to get more Republicans, was to make sure we'd lined up all the Democrats.

Aside from Kennedy's senator-to-senator contact, we had groups meeting with senators in their home state offices and in the Capitol, and we had Daschle conducting a whip count of Democratic senators and where they stood on the issue. (The expression grew out of the practice of "whipping" members into line with a party position on a given issue, and the count was conducted by the Senate whip's office.) The whip count process, however, at least among Senate Democrats, was not exactly tightly organized or very reliable. Senator Wendell Ford of Kentucky was the deputy leader, and it was his office that handled the whip counts. A group of senators took responsibility for contacting other senators and reporting back to Ford's staff. Whip counts conducted at the staff level were notoriously unreliable because in many cases senators had not decided how to vote, and if they had, they hadn't told their staff. If real precision was important, contact normally had to be made directly by one senator with another.

For some of the senators who were particularly influenced by the small business lobby, the minimum wage issue was not an easy one. We thought Senator Breaux would support the 90-cent increase because he was a member of Daschle's leadership team who had been brought around during the negotiations over the amount of the increase in January 1995. But many other votes were hard to predict. Some Democrats were still complaining that the message of the 1994 election was that the Old Democratic public image needed to be changed, and the minimum wage seemed to them to be a typical Old Democratic issue. Others thought increasing the minimum wage was hopeless in a Republican era. Some felt too much pressure from their small business lobbyists and the National Restaurant Association. Some thought it was too soon. Some simply did not want to get into the fray. So the whip count was inconclusive. We knew we had thirty-five to forty votes, but we did not know where the rest of the Democrats stood.

Ultimately, because the whip count indicated that some Democratic senators had not yet taken a position on the legislation, we felt we needed to go for an early vote in the Senate. That was the only way to force senators to take a position, and unless we could show Democratic strength, we would never get enough Republican support to prevail.

Our task therefore was to find an opportunity to get a test vote on the minimum wage. We wanted to put the increase in the most favorable form possible; that meant we probably should start with a sense of the Senate Resolution as opposed to an actual amendment. This simply puts the Senate on record as favoring something; it has no force of law. We thought we could make it easier for undecided members by drafting a sense of the Senate resolution stating that the Senate should vote on the minimum wage increase. Thus senators voting on the resolution were two steps removed from actually having to take a position. If they wanted, they could maintain the fiction that even if they supported the resolution, they had not yet decided what their vote would be. At the same time, though, a yes vote—even on this watered-down provision— would help smoke senators out and make it harder for them to ultimately vote against a real amendment.

Kennedy looked for opportunities to offer his sense of the Senate Resolution all during the spring of 1995. On July 31, on the State Department appropriations bill, he found his opening. Three senators were absent—Democrat Exon and Republicans Gramm and Frank Murkowski—and the resolution was defeated by a vote of 49–48. But voting with us were all Democrats, except for Bob Kerrey, and we won the support of four Republicans: Jeffords, Specter, Campbell, and Warner. Kennedy and the minimum wage campaign coalition were jubilant over the outcome.

Kerrey later told us that he had made a mistake. He thought the vote was on a motion to table the resolution, in which case his no would have been a vote favoring the increase. It was rare, but sometimes senators made such mistakes, usually when they made only a very brief appearance on the floor to cast a vote. For instance, sometimes a senator would stick his or her head in the door of the Senate chamber, catch the eye of the clerk, and give a thumbs-up or -down either confused about what the vote was on or not understanding the bill. And sometimes the clerk would mistake a thumbs-up for a thumbs-down. In an attempt to conceal the fact that they'd rushed down between points from the tennis court on the roof of the Hart Building, I've seen senators dressed in sneakers and tennis whites stick just a head and a hand through the door and vote by thumb sign. I've also seen senators in tuxedos voting on their way to a fundraiser.

With this near victory under our belt, we looked for the opportunity for another vote. Kennedy had always taken the position that once we could show we had the support of the majority of the Senate, it became much more difficult for the opposition to hold off a measure. At that point, the opposition had to rely on the use of the filibuster. Resisting a popular measure through a filibuster creates additional procedural problems for the opposition and feeds the public relations message. If a bipartisan majority of the Senate believed the minimum wage should be raised, why was the Republican leadership denying a vote on the measure?

The next opportunity came during the debates on the reconciliation bill in late October 1995. Normally the Republicans had procedural maneuvers available to keep us from actually getting a vote on a measure, but under budget rules any amendment filed within the fifty hours allotted for debate on the bill automatically gets a vote, even if there's no time to actually debate the amendment. If there is no debate and vote during the fifty hours, the amendment is lined up with all the others that were offered but not voted on and votes are scheduled every ten minutes until all amendments are disposed of. There are often as many as one hundred votes on amendments still to be held after the expiration of the fifty-hour period. It's a chaotic time; senators are often not even sure what they're voting on. The minimum wage increase was a perfect issue for such a vote because Republicans could not block the vote from occurring and it was not the kind of issue that had to be debated or explained. It was clear, and everyone knew what was at stake.

As the Democratic leadership team organized strategy for the debate on the reconciliation bill in October 1995, they settled on the basic issues they wanted to highlight: health care (Medicare and Medicaid), education (student loans, school reform, Head Start, and the like), the environment, and labor. The minimum wage increase was the key Democratic legislation of the jobs and wages component of the budget fight. Minimum wage was not precisely an issue for the budget, but the budget debate provided a clear-cut opportunity for a vote. A goal of the Democratic leadership was to assign key so-called message amendments to different senators to give as many senators as possible a chance to come to the floor and participate in this colossal fight with the Republicans. Senators competed for the opportunity to offer these high-profile amendments.

John Kerry, the junior senator from Massachusetts, was a logical choice. Kerry was a tenacious advocate and skilled negotiator who was best known for his work on intelligence, foreign policy, and international financial crime. He faced a tough campaign for reelection in 1996 against the popular Republican governor, William Weld. Kennedy enjoyed mentoring Kerry when he first arrived in Washington, and Kerry was known to Kennedy principally for his opposition to the Vietnam War. Over the next quarter century while they served as senior and junior senators from Massachusetts their relationship grew into a close and enduring friendship. When Kerry ran for president in 2004 Kennedy was one of his closest advisors, campaigning for him wherever the Kerry team asked him to go. Kerry was particularly solicitous and warmly attentive to the senator and Vicki after Kennedy fell ill.

In 1996 Kerry asked Kennedy if he could offer the minimum wage resolution on the budget, and Kennedy agreed. On October 27, at the end of the budget debate, Kerry offered a Sense of the Senate Resolution calling again for a vote on the minimum wage increase. The resolution was offered in the same form as in July because the budget format offered an advantage Democrats had not had earlier: an ideal opportunity for a test vote. Because the sense of the senate Resolution was not technically a budget amendment, under the rules it was subject to a point of order. That meant the amendment was technically out of order, and if Republicans raised the point of order—as of course they did—it would take sixty votes to override in order to move to a vote on the amendment itself. Since the resolution was not binding in any event, and since the purpose of the amendment was simply to show that we were making progress in picking up votes, offering the resolution in a context where it would take sixty votes to succeed made it easier for wavering senators to vote for the resolution; they could always tell the lobbyists on the other side that they knew it would not get sixty votes and therefore would not pass. To some degree, it was a free vote. But, like the earlier vote, once a senator had voted for a resolution favoring the minimum wage increase, in whatever context the issue was raised, it became more difficult for him or her to reverse course. So the budget was an ideal opportunity for another test vote.

Kerry raised the amendment. It was placed on the schedule to be voted on late in the night of October 31, but the vote was blocked by a point of order. A motion was made to waive the point of order, and that motion was supported by a 51–48 vote. We had picked up three more senators: Democrat Bob Kerrey (reversing his previous mistaken vote) and Maine Republicans William Cohen and Olympia Snowe. We now had a majority of the Senate on record for a resolution that a vote on raising the minimum wage should be held. We were elated. This vote represented major progress toward the goal of passing an amendment that would, if adopted, actually raise the minimum wage in 1996. The question now was how we could outmaneuver Dole and get the opportunity for a vote on that amendment.

Once again Senate rules played a critical role. As I explained earlier, if a single senator objects, no action can be taken in the Senate, no procedural step taken, without utilizing the cumbersome process of breaking a filibuster by obtaining a majority of sixty senators for a cloture petition. With the Republicans in control of the Senate, Democrats did not have the option of calling up legislation. They could offer amendments to bills called up by the Republican leadership, but those amendments could not be voted on unless Democrats could override the filibuster. So even though sixty votes would be required, at least there would be a vote. But if Dole were sufficiently determined, he could block even that opportunity by using his power of first recognition to fill up the amendment tree and prevent us from even offering a minimum wage amendment.

On the other hand, if forty-one senators are sufficiently steamed up about being denied an opportunity to offer and vote on an amendment, they can filibuster the underlying bill. As noted earlier, the majority leader then has a choice: to yield and allow the vote on the amendment or to pull from the floor the underlying bill to which the amendment had been offered. Thus the leader can block a vote on the amendment or get the bill passed, but not both.

Obviously the choice of the underlying bill on which to offer the amendment was critical. Unless the underlying bill was one enough Democrats were prepared to defeat or delay, Dole could use his power as majority leader to fill up the amendment tree before we had a chance to offer our amendment and force a vote to end debate on the underlying bill, which meant no more amendments could be offered, and we would be locked out. If it weren't something the Republicans cared about passing, Dole could simply pull the bill down.

As it turned out, Dole kept the Senate out of session until February 27, 1996, so that he could conduct his campaign for president and avoid exposing the disagreements among Republicans about their overall strategy. The prime responsibility for Congress when it came back into session in February was the budget and the appropriations bills. There had already been two government shutdowns and more than a score of temporary resolutions to keep the government operating. Anything that could be seen as a distraction from straightening out that situation would work against the minimum wage issue. Wavering members could simply be against it on the grounds that this wasn't the moment to introduce the amendment because the first priority was to get the government running again and work out the budget. So we kept waiting.

HEALTH INSURANCE REFORM

While the track was being laid for the minimum wage increase during 1995, a separate but parallel track was being laid for the Kassebaum-Kennedy health reform bill.

The strategy behind the bill was similar to the strategy behind the minimum wage bill, with one essential difference: Kassebaum-Kennedy was bipartisan from the beginning, while the minimum wage began as a Democratic proposal.

As I discussed earlier, Kennedy made a point of seeking a lead Republican sponsor on legislation before it was introduced because a bipartisan start was a major leg up to ultimate success. There's a different story behind each of these alliances. They grow out of friendship, respect, years of working together, a shared commitment to a particular cause, a desire for the public recognition that comes from legislation with your name on it—the reasons are different for each senator and for each issue. In the hyperpartisan climate after the 1994 election, finding a Republican partner for major legislation was no easy task, but for Kassebaum joining with Kennedy on the health insurance reform bill was simply a matter of doing what was clearly right and needed to be done and of trying to salvage some legitimate policy gains from the health care debates of 1993 and 1994.

The issues of preexisting condition exclusions and portability had been debated in the Labor Committee markup of the Clinton bill in 1994, when Democrats and Republicans had unanimously adopted legislative proposals in these areas. Thus arriving at the substance behind the Kassebaum-Kennedy health reform bill to be introduced in 1995 was not terribly difficult; Senators and staff simply went back to the legislation that both senators had supported in 1994 and used it as a starting point for negotiations on the new bill. The proposal the two worked out was a long way from Kennedy's goal of universal coverage but would make health insurance far more meaningful for millions of Americans by both making sure their insurance wasn't rendered largely worthless by preexisting condition exclusions and by allowing them to change jobs without fear of losing their insurance. The bill would also make coverage available for many small businesses that had been locked out of the market.

One gap in the legislation was that it did not provide any limitations on the amount insurers could charge the small businesses for which they were now required to provide policies or for individuals who lost or left their job and needed to buy coverage in the individual market. Kassebaum believed that other Republicans would see any such limitations as too great an intervention in the market. But we realized that this opened a large loophole. Insurers could still charge an exorbitant price for small business or individual coverage, rendering the actual availability of the policies somewhat moot. We reasoned that many states had already enacted limitations on the price adjustments that could be made to small business coverage and that we had included funding for state-run programs to provide subsidized insurance for individuals who qualified for coverage under Kassebaum-Kennedy but were priced out of the market. Moreover this issue was not relevant for workers in larger businesses. But the absence of provisions controlling costs was a disadvantage to Kennedy's strategy of working with Kassebaum.

Once the legislation had been developed, the next step was to build political support for it and increase public awareness of the issue. On the political front, Kassebaum and Kennedy, respectively, were assigned to round up Republican and Democratic cosponsors. Kennedy had the easier job: many Democrats wanted to become cosponsors. We decided to limit the number of Democratic cosponsors on the bill to however many Republican cosponsors could be found so that the ultimate product would not appear to be tilted dramatically in the direction of the Democrats. This meant that Kennedy, who'd started promoting the legislation at the Senate Democratic Caucus lunch the previous February, had to hold off Democrats while Kassebaum painstakingly obtained Republicans. Kennedy took an unsuccessful stab at obtaining support from Bob Bennett, who had been appointed chair of the Senate Republican task force on health care, but soon we had six Republican cosponsors: Frist, Jeffords, Hatch, Chafee, Gregg, and Gorton.

In addition to obtaining support from other senators (the inside game), Kennedy, as he had on the minimum wage, created an infrastructure of public interest groups that supported the legislation and would take the lead in the grassroots campaign. He met with all the key health groups during the spring of 1995 while the details of the legislation were being developed. He also met with numerous insurance company officials, as well as other large and small businesses to ascertain their views on the legislation and, hopefully, obtain their support. Over the years he had developed a veritable kitchen cabinet of experts in a slew of fields, but particularly in health care, and now he met with representatives of hospitals, physicians, and other health care providers and businesses from Massachusetts and elsewhere.

Kassebaum and Kennedy aimed to have forty cosponsors when the bill was introduced in the Senate and to have numerous public interest groups in place supporting it. These groups were asked to attend press conferences, hold rallies, and conduct grassroots activities in support of the legislation. Each week, or at least several times a month, the senators would convene public relations events to discuss and highlight problems with the current health care system that the new portability and preexisting condition rules would help to minimize.

Kassebaum was ultimately able to line up a total of twenty Republican cosponsors by the time the two senators went to the floor to introduce the bill on July 13, 1995. In her floor statement, Kassebaum said that the legislation would "promote greater access and security for health coverage for all Americans." For her Republican colleagues, she emphasized that the legislation "did not impose expensive regulatory requirements, create a new federal bureaucracy or federal spending, and did not require employers to pay for health insurance coverage." When it was his turn, Kennedy described the important problems the legislation was designed to fix and summarized how it would do so. He concluded, "I continue to support the goal of comprehensive health reform. This bill is not comprehensive reform, but it will eliminate some of the worst abuses of the private insurance market and provide greater protection for millions of our fellow citizens."

After the bill was introduced, Kassebaum moved quickly to report the legislation through the Labor Committee. This was possible because so much groundwork had been laid beforehand. On July 18, 1995, the Committee held a hearing on the legislation and on August 2 Kassebaum scheduled an executive session of the Committee to report it out. Modest changes were made, and the Committee voted unanimously to approve the legislation and report it to the Senate. The Committee then took the next step of finalizing the report, which was filed in the Senate on October 12. Once the report was filed, the bill was formally placed on the Senate calendar. That made it available to be called up by Majority Leader Dole at any time. The bill's fate was now in his hands.

Dole should have looked favorably upon the Kassebaum-Kennedy health reform bill. After all, Kassebaum was his junior colleague from Kansas and similar provisions had been included in health care legislation he introduced during the debates of 1993 and 1994. Moreover, the Labor Committee had reported the legislation unanimously. Nine Republicans had voted for it, including conservatives Gregg, Coats, and the Senate's only physician, Bill Frist.

By 1995, however, the dynamics in the Senate and in the country had changed. The Republicans were now in control of the Congress, and Dole was running for president. He believed that it was essential to his presidential strategy to win the support of the conservative wing of his party, and therefore supporting legislation that imposed new government regulations in health care would not be helpful. Moreover many insurance companies—important sources of funds and support for the Republican Party and for individual senators within his caucus—opposed the bill. So the pressure was on Dole from the right wing not to call up the legislation. And Kassebaum, although she clearly supported the bill, was reluctant to rock Dole's strategy in the months leading up to the initial primaries in 1996.

From the time the bill was reported, there was a steady series of press articles and public relations events that had the effect of drawing attention to the fact that Dole was not bringing the bill to the floor, even though it had been reported unanimously from the Committee. The public pressure on him to bring up the bill grew in intensity in the winter of 1995–96, but he still resisted. He had a ready-made excuse: the government was shut down and the Congress was not dealing with anything other than budgets and appropriations bills for essentially all of 1995. In early 1996 that excuse no longer worked because the government was operating on a series of continuing resolutions and there were other bills that he scheduled for action on the floor, including various bills creating new national parks that were important to senators and ultimately immigration reform legislation.

Again the Senate rules were an important factor. Any senator can object to almost any action of the Senate—in this case bringing a bill to the floor. If that senator refuses to back down, cloture on the motion to bring the bill to the floor needs to be invoked before debate on the bill itself can begin. As Senate procedures have evolved, senators can block bringing up a bill not by actually standing up and objecting but by notifying their party leader that they *intend* to object. This is called a "hold," and it can be done secretly; if asked by the member, the leader is expected not to reveal the source of the hold. Of course, if the majority leader wants to bring up a bill, he or she doesn't need to honor the hold but can force the senator to stand up on the floor and make his or her objection public. Republican senators opposed to the legislation, with Dole's acquiescence and likely encouragement, used this tactic of a secret hold to block the Kassebaum-Kennedy bill, giving Dole an excuse to avoid bringing it up.

In fact opponents of the bill engaged in a "rolling hold." That is, because the bill was so popular, no senator wanted to be fingered as the person who was holding it up, so a series of senators took turns blocking and lifting secret holds. This process can be repeated indefinitely, and it went on from October 1995 through January 1996.

President Clinton gave the bill a strong public push by urging its passage in his State of the Union speech on January 23, 1996, and that helped kindle press curiosity about the situation. Laurie Kellman, a reporter with the *Washington Post*, was interested about the delay in passing a health care bill that seemed to be supported so broadly in the Congress and had passed the Labor Committee unanimously six months before. She wrote several articles describing the process of the rolling hold and identifying some of the Republican senators responsible for it. The situation was raw meat for the press because it seemed to be such an obvious case of abuse: at the behest of special interests, the Senate allowed senators to secretly block a bill that had broad support without ever having to account for their actions.

The wider media picked up these articles, and Dole was asked why he was knuckling under to the rolling holds and refusing to bring the health care bill to the floor. A particularly embarrassing moment in the week before the February 20 New Hampshire primary was the tipping point.

Nightline with Ted Koppel on ABC was at that time one of the most popular news programs on the air. The program loved exposés, and this seemed like a good one. The producers did an on-camera interview with Kennedy, who explained why the bill was needed and placed the blame for failure to bring it up squarely on Dole. A *Nightline* reporter and cameraman tracked Dole down in New Hampshire, caught him walking along a motel corridor, and asked him why he was refusing to bring up the bill. Obviously uncomfortable, Dole kept walking. The reporter asked the question again. Dole quickened his pace, muttered over his shoulder that there were "holds, lots of holds," and ducked into a motel room, shutting the door in the cameraman's face.

Dole looked terrible, and he knew it. The day after the *Nightline* segment aired, he approached Kennedy on the floor of the Senate and offered to bring up the Kassebaum-Kennedy health reform bill before May 24, a date he selected in the hope that it would be soon enough to satisfy Kennedy and distant enough to get Kennedy to leave him alone during this critical time for his campaign. I'm sure his calculation was that by May 24 he would either have won the presidential nomination or not. For now, he could tell the conservatives that he had held the bill off for another four months.

When approached by Dole, Kennedy insisted on bringing the bill up earlier. He knew that because of the timing of recesses, May 24 might be too late to enact the bill that year. He, Kassebaum, and Dole settled on May 3 as the deadline for bringing up the bill.

Senator Kassebaum went to the floor and asked for unanimous consent that the Senate would consider the bill prior to May 3. But Senator Rod Grams of Minnesota lodged an objection. He wanted to make sure the bill would not be considered until after April 15 (not that there was any likelihood that Senator Dole would bring the bill up any sooner than he had to). Grams, presumably one of the Republican senators objecting to bringing the bill up at all in the months since October 1995, had the idea that somehow the momentum would turn around, perhaps somehow triggered by tax day on April 15, and the country would reject the idea of regulating health plans to increase portability and reduce preexisting condition limitations. On February 6 a unanimous consent agreement was entered in the Senate that not prior to April 15 but not later than May 3 the Senate would turn to consideration of S.1028, the Kassebaum-Kennedy Health Insurance Reform Act of 1996.

Chapter 20

THE CLASH OF THE TITANS: DOLE VS. KENNEDY

GRIDLOCK OVER THE MINIMUM WAGE INCREASE

Attention now turned back to the minimum wage increase. Through the first half of March, Kennedy had stoked interest in the issue by telling the press that he was going to offer the minimum wage amendment on the Senate floor, but as the end of the month approached we still hadn't found an opportunity to do so. Pressure built on Kennedy as the press began to question the seriousness of his commitment to force a vote.

The root of the problem was that a minimum wage amendment would likely prompt Dole to pull the underlying legislation from the floor to avoid a vote, so we needed to attach the amendment to a bill that members of the Republican Caucus wanted to pass and that Democrats were willing to block. For most of March, Dole had been offering routine bills that were as important to Democratic senators as they were to Republicans. One example from the week of March 20 was the Livestock

Grazing Act, important to western state Democrats because it regulated grazing on federal land. Other legislation Dole introduced was related to the debt limit or the government shutdown, and Democrats were unwilling to threaten the viability of those bills.

The week of March 25 would be the last chance to offer the minimum wage amendment before the two-week Easter recess, which would begin on March 29. Democratic Senate staffers met to discuss strategy on March 22. Joel Johnson, Daschle's new policy chief, had replaced John Hilley, who had become chief of the president's Office of Legislative Affairs. Johnson described the Senate schedule Daschle expected for the following week. Dole had brought a bill to the floor reported from the Energy and Natural Resources Committee, an omnibus bill dealing with the establishment of national parks and heritage areas as well as other Interior Department projects. It was variously referred to as the Presidio bill (for the first area the bill dealt with), the parks bill, and the Utah wilderness bill. Some Democratic environmentalists opposed the bill, but many senators had projects they wanted to add to it. By selecting a bill in which so many senators had a stake, Dole was trying to head Kennedy off.

Dole indicated he would lay down a cloture petition on March 25 to bring debate on the parks bill to an end, with a cloture vote scheduled for March 27. However, he had miscalculated. Enough Democrats were dissatisfied with the underlying bill, or eager to get a vote on the minimum wage, that Kennedy had enough votes to defeat cloture. The Senate would be stuck on the parks bill as long as Republicans wanted to keep it on the floor. Here was our opportunity. Daschle had secured an agreement to offer an amendment on March 26, with a three-hour limit for debate and then a vote. He would use this agreement to offer the minimum wage increase.

On Monday, March 25, Senator Lott, standing in for Senator Dole, who was not in Washington but campaigning on the presidential primary trail, made the statement on the floor that, "For the information of all senators, the Senate will resume the Utah Wilderness legislation tomorrow morning with the understanding that Senator Daschle or his designee would be prepared to offer an amendment at 10:30 a.m." The next morning, however, it became clear to the Republican leadership on the floor that they had missed signals when they agreed to allow the Daschle amendment. Now that they realized they would be facing a minimum wage vote, they needed a new strategy, so Lott asked for unanimous consent that a substitute parks bill be considered as original text, replacing the underlying bill. While the new text would theoretically be open to a minimum wage amendment, Lott planned to fill in the amendment slots on the new text before the minimum wage could be offered. As it turned out, however, Republicans would make a potentially ruinous mistake in implementing the strategy—a mistake that only Kennedy identified. After making his unanimous consent request, Lott asked that the Senate agree to go off the parks bill and enter a period of morning business until 12:30. Morning business was the period of speechmaking on any topic a senator chose, with no legislative business in order. Under his proposed consent agreement there would be no amendments offered or business conducted relating to the underlying legislation.

Kennedy objected to this procedure, reiterating his understanding that Daschle was to be recognized at 10:30 to offer an amendment. He stated that Daschle had designated him in his place and that the amendment they were seeking to offer was the increase in the minimum wage. He blasted the Republicans for saying, in effect, "We are not even going to permit you to vote. We are going to use all the parliamentary means [at our disposal to] deny working families the chance to get any kind of increase in the minimum wage." And he laid the responsibility for the strategy on the absent Dole.

Kennedy continued speaking on this theme, asserting that the Republican leadership could not justify not even allowing the Senate to vote on increasing the minimum wage at a time when CEO salaries were skyrocketing. "In the past we've increased the minimum wage and it's been bipartisan," he pointed out. "Why can't we do it now?"

Kerry and Wellstone joined Kennedy on the floor, speaking in morning business on the importance of raising the minimum wage. Conservative Republican senator Nickles responded, "The implication from the remarks of the senator from Massachusetts is that if we do not increase the minimum wage, we do not care about low-income people. I find that to be offensive."

Later that same morning Senator Dole was back in Washington, and by the time the Republican Caucus met at noon, the Republican leadership was comfortable that they had a plan to block Senator Kennedy from introducing the minimum wage bill. When the Senate session resumed at 2:00 that afternoon, Senator Lott and Senator Dole arranged to have two amendments filed to the Lott-Murkowski Parks substitute. They believed that by filling the available amendment spots in the substitute, they had closed off any opportunities for further amendments.

But Kennedy, with his wide knowledge of Senate procedure, thought otherwise. "I believe they've missed something," he told me. "There's an opening to offer the minimum wage to the underlying bill because there are no amendments to the underlying bill other than the substitute. They've substituted revised text, but that still leaves the underlying bill open for an amendment." He asked me to check with our Democratic floor strategists during the lunch caucuses without giving away our strategy to the Republicans.

The Democratic floor staff assumed that Senator Dole and the Republican Parliamentarian had eliminated the possibility of additional Democratic amendments and were skeptical of Senator Kennedy's interpretation of the rules. I relayed this to Kennedy, who was frustrated but undaunted. He said he knew he was right, and that I should check with other parliamentary experts. I phoned one of the experts at the Congressional Research Service who said he thought Kennedy was right. After I reported back to Kennedy he conferred with Daschle and they agreed that later that afternoon they would strike. Daschle would be recognized; he would yield to Kennedy; and Kennedy would offer the minimum wage amendment to the underlying original parks bill. Then, to make sure that there would be no second-degree amendment that would undercut a clean vote on the minimum wage increase, Kennedy would yield to Kerry, who would offer a second-degree minimum wage amendment, which would change the Kennedy amendment only very slightly, leaving a clean vote on the minimum wage as the order of business. Under Senate rules, a second-degree amendment can't be identical to the first-degree amendment it is amending. Both amendments raised the minimum wage to $4.70 an hour as of July 1996 and $5.15 an hour as of July 1997. But under the Kennedy first-degree amendment, the wage went up on July 4, and under the Kerry second-degree amendment the effective date was July 5. Following the Kerry amendment, Daschle would offer a cloture petition on the Kennedy amendment signed by fifteen Democratic senators, which would require a vote on the minimum wage amendment two days later, on March 28. While the Democrats were unlikely to get the sixty votes needed to invoke cloture, there would be a chance for a recorded vote on the amendment, and the process of actually raising the minimum wage would have taken a giant step forward.

After the caucus lunch, the Senate resumed debate on the parks bill. Dole came to the floor and, as expected, offered two amendments to the Lott-Murkowski substitute. Thinking that he had now blocked Kennedy's amendment, he confidently allowed Daschle to be recognized on the floor. "Sooner or later we will have a vote on the minimum wage," Daschle said. "Sooner or later it has to be resolved. Sooner or later this minimum wage increase must pass. We can do it sooner or we can do it later. Our preference is to do it sooner. This vehicle affords us the opportunity to do that, whether it is this vehicle or any other bill. I certainly hope that we can do it soon. I yield to my colleague from Massachusetts, Senator Kennedy."

Kennedy took the floor and, as planned, offered his amendment to the underlying original parks bill. Then Kerry stood up, Kennedy yielded to him, and he offered the second-degree amendment to the Kennedy amendment. Then Kerry moved to table his own amendment. A tabling motion takes precedence over any other matter and must be voted on immediately without debate.

When Dole heard what had just happened, he rushed back to the floor, highly agitated, and immediately put in a quorum call to block a vote on Kerry's tabling motion. For several hours the Senate was in a quorum call and no debate was allowed while Dole, taken by surprise and confused, explored his options. After three hours Dole came back to the floor with a strategy: he would persuade all Republican senators to vote with Kerry and the Democrats against Kerry's motion to table the minimum wage amendment. By doing so, he would deny the Democrats the ability to claim that they had had a meaningful vote on the minimum wage increase. All Republicans would have voted against the tabling motion, allowing the debate on the minimum wage to go forward but not voting up or down on the substance of the increase. The problem with this strategy, however, was that it still left the Kennedy and Kerry amendments as orders of business on the underlying parks legislation.

The Senate is truly a place where it is difficult to tell the players without a scorecard. At this point we had the Lott-Murkowski substitute with two place-holding amendments and the underlying original parks bill with the Kennedy and Kerry amendments. Before the parks bill could be passed, those amendments had to be voted on. So Dole announced that he would pull the parks bill from the floor entirely. He had avoided an up-or-down vote on the minimum wage, but only at the cost of sacrificing—at least for the moment—the parks bill. And he still faced a cloture vote on Kennedy's amendment when the cloture petition "ripened" on March 28.

The next day Dole turned to line-item veto legislation. Senator Byrd, the principal opponent of the line-item veto, gave a two-hour speech citing the Bible, Aristotle, Alexander Hamilton, Daniel Webster, the fall of Rome, and the U.S. Constitution. Despite this impressive list of supporters his arguments did not prevail, and he was defeated 69–31, though he was ultimately vindicated years later when the U.S. Supreme Court struck down the line-item veto legislation as unconstitutional.

The morning of the cloture vote, with the presidential campaign heating up, Kennedy raised the temperature of the cloture debate by putting the blame for blocking the minimum wage amendment squarely on Dole and linking him to the unpopular Gingrich: "Senator Dole is leading this filibuster. . . . Speaker Gingrich and Senator Dole make a remarkable couple. It is like Bonnie and Clyde writing the Republican platform. Newt Gingrich wants to repeal the ban on assault weapons,

Bob Dole wants to block any increases in the minimum wage. Democrats do not share these appalling priorities, and neither do the vast majority of the American people."

Senator Murkowski came to Dole's defense, complaining that Kennedy's strategy of putting the minimum wage amendment into the national parks bill was unconscionable, "political opportunism at its worst," because it was delaying the most significant environmental measure to come before the Senate. Senator Nickles followed: "This amendment does not belong on the national parks bill. You might say 'Well, why is it on this bill? Why was it offered by my friend and colleague from Massachusetts to put on this bill?' I will tell you. In my opinion it is all about politics. Why did they do it now? Well, presidential politics."

Kennedy took to the floor again, quoting Dole: "Bob Dole, March 28, 1974: 'I am pleased to support the conference report on the minimum wage bill. A living wage for a fair day's work is a hallmark of the American economic philosophy.' May 17, 1989, Bob Dole on the floor of the Senate: 'I have said as a Republican I am not going to stand here and say you can live on $3.25 an hour, or $4.55 an hour.' Bob Dole on the Senate floor, April 11, 1989: 'To be sure I am all for helping the working poor. I have spent most of my public life supporting causes on behalf of the working poor, and no one would deny that the working poor are the ones who most deserve a wage increase.'

"Mr. President, where is that Bob Dole?"

Shortly thereafter the cloture vote was held. The forty-seven Democrats picked up eight Republicans for a total of fifty-five votes for the minimum wage amendment, up from fifty-one on October 31, 1995. The Republicans joining with the Democrats were Hatfield, Jeffords, Specter, and Al D'Amato of New York, all of whom said they supported the increase. Snowe, Cohen, Roth, and Rick Santorum of Pennsylvania also voted to invoke cloture, although neither they nor their spokespeople said how they would ultimately vote on the minimum wage increase itself.

The Democratic strategy was working. Though we failed to obtain the sixty votes necessary to end the filibuster, we had made progress and were on the prowl for the next opportunity to strike.

Democrats went home for the Easter recess on March 29 with packets of talking points on why the minimum wage should be increased and suggestions for holding town meetings with minimum wage workers to highlight the issue in their districts. In Washington, Democrats used the Easter recess to organize a coordinated strategy with the White House for the presidential campaign. Following up on Stephanopoulos's visit to the Hill to talk about keeping Dole stuck on the floor, staff from seven Democratic senators in the so-called core group were invited to the White House Roosevelt Room to discuss strategy for the period after the Senate reconvened. Staff from Senators Boxer, Dorgan, Breaux, Daschle, Kennedy, Dodd, and Mark Pryor were invited. Present from the White House were Stephanopoulos, Hilley, Deputy Chief of Staff Doug Sosnik, and Susan Volpe, Hilley's deputy.

Hilley said we needed to have the mechanisms and the organization in place to take the presidential campaign to Dole on the Senate floor. Volpe explained that those present would be the core group, but there were other senators who would get involved on specific issues, for example, Senator Nunn on foreign policy and defense. Joel Johnson from Daschle's office observed that Dole's staff and his Republican colleagues in the Senate would be there on the floor protecting him, attacking the president, and Democrats needed to have planned responses. We needed to be ready with amendments to highlight the issues on which Dole was vulnerable, and we needed to keep him on the floor. When he was on the floor we needed to engage him in debate and colloquy on the issues on which he was weak. We needed to be in a position to respond when he attacked Democrats or the president. As always, the core issues for Democrats would be education, the environment, Medicare, Medicaid, tax cuts for working people, the minimum wage increase, and health care. We also needed to be able to defend against Dole's agenda: crime (where the legislation enacted by President Clinton to add 100,000 police was a strong counterargument), defense, welfare, taxes, and Whitewater.

At least for the moment, any thought of a triangulation strategy was a thing of the past. The White House badly needed strong support from Democratic senators—and they knew it. As Stephanopoulos had emphasized at the earlier meeting, because the Republican candidate was also the majority leader, the Senate had become a primary venue to fight out the presidential election. What happened on the Senate floor would be as critical to the outcome as all the traditional rallies and speeches and events in cities and towns across America.

There was an amusing sequel to the battle over the Parks bill. Six weeks later, shortly before Dole left the Senate and after he and Kennedy had been going at each other hammer and tongs on the floor day after day over the minimum wage bill and Kassebaum-Kennedy, they managed to get together on a little bill called the Nicodemus National Historic Site and the New Bedford National Historic Landmark Act. The bill established two national historic sites, one in Kansas, commemorating the only remaining African American settlement established in the West after the Civil War, and one in New Bedford, Massachusetts, commemorating the town's whaling history. The bill provided federal funds to develop and maintain the sites and presumably bring in tourist dollars. The bill was introduced and almost immediately passed by the Senate on May 2. Ultimately it was incorporated into that same omnibus parks bill that Kennedy's maneuvering had forced Dole to pull down.

THE HOUSE VERSION OF HEALTH INSURANCE REFORM

While the Senate had postponed action on the Kassebaum-Kennedy health care bill until at least April 15, the House had actually passed its own version of health reform prior to the Easter recess. The House legislation had some minimal protections for consumers concerning portability and preexisting condition exclusions, but also added a series of controversial special interest provisions backed by their friends in the insurance industry, the small business lobby, and the AMA. In our view, these provisions undercut the whole purpose of the bill, which was to make the health insurance system work better for patients, not for special interests. Democrats in the House opposed the legislation on the grounds that the add-ons overwhelmed the original purpose of the bill and the details of the preexisting conditions and portability provisions were so weak that they would actually hurt rather than help the problem. They offered the Kassebaum-Kennedy legislation, but it was defeated 226–192, with only ten Republicans supporting it.

Kennedy used the recess to study the fine print of the House Republican add-ons. One of these, medical savings accounts, or MSAs, became central to the fight to enact a good bill. Indeed, as events unfolded, the issue of MSAs threatened to overwhelm the favorable momentum we had generated for insurance reform and sink the bill altogether.

The impetus for the MSAs came from Patrick Rooney, CEO of the Indianapolis-based Golden Rule Insurance Company. Rooney was a generous contributor to the Republican Party. With his enthusiastic backing and support from a conservative think tank he had endowed, MSAs had become the conservatives' favorite remedy for the health care cost problem. Like other firms in the individual and small business health insurance market, Golden Rule's business strategy was to insure only the healthiest people. The healthier its clients were, the fewer the claims that were paid out and the higher the profits. Golden Rule had a dismal track record as a company notorious for denying claims based on even the flimsiest link to alleged preexisting conditions. In one particularly egregious case, cited by Kennedy in a floor speech, a patient's medical claim for treatment of a stroke was denied because the insurance company claimed he had failed to report a preexisting condition: the flu.[1]

Under the MSA concept, insurance companies could link high-deductible health insurance policies—which required patients to spend large amounts out of their own pocket before their insurance coverage kicked in—with a tax-free savings account. Any contributions to the account either by an individual or an employer and any accumulations from account investments would be tax-free, and withdrawals to pay medical expenses not covered by insurance, including the large deductibles, would be tax-free as well. Under the House bill, as an added sweetener, after an individual reached age sixty-five, tax-free withdrawals would not be limited to paying medical expenses.

For Rooney, MSAs represented an important new business opportunity. Golden Rule already marketed some high-deductible policies; in Rooney's view, that market would explode if a tax-free savings account were added. And as insurance reform and the growth of managed care made it more difficult for Rooney to compete by selling conventional policies only to healthy people, MSAs might be the only way he could keep his company viable.

Once the National Center for Policy Analysis laid out the arguments, conservatives embraced the concept. After all, unlike the Clinton plan or other Democratic programs, medical savings accounts didn't regulate payments to providers or cap insurance company premiums. There was essentially no government regulation of the health system at all. Instead, in the conservative view, individuals would be "empowered" to reduce costs by choosing less expensive providers and forgoing elective care they didn't really need. And the beauty of it, in their view, was that with MSAs to fill in the deductibles and other out-of-pocket payments, patients wouldn't lose a thing.

We didn't believe MSAs were a real answer to the health problem. When people are sick and need care immediately they aren't in a position to shop around for health care by analyzing the prices of different providers. Most health care expenditures are incurred by people with serious illnesses, and the costs of their care exceed even high deductibles. Moreover, most economists believe that any systemwide savings from higher deductibles are only one-time savings; they don't reduce the rate of increase in health care costs, which has been the real problem.

Our concerns about MSAs went far beyond the fact that they wouldn't control health care costs. If they really were successful in the marketplace, they would disproportionately help the healthy and wealthy while potentially harming everyone else. Studies indicated that high-deductible plans discourage appropriate, needed care as much as inappropriate care. Low- and moderate-income families, who couldn't afford to pay thousands of dollars out of pocket before their insurance kicked in, would be most likely to defer seeking help until they were so ill that they had no choice. People with serious or chronic illnesses would also be harmed by plans that exposed them to higher out-of-pocket costs. By contrast, high-deductible plans might be attractive to healthy people who didn't expect to get sick and would be willing to trade some risk of higher out-of-pocket costs for lower insurance premiums and the chance to open a tax-free savings account. And of course, the plan would be especially attractive to the wealthy, who would have the most to gain from the tax break the MSA provided and would be least worried about having to pay a high deductible if they got sick. The claim that the availability of MSAs to go with the high-deductible plans would leave patients just as well off was illusory. The reductions in premiums associated with higher deductibles were far less than the increased exposure to out-of-pocket costs, so any savings gained would not be nearly enough to fill the MSAs to a level that would provide similar protection to conventional insurance.

Conservatives might argue that no one was forced to sign up for MSAs, so what was the problem? One problem was that the program would have established another tax break for the wealthy worth billions of dollars. At a more basic level, based on consultation with insurance experts, we were concerned that MSAs would ultimately make conventional comprehensive insurance unaffordable. To be viable, insurance has to cover a reasonable mix of both healthy and unhealthy people; the premiums of the healthy subsidize the costs of those who are sick. This is fair because none of us stays healthy forever and all of us need protection against unforeseen events. If the healthy leave the insurance pool, premiums rise to unaffordable levels. Since MSAs disproportionately attract healthy consumers, they could set off what insurance actuaries refer to as a death spiral. As the healthy move away from conventional insurance, premiums for those who remain in the pool rise. As premiums rise, more people leave conventional insurance, until only the sick remain. The result: conventional coverage is not affordable for anyone.

Since we had developed Kassebaum-Kennedy to provide greater protection for patients, a provision that could make things much worse for people who needed protection the most—the sick and the low income—was totally unacceptable. Thus the outline of what was to become an intense struggle that would determine the future of health insurance reform was emerging: Republicans would push for MSAs as central to their

vision of health reform; we would oppose them just as strongly because
we thought MSAs would be harmful.

The Republican strategy for dealing with popular Democratic initiatives such as health reform and the minimum wage was becoming
clear. They would do all they could to weaken the provisions that the
Democrats supported in the underlying legislation and would then add
to the legislation a whole set of measures representing their right-wing
ideology—provisions they knew would be unacceptable to Democrats.
From the Republican point of view, this strategy was a no-lose proposition. If the Democrats accepted their changes, the Republicans would
have won legislative victories that would otherwise have been impossible.
If the Democrats refused, the Republicans would have killed a bill they
disliked all along without taking responsibility for opposing it.

Over the Easter recess several organizations released polls on the
presidential election and the approval rating of the congressional del-
egations for each party. The *New York Times*/CBS poll had Clinton ahead
of Dole by almost twenty points but found that Dole showed greater
strength on personal qualities.[2] A Pew poll found Democrats ahead by
five points in the generic congressional vote. Women supported Democrats by 55–40, seniors by 57–36, independents by 43–41.[3]

BACK TO THE MINIMUM WAGE

Congress reconvened on April 15, and the first bill on the floor of the
Senate was the immigration reform bill. Senator Alan Simpson would
manage the bill for the Republicans and Kennedy, the ranking member on the immigration subcommittee of the Judiciary Committee in the
Senate, would manage the legislation for the Democrats. That Kennedy
would be presiding during the time that the minimum wage and health
care reform efforts converged on the floor was to create an immense
problem for Dole.

For twenty years immigration matters had been worked out jointly
between Simpson and Kennedy, no matter whose party was in power and
who was the chairman of the subcommittee. But now, as the immigration

bill was prepared for the floor, the Republican right had forced Simpson to insert draconian provisions that Kennedy and other Democrats opposed. After one day of debate on the immigration bill, Dole was preparing to pull the bill from the floor because of Kennedy's attempts to offer the minimum wage amendment to it.

The grassroots effort in favor of the minimum wage increase was paying off. On April 17 Adam Clymer reported in the *New York Times* that "13 House Republicans are expected to announce Wednesday that they have broken ranks on the issue of the minimum wage. House leaders who spurned a Democratic demand for a minimum wage vote today are understood to be uncertain about whether they would win if they had to allow one." Clymer also reported a statement Dole had made to a reporter in Florida during the Easter recess about the minimum wage. According to Clymer, Dole said "he had not thought about what should be done on the minimum wage."[4] This comment was accompanied in many newspapers by pictures of Dole in a bathing suit at the pool in his condominium in Bal Harbor, Florida. The juxtaposition was not helpful to Dole's campaign.

According to the *Times*, the number of House Republicans prepared to vote for the minimum wage had climbed to twenty, and Gingrich informed House members at a closed caucus that they needed to be prepared because it was inevitably going to be forced to a vote. On April 18 the House Democratic leadership released details from a *New York Times/ CBS* poll showing that 84 percent of all Americans supported raising the minimum wage from $4.25 to $5.15 an hour: 94 percent of Democrats, 87 percent of independents, and even 71 percent of Republicans.[5]

Dole and the Senate Republicans, however, were still unwilling to move, although Dole seemed to be concerned about the political fallout from continued opposition. He appeared on the PBS *NewsHour* and told Jim Lehrer, "You can't explain it but the [minimum wage] increase is very popular politically."

DOLE GIVES IN

Also on April 18, Dole, still undecided on the minimum wage and resisting Kennedy's efforts and that of other Democrats to add a vote on the minimum wage to whatever legislation was on the floor, suddenly announced he was calling up the Kassebaum-Kennedy Health Insurance Reform Act for consideration, consistent with the agreement he had made with Kennedy several months earlier. Now we were off the minimum wage and back to health care reform.

Kassebaum and Kennedy, the floor managers for the legislation, started off by praising each other's efforts. Kennedy recalled the 1994 health care debates: "All of us who were part of that effort knew that Senator Kassebaum was trying to find areas of common ground on which we could move forward. . . . It is really [as] a result of her own particular skills, talents and energy that we are here today." Having emphasized the bipartisanship of the measure, Kennedy then turned to the substance. He said that the legislation would "end many of the most serious health insurance abuses and provide greater protection to millions of families." He gave examples of individuals who had lost their health insurance when they changed jobs or because one of their family members had gotten sick. He then listed the senators who had supported these provisions in previous years and the outside groups that were committed to this legislation: "The Independent Insurance Agents of America—the largest association of agents in the country—sees the tragedies created by the current system every day. They support this bill. Doctors, hospitals, and other health providers see those tragedies as well, and they support the legislation. It has been endorsed by the American Medical Association, the American Hospital Association, and over forty-four medical specialty societies. In fact, the only opposition to this legislation comes from those who profit from the abuses in the current system."

Anticipating a debate on MSAs, Kennedy then explained the agreement that he had reached with Kassebaum about certain provisions in the bill—an agreement that was to play a critical role in the upcoming debate. They had committed to these provisions in their negotiations with public interest groups and industry groups in order to obtain the groups' endorsement of the legislation. Many of the groups had been unwilling to endorse it unless Kassebaum and Kennedy agreed to resist all controversial amendments that would significantly alter the key provisions in the bill. It was not an uncommon practice for senators seeking to obtain support for legislation to agree that they would oppose changes to it on the floor or in conference. The Senate sponsors obviously could not totally control what happened to the legislation, but commitment to a good-faith attempt to keep the legislation to the terms that had been negotiated was an essential element in obtaining support from many outside advocates.

Kennedy had told me about his first experience with this process in the Senate, during the debates on civil rights in 1965. The Republican leader Everett Dirksen had broken ranks with Republican senators who opposed civil rights legislation and had pulled together a bipartisan group of senators to develop compromise legislation that they would support. Kennedy was in that group, so he met with Dirksen and other senators in a room off the Senate floor for more than a week, hashing out differences and settling on compromise language. When the process was over, the senators in the room agreed that they would oppose changes to the legislation, even changes they would normally support, in order to obtain the overall group consensus and the opportunity to move the legislation forward as drafted. This was the same procedure that Kassebaum and Kennedy adopted for the health care bill. As Kennedy asserted in his opening statement:

> Members of the Senate who are serious about insurance reform should vote against all controversial amendments—including medical savings accounts. Senator Kassebaum and I have agreed that we will vigorously oppose all such amendments—even those that we might support under other circumstances. The Democratic leader and many other Senators of both parties have joined us in this pledge. This is a test of the Senate's seriousness and ability to put the interests of the American people ahead of the special interests. . . .

This legislation is not comprehensive health reform. It will not solve all the problems in the current system. But it is a constructive step forward—a step that will help millions of Americans. I urge its adoption.

Following Kennedy, Kassebaum spoke again, this time about Senator Kennedy:

He is one who has been involved in health care issues for many, many years and cares deeply about it. He would, I am sure, like to have expanded this bill much further. But we worked hard to construct, as he mentioned, something that we felt could be passed and could be approved by the widest number in both the U.S. Senate and the House of Representatives. So I have greatly appreciated his leadership in the Labor and Human Resources Committee, as we have worked hard and constructively on both sides of the aisle in the Committee, as well as on the floor, to bring this to fruition today.

She then introduced Senator Frist, a member of the Committee who had also worked on the legislation and was the only doctor in the Senate. He said, "I rise to congratulate Senators Kassebaum and Kennedy for introducing what I consider to be a fair, balanced, focused, and excellent bill."

Dole rose to offer his amendment to the Kassebaum-Kennedy bill, revealing his strategy. After resisting the legislation for more than six months, now that he was forced to call it up, he would try to add his own initiatives to it and then try to take credit for it. The Dole amendment had several provisions developed in the Finance Committee, including expanding tax deductions for the self-employed and for people who buy insurance to cover the cost of long-term care or who spend their money on nursing home care, and simplification and automation of provider claims for insurance reimbursement. These measures were generally supported.

But then came the kicker: a provision to allow the establishment of medical savings accounts. Kennedy rose to oppose that portion of the

Dole amendment dealing with MSAs, and Kassebaum offered a second-degree amendment to strike the MSA provision from Dole's package. She also confided to Kennedy her disappointment that Dole had inserted the provision. "This is very bad of Bob," she said.

The debate on the Dole MSA amendment, carried on throughout the day and into the evening, was intense. Democrats argued that if the Dole amendment on MSAs passed, it would have the effect of killing the health care bill, but given the steam the issue had acquired among conservatives and the natural inclination of Republicans to support their leader and presidential candidate on a high-profile issue, it was unclear how the vote would end up. It was close to midnight when the Senate voted on the Kassebaum amendment to strike the MSA provision from the Dole amendment. In the end, five Republicans joined all forty-seven Democrats in voting for Kennedy over Dole. In retrospect it is surprising that Dole hadn't done a more accurate vote count before offering his amendment. For a man running for president in part on his proclaimed "can do" mastery of the Senate, a high-profile defeat like this was hardly good advertising.

It was supremely ironic that leading the battle against the Dole MSA proposal was his Republican colleague and good friend from Kansas, Nancy Kassebaum. But, like Kennedy, Kassebaum was one of those senators who believed her word was her bond. She told Kennedy she would oppose all controversial changes to the bill and honored not only the letter of her commitment but its spirit, fighting hard to keep enough of her Republican colleagues in line to defeat the amendment.

There was another controversial amendment offered to the bill: to prohibit insurers from discriminating against patients who need mental health care. Insurers had long attempted to hold costs down by putting severe limits on mental health benefits: the number of visits to a therapist that would be covered, the number of days of hospitalization that would be allowed, the total cost of mental health services, and more. Republican senator Pete Domenici of New Mexico, who had a child with schizophrenia, and Democrat Paul Wellstone, a liberal from Minnesota who was passionate about advocating for mental health services, teamed up on an amendment that would require insurers that offered any mental health coverage to offer it under the same terms as coverage for physical illnesses. Kennedy, who had a deep concern for mental health issues himself, would have very much liked to have supported the amendment, but, honoring his agreement with Kassebaum, voted against it.

In this case, though, the amendment carried, with substantial support from both sides of the aisle. The strong personal affection that so many Republican senators felt for Domenici caused them to vote for a requirement for insurers they might otherwise have opposed. In conference, Kennedy worked closely with Wellstone and Domenici to ensure that a provision, albeit a weak one, was included in the final bill. (Ultimately full mental health parity was finally included in the Troubled Assets Relief Act (TARP) in 2008. The key TARP bill conferees who worked out the agreement were Kennedy, who led the Senate effort on parity after Wellstone's tragic death in a plane accident in October 2002 and Domenici's retirement in January 2009, and Congressman Patrick Kennedy, who was the leader of the effort in the House. With his responsibility to represent the Senate position in the conference, Senator Kennedy had to argue against his son, who had the same responsibility in representing the House position. Presumably these different responsibilities led to lively conversations around the Kennedy dinner table.)

Following the vote to strike the MSA provision and the vote to adopt the remainder of the Dole amendment, one of those bizarre moments that often happen in the Senate occurred. Vice President Gore had been summoned from the White House to preside over the Senate in the event that the vote was a 50–50 tie and his vote would be needed to defeat the MSA provision. He was also present to provide the Clinton presidential campaign an opportunity to highlight the defeat of Dole's measure if that were to occur.

Daschle, Gore, and Kennedy stepped off the floor to hold an impromptu press conference to discuss the defeat of the MSA provision and herald the imminent passage of the bill now that the main obstacle had been removed. Both the presidential and the congressional press corps were waiting eagerly. Kennedy had made clear to Daschle that he would not participate in the press conference unless Kassebaum appeared with him, as they had been partners in the legislation from the beginning. She agreed to join him, but then she asked, "What about Senator Dole?" Her strategy all along, she reasoned, had been to get Dole to support the health bill, which he was now prepared to do, and there were many provisions in the bill that Dole had added and that had been accepted. Kennedy offhandedly agreed that Kassebaum should bring Dole along to the press conference, and she went over and spoke to Dole.

TV cameras, print reporters, and others were clustered around the vice president as he stepped from the Senate, followed by Daschle, Kennedy, and Kassebaum. Gore began laying into Dole for his attempt, as he put it, to kill the health bill by adding on the destructive MSA provision. He insisted that Dole had proposed MSAs largely to benefit a single insurance company, the Golden Rule Company, owned by one of Dole's largest contributors.

As Gore's diatribe was unfolding, out from the Senate came Dole himself, who apparently had accepted Kassebaum's invitation to join in the press conference for the purpose of claiming his share of the credit for the health insurance bill. He was undoubtedly surprised to hear the vice president attacking his provisions in the bill, but he nevertheless stood beside Kassebaum and behind Gore as the diatribe continued. Gore was unaware that Dole was standing behind him.

TV cameras were rolling to capture this remarkable scene. In the midst of a full-blown attack on the Republican attempt to kill the health care bill, Gore turned his head slightly to the right and out of the corner of his eye caught sight of Dole standing there. The diatribe ended abruptly, and Gore welcomed Dole to the press conference, explaining that he had not known Dole had been there during his most recent comments. The tone of the conference quickly changed. Gore moderated his remarks, offering general praise for the important Senate action in advancing the insurance bill.

While this was going on, Dole whispered to Kennedy, who was standing next to him, "What should I say?" Kennedy whispered back that he should talk about how great it was that the bill had gotten this far and that it would provide portability and limit preexisting condition exclusions. He suggested Dole also talk about his provisions for increased tax deductibility for insurance for the self-employed.

Each of the senators, including Dole, was given a chance to speak, and it ended up being a jolly event, with everybody praising everybody else for their role in moving the legislation forward. Vice President Gore, a tough partisan focused on the president's and his own reelection, was also a former member of the Senate who felt honor-bound to observe its traditional courtesies, and each senator was unfailingly polite and jocular in this group setting that they had been thrust into.

The health care bill was now ready to pass the Senate but was still a long way from completion. The fight to maintain the stronger Senate provisions in conference and to drop the House special interest add-ons, especially the MSA provision, had not even begun. Indeed, rather than quietly licking his wounds on the MSA issue and waiting to fight another day, Dole raised the ante just a few days later.

Now Kennedy and the Democrats in the House and Senate turned their attention back to the minimum wage. With twenty House Republicans indicating their support, it now seemed more likely that a minimum wage increase would pass. On April 21 Dole appeared on CBS's *Face the Nation* and essentially conceded the increase. "Will there be an increase? I assume there will," he said. "The House has already indicated they're going to pass the minimum wage." He announced that his strategy, as it had been with the health care bill, would be to add other measures to the legislation. He would focus on measures that would limit the powers of unions and the right of workers to receive mandatory overtime pay. In a breathtaking understatement, he remarked that the unions "aren't crazy about" these provisions.

By April 22 Kennedy was back on the floor pressing Dole for an up-or-down vote on the minimum wage:

On *Face the Nation* yesterday, Senator Dole was asked whether he would allow a straight up-or-down vote on the minimum wage. Senator Dole said, "No, our view is that it needs to be packaged with other things—maybe comp time, flex time."

Let me be very clear in response. There is no reason to delay or saddle the minimum wage with other controversial measures. I intend to offer a clean vote on increasing the minimum wage on the nuclear waste bill or any other bill this week or next week that is open to amendments. There is no excuse for further delay in raising the minimum wage.

He went on, laying out the facts supporting the minimum wage increase and emphasizing its importance to women. Polls were showing a growing gender gap favoring the Democrats, especially Clinton over Dole in the presidential contest. Kennedy was relentlessly hammering away on the importance of the Democratic agenda to women.

On April 23 the Senate finally voted, 100–0, to pass the Kassebaum-Kennedy health care bill without the MSAs but with Dole's other amendments. Kassebaum and Kennedy held a press conference celebrating the bipartisan spirit and the unanimous vote. Now they hoped that the bill could move quickly through conference without any other extraneous measures attached, as they wanted the president to be able to sign it as soon as possible.

Dole and his Republican colleagues also held a press conference to congratulate each other on the passage of the bill. There was a certain irony in this since Dole and the right-wing Republicans had opposed even bringing the legislation to the floor from October 1995 until April 1996, but now Dole was trying to make the best of a situation that he had badly mishandled from the very beginning. He said, "The important part of this bill is the tax provisions that I have added to it. We are now on the right track. The long-term care provision and increasing the deductibility of health expenses for the self-employed and small businesses are the important aspects of this legislation. I want to thank Senator Roth, chairman of the Finance Committee, for his effort in putting the bill together."

Roth focused on these same provisions but Senator Phil Gramm used the occasion to increase the pressure on his Republican colleagues. "Finally, we will stop discriminating against the self-employed and that's what Senator Dole and Senator Roth have achieved," he said. "There is strong support in the Senate to keep MSAs in the bill and, of course, the House bill already has MSAs included. There will be a strong push to adopt the House provision in conference with medical savings accounts."

Amid all the congratulatory rhetoric, there was an ominous note for Democrats. When asked about MSAs, Dole said he expected the conference to include them, and reminded reporters, "I appoint the conferees."

No Republican mentioned the portability and preexisting conditions provisions, the essential elements of the legislation from the beginning. But never mind, the Republicans were on board, and what could we expect? They wouldn't be so dumb as to carp over a bill that the Senate had just adopted 100–0.

Shortly after the health care vote I talked again with Tom O'Donnell, chief of staff for Congressman Gephardt. He reported that both Daschle and Gephardt had asked the president to veto the health care bill if it contained a substantial program of medical savings accounts. O'Donnell was concerned because Gore had responded that the president might not be able to veto the bill for that reason. Once again it seemed that progressive Democrats in the House and Senate might need to shore up the president. One could argue that it was important for Clinton to sign any bill that had the words "health care" on it. Since he had the largest megaphone, he could present any legislation as a step forward. He could have a signing ceremony, taking credit for presiding over the passage and enactment of a major new health care bill. The fact that the bill might include an unlimited program of medical savings accounts that many health care experts felt would be destructive would be a concern, but not necessarily a decisive one for him. And, of course, the House Democrats weren't without self-interest in this matter. A big signing ceremony would be good for the president, but it wasn't necessarily good for Democrats hoping to regain control of the House by campaigning against a do-nothing Republican Congress.

On April 25 Senator Lott, acting on behalf of Dole, went to the floor to appoint conferees for the health care bill. Normally these appointments are automatic; it can be an immensely cumbersome process if any senator chooses to exercise his or her right to object. When Lott asked for unanimous consent, however, Kennedy objected. He said he first wanted to know who the conferees would be. Lott told him the conferees would include Dole, Roth, and himself. The Democrats would be allowed two conferees.

The party ratio was standard, but Lott's tactics were not. In order to ensure that a majority of Senate conferees favored medical savings accounts, even though the Senate had voted to eliminate them from its bill, Lott bypassed normal Senate practices. He put himself on instead of Chafee, who was the next in seniority after Roth on the Finance Committee, and, in the most striking departure from normal practice, he excluded Kassebaum, who was not only the chief Republican sponsor of the bill but the chair of the committee that had jurisdiction over the key part of the bill.

Since the House Republicans and Lott's proposed Senate conferees favored MSAs, they would have been made part of the final legislation. We would have been put in the awkward position of having to do our best to block our own insurance reform and encouraging a presidential veto. Based on this information, Senator Kennedy renewed his objection to the unanimous consent motion to appoint conferees. Since, if unanimous consent is not given, this motion is debatable and subject to a filibuster, Kennedy's objection blocked, at least for the moment, the Republican effort to stack the conference in favor of MSAs.

This parliamentary skirmish was the first but not the last Kennedy had with Lott over the next eight years while Lott was majority leader. Although he started out in the Senate as a conservative firebrand, trained in the House under the leadership of Newt Gingrich, we soon saw the side of Lott that was committed to making the Senate work. He could be a tough opponent, but played by the rules we did, albeit seeking a different outcome. Despite wide differences with Kennedy on most policy issues, he partnered with Kennedy in 1997 to pass the Individuals with

Disabilities Education Act and in 2007 on the unsuccessful immigration reform effort among others.

Lott was a happy warrior for the very conservative agenda, as was Kennedy for the opposite. Lott would go to Daschle, the Democratic leader, with a long list of asks and demands—many reasonable, some outrageous. When the outrageous ones were caught, he would kind of chuckle, as if he were thinking, "Well that didn't work. I didn't expect it to, but a fellow has to try." Then after having fun with this back and forth, he would return to real negotiating. When he'd leave the leader's office, he would often whistle down the hall back to his office, as if he knew it had been a tough but fair fight and was not at all agitated that he had gone at it.

Lott obviously took his responsibility to the Senate very seriously, and in 2013 he began serving as a board member for the Edward M. Kennedy Institute for the United States Senate with, among others, Tom Daschle, the former Senate Democratic leader. The active involvement of the two former leaders on the board emphasizes the Institute's bipartisan spirit. When accepting his appointment, Lott said the Institute, "will help students, teachers and the public to learn more about their government and just how the work in Washington, DC is pivotal to our working democracy." At Senator Kennedy's memorial service in August 2009 at the JFK Library, then senator John Kerry commented on Kennedy's relationships with Republicans. He recalled that one of the framed notes in Kennedy's office was a thank-you from a colleague for a gift: a special edition of *Profiles in Courage*. The note said: "I brought it home and re-read it. What an inspiration. Thank you my friend for your many courtesies. If the world only knew." It was signed by Trent Lott. In March 2015, at the dedication of the Edward M. Kennedy Institute, Lott retold the story and provoked gales of laughter from the audience when he jokingly commented, "I didn't actually want the whole world to know."

After Kennedy objected to the Lott motion to appoint the stacked deck of conferees, Dole approached him, perhaps to try to work out some agreement. Dole often made offhand comments that were disarming in their frankness, but not necessarily politic. In the course of the conversation he said, "As a matter of fact, I'm not that crazy about medical savings accounts." Kennedy was not surprised by this remark because it was consistent with his view that Dole had no fierce ideological commitment to the right-wing agenda but was simply pushing it in order to appear responsive to some of his strongest supporters. Without thinking it through, Kennedy revealed the remark to reporters—a severe breach of Senate etiquette because it exposed what Dole had thought was a private conversation. It was very unusual for Kennedy to make a mistake like this. When he realized what he had done, he apologized to Dole. Later Dole told reporters, "I don't have to work it out with Senator Kennedy," emphasizing that he, not Kennedy, was the majority leader.

Kennedy called the Republican attempt to stack the conference in favor of MSAs an attempt to "hijack" the legislation; the MSAs were a poison pill that would kill the bill. Republicans would attempt several more times to appoint a stacked-deck of conferees, but Kennedy would always be there to object. Ultimately he insisted on "preconferencing" before he would allow conferees to be appointed, which meant that the key players on the health care issue needed to negotiate over the matter of MSAs and agree to a compromise before Kennedy would give up his leverage of holding up the appointment of Senate conferees. Republicans complained mightily that Kennedy was now the one holding up health reform, but each time he responded that in fact it was the Republicans who were blocking reform by attempting to bypass normal procedure to ensure MSAs would be included. And he returned to the floor again and again, week after week, to rail against MSAs and what he portrayed as an unholy alliance between Republicans, Patrick Rooney, and the Golden Rule Insurance Company to kill an essential reform to a system that was harming millions of Americans.

MORE SENATE GRIDLOCK ON THE MINIMUM WAGE INCREASE

At the same time the conflict over the appointments of conferees on Kassebaum-Kennedy was beginning, the struggle for the minimum wage increase was heating up. On April 24 Dole called the immigration bill back to the floor with orders for votes on various amendments, but with the path for a vote on a minimum wage amendment still blocked. The strategy was to deny recognition to any individual who had not pledged that the amendment he or she was going to offer would be relevant to the immigration bill.

Kennedy was ready and rose to his feet. "After these amendments," he said, "hopefully, we will have the legislation that will be open for amendment. I intend at the earliest possible time to offer an amendment on increasing the minimum wage. I would be more than glad to enter into a time limitation so that our side would have thirty minutes and the other side would have thirty minutes. It seems to me that the 13 million families that will be affected by the minimum wage are entitled to have at least thirty minutes of the United States Senate's time in order to make their case."

On April 25 some House Republicans conceded that they might allow an amendment on the minimum wage. It looked like the House might actually act. But House Majority Leader Dick Armey was still leading the resistance to the minimum wage increase, and House Republican whip Tom DeLay caused a furor when he declared, "Emotional appeals about working families trying to get by on $4.25 an hour are hard to resist. Fortunately such families don't really exist." As the House Democratic talking points declared, "DeLay's suggestion that minimum wage families don't really exist will certainly come as a surprise to many Americans who are struggling to get by."

On April 26 Democrats in the House tried again to require a vote on the minimum wage increase. Thirteen Republicans sided with the Democrats, but ultimately the motion failed 220–200. After the vote, House Democrats went public with comments by Republican leaders on the minimum wage. Dick Armey had said, "I will resist an increase in the minimum wage with every fiber of my being."[6] And John Boehner, the Republican conference chairman, promised, "I'll commit suicide before I vote on a clean minimum wage bill."

Meanwhile Dole had now figured out how to continue to block Kennedy from offering a minimum wage amendment to the immigration bill. Throughout the week he refused to allow any senator to be recognized who planned to offer any amendment other than one germane to the immigration bill, and on April 26 he filed a cloture petition, which would be voted on at 5:00 p.m. on April 29. Since the bill was an important one and had been amended to the point that it had broad bipartisan support, it could no longer be held hostage to the minimum wage amendment.

Kennedy was back on the floor on April 29, insisting, "The American people are overwhelmingly for [increasing the minimum wage]." Then he rehashed all the maneuvers Dole had engaged in to avoid a vote in the week before the Easter recess, when the national parks legislation was on the floor, then again after the Easter recess for the weeks of April 15 and 22, while the immigration bill was on the floor. Senator Kennedy reveled in mocking the lengths to which Senator Dole had gone to avoid a vote on the minimum wage:

> Last week we were dealing with the spectacle of a rarely used motion to recommit, but only to recommit to the committee of jurisdiction for an instant, a nanosecond, and then to report back to the floor. In other words, it was a sham motion to recommit.
>
> This was to avoid some member of the Senate rising and saying, "Let's have thirty minutes on the increase in the minimum wage, divide the time up between those who are for it and those who are opposed to it, and let the Senate go."
>
> On top of the motion to recommit, there had to be two separate amendments to fill what they call the amendment tree on one side of the bill. Then back on the bill itself, Senator Dole had to maintain two amendments, a first-degree amendment and a second-degree amendment. Therefore, we were in the absurd position last week where Senator Simpson had to offer a Simpson second-degree amendment to the Simpson first-degree amendment to the Simpson motion to recommit to the underlying illegal immigration bill.
>
> We also ended up with a Dole second-degree on illegal immi-

gration, a Dole second-degree to the first degree, a Dole first-degree amendment to the illegal immigration bill. Then after each of these amendments had been adopted, we had to go through a half dozen unnecessary votes to adopt amendments to fill each of these slots.

Senator Dole had to then undo each of the amendments that had been adopted. So we were then in the position of Senator Simpson moving to table the Simpson second-degree amendment. This is effectively the person who offered the amendment trying to table or effectively remove his second-degree amendment to the Simpson first-degree amendment to the Simpson motion to recommit the underlying bill. After that was tabled, Senator Simpson was in the position of offering the Simpson motion to table the Simpson first-degree [amendment] to the Simpson motion to recommit the underlying illegal immigration bill.

Then when that charade had been completed, we had to readopt all of the underlying first- and second-degree amendments, and then Senator Dole had to go back and fill the tree again by adding five new amendments.

Then Senator Dole has to get cloture. Then, finally, there may be the chance, after the cloture vote, to offer amendments on the immigration bill. However, only germane amendments will be allowed after the cloture vote when the amendment is adopted sometime tomorrow perhaps.

Senator Dole will then have to go through this whole process all over again on the underlying bill. We will then have a Dole motion to recommit, again a sham because it is only a motion to recommit for a nanosecond and then report back to the floor. We will have the Dole or Simpson first-degree amendment to the Dole motion to recommit. Then we will have the Simpson or Dole second-degree amendment to the Simpson or Dole first-degree amendment. This is truly an extraordinary parliamentary procedure. Its only purpose is to avoid a vote on the minimum wage. The result is to delay the passage of the illegal immigration bill.

While most people listening to Kennedy's remarks probably lost the thread of the action after the first few sentences, they certainly got the message that the Republicans were willing to pull out all the parliamentary stops to avoid voting on the minimum wage increase. Daschle joined Kennedy on the floor. "One day we will have our vote on minimum wage," he said. "If not today it will be tomorrow, this week, or next week. But we will have our vote." Not however, on the immigration bill, which finally passed the Senate with Simpson and Kennedy as floor managers on May 2.

Chapter 21

CLASH OF THE TITANS, ROUND 2

MORE GRIDLOCK ON THE MINIMUM WAGE

President Clinton knew what he was doing when he addressed the Democratic senators' annual retreat over the weekend of April 27, 1996, and conveyed personally the message his staff had already been pushing with Senate Democrats. He described what he called the "five stages" of his campaign for reelection: 1995 and the budget fight; the primaries; Dole's performance as Senate majority leader, which Clinton described as the most important stage and would define who won the presidential election; the convention; and, finally, the campaign itself. Dole's performance as majority leader would certainly be a crucial factor in the campaign, and Clinton gave it special emphasis before this audience of Democratic Senators because he wanted to enlist them in his reelection effort and to ensure that they were thinking of the broader political stakes behind the positions they took in the Senate. He knew that the assembled senators would be the front line in combating Dole in full view of the national press.

Dole's strategy to win his party's nomination and defeat Clinton for president was to show that he could get things done in the Senate and boost his campaign message that he was a doer, not just a talker—implicitly drawing a contrast with the super-articulate Clinton. Like Lyndon Johnson before him, he would be the "Master of the Senate." As it turned out, Clinton was correct in his analysis of the importance to the campaign of Dole's performance in the Senate. And Kennedy's fights to enact the minimum wage increase and health insurance reform were ultimately the lynchpins on which the success or failure of Dole's strategy depended.

Dole kept the Senate in recess for an inordinately long time, from January until February 27, while he campaigned in Republican presidential primaries. Once the Senate reconvened, Kennedy's goal was to force an up-or-down vote on the minimum wage increase, a strategy he had been building for over a year, since the beginning of the session. Dole did not want to allow a vote because he feared he might lose it and he did not want the minimum wage—strongly opposed by the conservative wing of his party and by many of his key supporters in the business community—raised on his watch. Dole knew Kennedy was waiting to offer his amendment to increase the minimum wage to whatever bill Dole brought to the floor and Dole was determined to prevent him. He did not want a repeat of the parks bill maneuver, which ended in forcing him to pull the bill down. Nor did he want another confrontation like that over the health insurance bill. Because of Kennedy, it was now the end of March and Dole had no legislative accomplishments on which to run for president: not the Contract with America or even the parks bill.

On the minimum wage, Dole would pursue a dual track. He would continue to try to block a clean vote and, to the extent that wasn't viable, would try to make the price for the Democrats too high by adding antiunion and antiworker provisions.

What had started out as a titanic struggle for votes between Dole and

Kennedy now turned into a tactical back-and-forth between the two. Dole tried to attach poison pills to the minimum wage bill. Kennedy wanted separate bills for each poison pill so he could defeat them or Clinton could veto them. After a year's worth of building support, Kennedy now thought he had the votes to win—if he could just get a clean vote.

In the House, Gingrich was facing more defections. After reversing course for the umpteenth time on allowing a vote on the minimum wage, in early May he told moderate Republicans that he would drop his resistance to a vote. As Congressman Christopher Shays of Connecticut, one of the leaders of the Republicans supporting the minimum wage increase, described it, there was disagreement between Armey and Gingrich. "One believes it is going to happen, and the other believes he can stop it," Shays said. "There is going to be a vote on the minimum wage. Let's face that fact. Every week we delay it, the more politically painful the outcome will be."[1]

Other Republicans, deeply worried about the upcoming election, lashed out at Gingrich and Armey. "It's a southern anti-union attitude that appeals to the mentality of hillbillies at revival meetings," Congressman Peter King, Republican from New York, said. "The Republican leadership has gone out of their way to appease wacko militias. . . . I don't know of any Republican leader who has attacked the militia leaders and yet they attack union bosses."[2] Senator D'Amato was quoted in the *New York Daily News* on May 7 as saying, "Newt Gingrich is a smart man, but he misread the elections entirely. People did not vote to cut education and cut funding for the environment and cut funding for programs they care about. People did vote for change, but not for this revolution. They want lower taxes and less spending, but not dirty drinking water."[3]

In early May gasoline prices increased across America. Republicans and some Democrats were urging immediate action to reduce gasoline taxes—creating another opportunity for a minimum wage amendment. When Dole latched on to the idea of repealing the 4.3-cent per gallon tax increase that had been included in Clinton's 1993 deficit reduction bill, he suggested that he might make repeal part of a package that would include a vote on the minimum wage increase. There was some support for repealing the tax among Democrats as well as Republicans. Daschle observed that Dole had supported two 5-cent increases in the gas tax between 1982 and 1992 and wondered if we should repeal these, which he called the "Dole dime," as well. Daschle said that Democrats would bring the minimum wage to the floor any way they could and he urged Dole to allow a clean vote on the minimum wage amendment within the next few weeks, arguing that the gas tax and other issues were really smokescreens to avoid a minimum wage vote.

On the Senate floor Dole offered the so-called TEAM Act, which would allow management-controlled unions, and discussed other poison pills he was planning to add to a package with the minimum wage. Senator Kit Bond of Missouri was prepared to add a national right-to-work law to Dole's anti-union package. Kennedy was afraid that all these bills would pass the Republican Senate, and if they were part of a minimum wage bill, Clinton would have to veto it.

On May 7 Dole offered his amendment to repeal the gas tax. Daschle had indicated that he would let the gas tax come up on the floor if Kennedy could in turn offer the minimum wage amendment, but Dole resisted. Dole and Kennedy argued about the implications of the TEAM Act. Dole proposed a unanimous consent agreement to take up the gas tax, minimum wage, and the TEAM Act. Daschle objected. Kennedy offered to take up just the gas tax and the minimum wage. Senator Dole objected. At the end of the dialogue nothing was agreed upon. The debate rambled on and on in that manner. From time to time, Senator Kennedy or Senator Dole came back to the floor, Senator Dole to argue for his proposal that the Senate take up the gas tax and the TEAM Act, and Senator Kennedy to argue for his proposal that the majority leader allow an up-or-down vote on just the minimum wage amendment.

While the minimum wage amendment stalled on the floor, Kennedy continued to work on the Kassebaum-Kennedy health insurance bill. On May 7, he met with White House staff to discuss options for compromise on medical savings accounts. The White House made clear that it preferred not to have medical savings accounts in the health insurance legislation, but since MSAs were likely the price of compromise, they urged us to consider limiting their number or limiting them to small business employees or to employees below a certain income.

The Senate had now been tied up for six weeks, since March 22, by Dole's objection to allowing a vote on the minimum wage. Democratic senators who were upset with Dole's actions on the floor met with the White House to review strategy and to unify their response to Dole. Everyone had different views. The White House staff were eager for the president to sign some bills. They guaranteed that he would veto the TEAM Act. Clinton said that the minimum wage would be a huge win for Democrats and it was worth letting Dole get away with his election year stunt on the gas tax.

After the White House meeting, Kennedy and Dole went back to the Senate floor. Kennedy reiterated his desire to work out an agreement to take up the gas tax and the minimum wage. He opposed conditions or restrictions being imposed on Democrats at the time of the consideration of the TEAM Act, which he continued to call "the anti–workplace democracy act." The state of play on May 8 was this: Dole had an amendment to the underlying bill then on the floor, a minor bill dealing with whether a single individual who had incurred legal fees in connection with the investigation of the White House travel office by the Justice Department should have those fees reimbursed by the federal government. His amendment combined the TEAM Act, the gas tax repeal, and the minimum wage increase as a package. Kennedy had his own amendment for the gas tax and the minimum wage standing alone. He insisted that there not be a vote on Dole's combined package, while Dole didn't want a vote on Kennedy's.

Senator Hatch came to the floor to resume his role of floor manager of the underlying bill and quickly threw his weight behind Dole. Never at a loss for an argument, especially with his friend Kennedy, Hatch said, "The demand that we can only deal with the minimum wage . . . without attaching anything else to it, that it is so important, so pristine, that it must go through without amendment, while everything else can be filibustered, that is a demand that is as unreasonable as it is unlikely to succeed," Hatch said. "My suggestion, Mr. President, is that we go forward, we have a debate on the merits [and] the shortcomings of the TEAM Act, on the merits and the shortcomings of a minimum wage increase, on the merits and the shortcomings of the gas tax increase, being the three elements in this amendment, and then vote on the amendment and determine whether or not we are for it, or, alternatively, as the majority leader has suggested without acceptance, that we vote separately on the first two, and if both are passed, they go out of this body together to the House of Representatives. If one is passed and one is defeated, the survivor goes out as it is."

Of course, Kennedy wasn't going to accept this approach; his strategy was to resist any arrangement that would have limited his ability to filibuster the TEAM Act. He was confident he could hold the forty-one votes necessary to maintain a filibuster on the TEAM Act, but knew he was likely to lose an up-or-down vote. He was also growing in confidence that he could get more than sixty votes for the minimum wage, and therefore any Republican attempt to filibuster the minimum wage increase would fail.

In the midst of the struggle between Senator Kennedy and Senator Dole, the two senators met and had a brief discussion on the floor. Dole asked Kennedy where the health care legislation stood, and Kennedy said he would follow up with Kassebaum. Then Dole said to Kennedy, "People don't think I like you." It is unclear whether this remark was simply a joking way for Dole to report to Kennedy that despite everything they really were old friends and did like each other, or that even though some people were given the impression that Dole didn't like Kennedy he really did, or whether it was just an offhanded jibe of the kind Dole was known to make.

On May 9 President Clinton got into the act, blaming Dole for gridlock and urging that the only way to break the gridlock was for Republicans not to "ruin these good bipartisan bills by adding poison pills" intended to force him to veto the bills so that Republicans could assert that he opposed them. In a news conference President Clinton called for the three bills in question, the TEAM Act, the minimum wage, and the gas tax, to be acted on separately. He said he supported the minimum wage increase and the gas tax, but not the TEAM Act.[4]

Dole was backtracking from a suggestion he had made at his own news conference that each of the bills be voted on separately. He returned to the position that they would remain linked in the single bill, thereby retaining the poison pill of the TEAM Act along with the minimum wage. Kennedy confronted him on the floor later that afternoon. When asked whether he would allow the Senate to proceed with three separate initiatives, Dole snapped, "I might, I might not. That will take care of that." Gridlock continued.

Kennedy kept after the minimum wage issue every day the Senate was in session. He introduced copies of editorials from all over the country, including the *New York Times*, the *Washington Post*, the *Atlanta Journal*, the *St. Louis Post*, the *San Francisco Chronicle*, the *St. Petersburg Times*, and the *Seattle Times*, supporting the increase. "With this depth and breadth of support among editorial boards for a higher minimum wage," he said, "and the broad support among voters for a higher minimum wage, the question is obvious: Why are Republicans obstructing action on the minimum wage?"

Thursday afternoon, May 9, was to be the last day of Senate activity for the week, and the White House travel office reimbursement bill was still the business on the floor. Lott announced that the Senate would not be in session on Friday and there would be no votes on Monday. It was Kennedy's last chance for the week, and he took the occasion to poke some pointed fun at the Senate's failure to act:

> Now, Mr. President, in recent days a number of commentators have pointed out that the Senate seems to be in the "doldrums." I thought it might be interesting to listen to some of the dictionary definitions for that word. The *Random House Dictionary of the English Language* defines it this way: "a state of inactivity or stagnation; a belt of calms and light baffling winds; or a dull, listless depressed mood, low spirits." The *Oxford English Dictionary* refers to the doldrums this way: "a vessel almost becalmed, her sails flapping about in every direction." It goes on: "a region of unbearable calm broken occasionally by violent squalls." The *American Heritage Dictionary*: "a period of inactivity, listlessness or

depression probably influenced in form by the word tantrum." That seems to fit the Senate precisely. First, our Republican friends have a tantrum over the Democratic efforts to raise the minimum wage, then our Republican friends go into the doldrums. The American people look to the Congress for action on the minimum wage, and all they see are cloture motions, quorum calls, and procedural gymnastics to avoid taking action. I say end the gridlock, end the deadlock, end the "doldrums." The way for Senator Dole to find his way out of the doldrums is clear. Raise the minimum wage.

A new *Time*/CNN poll showed Democrats with a seven-point lead over Republicans in the generic congressional vote across the country.[5] By May 15 Dole's presidential campaign was in such dire straits, sources reported to the *New York Times*, that he was removing himself from his day-to-day duties as majority leader to be free to campaign across the country. If the report was true, he was abandoning his plan to make his job as majority leader a showpiece of his presidential campaign.

On Friday, while the Senate was on its extended weekend recess and Dole was away campaigning, Lott came to see Daschle to discuss the possibility of having three freestanding bills with limited amendments to each. "We'd take the gas tax up on Tuesday and follow it up with the minimum wage and the TEAM Act," he offered. "On the minimum wage one of our amendments would be to impose a training wage similar to what was adopted in 1989, and in two weeks we'll bring up our other legislation." Daschle would not go along with the plan because he would not give up the right of Democrats to filibuster antilabor measures.

When the Senate returned on Monday, May 13, Kennedy summed up the situation to a reporter in a vivid set of metaphors. "The minimum wage," he said, "has caught fire because of the widening income gap and the feeling of economic insecurity affecting millions of Americans. That insecurity provided the kindling for the issue. The voters in the Republican primaries lit the match; now Bob Dole can't find the fire extinguisher." He concluded, "Raising the minimum wage is a classic example of an irresistible force. Democrats recognized that, and Republicans made a mistake when they tried to be an immovable object."

And then a shocking event occurred.

A DEFINING MOMENT

A defining moment of the 1996 presidential election occurred on May 15, when Dole surprised the political world with an announcement from the Senate floor:

> I'd just say, ladies and gentlemen, one of the qualities of American politics that distinguishes us from other nations is that we judge our politicians as much by the manner they leave office as by the vigor with which they pursue it. You do not lay claim to the office you hold, it lays claim to you. Your obligation is to bring to it the gifts you can of labor and honesty and then to depart with grace. My time to leave this office has come and I will seek the presidency with nothing to fall back on but the judgment of the people and nowhere to go but the White House or home.
>
> Today I announce that I will forgo the privileges not only of the office of the majority leader, but of the United States Senate itself, from which I resign effective on or before June 11th.
>
> I will then stand before you without office or authority, a private citizen, an American, just a man . . . for today I will begin to reconstitute our momentum until it is a great and agile force—clear in direction, irresistible in effect. Our campaign will leave Washington behind to look to America. As summer nears, I will seek the bright light and open spaces of this beautiful country and will ask for the wise council of its people, from the seacoasts of Maine and California to the old railroad towns in the Midwest, to the verdant South, from the mountains of Colorado to the suburbs of Chicago, and in places in between known mainly to you who call them home.
>
> I have absolute confidence in the victory that to some may seem unattainable. . . . To concentrate upon the campaign, giving all and

risking all, I must leave Congress that I have loved, and which I have been honored to serve. With all due respect to Congress, America has been my life.

It was a gracious speech full of poetry and simple, direct emotion. It also represented a belated recognition that Dole's presidential campaign was going nowhere on the floor of the Senate. Adam Clymer wrote in the *New York Times*:

There are two measures that may be strikingly affected by Mr. Dole's departure. One is the Kassebaum-Kennedy health insurance bill, written to make insurance coverage portable from job to job. Although it passed 100 to nothing in the Senate, it has been hung up for three weeks since Mr. Dole sought to get conferees to attach a medical savings account beloved by House Republicans, but rejected by the Senate. Only Senator Dole has the authority to back down to a compromise, something he has frequently told Senator Edward M. Kennedy of Massachusetts that he wants. Mr. Dole told Senator Nancy Landon Kassebaum and other Kansans the same thing today, saying that he wanted to see the bill passed before he left. It may have to be. Without him, the bill may be dead, because none of his potential successors are as inclined to compromise on health insurance as he. The other issue that his departure may affect is the one that has dogged him and symbolized the impossibility of his dual role since March—the minimum wage.

The realities of Capitol Hill enabled Democrats to keep him from running, as he expected, as the man who could get things done on big issues that mattered to ordinary Americans. Instead he was coming across as the man who could not get the Senate out of gridlock. He was not confronting Bill Clinton—he was scrapping with Tom Daschle and Mr. Kennedy.[6]

By the end of the week it was reported that Dole had actually decided to resign from the Senate in late April, following his loss of the medical savings account amendment to the health insurance bill and his inability to deal with the minimum wage issue.

Looking back, it was apparent Dole had lost control of the Senate to Kennedy because of Kennedy's two flagship initiatives. Even after it became clear that raising the minimum wage and the Kassebaum-Kennedy health insurance reform bill enjoyed tremendous popular support and majorities in the Senate, Dole continued to resist and proposed to weigh them down with poison pills. He lacked the vision to turn a losing hand into a winning hand. A different strategy would have recognized the handwriting on the wall and packaged the legislation in a way that he could enthusiastically support and claim credit for, or he could have made sure he kept control of the Republican defectors and won. In the end, he did neither. He was on the wrong side of the two issues—the wrong side substantively and the wrong side politically. And he got the worst of both worlds: he was tagged with opposing legislation the public overwhelmingly supported, and he lost control of the Senate, undercutting his claim to be an effective leader.

There were several reasons why Dole may have worked so hard to block these bills. As a candidate for the nomination—and as a nominated candidate as well—he probably felt he could not afford to offend the radical conservatives who had always been a powerful force in the party and who were newly emboldened by their 1994 election victory and their fight for the Contract with America. They were already angry with him because of his failure to get most of the items in the Contract with America through the Senate and his willingness to throw in the towel on the government shutdown while the House Republicans were still fighting on. In addition to the radical conservatives, interest groups powerful in the Republican Party wanted both bills blocked. Leaving aside his presidential candidacy, it is difficult for a Republican leader to be on the wrong side of a majority of his caucus on a major, controversial bill, which would have been the case if Dole had supported the minimum wage increase—although he did not need to go to such extremes to block it.

In working so hard to placate conservatives and Republican interest groups at the same time he was running as "a doer, not a talker," Dole made a huge strategic mistake. Given this dynamic, the longer he was on the Senate floor as majority leader, the more his campaign suffered. Nothing important was getting done, either in the Senate or on his campaign. The Democrats, and Senator Kennedy in particular, were dominating the agenda. There was nothing Senator Dole seemed to stand for—no vision, no mastery of the Senate. He was floundering in Washington when he should have been campaigning around the country.

But this outcome was not predictable or likely in November 1994—and none of it would have happened without Senator Kennedy. It was he who identified the minimum wage increase as a key issue of both principle and politics. It was Senator Kennedy who forged a consensus among sometimes reluctant Democrats both on the substance of the bill and on the importance of making it a priority. It was Senator Kennedy who put together the coalition and press strategy that made the issue salient to the public. It was he who relentlessly kept the issue alive with his knowledge of Senate procedures and willingness to go to the mat for what he believed.

The Kassebaum-Kennedy bill was uniquely a Kennedy product as well and would never have existed if Kennedy had accepted the conventional wisdom that health care was a dead issue for the 104th Congress after the health reform debacle in 1994. It was because he identified the set of issues on which common ground could be found that he was able to develop a solid alliance with Kassebaum. It was because the two of them were able to develop a compromise bill that it was possible to gain the momentum to pass the legislation unanimously through the Labor Committee. And it was Senator Kennedy's press strategy that ultimately made it untenable for Senator Dole to continue to bottle up the bill.

It wasn't Bob Dole who was master of the Senate; it was Ted Kennedy.

THE PRESS FOCUSES ON KENNEDY

By April 1996 the Washington press had begun to notice the impact Kennedy was having on the presidential campaign and the Republican agenda and, even more remarkably, his ability to advance his own Democratic initiatives on health care and the minimum wage. Washington insiders knew Kennedy as an impressive senator; many were aware that he had been the driving force behind reams of legislation in the thirty years he had been in the Senate. On civil rights, health care, education, and judiciary issues, no senator had been more influential, at least for the past two decades.

But the media in Washington had always paid much more attention to the Kennedy myth, to the senator's presidential aspirations and his personal life than to Senator Kennedy the legislator. Then, in 1996, it was as if the tectonic plates underlying and defining his reputation in Washington began to shift. The major newspapers assigned star reporters to write profiles of Kennedy, his legislative record, and his legislative strategies. Lloyd Grove's, in the *Washington Post,* was the first major profile to appear. The entire top half of the "Style" section was filled with a photo of Senator Kennedy and the headline "The Liberal Lion Roars Back."

> Despite being out on the leftward wing of the minority party, Kennedy is somehow still formidable—more, perhaps, than ever. This superannuated liberal has also distinguished himself as a legislator—that is, someone who can actually work with even his most ardent adversaries to write laws. In this regard, Kennedy is enjoying one of his best Senate sessions since he arrived in November 1962, when he was widely dismissed as a spoiled rich kid who owed his seat to the happy accident that one brother was attorney general and the other was President of the United States. This year, there has hardly been a scrap of domestic legislation—addressing problems ranging from health insurance to immigration to job training to church arson—that doesn't bear the Kennedy stamp.[7]

David Shribman, the Pulitzer Prize–winning Washington bureau chief of the *Boston Globe* who had come from the *Wall Street Journal* and had not previously written enthusiastically of Kennedy, now wrote:

So the Red Sox are hopeless, the Bruins are hapless, the Celtics are history, isn't there anybody from Massachusetts leading anything? It turns out there is and it is happening in the least likely place at the least likely time. Out there on the floor of the Senate is a familiar face: Kennedy of Massachusetts. The White House is occupied by a moderate Democrat; the Congress is controlled by devoutly conservative Republicans; and yet, Senator Edward M. Kennedy has the Senate lined up behind him on a health care bill and just might get the chamber to vote to raise the minimum wage. The last lion of liberalism is holding forth, holding everything up, and holding sway.[8]

Shribman quoted from Cal Thomas, the conservative commentator: "'[Ted Kennedy is] a great lesson for conservatives,' says Thomas. 'He is consistent, he's passionate, he keeps plugging on. In the majority or in the minority he says the same things. A lot of others from Bob Dole to Warren Rudman could take a lesson.'"

The *Los Angeles Times* followed, as did the *Chicago Tribune*, *Newsday* of Long Island, the *National Journal*, and *USA Today*, each of the pieces following the same theme: Kennedy was a master legislator, dominating the agenda and, ultimately, forcing Dole out of the Senate. Each of the stories quoted senators on Kennedy's record for achieving bipartisan support for his legislative proposals. Each quoted Republicans who conceded Kennedy's effectiveness.

In late spring, Elsa Walsh, the author and former reporter for the *Washington Post*, began her research for a comprehensive profile of Kennedy for the *New Yorker*. Walsh followed Kennedy over many weeks in the Senate, sitting in on staff meetings and other strategy sessions and speaking with him on a daily basis. The article, which appeared after the presidential election, in March 1997, took as its theme that Kennedy had saved the Clinton presidency. Walsh concluded that Kennedy had given the president and the Democrats the backbone to resist the Republican budget proposals and then had turned the Congress around on minimum wage and health care, in the process driving Dole from the Senate and essentially destroying Dole's strategy of showing that he was the person who could get things done in Washington.

By the spring of 1996 the reality of Kennedy's effectiveness was simply indisputable, and the press corps had finally caught on to the fact that the defining struggle of the presidential election was being fought out on the Senate floor, as Clinton had predicted it would be. And that struggle was, at bottom, a duel between Dole and Kennedy. Kennedy liked Dole on a personal level, and he was always uncomfortable with the statement from political analysts that he had "driven Dole out of the Senate." But the fact was that they had been eyeball to eyeball for months—and it was Dole who blinked.

Chapter 22

VICTORY

Shortly after Dole's announcement that he would leave his post as majority leader, Senator Lott announced that he would run to replace him. Lott
was a man of immense ambition—and ability to match—and had made
enemies even among Republicans as he rapidly climbed the ladder in
the Senate. He had started out in Mississippi as a Democrat but became a
Republican when there was an opening to run for Congress in 1982. He
served in the House for ten years, and knowing he was a strong Gingrich
ally, we were skeptical about how he would perform in this new leadership
role in the Senate. We were worried that Lott's strongly conservative views
would make it even more difficult to get progressive legislation passed. But
we ended up being surprised by Lott. He concentrated more on making
the Senate work than Dole, who was running for president.

Lott had challenged Alan Simpson, a good friend of Kennedy's, for the position of deputy to the majority leader when the Republicans took over the Senate in 1995. Dole worked hard for Simpson, but Lott defeated him by one vote with the support of all the new right-wing Republicans. So Lott was none too popular with the Old Guard Republicans in the Senate. From the day he began his run for the position of majority leader he said that he would do all he could to rein in Kennedy. He had watched Senator Kennedy dominate the Senate floor for three months and he had been heard more than once mumbling that he would not let Senator Kennedy run the Senate the way Dole had.

HOUSE REPUBLICANS PASS A MINIMUM WAGE INCREASE

Despite Dole's announced intent to resign, the Senate floor was still gridlocked. After eighteen months with Republican majorities in both houses of Congress, the Senate under Dole had few accomplishments, while the House had passed the entire Gingrich Contract with America in the first hundred days. Democrats had stalled Dole in the Senate, but they had a long way to go if they were going to pass their legislation. The minimum wage increase had not passed either the Senate or the House, and Republicans were still demanding that any minimum wage legislation include anti-union provisions as the price of allowing it to proceed. The Kassebaum-Kennedy health insurance reform bill had passed the Senate in April but was stalled over the issue of medical savings accounts.

In the House, where the leadership realized a minimum wage bill had become a political necessity, things were beginning to move. A vote was scheduled for the week of May 20, although, as in the Senate, the Republicans chose to try to give with one hand and take away with the other. Their bill would have expanded the number of small businesses exempt from having to pay the minimum wage and from having to pay new workers overtime. As the House Democratic leadership put it in their talking points on May 23, "10 million Americans will lose overtime and minimum wage under the GOP minimum wage hoax. In a giveaway to business lobbyists, the Republican bill effectively exempts two-thirds of American businesses from having to pay their workers the minimum wage or overtime." The president stated, "If Congress sends me a bill to eliminate the minimum wage and wage protection for millions of workers, I will veto it. Speaker Gingrich and Majority Leader Dole should allow an honest up-or-down vote on the minimum wage."

Later that day the House voted on the minimum wage, and the Republican strategy failed. Democrats, joined by moderate Republicans, defeated the expansion of the minimum wage exemption and the overtime provision and voted to pass a straight 90-cent increase.

The Senate Democratic talking points emphasized that Dole's time as majority leader was running out: "The week after the Senate's Memorial Day recess will be the final week of Senator Dole's nearly four decades in Congress. He deserves to leave a better legacy than the government shutdowns and gridlock that the Republican-led 104th Congress have produced so far. Democrats urge Senator Dole to join the fight to pass the minimum wage increase."

A new *Washington Post*/ABC poll showed Americans choosing Democrats for Congress by a 51–41 percent ratio, the largest majority in recent years. By a 60–35 majority, Americans disapproved of the Republican Congress.[1]

After the recess, Congress returned to work for Dole's final week. He decided to take one last crack at the constitutional amendment to balance the budget. The amendment had failed by one vote in 1995, but he had kept the matter open and was able to call it back at any time. Passing the balanced budget amendment was to be the highlight of his final week in the Senate. But the amendment failed, again—not by one vote, but by six.

A FLURRY OF HEALTH INSURANCE REFORM NEGOTIATIONS

Kassebaum, Kennedy, and their staffs began a feverish effort to resolve the disagreement on MSAs and free up the health care bill to go to conference. We were beginning to accept the idea that we would have to have something on MSAs to get the House to move, and both Kassebaum and the White House were pressing us to compromise. The issue became how to constrain the program. One approach was to limit eligibility. The Republicans wanted everyone to be able to buy an MSA; we wanted to limit the pool to those who were previously uninsured or to employees of small businesses or to people who lived in a limited geographic area. A second possible approach was to constrain the total number of MSAs that could be sold, whatever the eligibility criteria. A third approach was to make the program temporary, subject to a "sunset," meaning a new law would have to be passed and signed by the president for it to be extended. This would give us another shot at ending it if it had the negative effects we feared, and might also limit people's interest in joining. A subsidiary issue was the degree to which consumers purchasing the policies would be protected. The original Republican proposal had very high minimum deductibles, no limit on how high deductibles could go, and no required cap on out-of-pocket costs after the deductible had been paid and the insurance kicked in.

Kassebaum and Kennedy thought their best chance to get the bill passed was to do it while Dole was still in the Senate, before the more conservative Lott took over, so in Dole's final week they engaged in an intense series of meetings, floor speeches, and negotiating sessions. At the staff directors meeting on June 3, John Hilley said that the White House wanted to ramp up the effort to resolve the Kassebaum-Kennedy bill during what he called Dole's "Sayonara week."

Over the recess, informal discussions had begun among House and Senate Republican leaders on possible compromises regarding the MSA provisions. Kassebaum played the role of intermediary between Kennedy and Dole. When Congress reconvened, Dole held a meeting among Republicans to work on a compromise proposal regarding MSAs. Afterward he told Kennedy, "We have a couple of other ways to do it," and Kennedy took this as a good sign.

We were picking up intelligence from reporters. Congressman Bill Thomas, chairman of the health subcommittee of the House Ways and Means Committee, was reported to have said that his goal was to have a bill before Dole left. Chairman Bill Archer said that the House was close but didn't have a deal yet. One House staffer, though, said that insisting on limiting MSAs to specific geographic areas would kill the deal.

On June 3, Kassebaum called Kennedy. Kennedy was unavailable to take the call so she spoke to his chief of staff, Paul Donovan. "The latest Republican proposal is that an MSA option should be open to all employers who offered health plans," she said. "It would be a two-year study. After one year, everyone would be included in the option to purchase MSAs unless Congress voted it down." Hearing Donovan's discouraging report, Kennedy talked to Kassebaum, who said that she'd try to limit the MSA program to a certain number of states. "I'll offer this to the House Republicans. If Archer doesn't accept it, I won't sign on to it. Then you can go after them."

Later that evening Kassebaum called Kennedy again with news about the Republican plan. It would initially apply to all employers with more than one hundred employees. After three years, there would be an assessment, with an affirmative vote required to continue the program. If the program was not voted down, it would then be expanded to all businesses. Kennedy responded diplomatically, "You were wonderful to stick to this figure of employers with one hundred or more, but that's 75 million people, or almost 60 percent of the whole workforce. The bill is simply not worth taking the risk." After another meeting with the Republicans, Kassebaum reported to Kennedy that Phil Gramm had persuaded her to lower her threshold for MSA eligibility, opening the program to even more people. Congressman Dennis Hastert, the leader of the House Republican task force on health policy (and later speaker), had heard the White House wouldn't go for MSAs for employers with fewer than one hundred employees. Limiting the plan to several states was not acceptable to the Republicans. "The speaker thinks he can get a deal," Hastert said. Dole called Kassebaum to say that he wanted an even bigger pool; he would exclude only businesses with fewer than twenty-five employees. Hastert told Kassebaum that the speaker would "talk to Archer and see if they will go to fifty."

Kennedy said that fifty was unacceptable, that it would be hard for us and the president to explain why we let the bill go if this program were included with the kind of risk it represented. "MSAs are untried and untested," he said. "If they go to twenty-five I won't sign the report and I will actively lead the fight on it." He suggested identifying three to four states as locations for the test, with a vote on phasing it in.

Kassebaum and Kennedy were now at an impasse, and Kennedy was worried that the White House was more flexible than they should be. He talked to Dole, who said the Republicans were in constant contact with the White House, talking about changes in the MSA proposal. He hoped to pass this legislation by early next week.

Kennedy then talked to Daschle; his response to the hundred-employees limit was "Oh, no, that's way too large." Dole told Kennedy the White House had signed off at fifty employees or more. Kennedy called Hilley to check on this. "This is not a numbers game," said Hilley evasively. "But we think we've got the thing wrapped up."

On June 4 Kennedy took to the floor. "Senator Dole has said on several occasions that he would like to achieve final action on this legislation before he leaves the Senate. If Senator Dole is serious about such action, it is difficult to believe he cannot make it happen." He recounted the history of the legislation in the Senate, noting that Dole had proposed including MSAs, "a proposal that would kill the bill." Fortunately the Senate decisively rejected that proposal, and the amended bill, without MSAs, passed the Senate unanimously. "Since then, unfortunately, a major impasse has developed over this issue. If the impasse can be resolved, the bill will pass. If not, the bill will die."

By midweek a *New York Times*/CBS poll distributed by the House Democratic leadership showed that the congressional job approval rating had dipped to a record low of only 19 percent.[2] Kennedy went to the floor again to talk about the Kassebaum-Kennedy bill and indicated that the president would sign a bill if there were a proposal for MSAs that wasn't just an open door to wholesale marketing but a legitimate test to find out whether they worked and whether they had the negative impact on the overall health insurance system that critics were concerned about.

Later Kennedy gave a pessimistic report on the resolution of the

health care bill before Dole's departure the following week. "Senator Dole yesterday left the impression that meaningful negotiations for an acceptable compromise were taking place. It now appears, however, that the intransigence of the House Republicans has prevailed. When Senator Dole leaves the Senate next week, he can take his health insurance with him. Every American should have the same right."

Meanwhile senator after senator, Democrats and Republicans alike, were going to the floor to praise Dole. Nothing brings out the tradition of collegiality among senators more than the departure of one who has served with them for as long as Dole had.

The negotiations continued, ever more frantic. Key Republicans—Chairman Archer, Speaker Gingrich, Senator Graham—all had different views. Dole kept working on the spin to the press. "The White House is all over the lot on the health bill," he said. "Of course, we're going to offer our proposal and that's it."

Kassebaum continued reporting back to Kennedy. "We're still working away," she told him. "We're drafting a document to see if everybody can sign on to it. There are still some who would like to see it fail totally, but it's back on track because of Dole. I don't know what will happen." After she met with Dole and Gingrich, she called Kennedy back: "Gingrich, Dole, and I met on MSAs with the White House proposal. They have agreed to allow employers with fifty or more employees into the program. The plan would take effect full-blown unless Congress voted to stop it. Dole is gone. He's gone to Tennessee to campaign."

Kennedy went back to the floor utterly frustrated with the inability of House and Senate Republicans to agree on a compromise with Senate Democrats—and, although he didn't say it out loud, with the White House's continuing to back the fifty-employee plan. "Dr. Dole is prescribing a poison pill for this consensus legislation," he asserted. Kassebaum's spokesman sounded as frustrated as Kennedy when he told the *New York Times*, "It's unfortunate that we cannot agree on a bill that can be passed by the House and Senate and signed into law. We are not there yet."[3]

Kennedy held a press conference in which he attacked the Republicans for their intransigence on MSAs, declaring that he would have no part in MSAs possibly jeopardizing the health system or, because of the tax deductions, the federal Treasury. Lott, apparently frustrated by Kennedy's relentlessness, told reporters, "Ted Kennedy doesn't run the world. He ought to get with the program."[4]

In an effort to avoid any rift with Kennedy, the White House issued a statement saying, "There's no distance between Senator Kennedy and us on this measure." Still not understanding their position, I called the White House. They were ready to accept MSAs for the self-employed and for employers with more than fifty employees, starting immediately. But there should be a study and a sunset before it was continued. By midday the word was out that the Republicans were going forward with their proposal. Kassebaum, Hastert, and Archer had agreed on the fifty-employees limit. Kennedy issued his response: "I strongly oppose the latest Republican plan and I very much regret that Senator Kassebaum has bowed to the pressure of Speaker Gingrich and the House Republican leadership. MSAs should be tested responsibly first, not recklessly imposed on a massive scale. There's still time for a reasonable compromise and I hope it can be achieved."

On the Sunday talk shows, administration representatives emphasized the importance of working out a compromise agreement on the Kassebaum-Kennedy health care bill. Majority Leader Armey, however, threw a wet blanket on any compromise when he said, "I will not give up on the savings accounts."[5]

On Dole's final day in the Senate, June 10, he, Kennedy, and Kassebaum all went to the floor. Dole spoke first: "It seems to me that we ought to reach some accommodation on medical savings accounts and send this bill to the president for his signature. I assume he will sign it. There have been a number of different proposals made, some rather useless, and others that I think have some merit. Hopefully we can resolve this. I understand Senator Kassebaum will be sending us—and maybe it is in my office now—a counterproposal that I will discuss with my House colleagues in the hope that we will resolve that too before the day is out."

Dole yielded to Kennedy, who said, "Mr. President, I appreciate the majority leader yielding. I join with him in the eternal hope that perhaps while he is still here, there may be a successful conclusion of this legislation, or if not, at least an agreement can be made that can be followed up in his absence."

Dole spoke again: "I thank the senator from Massachusetts. I understand we have now received a proposal from my colleague, Senator Kassebaum. We are in the process of reviewing that proposal. I am not certain that the senator from Massachusetts has a copy of it. But it indicates that we might be able to reach some compromise. It should be done. And maybe—speaking for myself—I would like to have it done before I leave. But at least if that cannot happen, I would like to have the agreement before tomorrow at two o'clock, and maybe under the Senate rules we could deem it passed sometime after the House takes it up. I will have to check with the parliamentarian on that. But if we have something agreed on by everybody in the Senate—as the senator knows, the original bill passed unanimously—hopefully we could reach some agreement today and at least have the agreement entered."

Hours later there appeared to be no progress, and Kennedy went back on the floor. "Mr. President, the insistence of the House Republican leadership on forcing medical savings accounts into the Kassebaum-Kennedy bill has become the Trojan horse that could destroy health insurance reform. The Democrats and the White House have offered a fair compromise that would provide for a controlled demonstration of the MSA concept to see if it could be expanded. But the House Republican leadership has said that it will be their way or no way."

That night Republicans in the Senate and House apparently agreed on their version of a compromise proposal. Their latest plan would have opened MSAs to all small businesses and the self-employed—30 million people in all. All others would be eligible in the year 2000 unless Congress specifically voted to terminate the program. Kassebaum appeared to support the plan, but Kennedy denounced it. The White House, speaking through Legislative Chief Hilley, was more equivocal.

The next day, Kennedy went to the floor. "This is not a test," he said, referring to the MSA provisions in the bill, "it's a travesty."

"Mr. President, yesterday House and Senate Republicans announced a compromise on medical savings accounts," he said. "In reality this compromise is a capitulation to House Republicans, who are more interested in creating an issue and serving a special interest constituency than in passing a bill." Kassebaum came to the floor to express her appreciation to Kennedy for his efforts on the legislation and her regret that the compromise had not been accepted.

DOLE LEAVES, LOTT TAKES OVER: THE STALEMATE CONTINUES

At 2:00 on June 11, Dole made one last, long statement on the Senate floor, a generous and gracious speech, attended by all his colleagues on both sides of the aisle. Then he was gone, down the steps of the Senate, cheered on by his colleagues, out to campaign as "just a man." A week of frantic negotiations had produced nothing that Democrats and the White House could agree to. The Republicans still wanted a very large and open-ended MSA program. Dole hadn't produced any sort of meaningful compromise. He left behind a Senate that was as tied in knots as it had been in January, when health care reform first exploded in his lap, through March, when he lost control of the minimum wage on the floor, to June 11, when he left the Senate. There was still no vote on the minimum wage. There was no agreement on handling any of the antilabor measures the Republicans wanted to include in the minimum wage amendment. The gas tax hadn't been repealed. And although the health care bill had passed unanimously, it was nowhere near enactment because Dole had been unwilling or unable or simply not interested enough to force a compromise on MSAs that the Democrats could accept. There had been a lot of activity. There had been talk. There had been all sorts of optimistic predictions, but they had come to nothing.

On June 12 Trent Lott defeated Thad Cochran for the position of majority leader by a vote of 44–8. Despite our concerns that the gridlock would get even worse than it had been under Dole, Lott turned out to be as determined to get things done as he was to advance his conservative principles. And despite his identification with the Gingrich wing of the party, he was not held back by rigid ideology. His core beliefs were undoubtedly conservative, but he was also willing to make compromises if they were necessary to make the Senate work or achieve important goals.

But before he even began to try to get the Senate functioning again, he suffered a self-inflicted wound and created a minor disaster his first week on the job as majority leader. A vast asphalt plaza ran along the whole east side of the Capitol and was used for many purposes—access for senators and congressmen by automobile directly to the doors of the Capitol, parking for members of the House and Senate while they were in the Capitol, and a walkway for pedestrians on their way from one building to the next. Areas of the plaza were used for press conferences by members and occasionally by groups who had gotten special permission from the Capitol Police. Tourists wandered across the plaza to gain access to the tourist doors to the Capitol.

Lott didn't like all the coming and going on the plaza and issued a decree that pedestrians could walk only on narrow pathways directly from point A to point B. Police were installed all over the plaza to shepherd everyone onto these confined walkways. Lott claimed this measure was necessary so that senators and House members rushing to the Capitol in their automobiles wouldn't jeopardize the safety of pedestrians, but the decree seemed to symbolize a desire for control that worried members of the Senate who cared deeply about their independence and prerogatives. Since reporters were among those who most enjoyed the impromptu conversations on the plaza, the press on the Lott decree was terrible—and he quickly backed off.

Although he was unable to control the plaza, Lott was determined to show that, unlike Dole, he could control Kennedy. But he was taking on a big challenge. Kennedy was at the center of the action, controlling the legislative fate of upward of ten legislative matters: minimum wage, a series of antilabor issues, the gas tax, immigration, job training, Food and Drug Administration reform, the parks bill, and the Kassebaum-Kennedy health bill. To show that he could be effective, Lott began working through the leftover morass from Dole's attempt to show that he could be a presidential candidate and majority leader at the same time. The first big keys to unwinding this mess were the minimum wage increase, with the antilabor and gas tax repeal items that Republicans had sought to attach to it, and the Kassebaum-Kennedy health care bill.

As of early June, Kennedy had to face shifting ground. The White House was a problem. It seemed to us that they wanted a health bill at any cost. Although they understood the dangers of MSAs, they were willing to be much more flexible than we thought they should be. On the other hand, Daschle, who understood the dangers of the MSAs and was enormously loyal to Kennedy, would be a strong ally in keeping the White House in line and standing firm against the Republicans.

In addition, as Kennedy analyzed the situation, Lott wanted to prove himself, and Kassebaum wanted to get her bill no matter what. She had no particular investment in the way the MSA issue was resolved, but she didn't want to embarrass Republicans any more than Dole had already been embarrassed. Some of the House Republicans, on the other hand, didn't want a bill at all because they saw the bill as an inappropriate extension of federal authority and didn't want to give Clinton anything he could claim credit for. Others were deeply and genuinely committed to MSAs as the best direction for health care and were willing to swallow more federal regulation of insurance if they could get an MSA program.

Kennedy believed the lever that would ultimately pry open the door to passing an acceptable bill was that the key House Republicans were very concerned about the "do-nothing Congress" label that the Democrats were working hard to pin on them, and therefore their interest in passing this popular legislation would bring them around to what we saw as an acceptable compromise, as long as they could take back something on MSAs to placate their party members. Finally, even the House Democrats were split. Most didn't really want a bill; they wanted to run against House Republicans as the do-nothing Congress. In fact Majority Leader Gephardt met with Kennedy to urge that he postpone action on the bill until after the August recess. By that time, Gephardt argued, the "do-nothing" label would have become unshakable. While Kennedy was noncommittal in the meeting, he knew that every legislative issue has its moment—and if you miss that moment, you might never succeed. He didn't intend to allow the health insurance legislation to miss its moment.

It was unclear how all of this would play out over the summer. All the top Republicans in the House and the Senate were involved. It was almost impossible for Kennedy to negotiate when both houses had taken so many "final" positions, when so many Republican players were trying to be in charge, and when the "final" positions were always set out after a big meeting in which the Republicans had to compromise with each other instead of us—giving those who didn't want a bill inordinate weight. In the end, I counted up an astounding sixty-five offers and counteroffers that were put forward at various times. Poor Kassebaum had to be the intermediary throughout all this. What she told Kennedy depended on who she had talked to most recently in the Republican leadership, and Dole was so busy in his last week that he didn't really try to force a unified Republican position that could be the basis for a deal.

Gearing up for a new round of negotiations, Kennedy started meetings with representatives of the Consumers Union, the American Nurses Association, the National Council of Senior Citizens, and the Service Employees International Union, as well as experts on MSAs. He also talked to his Senate colleagues and then called Hilley at the White House.

"We've talked to the Republicans, and they've apparently had a good meeting," Hilley said. "Half the Republicans don't want to give Clinton anything he can take credit for. The president wants a demonstration program of MSAs. The original Republican proposal was completely untenable, but their new proposal goes a long way without compromising our core position." Lott, Hilley said, had agreed to a sunset and capping the program. Kennedy had another phone conversation with Hilley, who had apparently taken on the job of sweet-talking Kennedy and keeping him in the loop on the health care bill. Hilley said he hadn't had a response from the Republicans to our recent discussions but that they were batting around the different ideas, looking at the consumer protection issues, and were quite optimistic on the larger issues of requiring an affirmative vote of Congress to expand the MSA program and limiting the number of people eligible.

While the health care negotiations were going on, there was another set of discussions about the minimum wage increase and the antilabor provisions. Republican senators Nickles and Bond were floating a provision that would allow every small business with revenues of under $500,000 a year to pay less than the minimum wage, a so-called subminimum. Other Republicans were pushing the overtime proposal, and still others were pushing provisions to limit union spending on elections.

That same week Kennedy was talking to editorial boards, meeting with the press, meeting with advocates, making the case for holding the line on MSAs. On June 14 he returned to the floor, again attacking the Republicans on Medicare cuts, health reform, and the minimum wage.

Lott and Gingrich had a photo opportunity, during which the press asked them about MSAs. "We're continuing to work for changes," said Lott. "We're looking at medical savings accounts for small business and the self-employed. Liberals in the House and Senate should get out of the way."

Lott followed up with a proposal that Hilley said was clearly a step back. Lott hadn't talked to Hastert, with whom Hilley had been talking, and his proposal had no cap on the number of MSAs; Lott was shooting from the hip. We were also concerned about the information coming from Hilley. He was clearly talking to Hastert about a compromise, and we were worried that we were out of that loop.

Dodd opened a meeting of the Senate Democratic leadership group to discuss the strategy going forward. Everyone agreed that the minimum wage was a great issue for the Democrats. Dodd said, "We get the minimum wage. They get the gas tax. They get a vote on the TEAM Act."

"We are losing by our not keeping these issues out front," Senator Reid said. "Minimum wage and Kassebaum-Kennedy are really good issues. They have hit home. I have a twenty-three-year-old son who has a medical problem. I know just how important limiting preexisting condition exclusions can be. We need to be on the floor talking about these issues all the time."

The group concluded that Daschle should give Lott a final, best offer on a package to go with the minimum wage. If Lott rejected it, we'd go back to the floor and try to offer the minimum wage increase on every bill again.

Lott was trying to resolve the gridlock that Dole had left behind, but so far with little success. In a public discussion with Kennedy on the Senate floor about the minimum wage stalemate, he said he had been meeting with Daschle. "We have discussed other ways that we may be able to deal with this issue, but we are being extra careful because we want to develop a relationship that is one of trust and respect. We are making sure that when we talk about something, I understand what he is saying and he understands what I am saying. We are trying to reduce it to writing with both our staffs working on it. This Gordian knot that has been tied up here, we are trying to take it apart one string at a time and we are making progress. I ask our colleagues here to give us a little more time."

Kennedy responded, "Mr. President, I am unpersuaded by the senator's position that this is a Gordian knot and that it has been languishing here. It has been languishing because of those senators who for over a year and a half have denied this body the opportunity to vote on the minimum wage when we have been able to demonstrate in previous votes a majority will vote for the increase."

What Kennedy knew and Lott was obliquely referring to was that over the weekend the Democrats thought they had an understanding whereby the bills debated would be the package of tax proposals from the Republicans and the minimum wage from the Democrats. They understood at that time that the antilabor provisions, specifically the TEAM Act, would not be lumped in with the minimum wage increase and the tax provisions and that the Democratic senators would retain their right to filibuster the TEAM Act. But Lott, despite his representations to Daschle, discovered that he could not get his Republican colleagues to agree to drop the TEAM Act. He was hoping for an auspicious beginning to his relationship with Daschle, but at least as far as some Democrats were concerned, he had already backtracked.

Kassebaum reported to Kennedy on the latest on MSAs: "Trent is there. I am there. But the House Republicans are not going for any limit on MSAs. And we can't terminate the program. The Republicans won't agree to that. They'll never take a cap, the Republicans in the House. You'll just kill the bill because you're insisting on a cap. They will take the sunset, but they are digging in their heels on the cap."

We talked to Chris Jennings, the White House health advisor. "The House Republicans are being total assholes, driving negotiations," he reported. "The good faith is all bogus. The Republicans are riding high with Whitewater. They are beating their breasts. They are out of the negotiating mode. Shouldn't we start firing the bill up, go to the floor and start blaming the Republicans?"

On June 20 Kennedy met with Daschle to size up the negotiations on MSAs. They were both concerned that the White House would give too much ground to the Republicans. Hilley was talking about a test with up to a million MSAs. Daschle was as angry as I'd seen him. "We're not going to have triangulation on this issue," he said, as he picked up the phone to call Hilley at the White House. Daschle knew Hilley very well; he had worked for Daschle before going to the White House. But Hilley's style of keeping everything close to the vest and being willing to give much more ground to the Republicans than Kennedy or Daschle thought he should had reached beyond the tolerance of the normally mild-mannered, imperturbable, and calm Daschle. He fairly exploded at Hilley. "I won't let this bill go to the president with that large a test. I want a position that Democrats can walk with together. Limit it to 500,000 and no more. Make sure we have decent consumer protections."

Later that day Kennedy met with the experts from the RAND Corporation, the Urban Institute, and the Brookings Institute on the MSAs, focusing on the size of possible demonstration programs. How big can it get without jeopardizing the health insurance pools for everybody else, he asked? The consensus seemed to be that a million policies would be the tipping point for destabilizing the insurance market.

At the White House, word of Daschle's eruption with Hilley must have reached the president, because he called Kennedy. The senator was fast off the mark. "We've got to have a limit on the number of MSA policies that can be sold," he said. "It shouldn't be higher than 500,000. It should not be in the million-plus range under any circumstances. We need protections for consumers, and we need procedures to make sure that the test is properly studied and terminated unless it's seen to be an overall plus. As it stands, the MSAs are just a giant tax break for the wealthy. There are six to nine other issues related to this that we need to work out."

The president responded, "I guess they don't want me to get this bill."

"I'm still for compromise, but I don't think anybody can live with what they are asking," Kennedy answered. "We've also got immigration and job training and the minimum wage out there."

"I think they're wrong about health care," Clinton said.

"It's a winning card for us," Kennedy agreed.

"I told Hilley I didn't know why Teddy was so mad at me," Clinton said. "I was shocked. I'm calling to tell you let's get this thing done. I've told the Republicans, 'If you get Kennedy, you get it all done.'"

Now Kennedy was truly the point man. Clinton had made it clear that he had told the Republicans they had to make the deal with the senator. Daschle had done the same. The comings and goings and back-and-forth of negotiations had ended up with Kennedy in charge. It was his bill. The White House would not pull the rug out from under him.

The press was reporting that the negotiations on health care were further apart than ever. On the floor, Kennedy said, "It appears that there has been significant backtracking by Republicans from what we understood had been agreed to earlier. That reduces the likelihood of a compromise."

Chairman Archer complained, "Instead of listening to the forty Democrats in the House who support medical savings accounts, President Clinton is leaning toward Senator Kennedy's position and the tug of the left. By yielding to the liberals the president is endangering the entire bill."

There was another phone call between Hilley and Kennedy. "How big should the MSA trial be?" Hilley asked. "Would the test be designed so that it was sufficiently informative to be studied? How much disruption would there be to the existing market?" According to Hilley, "The big guys want to get it done. I love Tom Daschle dearly, but he has a thing about this, not wanting to lose the fight."

On June 24 Kennedy met with Kassebaum. Still no progress on MSAs.

There were very few senators in town, but Kennedy lost no opportunity to go to the floor and recap the events leading to the legislative stalemate. He reviewed step-by-step the Republican attempts to block a minimum wage increase for the past year and a half, and then he turned to the Kassebaum-Kennedy health care bill. For almost an hour he laid out the specific case, point by point, against MSAs. He quoted from editorials in newspapers across the country urging compromise on Kassebaum-Kennedy and raising questions about MSAs, including the *Seattle Times*, the *St. Louis Post-Dispatch*, the *Pittsburgh Post-Gazette*, the *New York Times*, the *St. Petersburg Times*, and the *Newark Star-Ledger*. He reviewed instances of patients who had been victimized by Golden Rule insurance policies.

MOVEMENT

Then suddenly, on June 25, there was a breakthrough on the minimum wage issue. Lott approached Daschle with a proposal. There would be an up-or-down vote on the increase in two weeks, on July 9. What Kennedy had fought for for over a year was finally going to happen. But the Republicans would get to offer one amendment, which would delay the implementation of the increase for six months for every new employee and would exclude millions of workers from any minimum wage at all. The amendment would be similar to the Goodling amendment that had been defeated in the House. The Democrats would also get one amendment. Daschle told Kennedy, "We will do everything to stop the amendment, and if we can't stop it in the Senate, we will stop it if it comes back in conference." Following the vote on the minimum wage the Senate would take up the antilabor right-to-work bill and the TEAM Act. Both of these would be voted on no later than July 10.

Daschle invited Kennedy to meet with Lott to clarify the proposal. The three men met in Daschle's office for almost an hour. Lott started off talking about the health bill. "Let's work something out on health care. There's broad agreement on portability and preexisting conditions. The only disagreement is on a small item on MSAs. We've given up on the wholesale program."

Senator Kennedy told Lott there were three principal concerns—the size of the plan, the procedures to determine whether the programs would continue after an initial test period, and the consumer protections—and asked how they would be resolved. Kennedy wanted eligibility to be defined narrowly and a limit of 500,000 policies. On the procedures Lott said, "To expand it you need a positive vote; to stop it you need a negative vote." Lott suggested a follow-up meeting to include Hastert in the House.

Later Kennedy saw Kassebaum on the floor. She said she was meeting with Hastert the next morning at 9:00. "They're back to fifty. I'll have to be with them. Can't you make a move?"

The follow-up meeting resolved nothing. It was one of a series of meetings we had with Hastert as the leader of the Republican health task force. Hastert was shadowed by Ken Kies, the director of the Joint Tax Committee, a highly skilled tax professional who was also effectively Ways and Means chairman Archer's representative. The Hastert meetings generally had a positive tone that left us optimistic about the chances for moving forward, but it turned out that it didn't much matter what Hastert said. The ultimate decision-making power rested with Archer.

Kennedy spoke again to Kassebaum, who told him, "Your plan is too bureaucratic. It won't ever fly with Republicans. The House Republicans are going to accept our earlier offer in the fifty-plus range. They'll jam you in the House. They'll jam you in the Senate with conferees. Our people are raising the temperature now."

I talked to Tom O'Donnell, the chief of staff in Gephardt's office. Leon Panetta had told him the White House wouldn't do anything on Kassebaum-Kennedy without Gephardt, Daschle, and Kennedy.

Kennedy spoke to Lott on the floor. Lott said he had told Archer and Hastert that they had to deal with Kennedy.

Congress was getting ready to adjourn on June 28 for the July 4 recess. Democrats in the House were trumpeting a new *USA Today*/CNN poll that showed Americans preferred Democrats for Congress by 50 to 43 percent. Democrats in the Senate heralded their victory in getting the Republicans to finally agree to hold a vote to raise the minimum wage after the July 4 recess. They also attacked the Republican amendment that would undercut the minimum wage increase for millions of workers. It would deny the minimum wage to all new workers, to employees of all companies with less than $500,000 in annual sales, and to employees who are tipped, such as waiters and waitresses. Approximately 10.5 million employees and two-thirds of all workplaces would be excluded, and the amendment would also delay the increase in the minimum wage until January 1, 1997, another six months after the date established by the House.

As the July 4 recess began, there was still no progress on Kassebaum-Kennedy.

Kennedy and his staff used the recess to line up votes against the so-called National Right-to-Work Act. Kennedy described it as a national freeloader act because it allowed nonunion workers to benefit from union negotiations over wages, working conditions, and union contracts without joining the union or paying dues to the union for these services and benefits.

Meanwhile the outside interest groups were running ads and lobbying on the minimum wage increase. The AFL-CIO expanded its ad campaign in districts of swing Republicans from the House. The National Federation of Independent Businesses responded with ads attacking the minimum wage increase.

On July 8 the Senate came into session at 12:30 p.m., Strom Thurmond, the president pro tempore, called the body to order. Following the morning business, Lott laid out the agreement that was to lead, at long last, to a clean vote on the minimum wage increase. The logjam was finally broken. Lott had cut the Gordian knot—but at the price of giving Kennedy the chance to pass the minimum wage increase that he had been fighting for since the 1994 election.

Kennedy spoke: "For eighteen months Republicans have refused to allow the Senate to vote. Now the long overdue vote is about to take place, but the Republican obstruction has not ended. Opponents of the minimum wage have devised a shameless trick to prevent as much of the increase as possible by delaying it and by denying it to large numbers of deserving American workers." He continued speaking for an hour. He referred to letters of endorsement from the NAACP, the National Urban League, the National Hispanic Leadership Institute, the Leadership Conference on Civil Rights, the Mexican-American Legal Defense and Education Fund, the Migrant Legal Action Committee. He had statements from over a hundred economists, including three Nobel Prize winners, who endorsed the increase. He reviewed all the arguments that he had developed over the past eighteen months, and new ones. He focused particularly on the minimum wage as a women's issue, because 65 percent of individuals receiving the minimum wage were women.

Daschle followed Kennedy to the floor. "This is a chance," he said, "for us to stop stalling, to send a clear message to people across this land that we recognize how important your paycheck and your long-term security is. We recognize how important your family is. We recognize that if we are going to urge you to stay off welfare and go to work that you need a wage to do it. This is what this does."

The debate continued after lunch the next day. The senators adjourned for their caucuses and returned to the floor. There were more speeches. Senators Gramm, Coats, and Hatch spoke against the increase. Senators Harkin, Bingaman, and Moynihan spoke for it. Two votes were taken, first on the Bond amendment allowing small businesses with yearly revenues of under $500,000 to pay less than the minimum wage, which lost, 52–46 when Senators Specter, Hatfield, Campbell, and Jeffords broke with Lott to oppose it. Senator D'Amato voted against the Bond amendment as well, but only after he knew it had already lost.

Later in the day, the Senate voted on the minimum wage increase itself. The vote was 74–24 in favor. Twenty-seven Republicans—almost half the Republican Caucus—joined all the Democrats.

The minimum wage increase was technically an amendment to the Small Business Tax Package, which had become a vehicle not just for the minimum wage increase but also for billions of tax provisions benefiting businesses—$19 billion in tax cuts over ten years for small and large businesses. Since the minimum wage legislation would turn out to be the only tax vehicle moving to enactment through the Congress in 1996, senators were eager to attach their pet tax cut provisions to it. Cider manufacturers would benefit, as would small businesses that purchased equipment, certain fisheries, and homemakers with IRAs. Finally, the Senate closed off the so-called Benedict Arnold tax loophole, which had reduced the taxes of very rich individuals who had renounced their U.S. citizenship.

But the bill wasn't finished yet. Senator Nickles announced that he would object to appointing conferees to work out the final details of the bill with the House until Kennedy had withdrawn his objection to appointment of conferees on the health bill.

The next day, the Senate debated and voted on the so-called National Right-to-Work Act. The amendment was defeated, 63–36, a decisive defeat for the National Right-to-Work campaign and a victory for labor. The vote on the TEAM Act went the other way, however. The vote was 53–46 to pass the TEAM Act, which Republicans characterized as simply allowing employers and workers to meet together to discuss issues in the workplace. We were not upset by this vote, because Kennedy had always insisted that the TEAM Act be a stand-alone bill and had fought back Dole's efforts to package it with the minimum wage. The president had already said he would veto a stand-alone TEAM Act.

When the Senate returned from the July 4 recess and with the minimum wage passed and the antilabor issues disposed of for the time being, Lott now seemed ready to make a renewed effort to resolve the health insurance standoff. Lott told Daschle that he had received a new Democratic proposal on MSAs and felt very positively toward it. Neither Daschle nor Kennedy knew what he was talking about. Lott told Daschle it was worth considering. "I've reviewed the proposal," Lott said. "It may have come from Senator Breaux. He's been very active on this issue." Daschle was startled. There were clearly backdoor channels between Breaux and Lott. Was the White House involved?

On July 12 the Democratic senators headed to Nantucket for their annual Democratic Senate Campaign Committee retreat. Prime contributors also attend this event. Coincidently, Patrick Rooney, CEO of Golden Rule Insurance Company, was waiting in the section of National Airport reserved for private planes. Rooney was on his way back to Indianapolis after a day in Washington. He was overheard to say to one of the senators that he could live with either the Democratic or Republican proposal on MSAs. This was very surprising in light of all the pressure exerted by the Republicans, not to mention the price Dole had paid for holding out for the Republican position. Rooney had spoken to the House that day and had also told Lott to just negotiate and get something done.

Senator Breaux reported this overheard conversation to Kennedy. "The instructions in terms of the specific consumer protections don't bother me—I can live with them," Rooney had said.

Who was negotiating for whom? Did the Republicans really want a bill, or was the whole exercise simply designed to kill the bill and make sure there was no regulation of the insurance industry enacted in a Republican Congress?

Then the Olympic Games began, and the consensus was that the attention of the American people would not be on Congress. Meanwhile the House Republicans had joined Nickles in blocking conferees on the minimum wage increase. Polls showed Clinton ahead of Dole by as much as twenty-five points with Perot in the race, and twenty-four points without Perot. The Democrats in the House were still bashing Gingrich on cuts to Medicare, food stamps, programs for legal immigrants, and for continuing to block the minimum wage.

KENNEDY AND ARCHER

On July 22 Lott told Kennedy he'd be moving that day or the next to appoint conferees on minimum wage and health care. Then Lott went out into the hall for a press conference, where he announced that he was closing out debate on the MSAs that day and would move the legislation within a day or two. Both sides had to give a little, he said and added, "[We are seeing a] typical Teddy tactic. An endless charade to block going to conference. If we waited for Ted Kennedy it would never get done."

Lott then told Daschle that Kennedy should talk to House Ways and Means chairman Bill Archer. They'd be the point men to work out the final details of the agreement on MSAs. In fact Archer, a hard-core conservative, had been the deciding Republican vote on this issue all along.

Kennedy phoned Archer: "Lott and Tom Daschle have talked and you are the person on MSAs. I would like to have our staffs instructed to work it out and then give us the items they can't work out, so that we can finish this at an early time."

Archer replied, "I understand there's a two-pager of what was agreed in part. Let's get that down to me."

"The staffs should make recommendations in terms of those areas as well, but we need to have language," said Kennedy.

Archer agreed to meet with Kennedy.

Kennedy prepared for the meeting as carefully as he always prepared for anything important. He talked to people who knew Archer and obtained and studied biographies of him from the various congressional research services. He learned that Archer had an aged mother to whom he was very close, and had the idea that perhaps Archer would be softened up if Kennedy brought a gift for her. Although the book was out of print, the senator located a new copy of Rose Kennedy's book, *Times to Remember*, written when she herself was in her nineties, and autographed it to Mrs. Archer. He also discovered that Archer was a fan of Bela Karolyi, a famous gymnastics coach who had defected from Romania and settled in Archer's district, where he trained Olympic gold medalist Mary Lou Retton, among others. Kennedy would come prepared to talk about gymnastics.

He then prepared option papers on each of the key issues, the place he wanted to end up, his opening position, and responses to each proposal or variation Archer might offer.

On July 24 Kennedy went to Archer's office in the House, accompanied by David Nexon and Dennis Kelleher, who had recently come aboard as the Labor Committee's deputy staff director. I stayed outside to keep the press current on what was going on with the negotiations.

The conversation opened cordially. Kennedy presented Rose Kennedy's book and mentioned gymnastics and Mary Lou Retton. Archer happily talked about Bela Karolyi. But the pleasantries only cleared the way for the hard bargaining on the MSAs. The key issues, as always, were the size of the eligible population, whether there was to be a cap and how big it would be, and whether the program would sunset. The deal was not settled after the first meeting, so Kennedy and his staff reconvened for a debriefing and development of the strategy for the follow-up meeting that was to occur early that evening. Two tax experts from the Treasury Department were assigned to help us on the technical issues.

While Archer had agreed at the first meeting to limit the types of businesses and individuals who could purchase MSAs, he wanted to avoid accepting a hard cap on the number of policies that could be sold and didn't want the program to sunset—issues we felt were critical. In preparation for the follow-up meeting, we continued intensive discussions on these issues at the staff level, with Nexon working directly with Ken Kies.

Following the second meeting, Archer and Kennedy announced publicly that they had reached an agreement on the MSA issue. We felt we had won on all our key issues. They had agreed to allow a national test of MSAs, which would be capped at no more than 750,000 accounts, below the million that we had been told would destabilize the insurance market and a limitation the Republicans said they would never accept. The individuals purchasing such accounts were to be self-employed or working for businesses with fewer than fifty employees. The test would be carefully structured and would include adequate protections for consumers and time for a study of the impact of the accounts. The program would sunset, another thing the Republicans had said they would never accept, but in a concession to Archer, if a business signed up its employees for an MSA policy, it would be allowed to continue to purchase the policies for current and future employees even if the program sunsetted. And we had achieved the consumer protections we wanted: more reasonable deductibles than the original Republican proposal and assurance that there would be a meaningful limit on the total financial obligation of enrollees. We had done so well because Kennedy had stuck to his guns, because the Kassebaum-Kennedy legislation was so popular with the public, and because Archer was under tremendous pressure from his leadership to make a deal that would enable the bill to pass so that they would not be tagged with obstructing it in the upcoming election.

Archer stated, "I am pleased to announce that Senator Kennedy and I have reached agreement on the medical savings accounts issue. As a result, millions of Americans will soon benefit from legislation making health care more available and affordable."

Kennedy said the agreement cleared away the largest single obstacle to enactment of the bipartisan health reform bill. "It's a true test, not a full-blown program."

On July 25 Lott and Kennedy went to the floor of the Senate to announce the agreement. Kassebaum and others spoke on the floor as well, heaping praise on Kennedy and others involved in the negotiations that led to the compromise. At long last, conferees were appointed in the Senate for the health care bill, and the first formal meeting of the conference was held in the House Ways and Means chamber. Members of the Senate Finance and Labor committees attended. Chairman Archer opened the meeting by extolling Kennedy's contribution to the compromise, and Moynihan expressed Kennedy's regrets at not being there; he had a previous commitment in Massachusetts he could not miss. Senator Roth congratulated both Kennedy and Archer on the MSA compromise, calling it a "splendid bipartisan compromise." "We promised," Roth said, "we would continue the effort to achieve health reform when health reform died in 1994. We're proud to have followed up on that commitment." In a variation on an old saying, defeat may be an orphan, but victory certainly has a thousand fathers.

THE LOGJAM IS BROKEN

At the next staff directors meeting, it was as if a dam had burst and legislation was rushing through: welfare, minimum wage, health care, the small business issues, immigration, food stamps, antiterrorism, safe water, the veto of the TEAM Act, nuclear waste, Medicare, the Democrats' Families First agenda, the labor Davis-Bacon issues, and transportation—all were discussed.

In the House the Democrats were taking a victory lap. While they might have wished that the minimum wage and health insurance reform had not passed, now they were determined not to let the Republicans get credit for bills they had tried so long to kill. After all, Democrats had provided the votes to pass both bills, and the Republicans had blocked both for almost twenty months. Democrats repeated over and over that the Republicans were finally passing all these bipartisan bills that they had earlier opposed only because they wanted to have a record to run on in the election in November.

On July 31 the House and Senate conferees on the minimum wage agreed on a final package of tax provisions that would be added to the minimum wage increase. On August 1, with the final compromises worked out, the Kassebaum-Kennedy health bill went to the floor of the House and was adopted by an extraordinary vote of 421–2. The Democratic Senate talking points trumpeted the victory using an Olympics metaphor: "Bringing home the gold on minimum wage and health care security: We're at the finish line. Today, Friday, August 2, the Senate is expected to vote on the final version of the minimum wage bill and the Kassebaum-Kennedy health portability bill, two of the Democrats' priorities." House Democrats emphasized the minimum wage in their talking points: "Democrats chalk up another victory with minimum wage."

A jubilant Kennedy spoke about the minimum wage. "This day has been a long time coming," he said. "Eighteen months ago, in February 1995, I introduced legislation to raise the minimum wage to $5.65 an hour in three 50-cent increments and joined Senator Daschle one month later to introduce S.413, which would have raised the minimum wage by 90 cents in two increments, on July 1, 1995, and July 1, 1996. A year ago, on July 31, 1995, I offered a resolution expressing the sense of the Senate that the Senate should take up the minimum wage increase before the end of last year. It received only two Republican votes and was defeated."

The back-to-back votes on the Health Insurance Portability and Accountability Act of 1996 conference report (H.R.3103) and the minimum wage increase conference report were sweet indeed. The roll was called. The votes were cast. The health insurance reform bill passed 98–0. The minimum wage increase passed 76–22. All Democrats and *more than half* of all Republican senators voted to increase the minimum wage from $4.25 to $5.15 an hour.

The saga of Kennedy and the minimum wage over the course of his Senate career is nothing short of legendary. Four times he led the fight to increase the minimum wage. Each time he faced fervent opposition, even from some Democrats. Each time he prevailed. History will record that he was responsible for increasing wages for the poorest Americans from $2.30 an hour in 1978 to $7.25 in 2009.

After the back-to-back votes, Kennedy was recognized: "Mr. President, in the last half hour, we have experienced a double-header victory for the American people: health care and a raise in the minimum wage. In a sense, both these bills had nine lives, and they needed all of them. But they have come to a successful resolution this evening and, hopefully, they will be on the president's desk in the very near future."

Then Kassebaum and Kennedy went upstairs together to the Senate Press Gallery to appear live on the *MacNeil/Lehrer NewsHour* to discuss the health care bill and the minimum wage.

So much that happens in public policy, as in life, seems after it happens, to have been inevitable. There was overwhelming popular support for both Kassebaum-Kennedy and the minimum wage increase. How could Congress not pass legislation to deal with those issues? It reminds me of other legislation that Kennedy got passed which now seems inevitable but in fact was not: the Americans with Disabilities Act, civil rights legislation in 1991, the Ryan White AIDS CARE Act. Today it is hard to imagine that we would not have laws on the books providing accessibility for the disabled, penalties for discrimination in employment, and funding for AIDS treatment and prevention. But in fact none of these laws was even close to being inevitable. What seems so obvious today all flowed from the fact that Kennedy believed these issues to be timely and critical both politically and substantively and had such a formidable arsenal of legislative and political skills to bring to the task of enacting them. In fact Kennedy's performance on minimum wage and Kassebaum-Kennedy was one of the most remarkable in the modern-day Senate. That he could pass two such important bills over such relentless and powerful opposition from the majority party in both the House and Senate had never been done before and hasn't been done since.

The president called Kennedy the next day to congratulate him for his two victories. Kennedy thanked him for speaking to both issues in his State of the Union Address at the beginning of the year and for standing firm on medical savings accounts. Now both men were thinking ahead. "What's the next step?" the president asked. "The unemployed? Allowing the uninsured to buy into a pool? Restoring coverage for immigrants? More money for community health centers, mental health, or do we need a broad-based public health program?" The senator did not have an immediate answer, but he was already beginning to mull over exactly that question.

CLINTON WINS REELECTION

After passing Kassebaum-Kennedy and the minimum wage bill on the same day, Kennedy had much to celebrate—but he was asked to take on an important political assignment. Many of us on the staff met him in Chicago for the Democratic National Convention in late August. Clinton's team had decided to make it a very emotional event: the first night featured Sarah and Jim Brady and Christopher Reeve. I will never forget Jim Brady getting up out of his wheelchair to walk across the stage and praise Clinton for supporting the Brady Bill limiting access to handguns, and Christopher Reeve, motionless in his wheelchair following the horseback riding accident that broke his neck, speaking about the importance of federal research that might some day find a cure for spinal cord injuries.

Clinton had asked Kennedy to speak on Thursday, the last night of the convention and the same night Clinton was to accept the nomination, because Kennedy was so popular with the Democratic base. Clinton wanted Kennedy to warm up the crowd with a funny, partisan, "red meat" speech. We had a great time writing it, trying out different clever ways of characterizing the Republicans, and on the night the senator delivered it, he was in an ebullient mood. The packed hall gave Kennedy a raucous welcome, and he whipped them up further with his full-throated denunciation of "the education-cutting, environment-trashing, Medicare-slashing, choice-denying, tolerance-repudiating, gay-bashing, Social Security–threatening, assault rifle–coddling, government-closing, tax loophole–granting, minimum wage–opposing Republican majority." He went on to describe Dole as "the compliant partner in the so-called Gingrich revolution; Newt thought it up, but Bob Dole swallowed it hook, line, and sinker."

Clinton went on to win reelection in an Electoral College landslide in November. On Election Night the president telephoned Kennedy again to talk about the Democratic agenda going forward. Clinton said he needed to get together with Kennedy and the Democrats after the election to put together an agenda that everyone could support.

Chapter 23

THE CHILDREN'S HEALTH INITIATIVE

The major political cause of Senator Kennedy's life was expanding health care. Every member of his staff knew it. We also came to feel that it was the major cause of our lives too.

After the 1994 elections, Senator Kennedy and his staff had surveyed the rubble of the failed attempt to enact universal health care as they planned the Senator's next big health initiative. Our first choice at that point had been to expand health insurance coverage to children. Senator Kennedy had a special feeling for children who needed help, and for most people children are an especially sympathetic group. Moreover, because children are generally in good health, they are a relatively inexpensive group to cover. But we could find no Republican willing to endorse a sizable new federal spending program, even for children, after their takeover of Congress. Because of this, we had turned to the program of insurance reforms that became the Kassebaum-Kennedy bill.

In the 1996 election, Clinton defeated Dole 49 to 40 percent in the popular vote, with Ross Perot getting about 8 percent. Despite Clinton's solid win, the Republicans actually gained two seats in the Senate and lost just eleven seats in the House, retaining solid majorities in both bodies. So the hostile Republican majority we had faced in the 104th Congress was still there, but much of the steam had gone out of Newt Gingrich's Republican revolution.

Building on the success of the Kassebaum-Kennedy health bill, Senator Kennedy decided to try again with the idea that he could not get traction for in 1995; he decided that expanded health insurance for the country's 10 million uninsured children would be his top health policy initiative for the 105th Congress. He wanted to target those uninsured families with incomes too high to allow them to receive Medicaid but too low to enable them to pay the costs of private health insurance.

Ironically, the struggles over the Republican revolution had in some ways improved the prospects for legislation for children. Democrats highlighted many of the Republican proposals that would have cut back assistance for children, and Republicans were roundly castigated for picking on the most defenseless members of society. Politicians of both parties emphasized family-friendly policies; Republicans spent hours of valuable TV time at their 1996 national convention focusing on how their policies would help America's children. But while the Republicans had emerged chastened from the 104th Congress, they were still committed to a balanced budget and opposed to new government social programs—especially new entitlement programs.

Like their initial characterization of the minimum wage increase and the Kassebaum-Kennedy health insurance reform bill, most political observers at the beginning of the 105th Congress viewed Kennedy's goal of a major new step toward universal health insurance as quixotic at best. But Kennedy had beaten the odds in the previous Congress and he believed he could do it again. He had shown he knew how to pass bills even in the minority. Moreover, ideas that capture the imagination and mood of the public can take on a life of their own, and Kennedy was a proven master at finding the right legislative moment. Improbable as our prospects might have seemed, we felt that if we pulled out all the stops, this could be the moment for children's health care.

On October 1, 1996, a month before the election, Kennedy began to lay the groundwork for the next Congress by introducing his first bill to provide comprehensive coverage for children. Because John Kerry, then the junior senator from Massachusetts, was facing a tough reelection campaign and had been working on the issue himself, Kennedy agreed that Kerry should be the bill's lead sponsor. The bill provided grants to states to set up a children's health insurance program. The federal government would pay 100 percent of the cost of the coverage, but to qualify the state had to assure a comprehensive benefits package with the premium subsidy and cost-sharing requirements specified in the bill. Federal funding was open-ended; if the states created the program, every eligible child would be entitled to coverage and the federal government would cover the cost.

The bill had no specific taxes attached to pay for it, but it included a sense of the Labor and Human Resources Committee, to which the bill was referred, that it would be financed by a combination of tobacco taxes and by eliminating undeserved corporate tax breaks. The sense of the Committee provision was really more of a placeholder than a serious proposal, since the committee had no jurisdiction over taxes, but it did indicate some of the options we thought might be attractive. Corporate welfare was something the senator had been talking about for a long time, and we were aware that a successful children's health insurance initiative had been passed in Massachusetts in 1993 with financing from increased tobacco taxes.

On November 8, 1996, just two days after the polls closed, Kennedy and I flew up to Boston and met with Dr. Barry Zuckerman, chief of pediatrics at Boston Medical Center and a leading national advocate for children's health, and State Representative John McDonough, a leading proponent of health reform in the Massachusetts legislature, to discuss the successful program they had spearheaded. We were interested in learning more about the political strategy that was used in Massachusetts to see what might be applicable in the very different environment of Washington.

The Massachusetts initiative provided health insurance for uninsured children, paid for by a 25-cent per pack increase in the state's tobacco tax. McDonough described the very broad support the legislation had engendered among health care providers, consumers, and business groups. The driving force behind the legislation, he said, had come primarily from two groups: children's advocates and the antitobacco health care lobby. Studies showed that an increase in the price of tobacco reduced use of tobacco products by children and teenagers more than for any other age group. This linkage between children's insurance coverage and a tax that would discourage children from smoking had created a powerful and compelling political formula.

In an early boost for the cause, Senator Daschle included a bill similar to Senator Kennedy's legislation from the 104th Congress as one of the ten leadership bills introduced at the beginning of the Congress. This was significant; while the leadership bills were not necessarily serious candidates for enactment, they were meant to highlight issues that had both broad public support and support within the Democratic Party. The Daschle bill, however, included no financing mechanism.

Based on the success of the program in Massachusetts, we could see the benefit of linking children's and antismoking advocates around a single program and solving the financing problem at the same time. But there was a downside: using the tobacco tax as a funding source would create a powerful new opponent to the bill. The tobacco industry was politically strong. The Republicans controlling Congress had received sizable campaign contributions from the tobacco industry; tobacco money fueled right-wing think tanks that were influential within the Republican Party; and there were many Republican members of Congress and some Democrats from tobacco-growing states who would oppose any legislation threatening the industry.

But the tobacco industry was struggling more than ever before. Testifying before Congress that tobacco was not addictive, tobacco executives had looked foolish and disingenuous. Lawsuits against tobacco companies had been filed by states across the country, seeking to claim damages for health costs incurred as a result of tobacco use. There were even discussions about the possibility of a national settlement that would roll up and resolve all the separate state lawsuits. The tobacco companies themselves were suggesting that they might even participate in campaigns to reduce cigarette smoking by children and teenagers.

SUBSTANCE, POLITICS, AND PUBLIC RELATIONS

As with all the senator's successful initiatives, there would be three areas to the campaign: the substantive side, the political side, and the public relations side. Much of the substantive work had been completed in preparing the 1996 Kerry-Kennedy bill, although Kennedy's staff would continue to meet with experts and interest groups over the course of the winter to sharpen our understanding of such issues as the federal role versus the state role, the scope of benefits, defining eligibility for the program, conditions that would encourage insurers to participate, ways to contain the cost of the program, how to mesh private insurance programs with the federal and state Medicaid programs, how to encourage families to enroll their children in the insurance plans, how to implement the tobacco tax increase, what tobacco products it would apply to at what level, and the like.

Once the substance was under control, the attention of the senator and his staff would turn to the inside and outside games, the politics of actually enacting the bill. The key requirement of the inside game was obtaining bipartisan support for the legislation. The outside game involved putting together as broad a coalition as possible, combining the reach, influence, and power of the children's lobby with other health groups, particularly those focused on reducing tobacco use, such as the National Cancer Society, the American Heart Association, and the American Lung Association.

The public relations campaign would not be ratcheted up in earnest until the politics were in place. However, Kennedy and others would begin making speeches and putting the word out that the next step in health reform was children's health insurance and that this would be a full-court press and a long-term effort, not unlike the effort that had led to the enactment of the Kassebaum-Kennedy bill the year before.

FINDING A REPUBLICAN LEAD SPONSOR

In December 1996 Kennedy began meeting with Republican senators he thought might be convinced to become the Kassebaum of the new children's health initiative. He drew up a list of possible targets: senators who had supported children's issues in the past and had been active on health care and senators who had shown some independence and might be willing to work with him even at the risk of crossing the Republican leadership. This was a real concern for any Republican, because Senator Lott, beginning his first full Congress as majority leader, was determined to prevent Kennedy from creating bipartisan alliances that would end up dominating the agenda as had happened under Dole's watch.

Senator Kennedy's list included Senator Jeffords of Vermont, Senator DeWine of Ohio, Senator Hatch of Utah, Senator Chafee of Rhode Island, Senator Bond of Missouri, Senator Frist of Tennessee, Senator Specter of Pennsylvania, and Senators Snowe and Collins, of Maine. He called the senators to set up one-on-one meetings. All of these meetings were uniformly friendly. Each Republican Senator said that he or she supported Senator Kennedy's goals, but each either refused or were noncommittal on co-cosponsoring the legislation with him. By the end of January 1997, the senator had not lined up a Republican cosponsor.

A ray of hope came from Senator Hatch, who seemed interested in doing something for children, although not necessarily the bill Kennedy had in mind. The two senators had an impressive track record together, particularly in health care. In addition to the strength of their personal relationship, they were able to work their way through liberal and conservative issues and arrive at a compromise middle-ground position. Hatch was a solid conservative who might be able to bring other Republicans along, and he was also independent: he was willing to take the heat from his leadership for something he believed in. And Hatch and Kennedy were both very effective advocates on the Senate floor.

An alliance between Hatch and Kennedy for this particular effort had a special logic: Senator Hatch was a devout Mormon, and, as Senator Kennedy was fond of noting, the Mormons have strict rules about tobacco use. Senator Hatch would surely be interested in legislation that would discourage the use of tobacco products, particularly among children. In addition, Utah had the highest percentage of uninsured children of any state in the country and more children per adult than any other state.

While Hatch had given us a ray of hope, it was by no means certain that he would be willing to collaborate with Kennedy on this project, which he knew could put him at odds with much of his caucus and strain his relationship with Majority Leader Lott. As usual Senator Kennedy was determined to leave no stone unturned. Patricia (Trish) Knight, Hatch's chief health staffer, was on a Harvard-sponsored trip to Poland and had, after two plane rides and a long bus trip, just arrived in the middle of the night at a small cabin in a remote village when a knock came at the door: there was an important phone call for her.

Trish was terrified that someone close to her had died or was seriously ill. She picked up the phone and heard Senator Kennedy's unmistakable voice. She couldn't believe he'd tracked her down—she wasn't really sure where she was herself!

"Trish—sorry to bother you. I really need help to convince Orrin that we need to do this health bill," Kennedy said. "It is so important to ten million children."

Whether the phone call to Trish had anything to do with it or not, in February Hatch gave the go-ahead to his staff to meet with Kennedy's staff to talk about possible outlines of a revised children's health initiative. Hatch said that if he were to sponsor the legislation, it would have to change; he could not take a position supporting anything that looked like the legislation Kennedy had introduced with Kerry. Trish reported that a number of staff members were concerned that working with Kennedy on this bill would be bad for Hatch politically, but when it was discussed internally Hatch told them, "You don't know what it was like to grow up as a poor kid. Help me to do it, but do it right." Hatch's staff initially suggested that the bill might be a block-grant program. Such a program would send additional federal money to the states but allow them to use the money for any children's health purpose. We firmly rejected that option; the bill had to be about expanding children's health insurance coverage.

As usual, the discussions between Hatch and Kennedy, although friendly and with much good-natured teasing back and forth, were initially inconclusive. They took place in Hatch's office, where he usually sat in one of two wing chairs in front of his desk; he was never sitting behind his desk when Kennedy came into the room. Senator Kennedy would be welcomed into the wing chair next to Senator Hatch, but the two of them would not face each other directly—instead, they sat at a slight angle, primarily facing toward the center of the room. Members of Senator Hatch's staff would sit on a couch against the wall; David Nexon and I, who led the Kennedy team, would sit on chairs facing the two senators at the other end of the room. The arrangement created a kind of circle, with the two senators at the top. It seemed to be Hatch's way of saying that the participation and contribution of everyone on the two staffs would be encouraged, and it would be a group process, but the final deal, if there was one, would be between Kennedy and himself.

Each time they sought to work together on legislation, Hatch and Kennedy went through an elaborate courtship dance, and this time was no exception. Hatch began every negotiating session by playing one or more of the patriotic or religious songs he had written and recorded on his large office sound system. This would be followed by friendly teasing on one subject or another, including politics, Senate activity, and whatever news coverage either of them had generated recently. Then Hatch would claim that Kennedy was pressuring him too much and was "taking him to the cleaners." Kennedy would listen and then keep going, suggesting new compromises that might appeal to Hatch. Hatch would say, "Teddy, I'll never be able to go back to Utah if I agree to any of the provisions you are proposing." Kennedy would reply, "But Orrin, there are so many children in Utah who can never see a doctor!"

The Hatch and Kennedy health staffs met for several weeks. They started with an outline of the Kerry-Kennedy bill and an outline prepared by Hatch's staff of the key aspects of that legislation he might support. Hatch accepted our approach that the money be provided by the federal government from the tobacco tax increase, but he insisted it had to be controlled by the states and, unlike the Kerry-Kennedy bill, that it not be an open-ended entitlement. We accepted that approach as long as the money had to be used for children's insurance and the requirements for the insurance and the subsidies provided were sufficiently detailed to ensure that the coverage would be affordable and meet children's needs.

Hatch also insisted that the program involve private health insurance; he was not for expanding government-operated health care through the Medicaid program. He also insisted that the tobacco tax increase would have to be considerably less than 75 cents per pack, our opening proposal, and that the target would not be all uninsured children but only a portion of them. The two staffs boiled down the differences to several pages, with charts listing the four or five key issues on which there was not yet agreement. Like the Kennedy staff, the Hatch staff was willing to work long hours—sometimes all night and all weekend—going over the details of each proposal.

One day, looking ahead on the Senate calendar, Senator Kennedy noted that the Children's Defense Fund (CDF), led by its passionate and extremely effective CEO, Marian Wright Edelman, was having its annual convention in Washington on March 11, 1997. It turned out that the Child Welfare League of America was also having its convention on that same day. There would be over a thousand delegates for each of these two conventions meeting in Washington. Kennedy had the ambitious idea that it would give the bill a terrific kickoff to announce the agreement at both conventions. An announcement would provide an opportunity for significant press and ensure that news of the legislation and its bipartisan sponsorship would be heard by children's advocates across the country. He also thought that an announcement in such a public forum would appeal to Senator Hatch, make it hard for him to back off from supporting the bill, and act as an incentive for him to speed up the nego-tiations and have the bill done in time for the announcement.

The week before March 11, Senator Kennedy told Senator Hatch of his strategy to announce their agreement on the bill. Hatch was skepti-cal that all the remaining differences could be ironed out by the date of the conventions but agreed to try. Both senators cleared their schedules in their home states and remained in Washington over the weekend. Their staffs prepared new draft outlines of the legislative proposals and the remaining areas of disagreement. It was agreed that it was best to conduct these final negotiations in writing so that there could be no misunderstanding. As the two staffs worked on the outlines and specific issues that needed to be reconciled, the two senators communicated with hand-delivered letters carried back and forth between them. The staffs would draft responses after talking to their respective senators. The senators exchanged at least four letters over Saturday and Sunday, each one shorter than the previous one as their differences shrank. By Monday morning, March 8, only two big unresolved issues remained: how large the program should be and how big the tobacco tax increase should be.

Senator Hatch clung to the idea of allocating a share of the tobacco tax money to deficit reduction so he could show his Republican col-leagues that he was fighting alongside them to balance the budget. We disagreed. We felt that any revenue from the tobacco tax increase, which we knew would be difficult to obtain and would require great effort from the children's health advocates, should be used only for children's health. In the end, though, we concluded that we would have to give Hatch something on this issue if we wanted an agreement.

On Monday and Tuesday Hatch and his staff proposed a program that would total $20 billion over five years, with half the money for health insurance and half for deficit reduction, which would have meant only $10 billion for children. Kennedy responded that we needed to cover at least 5 million children at $1,000 per child per year—that was $5 billion a year over five years, so we needed $25 billion for children. Hatch said he wasn't willing to go that high; he needed more deficit reduction and he couldn't live with a tobacco tax increase that was more than approximately 30 cents a pack.

We all digressed from the intense negotiations when Hatch wondered aloud what we should name the bill. Trish Knight, who was clever at acronyms, took out a piece of paper and started writing title options. Suddenly she let out a big laugh and suggested "the Children's Health Insurance and Lower Deficit Act of 1997," the C.H.I.L.D. Act. We all broke into applause. Hatch beamed. Though he still hadn't agreed to do the bill with Kennedy, the fact that we had agreed on the name was definitely a positive sign.

We still didn't have an agreement on the amount of funding and how it would be divided between children and deficit reduction. For the final, make-or-break meeting, Kennedy decided that he should spring a surprise on Hatch: I should learn one of Hatch's songs and, at the right moment, sing it to him in his office. I reviewed the cassettes that Hatch had given to Kennedy and me over the past year and settled on "Freedom's Light," a powerful patriotic anthem with an uplifting, soaring chorus. At the crucial moment, I would sing it to Hatch. Maybe that would break the impasse.

When we were next in Hatch's office, Kennedy sprang his surprise. I sang with as much fervor as if I were back on Broadway and gave it everything I had:

> *This land, the Arc, of freedom's light*
> *Is home to you and me*
> *And we must keep it burning bright*
> *From sea to shining sea.*
> *We'll feed the fire of freedom's flame,*
> *We'll keep the dream alive.*
> *So this great land can always feel*
> *The glow of freedom's light.*

When I finished, Hatch smiled. His only words were "Nice move, Teddy."

After further songs were played on Hatch's sound system and the meeting got under way, Hatch proposed $18 billion for children's health. That wasn't enough for Senator Kennedy, but we were getting closer. Kennedy suggested he'd settle for $20 billion for children's health and Hatch could have $10 billion for deficit reduction, i.e., one third of the funds for deficit reduction, two-thirds for children's health—a total of $30 billion. Hatch asked how high the tobacco tax would have to be to raise $30 billion. Nexon calculated an increase of approximately 41 cents per pack, and Hatch said he could live with that. The senators finally had agreement on the bill and it had only taken them six weeks.

The senators shook hands. Perhaps worried about the reaction of his Republican colleagues, Hatch was restrained in his enthusiasm, but Kennedy was elated. When we got around the corner from Hatch's office, far enough so that Hatch and his staff couldn't see or hear us, we high-fived each other and whooped with joy. If all went well, we had just concluded a bipartisan agreement that might result in access to affordable health care for virtually every American child. No work in public service had ever made me happier.

Hatch had been a very tough negotiator, and he cut the deal that he wanted from Kennedy: a federal-state program with capped funding allocated for both children's health and deficit reduction. Kennedy got his cosponsor on the biggest health insurance expansion since Medicare and Medicaid in the 1960s. They agreed to announce the legislation together in two days, first at the CDF and then at the Child Welfare League, and to hold a press conference in the Senate press gallery between the two events.

The morning of May 11 arrived. The staffs had jointly prepared the outline of the agreement, and each senator had written a statement describing the legislation. As I rode with Senator Kennedy in his van on the way to the Hilton in northwest Washington, where the CDF was having its plenary session at noon, we discussed what the Senator would say about Senator Hatch in praise of Senator Hatch's role in the legislation. I happened to have in my pocket the tape of "Freedom's Light" that Hatch had given me days before. On the back of the insert to the cassette were the lyrics. Kennedy picked out a verse to use in his introduction because he felt it showed Hatch's compassion.

Both senators arrived at the Hilton and were ushered to the front of the ballroom packed with advocates for children from all over the country. Marian Wright Edelman introduced the senators. She was full of praise for each of them, listing the issues affecting children on which they had taken the lead, bringing the large audience to its feet time and time again. She left no doubt that with the two of them on board, the children's health legislation could actually happen. She described it as the biggest advance for children in decades.

Senator Hatch spoke first. He talked about his relationship with Senator Kennedy being like that of brothers and about the importance of children's health care and limiting tobacco use, particularly among children. Kennedy followed, beginning with the lyrics he had chosen from Hatch's song:

In this dark day of discontent
So many feel despair
As poverty and dissidence
Cause sadness everywhere.

The two senators were interrupted by repeated standing ovations. The cameras were rolling. Out in the audience Nexon and I stood with Trish Knight and beamed with enthusiasm.

The senators returned to Capitol Hill in time for a joint press conference in the Senate Press Gallery. There, to reporters gathered for the announcement, the senators repeated their descriptions of the bill and their commitment to see it through that year. That evening they attended the banquet of the Child Welfare League of America's annual convention. Both repeated their remarks from earlier in the day and again received thunderous ovations.

It was an auspicious beginning, but there were many hurdles ahead: the certain opposition of the tobacco companies, the likely opposition of the Republican leadership, the inherent difficulty of starting a new social program of this magnitude, and the fact that we were still operating in an environment where Republicans controlled both houses of Congress and, as a party, wanted to shrink government rather than expand it.

Once the idea of the legislation had been announced and the basic format was structured, the task ahead was to actually draft the legislation and introduce it in the Senate. This process was much tougher than expected. The broad outlines had been agreed on: $20 billion to the states for child health insurance, with requirements for what that insurance would look like; a cigarette tax increase of 43 cents per pack (up from the back-of-the-envelope estimate of 41 cents to produce the needed $30 billion). But there were still a lot of details to be ironed out. What would the benefit package look like? What would be the state match? How would funding for abortion be handled? What would the level of subsidies be? There were revisions back and forth, night after night. As staff members worked to craft the final legislative product, at numerous points the tensions became so great there was concern that the whole effort would fail over the struggle to agree on the precise language of the bill. But somehow we finally reached an agreement on all these points.

Hatch had the task of wooing Republican cosponsors for the legislation, and he had decided not to introduce it until he had what he considered an adequate number. Kennedy had an easier time; his problem was not lining up Democratic cosponsors as much as keeping down the number so it would roughly equal Hatch's when the bill was introduced. As in the case of Kassebaum-Kennedy, the idea was to have the bill appear to be as bipartisan as possible. Throughout this process of drafting the bill and obtaining cosponsors, Hatch met with different senators. At several points, his effort looked as if it might collapse. He hadn't lined up cosponsors yet, and he was clearly nervous about going forward alone, but he had committed to Kennedy and we knew that he would keep trying.

Finally, almost a month after the initial announcement of the agreement to introduce the legislation, Hatch told Kennedy that he was ready to go. He wouldn't tell us who or how many cosponsors he had; all he would say was that he had several. The night before the bill was to be introduced, we still didn't know.

On the morning of April 8, Hatch and Kennedy held a joint press conference to announce the introduction of the bill and the names of their cosponsors. Hatch surprised us by delivering eight Republicans. The legislation was introduced on the Senate floor that night.

In the days leading up to the introduction of the legislation, Hatch had suggested that the tobacco tax provisions be introduced in a separate bill. Kennedy agreed with that strategy because it meant the health insurance portion could be referred to the Labor and Human Resources Committee, of which he was a ranking member. The tobacco tax provisions would need to be referred to the Finance Committee, which has jurisdiction over all tax matters. If the tobacco tax and the substantive part of the bill were introduced together, the whole bill would have gone to Finance, and Kennedy was not a member of that committee, although Hatch was.

On the following day, the *New York Times*'s lead story on the front page was the announcement of the legislation and its eight Republican cosponsors, a highly unusual level of attention for a bill introduction. This was a momentous occasion for health policy. Health care had been an enormous issue during 1993 and 1994, when the goal had been to achieve a comprehensive health reform plan and universal health care. This children's health bill represented the second major step in the new strategy adopted by Kennedy and the Democrats to advance the health care agenda by incremental steps rather than comprehensive reform. And anyone who followed the track record of legislation jointly cosponsored by Hatch and Kennedy would have known that each such piece of legislation over the past decade had become law. Moreover, with the Kassebaum-Kennedy bill Kennedy had shown his power to legislate in the health area, even in a Republican Congress.

There was considerable concern among the Republican Caucus when the Hatch-Kennedy legislation was announced. Lott, who had sworn that under his watch Kennedy "would not run the Senate," was particularly

agitated. "A Kennedy big-government program is not going to be enacted," he publicly vowed. As he tightened the screws on the members
of his caucus and condemnation poured in from the right wing, three
of Hatch's cosponsors asked that their names be withdrawn from the tax
bill, since they had only agreed to cosponsor the children's health provision. Senator Bennett, Hatch's colleague from Utah, withdrew his name
from both parts of the bill. Supposedly he had been sharply criticized by
Utah's governor Mike Leavitt, who said that the legislation had too many
federal strings attached to the funds and he was opposed to the federal
government's use of the tobacco tax as a funding source.

ANOTHER LEGISLATIVE INITIATIVE
FOR CHILDREN'S HEALTH

Senator Chafee was one of the Republicans that Kennedy had approached in late fall 1996, as he had in the fall of 1994, to support a new
children's health initiative. Chafee had told Kennedy that in his view
there was no chance that such an initiative could be enacted in a Republican Congress and he could not cosponsor it, although he supported
the principles that Kennedy was advocating. Meanwhile the coalition of
children's and health groups that had been put together in the fall of
1996 to support the Kerry-Kennedy bill and the general effort to increase
health insurance for children was working on encouraging Democrats
on the Finance Committee and Chafee to propose their own provision to
expand Medicaid to provide health insurance for poor children.

Chafee and Senator Rockefeller, leaders on children's health issues
on the Finance Committee, announced their own children's health bill
on April 30. Unlike the program we had negotiated with Hatch, it was
a straight expansion of the Medicaid program. Coverage through Medicaid, which was an open-ended entitlement, had some definite policy
advantages over the CHILD bill, but Medicaid was a program that the
Republicans had actually proposed to eliminate in favor of a block grant,
and we saw no prospect of getting a straight expansion through both
Republican-controlled houses. We obviously didn't want to give the im-

pression that the advocates for children's health were divided, so Hatch and Kennedy agreed that they would support the Rockefeller-Chafee legislation and describe it as complementary to, rather than in competition with, their own legislation.

Since the fall of 1996, Kennedy had been discussing strategy for obtaining support for this initiative with Republican friends and colleagues with whom he had worked for years. One such friend was Ken Duberstein, former chief of staff to President Reagan and now a very successful lobbyist in a bipartisan firm in Washington. Duberstein suggested that Congressman Bill Thomas, chairman of the House Ways and Means Committee, was a key player, so Kennedy arranged to meet with him. Thomas brought with him Nancy Johnson, a moderate Republican who was also on Ways and Means. Although Thomas said he could not personally take the lead, he left the impression that he would try to be helpful. Johnson listened attentively but was noncommittal.

Two days before Hatch and Kennedy were to introduce their legislation, I was told by Nancy Johnson's chief of staff that she would cosponsor the companion to the Hatch-Kennedy legislation in the House and was willing to find other Republicans to join her. This was a significant breakthrough because as chair of the House Ethics Committee and a member of Ways and Means, Johnson was known to have a good relationship not only with Thomas but also with Gingrich. Now the legislation was off and running in both the Senate and the House.

BUILDING GRASSROOTS SUPPORT

Once the inside strategy was under way, Kennedy's attention turned to the outside game: mobilizing the grassroots. The CDF and the American Cancer Society agreed to cochair the coalition of children's health advocacy groups. Starting in early 1997, the coalition met several times a week, exchanging information on the status of the various initiatives and developing strategies for working on congressional members to support the initiatives and ultimately to support the Hatch-Kennedy bill when it was introduced.

In addition to one-on-one contact with staff and congressional members and the job of mobilizing allied advocacy groups in the states and in Washington to create attention for the legislation, coalition groups were also focused on the public relations side of the effort. As with Kassebaum-Kennedy and the minimum wage initiative in the two previous years, the coalition and Senator Kennedy knew that it was essential to maintain a drumbeat of public activity around the legislative initiative generating as much press for the legislation as possible in Washington and in members' districts. The coalition groups organized op-ed pieces, letters to the editor, and participation in radio talk shows across the country. They also organized Washington press conferences, one to announce the coalition's formation and others within each of the sectors that formed the coalition: health care, children, nurses, community health centers, the American Heart Association, the American Lung Association, the American Cancer Society, and the antismoking sector.

During the recesses of the Senate and House, public events were scheduled in the districts of senators and congressmen who sat on key committees and others who we thought might be persuaded to support the legislation. While members of Congress were in their districts, meetings were scheduled with local advocates both on the children's health front and on the antismoking front.

As support for the legislation grew, the case against the tobacco companies was getting stronger. On June 26 a group of state attorneys general and the tobacco companies announced that they had reached agreement on a national settlement of all the tobacco litigation brought by individual states. Because it essentially amounted to an admission of wrongdoing by the tobacco companies, the announcement was very helpful to the children's health legislation. At that point, it became much harder for the pro-tobacco forces in Congress to stave off an increase in the tobacco tax.

The CDF under Marian Wright Edelman's leadership deserves the lion's share of credit for its role in the coalition. The Cancer Society, the American Lung Association, and the American Heart Association worked hard for the bill but they did not provide the level of resources that the CDF did. The children's health initiative was CDF's number one project for the spring of 1997, and the resources they provided in Washington and in field offices across the country were immensely helpful.

It would have been an important addition to the campaign if the coalition had been able to raise the funds necessary to run television and print advertisements across the country, but ads in the major daily newspapers—*New York Times, Washington Post, Boston Globe,* and *Los Angeles Times*—cost between $25,000 and $100,000 per page. There simply were no funds of that magnitude available. The coalition was constantly trying to raise money for its effort, but what it mostly had were in-kind contributions from hundreds of health and children's advocacy groups.

Kennedy was not about to give up trying to raise money for a modest advertising campaign to accompany the legislative effort. When he was next in California, he met with his friend Lew Wasserman and asked the retired entertainment mogul if he would contribute to the CDF children's health education fund. Wasserman responded with a $100,000 gift. The contribution was very generous, but it was not nearly enough for a full-scale advertising campaign. It did, however, enable the coalition to run one-page ads in *Congress Daily*. Circulated every morning to all members of Congress and their staffs, the eight- to ten-page daily was an invaluable crib sheet enabling members to keep abreast of each important piece of legislation, as well as the daily schedule of hearings and other events on Capitol Hill and at the White House. Everybody on Capitol Hill read it every day. The coalition ran its full-page ad on the back page of *Congress Daily* for as many days as possible once the legislation began to be considered by Congress. They had a clever idea for framing the issue. Each ad would lead with two pictures, a photograph of an all-American tyke who we decided to call "Joey" and a mock-up of Joe Camel, the advertising icon of Camel cigarettes, accompanied by a description of the legislative proposal. The headline varied from "Whose side are you on? Joey or Joe Camel?" to whatever the appropriate message was for the stage the legislation was in on the day in question. But the pictures remained the same and the question always came down to whose side the individual members of Congress were on. Posters of this advertisement circulated to the regional offices of the advocacy groups. The ads also ran in some of the smaller print journals across the country.

The budget for the whole advertising and public education campaign for the bill barely exceeded Wasserman's $100,000 gift. In size and scope, it certainly was no match for the budget the opponents of the bill had, but I suspect that its effectiveness and the sharpness of the message made this one of the more successful ad campaigns that Capitol Hill had seen. Public interest advocacy groups will never have the kind of funding necessary to compete in a national advertising campaign with private industry. But we learned from this experience that carefully targeted, carefully placed ads with a very clear message can have an important impact on the success of a campaign around an issue that is powerful in its own right.

The substantive effort, the political inside and outside games, and the public relations effort were all in place. Now the challenge was to work the Hill, work the White House, and move the legislation forward.

NEGOTIATING THE BALANCED BUDGET AGREEMENT

In the months leading up to May 1997, the central preoccupation of congressional Republican leaders was on reaching agreement on a balanced budget over the next five to seven years. President Clinton had proposed a balanced budget in his State of the Union speech in January, and though Republicans had criticized his proposal they agreed to negotiate with him. With the Chafee-Rockefeller Medicaid expansion proposal and the Hatch-Kennedy CHILD bill both attracting considerable public attention and contributing to the momentum for the cause of children's health insurance, that cause became one of the most visible issues as the White House and congressional leaders moved closer to announcing a bipartisan balanced budget agreement.

On May 2 the outline of a balanced budget agreement was finally worked out between the White House and Republican leaders. The agreement was embodied in a resolution that wouldn't include actual legislation but would set the spending and revenue limits within which Congress was supposed to operate and would include reconciliation instructions to draft legislation meeting the targets set by the resolution. The agreement included $16 billion over five years for children's health insurance. Seeing the momentum behind the child health insurance effort, the administration had essentially consolidated health funds included in its budget that had been spread across several initiatives into a children's health line and insisted that these funds be included in the deal. The details of the program were not worked out, and there was no tobacco tax increase, but bipartisan budget negotiators had signed off on the $16 billion for children's health. The White House and President Clinton deserve tremendous credit for insisting in the budget negotiations that there be funding for children's health and making children's health among the most visible of the new investments included.

The next step was for the balanced budget agreement to be prepared in the Senate Budget Committee and brought to the floor for debate and a vote. Members of Congress and advocates involved in the children's health campaign were not satisfied with the agreement as it stood; the additional funding of $16 billion was still significantly less than provided for under the CHILD bill. Plainly the budget would not get as close as we wanted to universal coverage for children, and we also wanted the tobacco tax because of its impact on reducing smoking among youth. So the Hatch-Kennedy forces escalated their public relations and grassroots campaign with the goal of increasing the funding for the children's health initiative and adding the tobacco tax increase as a key element of the program.

Once again there was skepticism across the Washington establishment about Kennedy and Hatch's ability to push their initiative any further. Sixteen billion dollars seemed like a lot. The president and Democratic congressional leaders had signed off on the budget agreement and were inclined to defend it—or at least the White House was. Kennedy kept hearing from the White House, "Why don't you just declare victory with the $16 billion and drop your initiative? It won't go anywhere at this point." But that position was not acceptable to him or to the advocates who were so committed to actually providing health insurance for as many of the 10 million uninsured children as possible. They saw that this was their moment to achieve that goal.

By mid-May the public relations drumbeat for the CHILD bill was intense. Kennedy realized that it might be now or never for the bill. If the additional funding for the CHILD bill were added to the budget resolution and included in the reconciliation instructions that were part of the resolution, it would be a huge leg up. The reconciliation bill could not be filibustered and, in view of the balanced budget agreement, was pretty close to a must-pass bill.

So Kennedy went to Hatch to persuade him to join in offering the CHILD bill as an amendment to the budget resolution. They met several times. Hatch's staff was concerned and skeptical. Republican leaders had their agreement with the president, which provided for both tax and spending cuts and achieved a balanced budget. They didn't want any distraction from their message on what they had accomplished, and while they had accepted $16 billion for children's health as one price of the deal, they certainly didn't want more money for a program they disliked.

The position of the White House was less clear: because they had made the budget agreement with Republican leaders, would they feel bound to oppose any new initiatives, even if they were paid for, as the CHILD bill was, by the increase in the tobacco tax? The Kennedy forces took the position that there was nothing in the balanced budget agreement that prohibited rearranging funding as long as the initiative was "deficit-neutral"—that is, did not increase the deficit—and the end result was still a balanced budget. But Kennedy was in an awkward position. He was afraid that if, during the debate, he asked the White House to support his attempt to add the CHILD bill to the agreement, the budget hawks in the White House would deny their support.

The issue was especially sensitive because, although the amendment would have been deficit-neutral, it would have reduced the total for tax cuts assumed in the resolution by the amount of the cigarette tax increase. Although the Republicans supposedly wanted income tax cuts for individuals and lower taxes for businesses—neither of which would have been affected by the tobacco excise tax—the bottom-line number of the total tax cut had assumed a sacrosanct status for them as a key part of the agreement. They did not want to reduce that figure.

Others at the White House did not feel the White House would be bound to oppose any new initiatives, as long as they were paid for. So Kennedy and his staff told our allies in the administration—at Health and Human Services, at the White House, and particularly in Mrs. Clinton's office—that we were intending to go forward with the children's health amendment to the budget resolution. We asked each of our allies to make the case to the budget negotiators and the president that they should support or at least be neutral on our effort to include the funds for the CHILD bill in the budget resolution.

In briefings to congressional staff members by the White House budget negotiating team, John Hilley expressed the "hope" that Kennedy and Hatch would not offer the CHILD bill as an amendment to the budget resolution. Looking back on what happened, it seems to me that Hilley preferred we not offer the amendment because he had decided that he was bound not to support it because of his role in the budget negotiations. But he didn't press very hard because he thought it would not be a huge problem even if we did offer the amendment—the Republicans would not vote for it, and therefore the White House would not have to take any position at all. They might even allow themselves to publicly appear to support the initiative so that they did not cross their allies in the children's health communities and look to the public as if they weren't really pro-child.

On May 21 the budget resolution was on the floor of the Senate. Kennedy and the CHILD bill coalition had worked hard to line up votes to add the bill's funds to the resolution. The *Congress Daily* ads ran every day: "Senator: Whose side are you on? Joe Camel or Joey?" It had been touch-and-go whether Hatch would agree to this strategy, but now he was on board. Early that morning, he and Kennedy went to the floor to offer the amendment. Kennedy delivered a rousing speech, pulling together all the arguments against tobacco and for children. Hatch followed with an equally rousing speech.

Then Lott and Domenici appeared on the floor, arguing angrily that the amendment would break the balanced budget agreement. "The agreement would fall apart" if the amendment were adopted. The president and the White House needed to oppose this amendment, or "the budget deal was off," they threatened. Domenici, in particular, hung the whole future of the balanced budget on the back of the children's health initiative.

Back in the Republican cloakroom, Lott was apparently counting votes to see whether or not he could defeat the CHILD bill amendment. A number of Republican senators indicated that they were committed to supporting the amendment. If all the Democrats who had already committed to the bill voted for it, and the five or six Republican cosponsors voted for it, it would pass.

Lott did not want a Kennedy victory in the context of the budget agreement. Even though the CHILD bill paid for itself with the tobacco tax and would not upset the end goal of a balanced budget, he was not going to support a tobacco tax increase or let Ted Kennedy "run the Senate." He had seen what had happened to Dole only one year before, and he was not going to let it happen to him.

So Lott called President Clinton and told him to pull Democratic votes from the amendment or else the budget agreement would be sunk and there would be no money for the new initiatives the president had negotiated as part of the deal. Of course, there would have been no money for the Republican tax cuts and no balanced budget either, but the president's budget hawks accepted Lott's threats and began calling Democratic senators to tell them they had to vote against the bill amendment because it jeopardized the entire budget agreement.

Nine Democratic senators who intended to vote for the bill received calls from the White House; by noon, five of them had agreed to vote against the amendment. Lott went to the Senate floor to announce that he had talked to the president, and the White House opposed adding the CHILD bill funding to the budget resolution.

Kennedy and his staff were dumbfounded. We had heard, possibly erroneously, that Vice President Gore was on his way to the Capitol in case he needed to break a tie vote on behalf of the CHILD bill to pass our amendment. How could the president suddenly switch gears and pull the rug out from under us on the most important health initiative introduced in this Congress?

But there was nothing that could be done. Senator Kennedy buttonholed Democrats whom we believed were the subjects of phone calls from the White House to make the point that the amendment was paid for, that it was deficit-neutral, and that it would not upset the balanced budget agreement. The advocates worked intensely as well, but our combined efforts were not able to hold the five Democratic senators. At 4:00 o'clock on May 21, the vote was taken. The question of amending the budget resolution to provide full funding for the CHILD bill was defeated 53–47.

TURNING DEFEAT INTO VICTORY

Following this debacle, our task was to create a positive spin and regain the momentum. We argued that a majority of the Senate had been prepared to vote for the CHILD bill, but that five senators had switched their votes in the belief that the parties to the budget agreement were bound to oppose all changes to it.

We asked reporters to call the Democrats who had voted against the CHILD bill to find out if they would be for it in a different context. Each said he or she would be. Reporters also talked to the Republican cosponsors of the legislation who had voted against it, and they too said they would be for the initiative in a different context. So we announced that in the next stages of the budget negotiation, a majority of the Senate was prepared to vote for the CHILD bill. It was only a matter of time until we prevailed. Or at least that was the way we spun the story.

Although the coalition groups and the staff working the bill were furious with the White House, it was very important to Kennedy that neither he nor any of his staff criticize the president. We hoped that sooner rather than later the White House would find a way to support us. This is not to say that Kennedy was not angry. He virtually never lost his temper over a floor vote, but the aide who drove him home that night reported that he was slamming papers around and complaining loudly about the president letting him down.

Kennedy and the coalition worked on several fronts to keep the bill alive. First, we worked the White House with the goal of obtaining a commitment from the president that he would support the CHILD bill at the next opportunity and in a different context. Our next target was the Senate Finance Committee; it would be marking up its parts of the reconciliation bill as early as mid-June. Could we get the CHILD bill included? The legislation was budget-neutral, and the Finance Committee members were not bound by the precise details of the budget agreement struck between the Republican leaders and the White House; there were certain to be changes to the deal included in the Committee's proposal.

On June 18, the Senate Finance Committee met to report its budget reconciliation provisions. There was great speculation about what would happen if Senator Hatch offered the Hatch-Kennedy bill in the Finance Committee markup. But first Chafee-Rockefeller and Hatch-Kennedy needed to consolidate their bills so that there would be support from a majority of the Committee. Hatch's staff and Chafee's and Rockefeller's hammered out an agreement before the markup. When the Republican governors got wind of the deal, however, they weighed in with a flurry of protests.

Yet another negotiation had to be carried out between the Hatch-Chafee-Rockefeller forces and Finance Committee chairman Roth. The biggest substantive change that emerged from this dual round of negotiations was that states were given a choice of enrolling the additional children funded by the new legislation in the existing Medicaid program or in private insurance, as provided in the CHILD bill. The money provided for covering children, however, was still at the original $16 billion level negotiated in the budget agreement—and there was no tobacco tax. The stage was set for another confrontation.

Kennedy, his staff, and the CHILD bill coalition were not privy to the Finance Committee markup. If Hatch offered the tobacco increase, how big would the increase be? And what would the increased revenue be used for? At one point in the evening of June 18 the Committee senators dismissed the staff and met by themselves behind closed doors. Everything hinged on what Hatch, our partner on the bill, would do behind those closed doors. Rumors spread that he was dropping the tobacco tax from 43 to 20 cents and that he had agreed that some of the money raised by the tobacco tax could be used for purposes other than children's health. Kennedy and his staff were frantic, but they couldn't reach Hatch.

In the fluid environment of the markup, things changed rapidly. First, Chairman Roth and ranking member Moynihan talked about including a lower tobacco tax and using the money for airport construction and maintenance. Hatch made an impassioned speech about the importance of insuring children and threatened them that he and Kennedy would "clean their clocks" on the floor if they went ahead with that proposal. Hatch then struck a deal. The Finance Committee would approve a 20-cent tobacco tax increase, which would raise $15 billion over five years, $8 billion of which would be directed at children's health. The remaining $7 billion would go to various infrastructure programs and tax breaks for corporations and other tax loopholes.

When the advocates heard what Hatch had done they were furious. Without consulting them, he had unilaterally agreed to cut the tobacco tax in half and give away almost half the revenue raised by it for purposes other than children's health. Kennedy told him it was the biggest betrayal "since Benedict Arnold."

But Hatch saw it another way, and he may have been right: we already had $16 billion in the Finance Committee bill for children's health as a result of the budget agreement. He managed to add on $8 billion more for a total of $24 billion. That was more than the original $20 billion that Hatch-Kennedy had sought. It was necessary, he said, to make these concessions to get the support of enough Republicans on the Committee to pass the proposal. Lott and Nickles were furious with him. They would under no circumstances support the tobacco tax. But he had a group of Republicans who were prepared to support the tax if he made these concessions.

Kennedy was still unhappy, but the decision had been made, and on June 19 the Finance Committee reported its budget reconciliation legislation: $24 billion for children's health insurance coupled with a 20-cent per pack increase in the tobacco tax.

Once the Finance Committee had completed its work, the next step in the process was for the full Senate to take up and vote on the reconciliation legislation and the associated tax legislation, which had been broken out into two separate bills. On June 25 the Senate passed the Balanced Budget Act of 1997, which included $16 billion for children's health over the first five years and extended the program for an additional five years from our original five-year authorization, for a total of $38.9 billion over ten years. On June 27 the Senate passed the Revenue Reconciliation Act of 1997, which included a 20-cent tobacco tax. Of the $15 billion raised by the tax, $8 billion was dedicated to children's health, making a grand total of $24 billion for children's health over five years and almost $50 billion over ten years. This was indeed $4 billion more than the original Hatch-Kennedy bill and $8 billion—50 percent—more than the balanced budget deal over the first five years of the program— and the extension of the program authorization to ten years was an additional bonus.

We were well on our way to a major success, but we weren't there yet. The reconciliation bill that the House Republicans had passed included only the $16 billion for children's health that had been negotiated with the White House. Now a Senate and House conference committee would have to work out the differences between the two proposals.

Our campaign intensified. We knew that in the final analysis the White House would be in the room negotiating with House and Senate Republican leaders on the details of the final legislation. The budget hawks in the White House were still smarting from the Lott controversy because all signs seemed to indicate that Lott and the Republicans would have backed down from their earlier threat to scuttle the balanced budget agreement if a children's health program were included in the legislation. Plus, the president had been put in the embarrassing position of securing a Senate vote against children. Yet it was unclear whether the White House would insist on the $8 billion add-on to the $16 billion that had been approved. Some at the White House seemed to be for it; others we couldn't count on. The concern was that those doing the final negotiation were those who couldn't be counted on.

So Kennedy and the coalition directed their efforts toward the White House as well as the broader group of Republicans. As negotiations continued into July, the White House seemed to be stiffening its resolve. Chris Jennings, now the White House chief health advisor, stated that the White House would fight hard for the $8 billion add-on, and Hillary Clinton and her allies were very committed to the $24 billion total.

When the results of the negotiations between the White House and the Republican leaders were finally announced, the White House had indeed insisted on the $8 billion add-on. Working with the coalition, the White House had also prevailed on the conference members to include a comprehensive benefits package and eligibility standards and requirements for the use of the funds that were acceptable to Kennedy and the coalition.

But the story was not quite over, at least as far as the tobacco tax was concerned. In the dead of night, as the conference papers were being drawn up in the House, the tobacco companies apparently prevailed on Republican conferees to reduce the size of the tobacco tax from 20 to 10 cents per pack starting in the year 2000, with a 5-cent increase starting in 2002. The revenue raised in this version would not cover the amount necessary to carry out the children's health initiative, so the conference members simply found the money elsewhere in the budget.

The House conferees took an additional step regarding the tobacco tax: they included a provision directing that any funds raised by the 10- and 15-cent increases would be subtracted from the overall tobacco settlement! It was clear that the tobacco companies still had their tentacles wrapped around Congress.

USA Today discovered this sleight of hand and wrote about it steadily during the August recess. It would turn out that the tobacco companies had overplayed their hand with the provision to deduct the revenue raised by these tax increases from the ultimate settlement level. Other journalists picked up on the issue, and by September one of the first orders of business for Congress was to repeal that provision from the overall budget bill.

Initially no House member was willing to acknowledge responsibility for including the deduction provision in the bill, but it was ultimately traced to the Ways and Means Republican staff. The repeal of the provision in September was unanimous—no one would stick out his or her neck to defend it. The tobacco companies had suffered a major setback. Their influence was not what many thought it was—at least at that moment.

President Clinton signed the Balanced Budget Act at a White House ceremony on August 5. He highlighted the Hatch-Kennedy initiative, now called the Child Health Insurance Program (CHIP), as one of its most important elements.

Kennedy moved quickly to capitalize on the momentum from enactment of CHIP. He opened discussions with Hatch about the possibility of another Hatch-Kennedy bill involving controlling tobacco use. This time there would be a $1.50 increase in the tobacco tax, with the funds to be spent on biomedical research and antismoking programs directed at children. Part of the rationale for the new tax was that the tobacco companies had entered into a multibillion-dollar court settlement with the states designed, in part, to reimburse states for the extra Medicaid costs they had incurred as the result of cancer and other diseases caused by smoking. The federal government had also incurred billions of extra costs for its share of the Medicaid program and for Medicare, so, we reasoned, the tobacco tax increase would be a logical form of restitution.

We had a long run-up to this tentative agreement, with the Hatch and Kennedy staffs meeting numerous times to come to agreement and draft a bill. But members of the Republican Caucus got wind of what was going on and put enormous pressure on Senator Hatch not to join with Kennedy on this legislation. We had one last meeting with Senator Hatch, in which we were going to try to seal the deal. Kennedy and

I talked about the meeting beforehand and I remembered the CHIP negotiations. I found an inspiring and appropriate song by Hatch called "One Voice" to sing at this meeting:

> *Let there be one voice that sings people's spirits*
> *Just one voice and others will hear it*
> *And that one voice that starts out all alone*
> *Will start a grand chorus and the world will come along.*
> *So be that one voice that starts out all alone.*
> *Sing the songs of heart and heaven*
> *And the world will sing along.*

The not-so-subliminal-message was that Hatch might start out as a lonely voice within the Republican Caucus, but since he had right on his side eventually everyone would sing along (at best, a somewhat dubious hope).

I dutifully opened the meeting with the song, giving it all the emotion I could. Hatch listened politely, then turned slowly to Kennedy and said with a rueful smile, "Senator Kennedy, I'm just not going to be able to do it."

Though we weren't able to get this new Hatch-Kennedy initiative off the ground, we were elated by the success of CHIP. This legislation was the largest new social program enacted by Congress since Medicaid and Medicare in the 1960s. What started as the Kerry-Kennedy bill introduced in the Senate on the last day of the 1995–96 session had, a mere ten months later and just four months after the introduction of the CHILD bill, become a giant step toward universal health insurance coverage for children and a milestone in Kennedy's quest for the day when health care would be a right, not a privilege, for every American.

After the Hatch-Kennedy CHILD (CHIP) bill was signed by the president, we began to watch the reaction in states across the country. It was both exciting and amusing. Republican governors—Paul Cellucci in Massachusetts, George Pataki in New York, John Engler in Michigan, Pete Wilson in California, Mike Leavitt in Utah—moved quickly to take credit for the new health insurance program in their states. Flush with cash from the emerging economic boom, every state in the country participated in CHIP. Republican governors all over the country would run for reelection touting their success in expanding health insurance coverage for children, even though most of them had fought the enactment of the program that made that success possible.

For the CDF and the other children's advocates, making sure that the program was implemented correctly became their number one project. Enrollment in the program was slow to get going, but eventually states hit the funding caps provided in the original bill and Congress extended and expanded the program. By the time the Affordable Care Act was enacted in 2010, 7.6 million children were covered through CHIP. In part because the recruitment efforts around CHIP's implementation spurred Medicaid enrollment among eligible but not participating children, the total number of children covered by the two programs had risen to 27 million, and only 10 percent of children in the United States were still uninsured—the lowest proportion of any age group in the country except the elderly covered by Medicare. President Obama made a powerful gesture toward recognizing the importance of CHIP for the nation's children and as a prologue to the fight for universal health care when he insisted that its reauthorization be the first bill delivered to his desk and the first one he signed. The date was February 14, Valentine's Day, and the president was in effect sending a Valentine to the nation's children.

The bill was wildly popular. In the first year of operation the Republican governors were concerned that some people might think that the Hatch-Kennedy program had something to do with Senator Kennedy or to think, correctly, that the bulk of the funding for the program had come from the federal government. So in the 106th Congress House Republicans included legislative language that specifically mandated that anyone who referred to the program in any federal context, had to refer to it as the State Children's Health Insurance Program (S-CHIP). The Democrats, in turn, changed the name back to CHIP in the Affordable Care Act. For us, the point wasn't the name; it was the fact that millions of children would now have access to health care. If the defeat of comprehensive health reform in 1994 was the prologue to the Republican revolution, the children's health legislation was its epilogue. The failure of universal health care had ushered in the Republican victory of 1994 and the ascendance of a radical right-wing antigovernment agenda. The passage of CHIP was a clear sign that even with Republicans still in control of Congress the tide was beginning to turn, at least temporarily, back to a more progressive view of government as an engine of social justice.

Chapter 24

A DREAM FULFILLED:
"WE OWE IT TO TED"

In the spring of 2008, Senator Kennedy made a swing through California on behalf of Barack Obama's campaign for president. I joined him and Vicki for a day of fundraising and speeches. With his usual energy and enthusiasm, he brought wildly enthusiastic crowds to their feet again and again.

Kennedy had endorsed Senator Obama for president because Obama inspired him. He wanted young people to be inspired, too, as they had been by President Kennedy. He was extremely hopeful that under President Obama it would finally be possible to enact universal health insurance, so that, in Kennedy's words, health care would be a right for all, not a privilege.

On that day in California, I remembered the speech Kennedy had given on the Senate floor the day the Clinton health bill officially failed, September 26, 1994. I thought it was one of his greatest speeches:

> I will never rest until every American has health insurance. I will never rest while any parent in America goes to bed not knowing what would happen if their child got sick. I will never rest while any senior citizen in America is left without home care or long-term care or prescription drugs. We have come a long way. We will not give up today. We will take the bill down today, but we will be back next year, and we will continue to fight and someday we will prevail.

It would take fifteen more years, but prevail we did.

Enactment of the Affordable Care Act secured President Obama's place in history as the president who had finally achieved a goal that had eluded generations of leaders going all the way back to Teddy Roosevelt. But this monumental achievement was also a monument to Senator Kennedy.

If Senator Kennedy had not kept universal health care as a central goal of the Democratic Party, it might never have ranked as high on President Obama's agenda. The senator's early and critical endorsement of Obama's candidacy was not conditioned on Obama's commitment to making universal health care a priority, but in many conversations with Senator Obama before his decision to run, Kennedy satisfied himself that the two shared a common interest and a common sense of urgency on the question of health care.

The success of the Affordable Care Act came in no small measure because Democrats had learned from the mistakes made in 1993–94. Even as Kennedy's health failed and he battled incurable brain cancer, he impressed on the White House and key congressional leaders the need to avoid repeating those mistakes. He spoke many times to former senator Tom Daschle, who had the president's ear and was originally slated to lead the effort for the administration until his nomination as secretary of Health and Human Services was derailed over personal tax issues. He spoke as well to Majority Leader Harry Reid and Speaker Nancy Pelosi, other key colleagues, and to President Obama himself.

The first lesson Kennedy urged, as he had urged Clinton, was to move fast and not allow the momentum of his election to dissipate. A crucial moment came at a meeting in the White House just three days after Obama's inauguration. The president's whole economic team and virtually his whole leadership staff, grasping just how desperate the economic situation in the country had become and how broad and sweeping an effective response needed to be, urged him to put health care on the back burner and concentrate fully on the economic crisis. After a discussion, the president asked everyone in the room who favored moving forward with universal health care to raise his or her hand. Only a former Kennedy staffer, Mark Childress, who was at the meeting representing Daschle, did so. Despite the absence of enthusiasm, the president said he intended to move forward. Perhaps he was thinking of his many discussions of the issue with Senator Kennedy.

At a second meeting a week later to reconsider the preliminary decision the same arguments against moving ahead were repeated. Once again Obama stated his determination to go forward, explaining, "We owe it to Ted." He sent his health reform proposal up to Congress almost immediately; had he not done so, the ACA may well have failed.

A second lesson that Kennedy emphasized and that Obama understood was that it was better to send up the outlines of a proposal to Congress, not a thousand-page, fully written bill. This encouraged the members of Congress, especially the chairmen of the key committees, to write the legislation themselves in their committees and take ownership of the proposal. This also encouraged the Democratic members of committees to support the bills that their chairmen wrote.

Kennedy was particularly vehement in urging "one bill," meaning that the committees act as partners in bringing a plan with broad support to the floor. The senator was determined that the committee rivalry that did so much to sink the Clinton bill would not be repeated, and after the election, invited Max Baucus, the chairman of the Finance Committee, to his house for lunch. They agreed that the Health, Education, Labor, and Pensions (HELP) and Finance Committees would work together this time for the common goal. Kennedy conveyed the message of the "one bill" agreement to Harry Reid, the White House, and Nancy Pelosi as well.

The Democrats in Congress managed to avoid the divisive rivalry between committees that hindered enactment of Clinton's Health Security Act. Under Obama, the committees worked as a team, with Finance and HELP dividing responsibility and working together in the Senate and the three House committees with jurisdiction over the program hashing out an agreement before the markups started.

Kennedy understood that in the fight over the Clinton health plan supporters had sometimes let the perfect be the enemy of the good. Obama did not make the same mistake: the proposal he sent up was something of a compromise to begin with, and he was willing to make whatever adjustments were necessary along the way to get the bill passed—most notably in dropping the requirement for a "public option" to compete with private insurance.

As Kennedy knew from bitter experience, passing comprehensive health reform was an enormously difficult political task and doing so while fighting the major special interests with a stake in the existing system was just too big a lift. Clinton lost his attempt in 1994 in no small measure because of the massive lobbying and public relations resources the interest groups opposed to the bill brought to bear. Over $100 million was spent on the battle, the vast majority coming from the opponents. The insurers spent $14 million on the Harry and Louise ad alone.[1] Beyond the financial resources they can bring to bear, interest groups also exert strong influence on legislators in many other ways. They are important employers in members' districts, they are often trusted sources of information, and the legislative scoring systems they use can affect campaign contributions and motivate voters.

So in the Obama effort to enact comprehensive health reform in

2009 Kennedy knew that gaining the support of the key health care and business interests—or at least minimizing their opposition—was critical. Before Kennedy's health became too poor he had initiated discussions with a number of the key interests, including hospitals, drug companies, doctors, and insurance companies. Although his health problems made it impossible for him to negotiate final deals with industry, he impressed upon the White House and other Democratic leaders the importance of working out acceptable compromises whenever possible. Obama and the congressional leaders took this lesson to heart. To the maximum extent feasible, the relevant interest groups needed to be conciliated, not confronted.

To help achieve this goal, at the senator's direction his HELP Committee staff convened the so-called work horse group, composed of representatives of all the major affected interests, and kept them at the table week after week trying to find consensus. In the end, most of the key interest groups—the hospital associations, the pharmaceutical industry, the American Medical Association—actively supported the program, and much of the business community was supportive or neutral. Those who ultimately opposed the bill—the Chamber of Commerce and the insurance industry—were kept in the negotiating room long enough so that their push to kill the bill came too late.

Even as Senator Kennedy's health declined, he continued to convey the lessons of the failed Clinton health plan to the president and the key congressional leadership and to provide encouragement and guidance. When he realized he no longer had the strength for day-to-day management he arranged for Senator Chris Dodd to act as his lieutenant to lead the effort to pass a bill out of the HELP Committee. Dodd served nobly despite the demands placed on him by his simultaneous chairing of the Senate Banking Committee at the height of the fiscal crisis. Kennedy also devised an effective strategy of breaking the bill into discrete subject areas, such as coverage and quality, and giving leadership of each area to Democratic members of the committee so that they would feel a special sense of ownership and commitment and would be in a position to reach out to committee Republicans in their area.

Kennedy insisted early and often that the budget resolution include reconciliation instructions allowing the Senate to pass a bill with fifty votes in case the normal process failed. This was resisted by many in Congress and in the White House, who felt that bipartisan support should be a prerequisite to passing something as big as health care reform. But the senator's views were vindicated after his death. In the end, not a single Republican was willing to support the Affordable Care Act. When Republican Scott Brown won the special election in Massachusetts to replace Kennedy, the Democrats lost their sixty-vote majority in the Senate, and only the availability of the reconciliation process made it possible to make the adjustments in the Senate-passed bill that were necessary to win a majority of the House.

Kennedy was thrilled when his HELP Committee was the first to pass the Affordable Care Act, and as the end of his life neared, he took great satisfaction in knowing that the cause that had been a central passion of his long career was finally on the cusp of victory.

To the end of his life, Kennedy was as determined as ever to give the fight for health care everything he had. He traveled to Washington from the Cape to cast his final vote for a bill to protect and improve Medicare and walked out onto the Senate floor for the last time to a thunderous ovation from both sides of the aisle. He died several months later knowing that his dream of universal health care was on the verge of finally becoming a reality.

Obama addressed a joint session of Congress on September 9, 2009, just two weeks after Kennedy's death, to urge enactment of the health care reform bill and rally the country to its support. The most dramatic moment of his speech came almost at the end. He read from a letter that Kennedy had written in May—a letter that he asked be withheld until after his death. In the letter, the president said, Senator Kennedy

> spoke about what a happy time his last months were, thanks to the love and support of family and friends, his wife Vicki, his amazing children, who are all here tonight. And he expressed confidence that this would be the year that health care reform—"that great unfin-

ished business of our country" he called it—would finally pass. He
repeated that health care is decisive for our future prosperity, but he
also reminded me that "it concerns more than material things. What
we face," he wrote, "is above all a moral issue; at stake are not just the
details of policy, but fundamental principles of social justice and the
character of our country."

The president went on to describe what the "character of our country"
meant to Kennedy and the fight for universal health care. He invoked
the senator's "large-heartedness—the concern and regard for the plight
of others" as a central reason that it was time for government to act. In
words that echoed Kennedy's deepest beliefs, the president continued:

> The concern and regard for the plight of others is not a partisan feel-
> ing. It is not a Republican or a Democratic feeling. It . . . is part of the
> American character—our ability to stand in other people's shoes, a
> recognition that we are all in this together, and when fortune turns
> against one of us, others are there to lend a helping hand; a belief that
> in this country hard work and responsibility should be rewarded by
> some measure of security and fair play; and an acknowledgment that
> sometimes government has to step in to help deliver on that promise.

Chapter 25

THE NEW
CHALLENGE AND THE
KENNEDY VISION

There can be little dispute about who emerged victorious from the struggles of the 104th Congress. The goal of the Gingrich Republicans was to undo the twentieth-century consensus on the role of government, a consensus forged in the Progressive era, the New Deal, and the Great Society and essentially endorsed and extended by Republican and Democratic presidents alike. Measured by the standard of achieving this goal, the Gingrich revolution failed.

Senator Kennedy was the crucial figure in the extraordinary effort to both defeat the Republican revolution and, at the same time, pass major progressive legislation through the Congress they controlled. He understood the importance of uniting his own party in defense of traditional democratic values and the programs that advanced those values; he was relentless in reaching out to his own party in the Senate, in the House, and to both the president and the people who surrounded him. He knew how critical it was to frame the issues and drive the message home to the press and the public. In his own reelection campaign he stated what he was for and what he was against. After the national election debacle, his speech at the National Press Club eloquently restated these beliefs for the country at large and, perhaps most importantly, for his colleagues in Washington.

Kennedy recognized more clearly than anyone the importance of the budget and believed that allowing the Republicans to define what was really a fight over the fundamental direction of government as a fight over deficit reduction would be a fatal mistake. So he pressed the president hard to present a budget that would provide the sharpest possible contrast to the Republican budget—no cuts to Medicare, Medicaid, or education. Kennedy also played a key role in encouraging the president to use his bully pulpit to draw public attention to what the Republicans were really trying to do—particularly when they moved to shut down the government.

In order to ensure that the Republican proposals were understood for what they were, Kennedy was tireless in organizing and pushing for events to highlight just how extreme these proposals were. The sheer volume of events was critical: scarcely a week went by without a forum, a hearing, a rally, or a speech highlighting what was wrong with the Republican program. He used floor amendments and debates in the Senate to draw contrasts between the two parties' points of view.

On November 9, 1994, the day after the midterm election, the idea that the conservative agenda would be defeated would have seemed scarcely credible, and the idea that Kennedy would be able to pass important progressive legislation through the newly elected Republican Congress even more preposterous. He was able to achieve this latter feat using many of the same ingredients that went into defeating the Republican agenda. He had both a remarkable tactical shrewdness about the workings of the Senate and a singular ability to reach across the aisle and achieve bipartisan compromise. While his victories on the minimum wage, Kassebaum-Kennedy health insurance reform, and the CHIP expansion of children's health insurance coverage all played out differently, they shared common characteristics. In each case he unified his own party behind his position, took his case to the public, made alliances that flew in the face of the partisan politics of the time, and used his encyclopedic grasp of Senate rules and procedures to outmaneuver even the best of his opponents. He knew when to compromise and when to fiercely hold the line.

THE NEW CHALLENGE

Between the time Senator Kennedy celebrated the passage of the CHIP legislation and the triumph of his vision that health care would be a right and not a privilege, he continued to press fundamental reforms in the face of a Republican Congress and, after the election of 2000, a Republican president. In partnership with President George W. Bush and John Boehner, who was then House Education Committee chair and subsequently speaker of the House, Kennedy passed The No Child Left Behind Act—an unprecedented expansion of the federal role in elementary and secondary education to narrow the achievement gaps for poor and minority students and raise educational standards for all children. While the legislation has been criticized as leading to an overreliance on standardized tests and is likely to be modified, the fundamental thrust will survive.

Working with Republican Senate Majority Leader Bill Frist and with an initially reluctant President George W. Bush, Kennedy engineered the largest expansion of social entitlement programs since the original enactment of Medicare—a $400 billion program to provide prescription drug coverage under Medicare for seniors and the disabled. He negotiated the terms of the bill with the pharmaceutical industry and controlled the strategy so skillfully that legislation passed the Senate with seventy-five votes in favor.

These achievements were possible, in part, because the Republicans had learned from the debacle of the Gingrich revolution. It was significant that George W. Bush ran as a "compassionate conservative." But in the 2010 election, the extreme conservative agenda came roaring back.

The Republicans captured the House of Representatives in a landslide even greater than that of 1994 and proceeded to advance a set of policy proposals that were virtually identical to the failed Gingrich agenda—privatize and cut Medicare, block grant and cut Medicaid, block grant and cut food stamps and other nutrition programs, slash education funding, and so on.

As the Gingrich Republicans had, the new Republican House majority tried to use the budget and appropriation process to force the president and the Democratic Senate to accept their agenda. Indeed, they proposed to advance this agenda using even more extreme tactics than the Gingrich Republicans—the threat to force the country into default at a time of deep economic crisis if their proposals were not accepted.

In the face of this threat, Democrats felt compromise was unavoidable. When the dust settled on the budget negotiation, the Republicans had failed to attain any of the restructuring of the government they sought, but they had forced deep cuts in discretionary spending. And, unlike the Republicans of 1997, these Republicans seem unchastened by their experiences. They continue to propose the same draconian budget each year. And in 2014, they expanded their majority in the House and seized control of the Senate.

THE WAY FORWARD

Senator Kennedy's legacy lives on in the programs he championed and the laws he enacted. He shone a spotlight on the disadvantaged and those who were hurting and demanded action. The rights of Americans have expanded steadily, and their lives have improved due in no small measure to his leadership. He played a key role in expanding health care, civil rights, and the rights of lesbians and gays, women, immigrants, and the disabled. He increased worker protections and wages, security for senior citizens, opportunities for children, availability of education, food and drug safety—the list goes on. He was a remarkably effective leader for almost fifty years and no other senator in the country's history has such a record of achievement. The vision of America he championed through good political times and bad was of a government that stood for justice, opportunity, and compassion. That vision was vigorously challenged in the 104th Congress, has been challenged since, and will continue to be challenged.

What Kennedy accomplished and how he led in the Senate provides an enduring example for anyone who holds or aspires to public office. No senator of our time is likely to have his combination of commitment, charisma, vision, and tactical and strategic shrewdness; but it is important to remember that these talents were honed during a lifetime of work in the institution he loved: the United States Senate. Success for him was not just about winning on an issue he cared deeply about, but about strengthening and sustaining the Senate itself, so that it could work for the American people. He believed in the strength of personal relationships, in being a colleague who could be trusted, and in finding common ground with those who disagreed with him on the most fundamental levels. His belief in the Senate and in making it work is one of the great gifts he offered to this country.

The dynamics of politics and government are ever changing: issues rise and fall; money and technology drastically alter the electoral landscape; the ideological center of the country moves left or right.

Kennedy's life and legislative successes are the stuff of history. But the challenges we face as we make our own history never end. As Senator Kennedy said in his speech to the Democratic Convention in 1980, "The work goes on, the cause endures, the dream shall never die."

There can be no greater tribute to his memory than to continue to fight for that enduring dream and no better model for success than his example.

EPILOGUE

Senator Kennedy and I saw each other often after I left the Labor Committee in 1998. That summer, Vicki and the senator made their annual August sail in Maine and came to dinner with Jenny and me in the small cabin without electricity or indoor plumbing that we had rented. We ate swordfish, corn on the cob, and at least two blueberry pies by candlelight. Kennedy cheerfully used the outhouse in the woods and announced that the cabin was one of the most beautiful places he had ever seen.

Some of my fondest memories of my evolving friendship with Kennedy are of my wife, Jenny, and me sailing with him and Vicki on his wooden schooner, *Mya*, off Cape Cod or on Penobscot Bay in Maine, usually accompanied by his portable CD player, Broadway CDs, and his beloved Portuguese water dogs, Sunny and Splash.

I had almost no sailing experience but learned to follow basic Kennedyesque instructions, such as "Grab the bluies and tie up the sail." Once we sailed from Hyannis Port to Monomoy Point, where he anchored and, after a picnic lunch, talked me into swimming off a nearby beach crowded with napping seals. Another time we sailed to Castine, Maine, to get crabmeat at Dennett's Wharf Restaurant, and he spotted Eaton's Boatyard next door. He told us that he and his brother Bobby had their boat repaired there while sailing by themselves up the coast of Maine in 1964, the summer after President Kennedy was assassinated. Mr. Eaton must have been in his nineties, but came out to greet the senator, then went back into his office and found a dog-eared photograph he had taken of the two brothers that summer. We sailed from Isle au Haut to Stonington, Maine, where the senator was surprised to see the same weather-beaten pay phone, near the town dock, that he had used in August 1968, months after his brother Bobby's death, to call Steve Smith, his brother-in-law, at the Democratic Convention in Chicago to say, finally, that he would not run for president that year.

On one sail with him down the Massachusetts coast from Gloucester to the Cape he pointed out landmarks along the way, including the Nahant Beach Club, which had refused membership to his father. He remarked drily that if that had not happened there would have been no Kennedys in Hyannis Port. "We would have been the Kennedys of Nahant." Often on these sails he thought about what he needed to get done in the Senate; that day I jotted down a list of what he wanted to do in the next week; there were twenty-nine items.

On May 17, 2008, Eric Mogilnicki, Kennedy's chief of staff, called me around noon to tell me the senator had lost consciousness right before his morning routine of hitting tennis balls to his dogs on the lawn in Hyannis Port. He was airlifted to Massachusetts General Hospital. It initially appeared that he had suffered some sort of stroke, but later we learned that the doctors had discovered a brain tumor, which had to be removed immediately. He had been such a big part of my life for so long that I could not imagine a world without him.

Kennedy was always enthusiastic about his birthday parties and Vicki planned something special each year. She held the last one, his seventy-eighth, on February 22 of 2009, at the house they had rented on the water in Miami, where they could see the *Mya* moored below their bedroom window. Vicki invited Christine Baranski, the star of the musical *Mame*, which was about to be revived at the Kennedy Center, to fly down and sing Broadway songs for the senator. Vicki made a beautiful dinner, as she always did, and afterward we sang for hours and spent much of the next day sailing. Although he had only eight months to live, he captained *Mya* in the crowded Miami Harbor, navigating her with the ease of the seasoned sailor he had always been, sailing through narrow channels and guiding her perfectly to the mooring in front of the house.

The morning after he died Vicki called to ask me if I would sing one of his favorite songs, "Love Changes Everything," at the service for him at the JFK Library the next evening, the night before the funeral. I had always thought that the song, which he loved and we had sung together many times, was about what he felt for Vicki and the difference she had made in his life. But as I stood waiting backstage, I also thought that the song was about the love he felt for his children, family and friends, for his country, and for people everywhere, especially those who were hurting and needed help. Up at the podium, I felt it was also about the love we all had for him, and how he had changed everything in our lives.

> *Love, love changes everything, hands and faces, earth and sky.*
> *Love, love changes everything, how you live and how you die.*
> *Love can make the summer fly, or a night seem like a lifetime.*
> *Yes, love, love changes everything, how I tremble at her name.*
> *Nothing in the world will ever be the same.*

I felt I was singing to him, as he lay in state at the foot of the podium, his casket covered by the American flag.

Acknowledgments

I have benefited from the help of many people since I began work on this manuscript in 1998. Originally known as "Stalling the Juggernaut," in reference to the Republicans in Congress, the project was soon known simply as "The Juggernaut" for the amount of space and time it took up in our house and lives. In the intervening seventeen years, interns have grown into senior staff, older folk, including myself, have retired, my grandchildren have been born and grown into very bright young people: Addie, Emmett, Stella, Sam, Calleigh, and Henry. I want to thank each of the people who helped with the book directly, as well as the people who helped Senator Kennedy with his work described here. If I have overlooked anyone, I apologize. Please know how grateful I am for your contribution.

First and foremost, I want to thank Senator Kennedy. When I asked him in the summer of 1998 if it would be okay for me to write a book about him and our work together, he generously said yes right away. I hope the book does justice to his work, the strength of his convictions, the breadth of his skills, and the warmth of his personality. My deepest thanks also to Vicki Kennedy, whose love changed everything for him and who had so much to do with the work described in this book. Thank you, Vicki, for your special friendship and your support.

I wrote the first outline for the book only months after I had left the Senate in the beginning of 1998. I showed it to one of my best friends, Steve Morgan, and to my writer son, Tom Lowenstein; both were encouraging and made useful suggestions. During my summer vacations at our rented cabin in Maine I dictated from some of the copious daily notes I had taken at nearly every meeting during my nine years on the Labor Committee. This process helped to fill in a lot of detail. Seth Hanlon, whom I met when he was an intern in Senator Kennedy's office from the Institute of Politics at Harvard, and Jeff Huang, who was a very able assistant to me on the Labor Committee and remains an invaluable friend, transcribed those notes over the summer and fall of 1998. Brian Carey, my superb colleague and trusted advisor both on the Labor Committee and in my law practice, and Patrick Manseau, a close partner and remarkably industrious assistant, provided important insight into the manuscript, as did the indefatigable Matt Selig, my first assistant in the staff director's office. Their long hours, intelligent input, and tireless dedication in Kennedy's office as well as in the writing of this book were indispensable.

I began to work on the book with my friend Don Cutler, a mentor to many writers far more experienced than myself. He helped me turn the notes that I had dictated into a narrative and patiently taught me something about how to write a book. I will be forever grateful to Don for his guidance. Charlene Crocker, a secretary at my law firm, Foley Hoag in Boston, on her own time typed hundreds of pages, which I had developed with Don's help. Jan Nugent, also an assistant at Foley Hoag, typed many drafts. Thank you both.

After several years of being able to work on the book only on weekends, I finally had to put it aside due to the growing demands of my law practice. But when Senator Kennedy died in 2009, I knew I had to finish this important story and took up the manuscript again with renewed determination. In the fall of 2012, on leave from my law practice and later retired and working on the manuscript full time, I was fortunate to enlist the help of my friend David Nexon, who had run Kennedy's health office for twenty-two years and therefore knew the details of the whole story firsthand. His cowriting, editing, and fact checking were essential. Without David's hard work, patience with me, and scrupulous attention to detail, this book would not have happened, and I am forever grateful to him.

As the manuscript neared completion over the last few years, my wife, Jenny, whose support had been critical in every way, also took on editing. She is a wonderful editor with an uncanny feel for how I should describe events and what I should include and leave out. My daughter, Kate Lowenstein, who has an inspired sense of how to tell a story that will engage the reader on an emotional level, also stepped in. She endlessly and selflessly devoted more time and effort to the manuscript than anyone. Without her the book would be much drier, less personal, and less vital. Eventually I showed the manuscript to my old friend, the accomplished writer John Kemp, who gave me the encouragement I needed to take the book to the next level.

My friend Jim Carroll, the distinguished American author, read the new manuscript and urged me to submit it to a publisher. David and I were overjoyed when Simon & Schuster agreed to publish the book, and we want to thank Jonathan Karp, Alice Mayhew, and Stuart Roberts for their invaluable guidance in the complex world of modern publishing and for shepherding the book to completion.

In the summer of 2014 in Maine (this time in our own house with lots of electricity), we prepared the final draft for submission. Kate and Jenny continued to be my mainstays, reading every word and when they came up to visit, my son Tom applied his writing talent to the manuscript, and my son Frank taught me the importance of emphasizing "moments" in the writing and pushed me to include more details about life with Kennedy in the Senate. Frank, Tom, and Kate have come home many weekends and continued their invaluable editing help. I would also like to thank their spouses Peyton West, Bridget Bagert, and Doug Bellow too for their love and support.

I found wonderful assistants in Maine. Jenny Powell was a true partner. John Ludlow, George Holderness, Michael Aikens, and Retta Crews all helped transcribe and edit the draft. For the final editing process, I was lucky to find Christian Schwebler and Brock Groombridge in Cambridge, and their help during these last few months has been crucial.

Thanks also to my sisters, Anne and Mary Littlefield, for their loyalty, support, love, and willingness to do whatever was necessary. Mary found, gathered, and secured permission to use all the photographs in the book. Anne put in endless hours on the final editing process. David's and my friend, the invaluable Mark Childress, who was my first hire to the Labor Committee in 1989, gave his special talents to health care while he worked (in order) for Senator Kennedy, President Clinton, Majority Leader Daschle, President Obama, and again for Kennedy in his final year of the Senate. Mark was very responsive and provided us with several wonderful anecdotes. Jeff Robbins and Chip Phinney were enthusiastic supporters of the project, providing help whenever we needed it. Sixteen years after they first transcribed the tapes for the book, Seth Hanlon updated a chapter and Jeff Huang organized the text for submission to Simon & Schuster. Dianne Cabral and Christine Donovan, my assistants at Foley Hoag, helped all the way along.

Doris Kearns Goodwin, the prolific and universally acclaimed historian, provided valuable feedback. I was surprised and honored by her offer to write the introduction and cannot thank her enough for her support and generosity.

Since singing and the happiness it brings is a central factor in the story I tell here, I can't help but take this opportunity to mention the many artists who came to Boston or Washington with their music and brought a joy so essential to Senator Kennedy's life—and therefore to his work in the Senate. They include Audra McDonald, Brian Stokes Mitchell, Kelli O'Hara, Glenn Close, Marin Mazzie, Betty Comden, Adolf Green, Yo Yo Ma, Marvin Hamlisch, Keith Lockhart and the Boston Pops, John Williams, and Hershey Felder. Thank you for your artistry.

I dedicate *Lion of the Senate* to my family: Jenny, Frank, Tom, and Kate. Words cannot adequately describe my love for you and my appreciation for your support during the years that I worked in the Senate, when we lived together on Capitol Hill seven blocks behind the Capitol. For those years and for all the years since that I have spent writing the book, I thank you. This book is for you.

—Nick

In addition to all the special people who assisted Nick in his writing of the book, I want to thank my neighbors and friends, Addison and Ron Ullrich, who were kind enough to read the manuscript at an earlier stage and provided invaluable reactions and comments from the viewpoint of critical readers. Rachel Santos and Christopher Schorr were efficient and effective research assistants verifying facts and locating citations. Thanks also to Erin Miller for her efficient and careful work entering my edits into the galleys in the appropriate format. Mary Ella Payne provided important insights on the Senate Finance Committee activity around children's health. Michael Myers, Nick's successor as staff director, provided invaluable information on Senator Kennedy's role in the enactment of the Affordable Care Act. Mark Childress provided helpful information on some key points. My cousin, Ben Heineman Jr., gave me good advice about publishing in general. Thank you all.

I want to dedicate this book to my family: my wife, Lainey, who was always supportive of the long hours and forgone family time that my work with Senator Kennedy required and of my decision to move to part-time status in my day job to put more time into the book, my son, Dan, my daughter-in-law, Maia Gemmell, and my lovely granddaughter, Lyra Gemmell-Nexon. All of you enrich my life immeasurably.

—David

The authors also want to mention some of the many people who worked for Senator Kennedy and whose incredible dedication made the successes described here possible. One of Kennedy's great skills was marshalling the talents of many people who shared his goals, and every accomplishment described in the book was a team effort.

The stalwart staff who worked with Kennedy during the period described include Paul Kirk, former chief of staff, who contributed valuable advice from outside; Carey Parker, legislative director; Ranny Cooper, chief of staff; Bob Shrum, a former press secretary and speechwriter and an ever insightful advisor; Paul Donovan, chief of staff; Michael Myers, head of immigration policy and later HELP Committee staff director; Dr. Van Dunn, head of public health programs; Paul Kim, FDA advisor; Terry Beirn, AIDS advisor; Lauren Ewers Polite, Cybele Bjorklund, Mary Beth Fiske, and Darrel Jodrey, deputy directors in the health office; Mark Childress, advisor on FDA and investigations and general counsel; Mary Jeka, general counsel; Ricki Seidman, investigations; Michael Iskowitz, head of poverty, family policy, and AIDS policy; Connie Garner, head of the office of disability policy; Clayton Spencer, Ellen Guiney, Jane Oates, and Danica Petroshius of the education office; Sarah Fox and Ross Eisenbrey of the labor office; Marsha Simon, appropriations policy; Ron Weich, head of criminal justice and mental health policy; Theresa Bourgeois, director of communication; Chip Phinney, counsel and speechwriter; Chris Murphy, national service advisor; Dennis Kelleher, economic policy; Bill Dauster, deputy staff director and parliamentarian; Gerry Kavanaugh, Massachusetts economic advisor and later chief of staff; Jeff Teitz, chief counsel; Nadine Arrington, chief administrator of the Labor Committee; Carolyn Osolinik and Jeff Blattner from Kennedy's Judiciary Committee were key staffers on the Americans with Disabilities Act and the Civil Rights Act of 1990. From Kennedy's Boston office, Barbara Souliotis, chief of staff, and Graham Shalgian, policy director. Other staffers, including our tireless staff assistants, who contributed so much during this period, include Jim Manley, the valiant deputy press secretary, Angela Leon, Kathy Malowney, Steven Spinner, Gregory Young, Kristi Kimball, Brian Moran, Stephanie Williams, Susan Green, Jonathan Halpern, Marianna Pierce, Colleen Richards, Addy Schmidt, Carrie Coberly, Shiela Maith, Heidi Mohlman, Jonathan Press, Stephanie Williams, and Stephanie Robinson. Beyond the paid staff, a host of fellows, detailees from federal agencies, and interns were critical to our efforts. Thank you, one and all.

Many Republicans were Senator Kennedy's and our colleagues. Some became personal friends in these years. Chief among them all is the senator from Utah, Orrin Hatch, who made possible some of the greatest thrills and accomplishments of my years in the Senate. His friendship with Kennedy was unique. He was assisted by the extremely able and hardworking Patricia Knight, his chief of staff, who was essential to the work on CHIP and to this day remains a good friend of both of ours. Trish was also kind enough to help in the preparation of this book by finding photos of Hatch and Kennedy and offering some valuable memories. Bruce Artim, a tireless ally on the Labor and Health Committee and staff director of the Judiciary Committee, also remains a good friend. Thank you to Kris Iverson, former chief of staff for Hatch; Rob Foreman and Dr. David Russell, health advisors for Hatch; and Nancy Taylor, formerly chief health advisor for Hatch; Senator Nancy Kassebaum of Kansas, who succeeded Kennedy as chair of the Labor Committee and continued cooperation with us on key social issues; Susan Hattan, chief of staff for Kassebaum; Dean Rosen, health advisor to Kassebaum; Senator Jim Jeffords of Vermont, who succeeded Kassebaum as chair of the Labor Committee and continued cooperation with Kennedy; Mark Powden, chief of staff for Jeffords; and Howard Cohen and Mary McGrane, Republican health staff in the House of Representatives. Without these and other Republicans, many of the achievements of those years would never have happened.

INTRODUCTION

1. R. W. Apple Jr., "The 1994 Elections: Congress—News Analysis: How Lasting a Majority? Despite Sweeping Gains for Republicans, History Suggests the Power is Temporary," *New York Times*, November 10, 1994.

CHAPTER 1: ELECTION DAY

1. Scott Lehigh and Frank Phillips, "Poll Sees Drop-off in Kennedy Support," *Boston Globe*, May 14, 1994.

CHAPTER 2: THE CONTRACT WITH AMERICA

1. Bill McAllister, "Politics: Gingrich Is Selling Out, White House Chief of Staff Says," *Washington Post*, October 15, 1994.

2. Robert W. Merry, "CQ Roundtable: Jacksonian Politics and Newt Gingrich," *CQ Weekly*, October 22, 1994, 3078.

3. Michael Weiskopf, "Playing on Public Pique," *Washington Post*," October 27, 1994.

4. Ibid.

5. R. W. Apple Jr., "The 1994 Elections: Congress—News Analysis: How Lasting a Majority? Despite Sweeping Gains for Republicans, History Suggests the Power Is Temporary," *New York Times*, November 10, 1994.

6. Ibid.

7. William Safire, "No Nyah-Nyah," *New York Times*, November 10, 1994.

CHAPTER 3: THE FAILED STRUGGLE FOR HEALTH REFORM

1. Adam Clymer, *Edward M. Kennedy: A Biography* (William Morrow, 1999), 547. Clymer's book is the definitive biography of Senator Kennedy and his career.
2. Curtis Gans, cited in Richard Berke, "The 1994 Elections: Voters the Outcome; Asked to Place Blame, Americans in Surveys Chose: All of the Above," *New York Times*, November 10, 1994.

CHAPTER 4: KENNEDY IN THE MINORITY

1. Clymer, *Edward M. Kennedy: A Biography*, 490.
2. Maureen Dowd, "The 1994 Elections: The House the Republican Leader; Vengeful Glee (and Sweetness) at Gingrich's Victory Party," *New York Times*, November 9, 1994.
3. "The 1994 Elections: In Their Own Words; Republican Leaders: Setting Congressional Agenda with 'Contract' in Mind," *New York Times*, November 10, 1994.
4. Maureen Dowd, "The 1994 Elections: The G.O.P. Leader; G.O.P.'s Rising Star Promises to Right Wrongs of the Left," *New York Times*, November 10, 1994.
5. Dan Balz, "Party Controls Both Houses for First Time Since '50s," *Washington Post*, November 9, 1994.
6. Mary McGrory, " Lonelier Than Usual at the Top," *Washington Post*, November 10, 1994.
7. Bill Clinton, "The 1994 Elections: In Their Own Words; Clinton: Voters Are Demanding That the Parties Work Together," *New York Times*, November 10, 1994.
8. Catherine Manegold, "The 1994 Elections: The G.O.P. Leader, Gingrich, Now a Giant, Claims Victor's Spoils," *New York Times*, November 12, 1994.
9. George Gordon, "Children Face Orphanage in U.S. Purge on Single Mothers," *Daily Mail* (London), November 14, 1994.
10. Ann Devroy, "White House Conciliatory toward GOP," *Washington Post*, November 16, 1994.
11. Julian Beltrame, "How Much Harm Can Helms Do? Loose-lipped Senator Sparks Debate about How Fit He Is for Top Job," *Gazette* (Montreal), November 26, 1994.
12. David Rosenbaum, "Washington Memo: A Balanced Budget: What One Looked Like," *New York Times*, November 28, 1994.
13. Richard L. Berke, "Democratic Party Struggles to Find New Equilibrium," *New York Times*, November 27, 1994.
14. "66% of Democrats Want Clinton Nomination Challenged, Public Expects

GOP Miracles," Times Mirror Center for The People & The Press, December 8, 1994.

15. Todd S. Purdum, "The 104th Congress: The President; Clinton Hints of a Tax Cut as He Meets G.O.P.," *New York Times,* December 3, 1994.

16. R. W. Apple Jr., "Comeback Kid's Tightest Corner Yet," *New York Times*, December 15, 1994.

17. Robert Pear, "Clinton Is Reported Set to Seek Revolution in Mortgage Agency," *New York Times*, December 14, 1994.

18. Keith Bradsher, "Many White House Employees Used Drugs, Gingrich Asserts," *New York Times*, December 4, 1994.

19. Adam Clymer, "Republicans All for One, and the One Is Gingrich," *New York Times*, December 5, 1994.

20. Nicholas Confessore, "Welcome to the Machine," *Washington Monthly,* July–August 2003; Ron Fournier, "'The Hammer' Checked Every Sleazy Box," *National Journal*, October 4, 2013.

CHAPTER 7: ORRIN HATCH

1. Senator Edward M. Kennedy, *The Health Care Crisis: A Report to the American People* (U.S. Government Printing Office, 1990).

2. Executive session in the context of today's Congress does not mean a closed session from which the public and press are barred. Rather it is a generic term for a committee session in which a bill is debated, amended ("marked up"), and voted on.

3. Eric Bates, "What You Need to Know about Jesse Helms," *Mother Jones*, May–June 1995.

CHAPTER 9: THE FIGHT BEGINS

1. Senate Committee on Labor and Human Resources, "The Health Insurance Reform Act of 1995," Senate Report 104–025.

2. Ibid.

3. Todd S. Purdum, "President Will Seek a Higher Minimum Wage, Senior Aids Say," *New York Times*, January 24, 1995.

CHAPTER 10: THE REPUBLICAN ATTACK

1. Manegold, "The 1994 Election."

2. Rene Sanchez, "GOP's Power of the Purse Put to the Test," *Washington Post*, September 26, 1995.

3. Congressional Budget Office, "Cost Estimates for H.R. 2425 as passed by the House on October 18."

4. Marilyn Moon, et al., "Protecting Low Income Medicare Beneficiaries," The Commonwealth Fund, December 1996.

5. Congressional Budget Office, "Cost Estimate for H.R. 2425 as passed by the House on October 18."

6. House Republicans originally planned even stronger incentives to move seniors into HMOs and more extensive increases in out-of-pocket costs, but backed away for fear of public reaction. *Baltimore Sun, New York Times News Service*, "Republicans Backed Away from Their Initial Proposal to Create Strong Financial Incentives to Elderly People to Join HMOs," September 10, 1995.

7. Government Accountability Office, "Medicare+Choice: Payments Exceed Cost of Fee-for-Service Benefits, Adding Billions to Spending," August 23, 2000, Publication No. HEHS-00-161.

8. "Politics: Gingrich on Medicare Medicaid," *New York Times*, July 20, 1996.

9. Elizabeth Drew, *The Struggle Between the Gingrich Congress and the Clinton White House* (Touchstone, 1997), 318. The Drew book is an invaluable source on the budget struggle from the points of view of Gingrich and the White House.

10. "For Republicans, It Is Still About Medicare," *Huffington Post*, October 17, 2013.

11. John Holihan and David Lisha, "The Impact of the 'Medigrant' Program on Federal Payments to States," Urban Institute Report, December 1995.

12. Bruce Meyer and Dan T. Rosenbaum, "Welfare, the Earned Income Tax Credit, and the Labor Supply of Single Mothers," NBER Working Paper 7363, September 1999.

13. Michael Weisskopf and David Maraniss, "Forging an Alliance for Deregulation; Rep. DeLay Makes Companies Full Partners in the Movement," series: "Inside the Revolution: Business and the House Republicans," *Washington Post*, March 12, 1995.

14. "Abortion Foes Press Their Agenda," *Congressional Quarterly*, July 29, 1996.

CHAPTER 12: WILL THE DEMOCRATS UNITE?

1. Robin Toner, "Gingrich Vows Total Review of Medicare for Cost Savings," *New York Times*, January 30, 1995.

2. Newt Gingrich, "Excerpts from House Speaker's Address on the First 100 Days," *New York Times*, April 7, 1995.

3. William J. Clinton, "Excerpts from President's Speech," *New York Times*, April 7, 1995.

CHAPTER 14: EXPOSING THE REPUBLICAN
BUDGET BEFORE LABOR DAY

1. Todd S. Purdum, "Clinton, at Conference on Aging, Assails G.O.P. Medicare Plans," *New York Times*, May 4, 1995.
2. Marian Burros, "Congress Moving to Revamp Rules on Food Safety," *New York Times*, July 2, 1995.
3. Ibid.
4. John H. Cushman, "G.O.P. House Leaders Succeed in Advancing Limits of E.P.A.," *New York Times*, August 1, 1995.
5. Alison Mitchell, "Cost of G.O.P.'s Medicare Plan Draws Criticism," *New York Times*, August 9. 1995.

CHAPTER 15: THE SENATE RETURNS TO
THE BUDGET AFTER LABOR DAY

1. "Remarks to Representatives of Senior Citizens Organizations," September 15, 1995, Weekly Compilation of Presidential Documents 31, no. 38 (1995), http://www.gpo.gov/fdsys/pkg/WCPD-1995-09-25/html/WCPD-1995-09 -25-Pg1569.htm.
2. Robert Pear, "G.O.P.'s Plan to Cut Medicare Faces a Veto, Clinton Promises," *New York Times*, September 16, 1995.
3. David, E. Sanger, "Gingrich Threatens U.S. Default If Clinton Won't Bend on Budget," *New York Times*, September 22, 1995.
4. Carl M. Cameron, "Clinton Admits Tax Mistake, but Still Blames Republicans. Leaders on Both Sides Perplexed by Views," *Baltimore Sun*, October 19, 1995.

CHAPTER 16: THE FIRST TRAIN WRECK

1. Adam Clymer, "Americans Reject Big Medicare Cuts, a New Poll Finds," *New York Times*, October 26, 1995.
2. Frank Greve, "Poll On GOP Contract's Support Flawed. Pollster Frank Luntz Reported 60 Percent Backing. He Had Not Scientifically Surveyed Public Opinion," *Philadelphia Inquirer*, November 10, 1995.
3. Drew, *Showdown*, 322.
4. William J. Clinton, Remarks by the President in Signing Veto Legislation, Office of the Press Secretary, November 13, 1995.

CHAPTER 17: THE SECOND TRAIN WRECK

1. Drew, *Showdown*, 340–41.
2. David E. Rosenbaum, "G.O.P. Rebellion Scuttles Accord on Budget Talks," *New York Times*, December 21, 1995.

3. Robert Hershey Jr., "G.O.P. Talking of Abandoning Weapon in Budget Battle," *New York Times,* January 15, 1996.

4. Adam Clymer, "G.O.P. Revolution Hits Speed Bumps on Capitol Hill," *New York Times,* January 21, 1996.

5. Drew, *Showdown,* 363.

CHAPTER 18: A NEW "BIG IDEA"

1. Richard L. Berke, "Candidates Clash Over Trade Issues Heading into Vote," *New York Times,* February 19, 1996.

2. Martin Walker, "Dole's Campaign Goes to Congress; Capitol Hill Becomes Presidential Election Arena," *Guardian,* March 14, 1996.

CHAPTER 20: THE CLASH OF THE TITANS

1. For information on Rooney, his company, and Golden Rule's business practices, see Robert Dreyfuss and Peter H. Stone, "News: Golden Rule Insurance Company Has Lavished Funds on Gingrich and the G.O.P. in Order to Promote Its Medical Savings Account Scheme and Destroy Medicare," *Mother Jones,* January–February 1996; Larry McIntyre, "Golden Rule Has a Keen Interest in Insurance Bill," *Indianapolis Star,* June 22, 1996; Statement of Senator Kennedy, *Congressional Record,* June 24, 1996, pp. S6754–S6758.

2. Richard L. Berke, "New Poll Finds Strength for Dole on Personal and Political Traits," *New York Times,* April 6, 1996.

3. Pew Center for People and the Press, "Democratic Congressional Prospects Improve," April 15, 1996.

4. Adam Clymer, "Dole Pulls Bill on Immigration over Side Issues," *New York Times,* April 17, 1996.

5. CBS News, CBS News Monthly Poll 4 April 1996. ICPSR04478-vl. New York, NY: CBS News [producer], 1996. Ann Arbor, MI: Inter-University Consortium for Political and Social Research [distributor].

6. Dick Armey, CNN News interview, January 24, 1995.

CHAPTER 21: CLASH OF THE TITANS, ROUND 2

1. Jerry Gray, "Gingrich Said to Vow Wage Vote Soon," *New York Times,* May 2, 1996.

2. Helen Dewar, "Senate Battle Pits Gas Tax, Wage Increase; Intense Partisan Maneuvering Leads to Partisan Impasse," *Washington Post,* May 8, 1996.

3. Dave Eisenstadt, "Newt Spoils Party, Sez Fonz," *New York Daily News,* May 3, 1996.

4. Robert A Rankin and David Hess, "Clinton Says Gas Tax Cut OK with Him;

The President, However, Linked It to an Increase in the Minimum Wage," *Philadelphia Inquirer*, May 9, 1996; David Dahl, "Clinton Offers Gas Tax for Minimum Wage," *St. Petersburg Times* (Florida), May 9, 1996.

5. Josh Dubow, "Time/CNN Poll: Clinton Increases Lead Over Dole," *Time*, July 12, 1996.
6. Adam Clymer, "Inside: Ties That Bind," *New York Times*, May 16, 1996.
7. Lloyd Grove, "The Liberal Element; Ted Kennedy Is in the Minority but Senate Republicans Are Finding Him Mighty Hard to Ignore," *Washington Post*, July 9, 1996.
8. David Shribman, "Kennedy's Week of Opportunities," *Boston Globe*, April 26, 1996.

CHAPTER 22: VICTORY

1. ABC News/Washington Post Poll, May 1996. ICPSR version. Radnor, PA: Chilton Research Services [producer], 1996. Ann Arbor, MI: Inter-University Consortium for Political and Social Research [distributor].
2. CBS News and the New York Times. CBS News/New York Times Monthly Poll #1, June 1996. ICPSR02300-v3. Ann Arbor, MI: Inter-University Consortium for Political Social Research [distributor].
3. Adam Clymer, "Health Care Bill Fails over Dispute between Parties," *New York Times*, June 8, 1996.
4. Ibid.
5. Adam Clymer, "White House Says Provision Endangers Health Bill," *New York Times*, June 10, 1996.

CHAPTER 24: A DREAM FULFILLED

1. The $100 million figure is from The Center for Public Integrity, "Inside Lobbying for Heath Care Reform," July, 1994; the Harry and Louise figure is from Theda Skocpol, *Boomerang: Clinton's Health Security Effort and the Turn Against Government in U.S. Politics* (Norton, 1996), 137–38.

NICK LITTLEFIELD was Senator Edward M. Kennedy's Chief of Staff for the Senate Health, Education and Labor Committee from 1989 to 1998. Recognized as one of the best-respected and most powerful staff members in Congress during his tenure on Capitol Hill, Littlefield was at Senator Kennedy's side while he spearheaded historic legislation in health care and civil rights.

Before joining Kennedy, Littlefield was a federal prosecutor in New York, chief counsel to an anticorruption commission in Massachusetts, lecturer at Harvard Law School, and a partner in the law firm Foley Hoag. After leaving Washington in 1998, he returned to his law firm in Boston, where he continued to work on expanding access to health care but now from the private sector. Nick retired in 2012. He and his wife, Jenny, live in Cambridge, Massachusetts, have three grown children, and six grandchildren.

DAVID NEXON served as Senator Kennedy's senior health policy advisor and directed Kennedy's Senate HELP Committee health staff for twenty-two years, from 1983 to 2005. Nexon was the lead health staffer on the Kassebaum-Kennedy Health Insurance Reform Act, the Child Health Insurance Program, and Medicare prescription drug coverage, among many other Kennedy initiatives.

Nexon joined Kennedy's staff from the Office of Management and Budget, where he was responsible for Medicare and Medicaid. He is currently a senior executive at the Advanced Medical Technology Association and lives in Alexandria, Virginia, with his wife, Lainey.